BRADMAN

And The Summer That Changed Cricket

BRADMAN

And The Summer That Changed Cricket

The 1930 Australian tour of England

Christopher Hilton

First published in Great Britain in 2009 by
JR Books,
10 Greenland Street,
London NW1 0ND

A catalogue record for this book is available from the British Library.

ISBN 978-1-906779-02-3

1 3 5 7 9 10 8 6 4 2

Printed by MPG Books, Bodmin, Cornwall

Contents

	Introduction	viii
One	Innocents Abroad	3
Two	Home	26
Three	Murder in May (Act I)	38
Four	Murder in May (Act II)	59
Five	8 and 131	86
Six	254 and 1	111
Seven	334	131
Eight	14	165
Nine	232	187
Ten	Life In The Hard Place	225
	Appendix 1 Every ball Bradman faced in the Tests	245
	Appendix 2 The matches Bradman didn't play in	264
	Appendix 3 The terms of the tour	269
	Appendix 4 The tour averages	274
	Bibliography	276
	Footnotes	278

Acknowledgements

I'm grateful to Shane Cahill of Melbourne University for finding what things cost in 1930, so putting the players' earnings into context; John Kobylecky for providing photocopies of Bill Ferguson's original score-books, some of his own research and, at least once, solving a genuine scorebook puzzle; Trevor Jones of Surrey for, literally, logistical support; leading cricket historian Peter Wynne-Thomas, for finding and photo-copying the Nottinghamshire scorebook pages for the Trent Bridge Test; Don Woodward, my reader, for all manner of background information; the British Newspaper Library at Colindale; Joan Grundy of Worcestershire for trying to help locate a missing scorebook; Chris Webb of the AA; Paul Livingston, Senior Reference Librarian, National Library of Australia; Michael Pascoe of W & F Pascoe, Balgowlah, NSW for making the process of getting me microfilm so easy; Lisa Dowdeswell of the British Society of Authors and Dr Jeremy Fisher of the Australian Society of Authors for invaluable copyright advice.

I pay my respects to the many authors who've written books about the tour or covered aspects of it. There is a full Bibliography at the end and footnotes show wherever I have consulted these books or quoted from them.

I pay my respects equally to the many newspaper men, unrecognised because mostly stories rarely carried by-lines, who wrote about the tour from its very beginning to end. I am especially in debt to the local paper reporters – from Tasmania to Perth, from Colombo to Glasgow – for providing so much colourful material which has helped, I hope, to bring the tour alive again. I have quoted extensively and unashamedly. Again the footnotes show from where.

The *cricinfo* website, like *Wisden* itself, is an extraordinary resource of basic information and I have used both to the full. To all concerned in compiling them, heartfelt thanks.

Note: * = not out in the text. * = captain and + = wicket keeper in the scorecards.

'West Indians such as Weeks, Sobers and Richards have on occasions played at the highest level with something approaching contemptuousness in the way they have dismissed the ball with apparent ease to the boundary. This mark of utter and merciless domination was born in Test cricket at Lord's in 1930, and it was Bradman who gave birth to it.'

Irving Rosenwater, *Sir Donald Bradman: A Biography* (1)

'This "Birth of Bradmanism", as it was called, helped the Australians from 161 to 404 in 165 minutes.'

Vic Richardson, *The Vic Richardson Story* (2)

'We must, if possible, evolve a new type of bowler and develop fresh ideas on strategy and tactics to curb his almost uncanny skill; he made his 334 out of 508.'

Percy Fender, *The Tests of 1930* (3)

'He had a very lucky escape when he had made 202, and again, at 273, he should have been caught at the wicket, but he had made cricket history and had established a new era in the game.'

The Times, 14 July 1930

'No one in England had forseen the strength of the Australian resurgence, led by the phenomenon of Don Bradman. Since their defeat in the first Test Match at Trent Bridge the Australians, largely due to Bradman, the perfection of the English pitches and the added fourth day, had transformed the nature of international cricket in England.'

Ian Peebles, *Spinner's Yarn* (4)

Introduction

HE SAYS HE WAS PERFECTLY CALM WHILE WAITING IN THE SMALL, quiet community of Bowral. His family weren't.

Bowral, a convenient escape from Sydney when the railway arrived in the 1860s, had a population of a thousand by the First World War. It was solid, hard-working, church-going – heartland Australia – and he'd call it a lovely place to live.

The whole of Bowral, all 3,000 of them, waited.

He kept his own counsel, even at the age of 21, as he waited with a mixture of fatalism and self-confidence. He seems to have been absolutely remote from self-doubt.

The announcement was due at 3.15 on the afternoon of 30 January 1930 and rather than stay for that he and his brother went off into the country to shoot rabbits. As they were coming back friends told him *you've made it, you've been picked to tour England.*

For once he'd express himself in something approaching unconcealed emotion writing about how he couldn't quite grasp the news at first and he needed time before he understood. He really was going 'Home, to begin an adventure upon which every Australian, whatever his station, sets his heart; I knew not a soul in the Old Country; but it did not matter – my ambition was to be fulfilled. The anticipation of such a glorious trip naturally filled me with a great delight.'[(1)]

To the modern reader these words appear almost childlike, arguably trite and certainly drawn from a world long vanished, but there is no reason to question their sincerity. Donald George Bradman did not deal in frivolity, whether he held a pen or a bat.

Beyond Bowral the selection provoked controversy and outrage across Australia. The established captain, Jack Ryder, was dropped and of the fifteen selected only four had been to England before. The manager, a man with a truly magnificent name – William Lucius Usna Kelly – hadn't been before, either. The players were young, eager, fresh faced and could be, the feeling went, lambs to the slaughter.

The day after the announcement Bradman received instructions from the Board on things which had to be done before the tour began on 7 March.

The historian always has an unfair advantage by knowing what happened next but, of course, the people living it didn't. The events of the following day were as unknown to them as our tomorrows are to us.

In these early days of 1930, with the tour several weeks away, Bradman was already more than an ordinary batsman but nobody – and in this he must surely be included himself – had the remotest notion of the extent of what would happen next, if for no other reason than nothing like it had happened before. There were clues in the background, however, as we shall see.

Cricket has two currencies: runs and wickets. Batsmen are free to make as many runs as they can but, in an innings, the bowler can take no more than ten wickets. Across the generations from the dark ages to 1930, with wickets improving, batsmen prospered in a way that bowlers never could and, by the 1920s, Test centuries were common although the highest of all in the long Ashes series, 287, had been made by an Englishman, R.E. Foster, at Sydney in December 1903. It loomed year after year as a sort of freak of circumstance, a mountain perhaps never to be scaled. The next highest stood at Walter Hammond's 251 at Sydney in 1928, then Bill Murdoch's 211 at The Oval in 1884, followed by 201s by Syd Gregory at Sydney in 1894 and the same Jack Ryder – who'd not been selected – at Adelaide in 1925.

Bradman, born in Cootamundra in August 1908, grew up in Bowral. In his youth he'd spend many hours hitting a golf ball against a curved brick wall with a stump and hitting it again at whatever angle it came back to him. You can read too much into such things, especially when you do know what will happen next, but it does allow three observations: he had the determination and desire to keep on hour after hour; he had the ability to hit a golf ball with a stump repeatedly; and doing this must have sharpened his reactions to the point where adjusting to the angles became purely instinctive.

It was to prove a combination of extraordinary and enduring power.

He was tempted by tennis but, faced with one clash of events, decided to go to the cricket and that was that. He played for Bowral, at 18 had reached grade cricket and, soon enough, New South Wales picked him. At 20 he was playing Test cricket against the 1928–29 visiting England team.

In the First Test at Brisbane, which England won by 675 runs, he made 18 and 1. Percy Fender – Surrey player, arch strategist and journalist – was covering the tour for the London *Star* newspaper and afterwards wrote a considered account of it, *The Turn of the Wheel.* (2) The Second Test was to be at Sydney and Fender said: 'Bradman, though a Sydney player and the idol of the moment of the Australian public, was the only one who had really failed [at Brisbane]. His batting had not even been promising . . . his fielding was far from being above reproach, and he entirely lacked experience.'

The selectors dropped him and England won by eight wickets. They recalled him for the Third Test and he responded with 79 and 112 although England won by three wickets. England won the Fourth Test by twelve runs (Bradman 40 and 58) but during Australia's first innings a young batsman called Archie Jackson made 164.

Here was, by common consent and expectation, a theme. Jackson (born September 1909) was slightly younger than Bradman and widely expected to be a very great success. The 164 is *still* remembered as exquisite, enchanting, brilliant, something like a Keats poem. Fender wrote that Jackson showed 'us every conceivable stroke, and made them all with a perfection of timing and a crispness which stamped him as a really class player'.

The innings lasted five hours, eighteen minutes and Jackson became the youngest player to score a century in Ashes history.

Bradman made another hundred in the final Test but England took the series 4-1. Several critics accepted that Bradman would always make runs on reliable Australian wickets (his aggregate, 468, represented a record for a batsman still under 21) but they insisted that his technical faults would be mercilessly exposed when the wily old English professionals – so adept at exploiting shifting, unreliable conditions in England – got their hands on him. Such criticism did not trouble him at all.

That final Test of 1928–29 had been at Melbourne and after it the great (and genial) England medium-pace bowler Maurice Tate took Bradman to one side and said: 'Don, learn to play a straighter bat before you come to England or you will never get any runs.'

Bradman considered himself no stylist and said so but he felt that having proved he could make runs his own way in Australia he could do that in England too, even if it meant adapting his technique.[(3)]

He did not, I repeat, suffer from self-doubt even when Fender, summing up the 1928–29 tour, wrote:

> *'Bradman was one of the most curious mixtures of good and bad batting I have ever seen. In Brisbane he made one grand shot off Tate to the square-leg boundary in the first innings and a collection of others of a most inferior brand. During the rest of the series he improved, making more shots of the truly magnificent type, but never being able to avoid either the really bad ones or the badly made ones. One would see him cram half a dozen or more shots, worthy of the greatest, into a couple or three overs, then two or three times running he would completely mis-time, mis-judge, and mis-hit the ball. One minute one would think him a grand player, and the next he would look like a schoolboy.*
>
> *'If practice, experience, and hard work enable him to eradicate the faults and still retain the rest of his ability, he may well become a very great player; and if he does this, he will always be in the category of the brilliant, if unsound, ones. Promise there is in Bradman in plenty, though watching him does not inspire one with any confidence that he desires to take the only course which will lead him to a fulfilment of that promise. He makes a mistake, then makes it again and again; he does not correct it, or look as if he were trying to do so. He seems to live for the exuberance of the moment. Only time will show whether the mellowing and steadying effect of experience will make or mar.'*[(4)]

Fender did not know what was going to happen next. Neither did Fender know what was going to happen to him – *Fender* – on a cloud-masked, chilled day at The Oval when the 'brilliant if unsound' country boy, bat not pen in hand, caught up with him. There'd be slaughter, but not of the lamb.

By the end of the 1929–30 season, *Wisden* was describing Bradman as 'the outstanding batsman of Australia'. In the Test Trial at Sydney in early December he made 124 and 225. For New South Wales: 48 and 68 against Queensland in Brisbane, 2 and 84 against South Australia at Adelaide, 89 and 26* against Victoria at Melbourne, 3 and 452* against Queensland in Sydney – the highest score in first-class cricket and taking him only five minutes under seven hours – 47 against South Australia at Sydney and 77 there against Victoria.

Now he'd been picked to tour England.

The party faced an itinerary of thirty-four matches and with only fifteen players they'd all get plenty of cricket.

Australian cricket was in transition from the mature and successful sides of the early and mid-1920s. The four who had been to England before were captain Bill Woodfull (Victoria), prolific batsman Bill Ponsford (Victoria), wicket-keeper Bert Oldfield (New South Wales), and wily leg-break bowler Clarrie Grimmett (South Australia). The selectors might have chosen experienced players in the Sheffield Shield, Australia's domestic competition, but didn't. When some of the critics in England saw the party – and one does not want to over-emphasise this because the critics added a lot of caveats – they thought it too young and too raw to have a chance. Yes, lambs.

The other eleven:

E.L. (Eddie) a'Beckett (Victoria), all-rounder.
Vic Richardson (South Australia), vice-captain and pugnacious batsman.
Tim Wall (South Australia), opening bowler.
Charlie Walker (South Australia), deputy wicket-keeper.
Alan Kippax (New South Wales), noted stylist.
Stan McCabe (New South Wales), youngest of the party, dynamic batsman.
Archie Jackson (New South Wales).
Alan Fairfax (New South Wales), all-rounder.
Percy Hornibrook (Queensland), left-arm bowler.
Alec Hurwood (Queensland), medium-pace bowler.
And Bradman.

The players had to sign contracts full of draconian clauses (see Appendix 3) and were paid £600 each, a considerable sum. Bradman would earn and be presented with a great deal more, as we shall see.

Australia inherited from Britain the surprisingly effective but archaic monetary system of three units: the £, which divided into 20 shillings, each of which divided into 12 pence. To find the context of the £600, consider: the basic weekly wage to keep a man, his wife and three children was £4 2/6 – four £s, two shillings and six pence. You could have a new flat at Bondi for £2 10s a week so the £600 represented five year's rent.

The most expensive seat at the Roxy, Sydney, was 3/5 (three shillings and five pence), the cheapest 1/- (one shilling.) Country Life cigarettes cost 1/6 for 23. A 26-ounce bottle of beer 1/1 in a pub, a 7-ounce glass 5d, a 10-ounce pot 9d (today $3). Hotpoint electric irons ranged from 28/6 to 35/- and a discounted suit £5 5s. The £600 bought a lot of those things.

Cars, however, were something of a luxury. A little Singer (and Bradman would drive one to a match in England) cost £215, a Plymouth Tourer £250, others as much as £850.

The real calculation, of course, must be based on the family's £4 2/6, which is slightly under £200 a year. If any of the tourists had a wife and three children, the £600 would have kept them for three years. The average wage in Britain, incidentally, was about £3/10/0.

A single alphabetical letter in Bradman's account of being selected – the capital H in Home – is extremely revealing because it sets out the relationship between Australia and Britain in 1930. That is immediately reinforced by his statement that he knew nobody there and was unaware of any family roots there, either. In no way did that prevent him from seeing this cold, frequently wet island on the other side of the world – which would fit inside New South Wales eight times – as something much more than a place of common language, heritage and basic attitudes. Britain represented Home to Australians as much as to British people themselves. Even a detailed reading of Australian newspapers of the time is deceptive because in layout, character and language they could just as easily be British. They carried lengthy parliamentary reports from London because such things mattered to them.

The British Empire reached its maximum extent in 1919 and was claimed to cover a quarter of the earth's surface with a quarter of the earth's population in it. The sun, as the saying went, never set on it.

Australia, completely a British possession, had a population of some six million, almost all of them of British origin.

The distant future – mass immigration by non-British citizenry, republican movements and aggressive nationalism built on multiculturalism – were completely unimagined. They would no doubt have been incomprehensible and thoroughly disliked if they had been. The average Aussie would have called all of it treason – treason against themselves, and what they understood themselves to be.

The position of sport was subtly different if for no other reason than here adolescent, raw-boned Australia could meet the mother country on equal terms, and beat the mother country *without sacrificing any of their Britishness.* Consequently, as the party made a mini farewell tour of Australia before they set off on the real tour, they were greeted with widespread acclaim (and despite their inexperience). Whenever Woodfull spoke publicly of winning the Test series his voice was drowned by cheering. Even as the party travelled by train across the continent from Melbourne to Perth, thousands came to stations along the way to glimpse them and, by definition, support them, associate with them.

A tour of England consisted of many interwoven strands and, all unknowing, a picture of Australia's future as a country. This tour of England, as the February days went by and all fifteen players counted how many days were left, would present a picture of cricket's future, too.

Cricket's present, in 1930, was genteel and rather charming off the field.

On the Saturday of the week they left, *The Observer* in Adelaide reported:

> *'The directors and staff of Clarkson, Ltd., entertained C.W. Walker at a smoke social at the Covent Gardens. Walker, who last week was 21, started work at Clarkson's when 13. Walker thanked the management for allowing him time off duty to play first-class cricket. V.Y. Richardson, vice-captain of the Australian team, said Walker had been chosen as one of the wicket-keepers, not as second wicket-keeper. Sir Wallace Bruce, on behalf of the directors, presented Walker with an engraved gold wristlet watch, and on behalf of the employees, Mr F.B. Penhall presented him with a camera.*
>
> *'Members of the Prospect District Cricket Club said farewell to their vice-captain, T.W. Wall, at a dinner at the Victoria Hotel. The president of the club presented him with a travelling rug.'*

And so it went. In fact, the future nobody knew would *really* look like the small, neat 21-year-old from Bowral. He wasn't about to redefine the batsman's currency because nobody could do that, but he was about to alter the rate of exchange beyond all recognition, and for ever.

BRADMAN

And The Summer That Changed Cricket

Chapter One

Innocents Abroad

ON THURSDAY 6 MARCH, BRADMAN TRAVELLED FROM SYDNEY TO Bowral to eat a final meal at home with his family. It gave him his 'sweetest memories' and he'd write of how proud and happy his parents were, and how much he felt it. [(1)]

The tour, lasting until November, was an immense adventure. The New South Wales players – except Bradman – and the two Queenslanders would embark from Sydney while Bradman supped with his family. He'd pick the train up at a station along the way called Moss Vale.

They were bound for Melbourne, then Tasmania for two matches, then Adelaide and the long train journey to Perth. There'd been extensive floods and the line hadn't re-opened, making the planned match against Western Australia problematical. The floods were so bad that the Western Australian Cricket Association decided not to make further arrangements 'until information is received as to whether the visit can be made or not'. A plan to fly the Australians to Perth had been abandoned. The real adventure would began at Perth, where they'd embark for Colombo and a match there, then visit Cairo and, for some of them, disembark at Naples and travel across the Continent to England, calling at Rome and Paris.

In Sydney, in the final few moments before it all began, 'barriers were needed to hold back the crowd at Central Station. Immediate relatives

[. . .] jostled with earnest well-wishers in the struggle for a final view. Many cricketers were present. Bradman was to hear of this hearty send-off three hours later, as he joined the train at Moss Vale. Oldfield and Jackson had many friends from Gordon and Balmain respectively. Kippax and Tom Howard had as big a contingent of well-wishers as the rest combined.' (2)

Howard was the 'modest' treasurer, Kippax a selector as well as senior player. Questioned by a reporter, Kippax said: 'We are merely going to join a team prepared to do its best for Australia. We want to dodge fuss. Judge us by our achievements. I'm confident every member of the team is a trier and a sportsman.'

The words Kippax used would, in tight variations, become a kind of mantra for the team. They'd mouth them repeatedly, not least captain Woodfull who also incorporated the major elements into a speech which he wielded with almost no variations at several places in Australia and all over England. Woodfull said that he had a fine young team and win, lose or draw they would play cricket in the spirit in which it was intended to be played. That was *the* speech.

Perhaps there were misgivings about the lambs and the slaughter. 'The scene as the carriages were drawn past an ecstatic throng was not quite typical of the despatch of an Australian Eleven. Though there were calls of encouragement, there were none of those rousing cheers common on such occasions in the past. They were not called for.' (3)

From Bowral, Bradman, his parents, sisters and brother went the six miles to Moss Vale. Many of Bradman's friends gathered there, joining the family in bidding him farewell. When they saw him again in November he'd have experienced a great deal of the world and a great deal of Britain, too, from angelic Worcester through industrious Leicester to the fastness of north London, from the chimneys of Sheffield through the outskirts of Liverpool to the imperial presence of Lord's, from the twisted spire at little Chesterfield through The Oval set in the urban sprawl of south London to Oxford's charmed colleges, from bustling Southampton on the coast through Cambridge's dreaming spires to the working city of Nottingham.

At Melbourne, the Victorian and South Australian players joined them so that they became a touring party for the first time. a'Beckett, however, wasn't present because his father had died.

The following day they were entertained by the Commercial

Travellers' Association. Manager Kelly suggested that the team's motto might be 'In the bright lexicon of youth there is no such thing as failure'. He added that 'the team compares favourably with others that have left Australia' and finished with 'I am satisfied we have a very good chance of returning with the Ashes'.

The President of the Association ruminated aloud that many people might wonder why they were giving the tourists a farewell party but pointed out that they – the tourists – were commercial travellers 'in the highest sense'.

This formal occasion set a tone because, wherever they went, the tourists would be greeted by dignitaries and hospitality, speeches and toasts.

Tasmania

In the afternoon they left Port Melbourne on the *Nairana* for Launceston and the matches in Tasmania. Bradman had not been on a ship before and discovered almost immediately that he suffered from debilitating seasickness. He had no dinner and was happy the next morning just to be alive.

The local Tasmanian paper, *The Mercury,* wrote that 'no previous visit of an International team has aroused more widespread interest than that of Woodfull's XI. It is thought probable that Bradman will play at Launceston and Hobart. To date this season he has made 1,400 runs in first-class cricket, and requires another 200 to equal the record he established last season. By playing in both matches his chances of breaking his own record would be enhanced. Bradman is the most popular cricketer in Australia today, and is certain of a flattering reception on the occasion of his first appearance in Tasmania.'

The mini tour there served two functions: to fashion the touring party into a team and to encourage cricket.

The *Nairana* sailed down the broad Tamar River to Launceston but Bradman, recovering from the seasickness, felt in no mood or condition to appreciate the scenery properly.

The *Nairana* docked at nine in the morning and a big crowd waited to greet the tourists, including several prominent Tasmanian cricket officials. They went to the Brisbane Hotel, a solid and imposing three story edifice with arched windows, where Kelly said he 'honestly believed' the team could surprise its critics when it reached England.

After this reception they went to the 'pretty' ground and began the match against Tasmania, who won the toss and, in perfect weather, batted. The tourists used five bowlers and Fairfax took 4 for 36, Tasmania all out for 157. Ponsford and McCabe began the reply. McCabe attacked immediately and, although Ponsford was out when he'd made 36, McCabe finished the day on 93 and Kippax 8.

That was the Saturday. On the Sunday they did some fishing in the Great Lake south of Launceston but, according to Bradman, didn't catch much.

Resuming on the Monday, McCabe moved urgently to his initial first-class century. Kippax was lbw for 17 and Richardson came in but McCabe, on 103, was bowled almost immediately. Bradman joined Richardson. He began by snicking the ball for a single through gully, and this ungainly, unsure shot launched his tour. Before he saw Bowral again he'd have made 3,395 more.

He settled and moved into double figures with a late cut through the gully but this time intended and worth 2. He showed his 'gracefulness' when he 'glided' medium-pacer Gerald James to fine leg for a couple.

Right-arm fast bowler Laurie Nash came on and during his second over Bradman went across his stumps and was lbw – the third appeal for that, although whether all three were against Bradman is not clear. He'd made 20 in twenty-four minutes but at no stage 'got properly going'. [(4)]

The Australians were all out for 311 and at the close Tasmania had made 109 for 6.

Next morning Oldfield and Hornibrook visited Church Grammar School, the oldest continuous public school in Australia, and had breakfast with the school's first XI. Oldfield said how impressed he was by the school's setting and *The Mercury* quoted him insisting 'cricket was one of the greatest assets for binding Australia and the Motherland'.

Tasmania were all out for 158 although a ball from Fairfax laid out wicket-keeper Oldfield.

The players and officials left in three cars at 11 o'clock the next morning to cover the 120 miles (190 km) to Hobart and the second match.

That was the Wednesday and *The Mercury* reported: 'A series of mishaps on the road from Launceston delayed the arrival of the Australian XI [. . .] and the official welcome arranged by the T.C.A. [Tasmanian Cricket Association] at Hadley's Hotel, where the team is

TASMANIA V AUSTRALIANS

Launceston, 8, 10, 11 March. Australians won by 10 wickets.

TASMANIA

J. Atkinson	c Oldfield	b Fairfax	50	c Hornibrook	b Wall	2
D.C. Green		b Fairfax	7		b Hornibrook	16
N. Davis	c Hornibrook	b Fairfax	2	c Hornibrook	b Fairfax	4
G.W. Martin		b Hornibrook	5	lbw	b Fairfax	29
L. Nash	c Fairfax	b Hurwood	31	c Oldfield	b Fairfax	49
A.C. Newton		b Fairfax	6	run out		0
J. Badcock	c Oldfield	b McCabe	9	c Hornibrook	b Fairfax	5
G. James		b Hornibrook	21		b Hornibrook	4
V. Hooper	lbw	b Hurwood	1	c Ponsford	b Hornibrook	22
R.C. Townley		not out	11	c Ponsford	b Hurwood	16
E. Pickett	c McCabe	b Hornibrook	9		not out	0
Extras	(lb 2, w 1, nb 2)		5	(b 6, lb 3, nb 2)		11
Total			157			158

1-50, 2-57, 3-68, 4-68, 5-78, 6-115, 7-121, 8-130, 9-143

1-2, 2-52, 3-57, 4-106, 5-106, 6-107, 7-114, 8-118, 9-141

	O	M	R	W	O	M	R	W
Wall	7	1	19	0	8	2	28	1
Hurwood	12	2	41	2	6.2	2	13	1
Fairfax	13	3	36	4	17	1	43	4
Hornibrook	14.2	3	38	3	15	2	51	3
McCabe	7	2	18	1	3	0	12	0

AUSTRALIANS

W.H. Ponsford	lbw	b James	36			
S.J. McCabe		b Hooper	103			
A.F. Kippax	lbw	b James	17			
V.Y. Richardson	c Martin	b Townley	33			
D.G. Bradman	lbw	b Nash	20			
A.G. Fairfax	c Pickett	b James	18			
W.M. Woodfull		not out	50			
W.A. Oldfield		run out	4			
A. Hurwood		b James	1		not out	2
P.M. Hornibrook		b James	12			
T.W. Wall	c Atkinson	b Townley	4		not out	4
Extras	(b 3, lb 4, nb 6)		13			0
Total			311			6

1-120, 2-163, 3-163, 4-199, 5-220, 6-249, 7-268, 8-273, 9-293

	O	M	R	W	O	M	R	W
Nash	13	0	82	1				
James	22	1	97	5				
Hooper	13	0	68	1				
Newton	5	0	34	0				
Townley	3	0	16	2				
Atkinson					1	0	2	0
Martin					1	0	2	0
Green					1	0	2	0

staying, had to be dispensed with. Quite a crowd gathered outside Hadley's to witness their arrival and although the two last cars did not arrive until shortly before 6 o'clock, two hours behind time, many stayed on determined to see the players.'

They saw Oldfield 'wearing a piece of sticking plaster on the spot where he was struck, and his right eye was also slightly blackened. However, he stated he had fully recovered.

'There was a feeling of unrest among officials at the T.C.A. when the last two cars did not put in an appearance until nearly two hours after the expected time of arrival and the secretary of the Association had only a few minutes previously set off in his car, accompanied by the chairman, with a view to ascertaining the cause of the delay when they arrived.'

For the match, 'up to 4 o'clock yesterday afternoon over 1,000 special concessions for parties of school children had been sold, including 450 to the Hobart State High School. Arrangements have been made for a special bus service to the ground and a souvenir programme, that includes the averages of the Australian players, has been issued by the T.C.A. The Governor will attend the match and extend a welcome to the visitors during the luncheon at the pavilion. Play will commence at noon.'

The match was due to be played over the Thursday, Friday and Saturday but overnight rain destroyed the Thursday. The wicket was not the problem because it had been covered, for the first time, by galvanised iron. Tarpaulin sheets draped over its sides stopped the water getting under it and spouts drained the water away. Elsewhere, however, the turf was boggy and slippery.

Arrangements had to be altered. The luncheon welcome was postponed until the Friday and, play abandoned, the tourists were driven down to Brown's River at nearby Kingston. During the afternoon some of them played on Kingston's links golf course. Because so much time had been lost, the Saturday departure on the *Orford*, a 20,000-ton liner owned by the Orient Steam Navigation Company, would be delayed until 8 o'clock in the evening so play could continue to 6 o'clock.

Before Friday's play the tourists were taken on a visit to a local landmark, the Springs, by car. Mist lifted shortly before they arrived and they were 'able to obtain an excellent view of the city, the river and the bays'.

The weather was hot enough to dry the pitch completely and a crowd of 3,000 watched as Tasmania, who'd won the toss, batted. Grimmett spun his web, bowling twenty-two consecutive overs to take 5 for 30. Tasmania struggled to 131 all out – they'd been 80 for 3 at lunch when the Governor made a speech and many others did, too, all couched in the language of purity and innocence.

Ponsford and McCabe opened the Australian innings after tea. McCabe was caught for 18 after twenty-five minutes and Bradman was given a rousing welcome as he came out to join Ponsford. He was not, however, comfortable against Gerald James, who he'd played in the first match, and his first five scoring shots were all singles. He broke this sequence in James's sixth over when he 'sweetly' square-cut the last ball for 4.

At 13, James made a 'brilliant attempt' to catch him off his own bowling. 'The ball was travelling at a terrific rate and he got his hands to it but it was a little too high for him.'

Three runs later Laurie Nash, another he'd played in the first match, induced him to snick the ball hard and low to Alfred Rutherford but it travelled so fast Rutherford couldn't hold it and it struck him on the knee.

Bradman moved to 20 by working the leg side: he placed a ball from Nash into a gap and they ran 2. This would become a staple diet among the 3,396 runs, a shot of perfect safety here in Tasmania and then all over England, rarely timed – or intended – to reach the boundary but, rather, a device to maintain the tempo of an innings, constantly keeping it in motion. Here, Bradman and Ponsford demonstrated the art of placement, sending the ball into gaps in the field with mechanical efficiency.

Ponsford reached 50 in an hour. Bradman brought the Australians' total up to the 157 of Tasmania with an off-driven single in the eighty-third minute of the innings. Now Tasmania had their leg-break bowler, Reginald Townley, on and Bradman was using his feet nicely to him, once playing an exquisite off-drive to the boundary.

Runs came quickly all round the wicket and both batsmen looked at ease. Bradman reached 50 after sixty-seven minutes with a cut single through the gully, Ponsford then reached 75. Bradman opened up, square-cutting and on-driving boundaries so that, at the close, he'd scored 70 not out in eighty minutes, including six 4s. Ponsford was on 83.

In the evening a crowd gathered at the Prince of Wales Theatre to see

Bradman be presented with a miniature bat in Tasmanian blackwood, the handle made of Tasmanian oak, for the 452 not out at Sydney against Queensland. A gold plaque in the centre recorded the score. Bradman made a speech saying he'd had other presentations but none he would value as highly as this. Afterwards the tourists and local dignitaries had supper in the theatre foyer while a local orchestra played.

Next day they attended a reception at Government House and when play resumed, in front of 3,062 spectators, Ponsford initially dominated the partnership while Bradman worked a path to his century. He slowed within sight of it, finally reached it by pulling fast-medium bowler Arthur Burrows to the boundary. It took two hours seven minutes and included nine 4s.

Townley's leg spin replaced James and Bradman, springing out to make the balls into full tosses, took 13 off the over. This would become a deliberate tactic among the 3,396 runs: the speed of his footwork allowed him to decree what length he wanted the ball to be, giving him instant domination. He'd use it to astonish a miserly old professional at Lord's and deflate a rotund old professional at Leeds.

Ponsford's innings at Hobart ended unfortunately. Bradman moved into a powerful drive from Newton and, as the ball went to mid-on, called for a run. Burrows fielded fast and returned the ball with Ponsford just short. His 166 had taken four minutes short of three hours. Shortly after, Bradman lofted a ball to long-off and was well caught by Alfred Rushforth. His 133, with sixteen 4s, had taken two hours, thirty-two minutes.

The tourists declared at 419 for 4 and Tasmania batted the match out, finishing on 174 for 5.

The Age in Melbourne carried a brief match report, and it said that Ponsford and Bradman 'provided sparkling cricket – quite the best seen in Tasmania for years'. That might have been expected, and so might the fact that at one 'hectic' stage they scored 62 from five overs in barely a quarter of an hour.

Ponsford, eight years older than Bradman, had been a heavy scorer from the beginning of his first-class career – the first of the serious, consistent heavy scorers in the history of the game. He made a world record 429 in 1923 and improved it to 437 some two years before Bradman's 452. Like Bradman he had an insatiable appetite for runs and thought of an innings in *days* rather than hours. Whether he regarded Bradman as a usurper has never, I think, been revealed. Nor has the degree of direct rivalry between them, or even if it existed. It's hard to believe it didn't.

Ponsford toured England in 1926 but did little in two Tests, and was hurt in the second Test of the 1928–29 series. An England bowling attack had yet to feel his weight and if it came at the same moment that Bradman, at the other end, was feeling monumental, the county and Test grounds of England were going to need bigger scoreboards.

In that context, brave little Tasmania conceding 62 in five overs represented not just an escape but deliverance itself.

Western Australia

That Saturday evening about 3,000 people watched the *Orford* – which, from Fremantle, would take them on the trip to England – sail for Melbourne. She travelled north on a calm sea during Sunday and arrived slightly before midnight.

The players spent the night on board and on the Monday morning moved through the inevitable farewell ceremonies beginning at noon at the Town Hall and then luncheon at the Alexander Hotel. The Lord Mayor spoke, the assistant Minister of Labour said that the Cabinet had decided Woodfull (a Civil Servant) would not lose any pay – great cheering – and proposed the toast. Woodfull, replying, gave *the* speech, saying that whatever happened they would play in the right spirit. That drew more great cheering.

The tourists went to Melbourne station for the 4.30pm trans-continental Great Western Express and the 2,000 mile (3,200 km) journey via Adelaide to Perth. They'd be on the first train since the floods and the three-day match at Perth would be played.

At the station they were given a great send off. People from the cricket world as well as ordinary supporters crowded the platform, and a little, rather sad cameo played itself out. Jack Ryder – the man who wasn't going – busied himself shaking hands with each member of the touring party and they, in turn, said cordial things to him. Cricket lovers were congratulating him on the sporting way he'd taken what *The Age* described as 'unjustifiable rejection'. As the Great Western Express pulled out, the crowd gave three hearty cheers – and cheered Ryder afterwards.

Between Melbourne and Adelaide the tour selectors – Woodfull, Richardson and Kippax – pondered what had happened in Tasmania and concluded that their bowling, on the almost English type of pitches,

TASMANIA V AUSTRALIANS

Hobart, 13, 14, 15 March. Drawn.

TASMANIA

J. Atkinson	b Hornibrook		25	c Walker	b Fairfax	19
A.W. Rushforth	c Hornibrook	b Grimmett	25	lbw	b Grimmett	11
L. Nash		b Hornibrook	0	c Hornibrook	b Hurwood	93
D.C. Green		c&b Hurwood	47	b McCabe		18
A.O. Burrows		b Hornibrook	0	c Walker	b Hornibrook	0
G. Martin	lbw	b Hurwood	9	not out		20
A.C. Newton	c Kippax	b Grimmett	6	not out		11
J. Badcock	st Walker	b Grimmett	1			
D. Vautin	st Walker	b Grimmett	0			
G. James	st Walker	b Grimmett	2			
R.C. Townley		not out	0			
Extras	(b 12, lb 3, nb 1)		16	(lb 2)		
Total			131	(5 wkts)		174

1-40, 2-40, 3-80, 4-81, 5-105,
6-112, 7-115, 8-121, 9-125

1-19, 2-46, 3-88, 4-89,
5-154

	O	M	R	W	O	M	R	W	
Fairfax	5	0	19	0	8	1	27	1	
Hurwood	13.4	4	24	2	10	1	40	1	
Hornibrook	14	1	42	3	9	4	17	1	
Grimmett	22	6		30	5	7	2	20	1
Bradman					4	0	21	0	
McCabe					6	0	30	1	
Richardson					2	0	17	0	

AUSTRALIANS

W.H. Ponsford		run out	166
S.J. McCabe	c Rushforth	b James	18
D.G. Bradman	c Rushforth	b Atkinson	139
A.F. Kippax	not out		53
A.G. Fairfax	c Martin	b Atkinson	33
Extras	(b 4, lb 6)		10
Total	(4 dec)		419

1-36, 2-332, 3-332, 4-419

	O	M	R	W
Burrows	19	0	113	0
James	18	0	109	1
Nash	10	0	78	0
Newton	9	0	38	0
Townley	5	0	36	0
Atkinson	3.2	0	35	3

had been 'significantly unimpressive'. [5] They decided that when they reached Adelaide they'd approach the South Australian member of the Australian Board of Control to try and get Bert Ironmonger, the very mature (born 1882) Victorian left-arm spinner, included. The tourists, of course, numbered only fifteen anyway.

The three selectors were encouraged by the response and, between Adelaide and Port Augusta on the edge of the desert, wrote to the Board. Kelly and Howard also signed it. The letter was posted in Port Augusta. Meanwhile officials of the West Australian Cricket Association wrote to Woodfull asking him, for the match, to select players who hadn't played at Perth before.

On this Monday, as the tourists left Melbourne, two 'country players' – Harold Lang, a right-hand bat of Wyalkatchem, and right-arm fast-medium bowler Harold Fidock of Woodanilling – reached Perth. They needed 'turf practice' and when they did that on the match wicket both showed good form. Their moment of immortality was not far away.

The Great Western Express reached Adelaide early on Tuesday morning. The tourists weren't disturbed for an hour and then given breakfast in the railway dining rooms by the South Australian Cricket Association, whose president said: 'Teams went to England to get inspiration and education, while the interchange of visits helped to keep the game alive and cement the Empire.' The Lord Mayor wished the team well. Woodfull, replying, gave a gentle variation on *the* speech. 'It will not be our fault if the Ashes do not come our way. The team is a young one, but the matches in Tasmania indicated that it will weld into a fine combination.' [6]

Then they prepared to leave for Perth. The Adelaide newspaper *The Observer* reported: 'Despite the fact that a crate of ducks was placed on top of their luggage at the railway station, members of the team [. . .] refused to accept the presence of these birds as a sign of ill luck.'

Walker, seen off by his fiancée, wore a hat, suit, collar and tie. A photographer caught Kelly and Ponsford gazing out of an opened train window. Kelly smiled but Ponsford looked serious. He generally seems to have done, even when he wasn't batting.

Kelly telegraphed the names of the Australian team to Perth, and it did include those who hadn't played there before so that Western Australia would have a chance to see them. The team: Richardson,

Jackson, Bradman, Kippax, Walker, a'Beckett, Grimmett, Hornibrook, Hurwood, Fairfax, McCabe.

When the Great Western Express reached Peterborough, some 157 miles (253 km) north of Adelaide, it was given a tremendous reception, and Kelly wouldn't forget it.

As it steamed out on to the plains and reached the flooded section, the players could see thousands of wild fowl on water stretching away on both sides of the repaired track. They saw seagulls from the coast a hundred miles away. They saw sheep being trucked up the line to find luxuriant – and unflooded – pastures.

The train, and the team, represented a considerable event and at every wayside station local people gathered to witness both. Kelly commented, in his best public relations mode, that 'all along the route the enthusiasm of the people had been splendid'. (7)

On Thursday afternoon the Great Western Express reached Kalgoorlie and a large crowd waited at the station for them there. The transcontinental railway authorities, meanwhile, had 'received a telegram' from the train saying that, although it was the first crossing since the floods, 'the journey surpassed the steadiness and comfort of all previous trips, and that members of the Test Team had enjoyed themselves'.(8) It's not clear who sent this but it could well have been Kelly.

The tourists were taken to the Town Hall for a reception and the Mayor, with a terrible inevitability to be replicated throughout the tour, spoke. Kelly responded and Woodfull gave *the* speech.

Later that afternoon the platform was crowded as the train steamed out for the last big leg to Perth accompanied by more great cheering. During the evening, a special dinner menu was provided by the State Railway Department's dining car service in honour of the team. After that they'd need a good night's sleep because Perth was going to be busy.

The itinerary:

Friday – arrive 8.47am on the Great Western Express. 12pm, match against Western Australia starts. 1.30pm, lunch and informal welcome by the Western Australian Cricket Association. 2.15pm, match resumes. 6pm, stumps. 8pm, guests of the Hawaiian Troubadours at Theatre Royal.

Saturday – 10.30am, civic reception. 12pm, match resumes. 7.30pm, guests of the Western Australian Trotting Association.

Sunday – 1pm, guests of the Governor at Government House. 2.30pm, guests of the Western Australia Cricket Association on river trip.

Monday – 12pm, match resumes then departure by the *Orford.*

On a dull, oppressive morning the train pulled into Perth central station with a vast crowd waiting – so vast the town hadn't witnessed anything like it for years. The train's whistle played 'Cock-a-doodle-do' as it slowed and instinctively the crowd roared out three cheers. The people were so densely packed that the players had to force a path through them to the waiting cars which would take them to their hotel. When they reached it they rested briefly.[9]

A crowd of 4,600 were at the ground. Before noon, Richardson won the toss and put Western Australia in. At lunch they'd reached a respectable 62 for 2.

During the lunch interval, the informal welcome turned out to involve a speech by the Governor, who spoke on the Empire-binding theme. Woodfull responded with *the* speech, of course, and Kelly did the same although he also gave an interview. In it he reiterated how enthusiastic the crowds had been, particularly at Peterborough.

After lunch Grimmett (6 for 75) destroyed the Western Australian innings and they were all out for 167.

Beginning the reply at 4.40pm, Jackson and McCabe put on 52 before McCabe was stumped and Bradman came in to a cheer. *The Age* described him as 'short and thick-set,' adding that it was 'a characteristic of him that he should hit the first ball good and hard with a rather ugly crossbat. His next scoring stroke was a leg glance.'

The crowd showed what they thought about an appeal against the light at 5.35pm. It was refused but another ten minutes later was upheld, with Australia 59 for 1 (Bradman 4 not out, made by lightly tapping the ball onto the leg side).

On the Saturday, Walter Evans bowled his right-arm medium pace from the northern end and Bradman hit the fourth ball so hard to Dick Bryant at cover that he almost ran Jackson out. The next ball struck Jackson's pad, Evans made a sharp appeal and the umpire signalled out. Jackson's 23 contained one boundary and lasted an hour and ten minutes. The crowd warmly applauded Evans but there was no mistaking their regret at not seeing Jackson in full, glorious flow.

Kippax came in and *The West Australian* report noted that Jackson had founded his style on Kippax, whose 'slight, willowy figure closely resembles that of Jackson'.

Fidock, the very tall paceman, reached for his full pace but Bradman weighed into him with a sudden, savage assault: cut him crisply behind point for 4, pulled him hard for 4 and on-drove him for 4 off successive balls. That made 13 in the over and the crowd hummed. Bradman thumped Evans past mid-off and a fielder was despatched there to block that gap. Fidock, meanwhile, scattered his off-side fielders to the deep to try and block all the gaps there.

Still Evans persisted and Bradman played an exquisite leg-glance which was well fielded. He seemed to be in a cavalier mood and it led to his downfall. Evans conjured a slower ball which deceived him and he hit a comfortable catch to Dick Bryant who was delighted to accept it.

Australia were 83 for 3, and Bradman's 27 had been made in as many minutes with four 4s. As with Tasmania, judging by the fragments of action in the contemporary newspaper accounts – shots played and missed, runs run – there was no sense of a great force beginning to gather. That in itself is tantalising.

Kippax gave a beautiful display of batsmanship, scoring 114 in 155 minutes, Richardson contributed a useful 45 and Australia made 324. Western Australia reached 67 for 4 by the close.

The tourists took the river trip on the Sunday, and during the day both Woodfull and Kelly made *the* speeches.

Negotiations had been going on to try and delay the departure of the *Orford* for an hour and a half in order to complete the match and give the players ample time to reach nearby Fremantle for embarkation. These negotiations hadn't been successful and stumps would officially be drawn at 4pm but given the state of the match this was now academic. Western Australia, resuming at 67 for 4, didn't last long.

The West Australian captured the human aspects of the leaving and their description deserves to be quoted in full.

> *'Taking with them the good wishes of every enthusiast in Australia, the members of the Australian Eleven left Fremantle last evening by the Liner Orford. As the vessel moved into mid-stream to commence her voyage to London, the crowd on the quay sent cheer after cheer across the water. With the exception of Bradman, all the players were grouped within a few yards of each other on two decks, and the wharf below that vantage point was black with people seeking to have a last look at the men they particularly admired.'*

WESTERN AUSTRALIA V AUSTRALIANS

Perth, 21, 22, 24 March. Australians won by an innings and 25 runs.

WESTERN AUSTRALIA

F. Bryant	st Walker	b Grimmett	18	lbw	b a'Beckett	4
H. Lang	c Hornibrook	b Grimmett	29		b Hornibrook	2
W. Horrocks	c Richardson	b Grimmett	7	c Walker	b Fairfax	15
R. Wilberforce	c Hornibrook	b Hurwood	22	st Walker	b Grimmett	25
E. Bromley	st Walker	b Grimmett	0		run out	12
*D. Bryant	c Walker	b Fairfax	17		run out	21
M. Inverarity	c Hurwood	b Hornibrook	25		c&b Grimmett	30
W.A. Evans	st Walker	b Grimmett	8	c Walker	b a'Beckett	2
H. Fidock	c Walker	b Grimmett	35		b a'Beckett	0
+W. Truscott	c Richardson	b Hornibrook	0		b a'Beckett	2
R. Halcombe		not out	0		not out	14
Extras	(b 4, lb 2)		6	(2)		2
Total			167			132

1-33, 2-56, 3-69, 4-69, 5-95, 6-105, 7-119, 8-167, 9-167

1-9, 2-9, 3-29, 4-44, 5-69, 6-101, 7-108, 8-108, 9-112

	O	M	R	W	O	M	R	W
a'Beckett	10	3	13	0	10	2	26	4
Hurwood	11	4	20	1	3	1	2	0
Hornibrook	9	2	24	2	12	0	34	1
Fairfax	9	1	29	1	5	1	10	1
Grimmett	14.2	1	75	6	18.2	4	53	2
Bradman					1	0	5	0

AUSTRALIANS

A.A. Jackson	lbw	b Evans	23
S.J. McCabe	st Truscott	b Inverarity	28
D.G. Bradman	c R. Bryant	b Evans	27
A.F. Kippax	c Bromley	b Wilberforce	114
* V.Y. Richardson	c & b Bromley		45
A.G. Fairfax	lbw	b Bromley	11
E.L. a'Beckett		c & b Evans	24
C.V. Grimmett	c F. Bryant	b Inverarity	40
A. Hurwood	lbw	b Fidock	1
+ C.W. Walker		not out	3
P.M. Hornibrook	lbw	b Fidock	0
Extras	(b 4, lb 4)		8
Total			324

1-52, 2-60, 3-83, 4-154, 5-174, 6-215, 7-312, 8-313, 9-324

	O	M	R	W
Bromley	7	1	43	2
Halcombe	9	0	47	0
Evans	19	2	71	3
Fidock	11.6	0	54	2
Inverarity	10	0	84	2
Wilberforce	1	0	17	1

'Because the match with the local team finished early the players were on the vessel earlier than anticipated, but not too early to defeat the object of a handful of enthusiasts who gave them a cheer as they went on board. Woodfull, Richardson, Ponsford, Hornibrook, Jackson, Bradman, McCabe, Hurwood and a'Beckett arrived practically simultaneously. Wall followed carrying a bouquet that earned the comments of the crowd, and the last to go aboard was Grimmett.

'When the official farewells had concluded on the deck of the liner the members of the team scattered into groups. There was cricketing history in one such group when Woodfull, Ponsford and Jackson took up a position on the rails next to C.G. Macartney and Warren Bardsley,[10] *who were passengers on the vessel.*

'At the last minute an importunate youth pressed forward to secure Woodfull's signature on a new bat and bore it off proudly when the Australian captain had smilingly signed.

'Vic Richardson was the centre of a group of well-wishers. His right hand must have pained him when he had concluded the informal leave as the handshakes he received were many and earnest.

'When all friends had left the ship and were gazing upwards to the decks of the liner, there began a friendly contest for the possession of streamers flung to the players from among the crowd. Woodfull, Ponsford, Hornibrook, Fairfax and Kippax were in one group but the honours – which meant most of the streamers – went to Hornibrook, whose long arm shot out further than that of any of his comrades to gather in the flying streamers. There was a cheer when one streamer intended for Jackson was caught and well held by a lady passenger.

'On the lower deck Grimmett and Walker were close together. Hurwood, Wall and Richardson were a little further along and the fair-haired a'Beckett was a lone figure on the foredeck. Withdrawn from the rest of the players, Bradman stood alone looking over the heads of the crowd. McCabe and Oldfield were not to be seen. The usual advice was shouted by individuals in the crowd to the players. Ponsford, called familiarly "Ponny", was urged not to be frightened of Larwood, and Woodfull was advised "not to get reckless in England". Hornibrook greeted a cry of "bowl 'em good and often, Horni" by kissing his hands to the crowd who laughed merrily but they roared when a lazy voice called out to Jackson to "watch them English girls don't bowl yer, Archie". There was a scramble for pencils among the team when autographed streamers

were suggested, and as the boat moved out from the quay many streamers were hastily pulled in to secure the souvenirs.'

Treasurer Howard had a narrow escape when the car he was in reached the wharf and a motorbike crashed into the side of it, on the side he was sitting. The pillion rider, however, was badly hurt and Howard had to go to the police station to make a statement. He got back to the wharf only five minutes before the gangway was hoisted and the *Orford* began her eight-day journey to Colombo, Ceylon [Sri Lanka] where the team were due to play a match.

Fortunately for Bradman the sea was calm all the way and, in any case, the ambience of steamships in those days induced calm all by itself, with impeccable service, stately rooms and an overt suggestion of luxury. The decks were big enough to allow all manner of sports and the tourists made full use of that to pass the time, keep fit and maintain sharp reactions.

A journalist, Norman Tebbutt, covered the tour for the *Australian Press Association,* a service taken by newspapers so that what he wrote appeared in several different outlets. Unusually for an agency man, he filed colourful and sometimes whimsical copy, had a neat turn of phrase and, at the end of the tour, produced a book on it which remains a delight to read [(11)]. Most unusually for the era, in the book he probed areas generally regarded as too sensitive to go near, and the chapter including Bradman's strained relationship with the rest of the team captures dispassionately something of prime importance. His reports to the *Australian Press Association,* however, were unsigned.

Tebbutt doesn't seem to have filed from the *Orford* – even if he could have done – but he was not idle. He knew that the circumstances in which the team left Australia did not create 'any great feeling of optimism'. There was the absence of Ryder, there was the team's youth, there was their inexperience of English conditions and over Bradman, the merciless record-breaker, there were many, many technical questions as well. At one point, while the *Orford* 'was sliding through tropical seas', Tebbutt sought out Macartney and said to him: 'This team is such an experiment, Charlie, that it seems to me our chaps might either be a tremendous success or a colossal failure.'

Macartney pondered and replied: 'They might easily be a colossal failure. I don't see how they can be a tremendous success. They might just about pull through, but that is about the most to be hoped.' [(12)]

This seems to have been a general sentiment and no doubt explains why, in *the* speech, Woodfull constantly reiterated one of his mantras: whatever happened, the team would play in the spirit of the game – perhaps subconsciously, for all his public assurances, because he thought that that's all they might emerge with.

Bradman, as it seems, had no such forebodings and was thoroughly enjoying himself aboard ship, not least at the deck games. [(13)] In his meticulous way he'd note who won what – Jackson the peg quoits, for example – while he himself took the deck tennis prize, beating Alec Hurwood. He regarded the days on the *Orford* as like a 'rollicking' holiday although, being the man he was, he took care to exploit the presence of the pool to improve his swimming.

It may be that during the journey Kelly profited from the time available – there must have been *some* empty hours – to give the tourists a code of conduct, or more properly a code of discipline. They were not to speak to the Press but refer all questions to him. There was a protocol for functions, because any touring team could be overwhelmed by invitations and Kelly seems to have been determined not to repeat the mistakes of the past, when invitations were accepted and only three or four players turned up. He decreed he would decide which functions were 'official', making attendance mandatory (or else), and which were at the discretion of the players. Wisely, Kelly kept the 'official' list to a minimum because, he must have sensed – and if he didn't, he'd soon understand – these young men preferred the cinema and theatre to dinner jackets, banquets and speeches. They were, in short, quite normal.

Ceylon

The *Orford* arrived at Colombo on the morning of Wednesday 2 April and the tourists took breakfast before they went ashore. Soon enough 'the strange sights and sounds [. . .] would fascinate them'. [(14)]

The non-first-class one-day match against Ceylon was due to begin at 11am but they asked for a little more time to get their land legs, so it started 25 minutes late. The ground, 'one of the most picturesque in the world', delighted all the Australians.

Ceylon won the toss and put them in because there was no doubt who the big crowd wanted to see, especially Bradman. On a slow, neutral wicket Ponsford and McCabe attacked and reached 30 in thirteen minutes. Both had 20 when McCabe was caught at mid-on with the total at 52.

That brought Bradman in and when his number – 3 – went up on the scoreboard a 'rousing cheer' rose all round the ground to greet him. The world record 452 had clearly preceded him, exciting anticipations.

He got the final ball of this first over he'd faced down to fine leg. That was from Frederick Siedle. A man with a complete Empire of a name, medium-pacer Churchill Hector Gunasekera, managed to bowl Bradman a maiden, only the second of the innings.

Ponsford pushed a single, Bradman got into his stride with a straight driven boundary and, when both batsmen had taken a single, drove Gunasekera to the cover boundary to bring up Australia's 60. It had taken a bare thirty minutes. Bradman proceeded with a 2 and a single, and Ceylon made a second bowling change, Edward Kelaart taking over from Gunasekera with his off-breaks. A single by Bradman gave him double figures.

For a moment Ponsford and Bradman were quiet and in Kelaart's second over Bradman reached too far out, nicked the ball and it fell just short of first slip. It ran on for a single. After forty-five minutes he reached 20 and sent up Australia's 80 before, to the last ball of Kelaart's fourth over, Ponsford cocked the ball up and was almost caught and bowled.

William Brindley came on and Bradman kept hitting him straight to fielders although he played a 'delightful' late cut for a single and the Australians had 100 in five minutes under an hour – Ponsford 62. He, however, was out like McCabe, caught at mid-on, bringing Woodfull to the wicket.

Bradman late cut a ball for a couple to reach 30, reached 38 with a pull and was then dropped off a ball which nipped in at him. He moved to 40 with two singles and at 12.55pm Neil Joseph, an occasional bowler – nobody seems to know what he actually did bowl – came on at the pavilion end. Bradman went back to his first ball and played on, something he would only do once in a first-class match, and that after the War. His 40 had occupied him an hour and five minutes, and contained only three 4s.

The Ceylon Daily News reflected gently that 'Bradman was a disappointment from the point of view of the spectators. He started well but slowed down considerably, almost painfully, after Siedle and Kelaart took up the bowling. He was the chief attraction that drew thousands to the ground, but he played an innings that one would have associated with Ponsford or Woodfull.'

Australia were all out for 233 by 3.30pm but the weather drew in – drizzle, fading light – and they came off with Ceylon on 52 for 1 after 19 overs.

The four Australians who didn't play enjoyed themselves having a rickshaw race, which Kippax won and Grimmett finished last by a long way.

The two teams dined at the Galle Face Hotel, an opulent olde-worlde place (built 1864) in the middle of Colombo with a worldwide reputation. Contemporary reports make no mention of any speeches but it's extremely difficult to imagine there weren't any, or that Woodfull didn't have to rise to make a reply. If he did, he certainly wouldn't have required notes. He'd surely learnt it by rote and memorised it by heart now. It would serve him well from the moment the team reached England.

As the *Orford* steamed out into the Indian Ocean, next stop Egypt, Bradman had played four innings: the two in Tasmania, the one at Perth and the one here. He'd made 139 at Hobart but the others seemed slightly bewildering cameos, not least the disappointing 40 here – the first innings he had ever played outside Australia. He might have been a world beater but on this form he didn't look like one.

As the *Orford* steamed further and further out, it's tempting to wonder if anyone on board – especially Bradman himself – had even a fleeting thought that English wickets and English bowlers might crucify him, slowly and endlessly.

The day after the Colombo match, England began the First Test against the West Indies in Kingston, Jamaica. England batted and Surrey opener Andrew Sandham spent the day compiling 151.

As the *Orford* steamed on and on, Sandham batted on and on, totalling 309 by the close of the second day. On the third he reached 325 before he was bowled. No man had ever scored a triple century in a Test before; it beat Foster's record. The fact that it was against the West Indies, who England had only begun playing in 1928 and whose provenance as a genuine Test-playing side was by no means established, gave this innings a curiously ambivalent reputation. Many people regarded Foster's 287 as the *real* record and across the 1930 season poor Sandham's feat was scarcely mentioned at all, even when it was most relevant.

The *Orford* steamed the eight days from Colombo to Suez, which it reached on Saturday 12 April, berthing in the harbour. The tourists took breakfast before they went ashore. Tebbutt cabled: 'Arrived here at

CEYLON V AUSTRALIANS

2 April. Drawn.

AUSTRALIANS

W.H. Ponsford	c van Geyzel	b Kelaart	62
S.J. McCabe	c Horan	b Siedle	20
D.G. Bradman	hit wicket	b Joseph	40
*W.M. Woodfull	c Kelaart	b Horan	54
V.Y. Richardson	c de Silva	b Kelaart	6
Percy A.G. Fairfax	c Horan	b Kelaart	19
E.L. a'Beckett		b Kelaart	10
T.W. Wall	c Gunasekera	b Joseph	5
A. Hurwood		b Kelaart	10
W.A. Oldfield		not out	1
+C.W. Walker		b Kelaart	4
Extras			2
Total			233

1-52, 2-105, 3-137, 4-154, 5-186,
6-204, 7-213, 8-220, 9-229, 10-233

	O	M	R	W
Horan	21	4	73	1
Gunasekera	7	2	31	0
Siedle	12	0	38	1
Kelaart	29.5	4	65	6
Brindley	3	1	10	0
Joseph	5	0	14	2

CEYLON

W.T. Brindley	lbw	b Fairfax	13
M.K. Albert		not out	25
L.D.S. Gunasekera		not out	14
Extras			0
Total	(1 wkt)		52

Dnb: F.C.W. van Geyzel, J.A. de Silva, +V.C. Schokman, *C.H. Gunasekera, C. Horan, N.S. Joseph, F.J. Siedle, E. Kelaart.

1-30.

	O	M	R	W
Wall	4	0	7	0
a'Beckett	7	0	16	0
Fairfax	5	1	19	1
Hurwood	2	0	6	0
McCabe	1	0	4	0

daylight. The Australian cricketers, except Woodfull and Oldfield, proceeded to Cairo by train, and are re-joining the *Orford* at Port Said tomorrow.'

The *Orford* sailed up the Suez Canal, taking Woodfull and Oldfield with it, while the others booked in to Shepherd's Hotel in Cairo, where a band played and you could sit in the beautiful gardens. The tourists, now literally tourists, faced a crowded day. They visited a museum to gaze at Tutankhamun relics, the famous Mosque Mahometali where Muslims were reading the *Koran*, and a bazaar. In Cairo, they even glimpsed King Fahd driving through the streets and Tebbutt noted that 'they were greatly amused at the natives in the suburbs of Cairo beating kerosene tins to scare off locusts and grasshoppers, of which there is at present a plague'.

They set off for the Pyramids and that involved riding camels. Richardson remembered [(15)] that they all did it except Grimmett who chose a donkey because there was less distance to fall. On the way back a camel race developed and Ponsford's broke loose from its handler. Despite Ponsford's cries of '*Halt!*' it headed out towards the desert. Richardson does not go into detail about how Ponsford was rescued or who did it. Tebbutt recorded how the tourists returned to their hotel 'considerably shaken' by the camel riding and Bradman wrote that he'd made his debut on a camel and never intended to get on one again. [(16)]

They started early next morning, Sunday 13 April, for Port Said and the *Orford*. As the ship steamed out into the Mediterranean for Naples, Tebbutt ruminated in a cable: 'In view of the small number of official engagements accepted, and also the retiring nature of the majority of the team, it appears that any attempt to make the cricketers social lions in England will not be encouraged. Woodfull does not drink, dance or smoke, and his example is being followed to a lesser degree by a number of others, who have rarely seen the dance floor on board the liner. Bradman is especially reluctant to dance, though he often entertains his friends with music. Jackson apparently prefers history books and Grimmett is busy finishing his book on cricket. a'Beckett is the team's keenest bridge player.'

Still they kept fit by playing deck sport and a'Beckett, Bradman, Fairfax, Hurwood, Jackson, McCabe, Ponsford and Oldfield won fourteen prizes between them.

Each moment brought the *Orford* nearer to Europe and Bradman's luck held. The Mediterranean was calm, too, although on the Wednesday, as Naples hoved into view on a bleak dawn, the weather was lousy. Clouds shrouded Vesuvius and a hail storm drummed out a very cold greeting.

Chapter Two

Home

THE PLAYERS PETITIONED THE AUSTRALIAN BOARD OF CONTROL TO be allowed to leave the ship when it docked and make their way overland to England, opening up the delights of the Continent to them. The Board agreed, stipulating only that they reach England at the same time as the *Orford.* The intrepid Tebbutt went continental walkabout, too.

The tourists disembarked and visited Pompeii and Vesuvius before, in the evening, catching the train to Rome. Bradman recorded how all this came as a wonderful revelation to him, in the sight-seeing sense. [(1)]

Rome exercised a profound effect on all of them. Their first experience, Tebbutt cabled:

> *'. . . was to follow a monk, clad in medieval garb, through the dark labyrinthine passages of the catacombs of Saint Sebastian, in which lie stone coffins and occasional heaps of bleached bones. The weird atmosphere was heightened by the fact that each member of the party carried aloft a lighted taper.*
>
> *'The team placed a wreath on the grave of the unknown warrior, and afterwards – sound evidence of cricket's appeal to Britishers everywhere – the British ambassador, Sir Ronald Graham, entertained the players at tea at the embassy. [He] expressed regret that he did not know of the visit*

earlier [because] he might have arranged for the Australians to meet Mussolini.

'The Australians were fortunate at seeing Rome in Holy week. They breakfasted within the sound of pealing bells to which the whole of the Eternal City echoed. Bradman surprised the waiter by asking for tea, the request immediately stamping him as an Australian. The team is rapidly becoming accustomed to the Continental diet with the exception that none is able to master the elusive macaroni!

'In delightful weather the Australians hustled through Rome, visiting the Forum, St Peter's, the Vatican and the Appian Way. In schoolboy fashion they are enjoying the colourful pageant of Italian life fascinated by the number and variety of the uniforms they see.'

Bradman recounted almost breathlessly the sites they visited, including John Keats's grave and strolling round at night proved 'an education'.

On the Friday, before they boarded the train for Milan, the Roman Catholic members of the team attended a Good Friday mass. During the journey – 'a wonderful panorama of mountain and coastal scenery'– the tourists gazed from their windows and were impressed by how profoundly British sport had penetrated Italy. In the shadow of the Appenine mountains, they saw 'many muddy football fields' and 'at the foot of one snow-clad peak, 2,000 excited Italians watched a rugby match as the train passed by'. (2)

After Rome's sunshine the gloomy weather closed in again but Richardson kept them entertained with a mimick-Italian language he had invented. Evidently they thoroughly enjoyed it but the Italians themselves were less than impressed, which must have made for even more hilarity.

After Milan they took the train to Lucerne, delighted by the picturesque scenery of the Swiss lakes and fascinated – especially Wall and Hurwood, who hadn't seen it before – when the train 'wound between towering peaks of the Alps, which were covered by a recent heavy fall of snow, which recommenced as the train emerged from the St. Gothard tunnel'.

When they arrived at Lucerne they bought gloves and sweaters – and they'd need them in England, too.

From Lucerne, Tebbutt cabled:

'The Australian cricketers, who a few days ago were sweltering in the tropics, today rejoiced in snowballing on the summit of Montrigi, 6,000 feet (1,800m) above sea level. The manager and the treasurer went to Interlaken, but the players proceeded to Lake Vitznau, ascended the cog-wheel railway to the peak, and bathed in brilliant sunshine. The team saw some magnificent panoramas in Lake Lucerne during respites in the snowball battles, which were waged with an unlimited supply of ammunition, even press representatives coming in for a share of good-natured bombardment.

'During a skirmish, T. Wall accidentally bumped a cigar from a German tourist's mouth, which evoked a torrent of unintelligible protest, the German apparently demanding 15 cents compensation for the ruined cigar, but international complications were averted.'

On the Monday they took the train for Paris. They hastened to the *Folies-Bergère* and its special delights, and revelled in a sketch lampooning British tourists in the city – not least, as Tebbutt pointed out, because it 'reminded them of their own language difficulties since their arrival in Europe'. The applause which greeted the lampoon made him think half the audience were English or American to have understood it.

There'd been thoughts of making a talkie film of them while they were there but it came to nothing, probably, Tebbutt thought, because they were too shy. Instead they became literal tourists again: the Louvre, Notre Dame, the Pantheon, Place de la Concorde, Champs- Élysées, Eiffel Tower and the Arc de Triomphe where Woodfull and Kelly placed a wreath in Australian colours on the tomb of the unknown soldier.

They stayed in style, a splendid hotel on the Champs-Élysées and, for Kippax and Richardson, the bedroom once reserved for Napoleon, complete with four-posters and oil paintings. Kippax said 'all we need now is for Napoleon to walk through that door' and at that moment McCabe did. He *looked* like Napoleon and from that moment on was known as 'Napper', a contraction of Napoleon.

They went to the races at St. Cloud, although as rather less than tourists because they'd made contact with an Australian trainer who had a good horse and an Australian jockey to ride it. The trainer gave them a 'patriotic' tip to back it – it was in the last race on the card – and six of them (Richardson, Kippax, Ponsford, McCabe, Kelly and Howard) did, winning £300. The trainer's young daughter joined the tourists in cheering the horse home, much to the bemusement of the silent French crowd. Reportedly, the nightclubs of Paris took care of the £300.

The London *Daily Telegraph* sent their correspondent over to interview the players, only to be told (no doubt to his anger and amazement) that they weren't giving any until they reached London. This was the first outside intimation that stern controls were to govern the tour – and, of course, they wouldn't be giving any interviews in London either.

The correspondent, Philip Trevor, wrote: 'My first impression was the remarkable youthfulness of the team. They were enjoying Paris, and are capable of enjoying anything. There is every reason to suppose that these boys will show England something well worth watching. Of Bradman and Jackson, I think Bradman has the greater future.'

It was extremely prescient, not least because it was very much a minority view.

As they prepared to board the midday train at the Gare du Nord for Calais, on Wednesday 23 April, Kelly said: 'Our little holiday in Europe is over.' He talked about getting into training and preparing for the job. Then the train pulled out across the pasturelands of northern France to Calais where they caught the cross-Channel ferry *Maid of Kent.* They were dressed formally – collars and ties, overcoats and hats. Still Bradman's luck held, with a calm crossing.

They watched as the white cliffs of Dover drew nearer and nearer. Although most of them had never seen England before the imagery of the cliffs, like so much else, was woven deeply into them.

The change began then. They'd been fêted at dinner in Colombo but after that they'd become anonymous. Which citizen of Rome knew of any of them, or cared about leg-breaks and googlies? Which solid burgher of Lucerne knew of any of them, or cared about swing bowling and sticky wickets. Which Parisienne, so slender and chic, would have known Richardson, Kippax, Bradman or any of the others wandering the Champs-Élysées? As *The Age* commented: 'The Continental tour was an eye-opener to the Australian cricketers. Some of their fellow passengers [on the trains] had not heard of the game of cricket, and were not even aware of the existence of Australia.' This brought one benefit: 'The fact that cricket has not the least interest to Continental people has enabled the team to enjoy a holiday as private people.'

The sense of change sharpened at Dover docks. At Dover everybody knew and everybody cared. *Maid of Kent* docked in the harbour shortly before 5pm. The town's Mayor and Lord Harris, a venerated cricket figure, officially greeted them in front of a large, enthusiastic crowd. (3) As the seagulls wheeled and cawed, the Mayor, wearing his robes of office and accompanied by an attendant in livery, briefly welcomed the team.

Bradman wrote in *Don Bradman's Book*: 'The feeling that at last we had come Home was indescribable. [. . .] to be among folk who claimed us as their very own captured us entirely.'

The train pulled out of Dover and, as Bradman would insist, only those making this journey for the first time could understand 'how soul-stirring it is, how immensely different from any other journey. The green, its richness, the colour of the countryside, the perfect peace of it all – never have I beheld nor yet have I been so moved by the picture that was painted.' (4)

Within thirteen days he would have taken by storm, no less, this country he did not know and yet knew so well; and within eleven weeks he would have reshaped the possibilities of Test cricket to the point where it has never been the same since. Other batsmen, *all* the others, had 'inhibitions he never knew'. (5)

The train journey through Kent's natural riches – the trellises of fruit, the hop kilns and chimneys, the cottages – had a profound effect. Another of the newcomers wrote that as the train neared London 'a hush of expectancy overcame us all. We were arriving very soon in the heart of what Britishers in overseas Dominions then still knew as "Home". One after another, we rose quietly from out seats and donned our hats and coats. Silently, we stood and waited for the great event.' (6)

They were so eagerly anticipated there were fears that if their carriage formed part of the normal train, arriving at a normal platform, it would be over-run. To circumvent this, a private platform had been chosen. The train, due at 7.15pm, was seventeen minutes late and as it reached the London suburbs grey drizzle fell.

At Victoria – an august, imposing edifice – a great host of cricket notables waited. Platform barriers and a large number of police 'kept back the main crowd of spectators, and only a few privileged persons and an army of reporters and photographers were allowed inside', *The*

Age reported. 'In view of the fact that 4,000 Londoners were barricaded well away from the reception platform, the arrival of the team must have been one of the quietest recorded in the history of Test cricket. Immediately the train stopped Mr. Kelly stepped down and shook hands with Lord Plumer [President of the MCC].

The tourists 'filed out one by one amid a silence that was so pronounced that Mr. Kelly could easily be heard introducing each member. While Percy Chapman sought out Woodfull and shook hands with him, Jack Hobbs and the other English players were giving a welcome to the others. There was a crowded jostling mass on the platform for at least five minutes and then the photographers took charge.'

Mr Fenton, the Australian Minister of Customs who 'had been struggling to get a close glimpse of his countrymen, took off his hat and shouted: "Three cheers for the Australians."

'When the cheers died he shouted again: "Good luck to the Kangaroos."'

The tourists 'drifted in ones and twos across the platform towards a fleet of private motor cars'. (7) When they were in them the cars moved so fast that the crowd couldn't pick out the players but they cheered all the same. Within a minute the drizzle and the London traffic swallowed them as they turned north for their hotel, the Midland Grand at St. Pancras Station.

In the past Australian tours stayed at the Cecil on the Thames Embankment, built during the 1890s and the largest in London with 800 ornately decorated rooms, but it had been demolished.

The Australians would have to make do with the Midland – an 'incredible, High Victorian Gothic tour-de-force' dating to 1876 (8) in unfashionable Euston Road. Tebbutt described it as a 'an immense railway hotel, with corridors so long that the glimmer of daylight at the other end made them appear to stretch for miles'. There was a drawback: the noise of trains arriving and departing at all hours.

When the tourists woke next morning, the location of the hotel might have shattered 'a dream of London', Tebbutt felt. 'True, the red busses of London – those blurs of scarlet that had been familiar pictures from boyhood – thundered past, but this world of gigantic [advertising] posters, shabby women, and oppressed-looking men in an estuary of dull grey streets – was this London?' (9)

The more fashionable areas, as they would learn, were not far away and, precisely because of its location, the hotel offered sanctuary despite the train noise. They'd come to regard its architectural 'freakishness' and 'profusion of spires and ornaments, and almost church-like interior, as home'.

They'd also have to make do with their fifteen players because the Board refused their request for an extra bowler.

On the first morning, all of them emerged for a full day of engagements except McCabe, confined to bed with an infection. A doctor who attended him diagnosed something he'd eaten and said he should be fine in a couple of days.

The official day began at Australia House, a massive stone pile on The Strand where the High Commissioner, Sir Granville Ryrie, bade them welcome. Pelham Warner, [10] spoke on behalf of England and Woodfull gave a brief version of *the* speech before Kelly responded.

'We like hospitality,' he said. 'Everyone does. From the moment we landed at Dover yesterday we have been given a marvellous reception but we are here as cricketers. We are here to win back the Ashes. We know that you good English people do not want to destroy our chances by giving too much hospitality.'

London's *Evening News* carried a front-page story which brought it alive.

> *'Up in the library of Australia House they were all jammed together today, all shaking hands in a cramped sort of way and all talking at once – men who were giants in the days gone by, men whose names will be legends in days to come. Somewhere, in the crush, were the Australian team because this was their first reception in London. Over there, towering above the heads, was Mr. Chapman, with the curly hair and boyish smile, and just nearby was Lord Harris of the grizzled little beard, and over someone's shoulder you could catch a glimpse of "Plum" Warner's pleasant face. But where were the Australians? One by one you picked them out . . .*
>
> *'There, standing as a tall young schoolboy near the wall, was Woodfull, the unbowlable captain, looking round him with his calm brown eyes. Jackson, willowy and graceful as a tall young schoolboy, talked to Oldfield, the veteran wicket-keeper, who was quite invisible amid the throng, and Vic Richardson laughed in that merry way of his, the laugh quite unheard in the din. Ponsford was near the door, hemmed in by the crowd. Ponsford was not saying much. Ponsford never does say much. He was just listening to the fragments of talk that filled the room.*

'Sir Granville Ryrie, the High Commissioner, mounted an impromptu dais and began to speak in that breezy, devil-may-care way of his. "I hope the older members of the team will point out the pitfalls to the youngsters," he said. "To play good cricket they have got to get to bed early and – you know, avoid the pitfalls." The youngsters laughed. "I'm pleased to see among the team a lot of young fellows," added Sir Granville. "In fact they look like mere boys. But I think they're pretty good boys."

'Warner mounted the dais. "Well," he said, "for the moment we hold the Ashes. I see Mr. Chapman in the room. I don't want to destroy your morale with the first over – but you know what Mr. Chapman has done both in this country and in Australia! We hope to see him in command again this year. He is a great captain and has that happy and charming manner which endears him both to his own side and his opponents."'

The tourists were given a lunch by the British Sportsman's Club at the Savoy Hotel. The King sent a message: 'Please convey to all present my sincere thanks for the loyal and friendly greetings you have sent me. I am glad that my son [the Duke of Gloucester] is present on this occasion, which I trust may be a happy beginning of an enjoyable tour for your guests, to whom I offer a hearty welcome.'

Lord Harris proposed the toast. Woodfull, responding, said: 'Most of the team have never had the pleasure of meeting the King. If they are able to catch a glimpse of him during the summer I can assure you it will be one of the great days of their lives.'

Later in the afternoon they went to Lord's for a net. Understandably Bradman had been impatient to see the ground but it didn't look quite as he had imagined it would. He was impressed all the same and cast a close eye on the turf, which he found quite unlike anything in Australia. He remembered particularly how soft it was. (11)

The Times, describing the practice wickets as so dead no reliable first opinions could be formed, wrote that this preliminary session 'could not be regarded as anything more than an opportunity to open their shoulders and to run about in fresh air'. Hurwood and Walker, neither regarded as batsmen, went in first. *The Times* added in its own austere way: 'There were just one or two bright moments. The first was when Jackson was batting. Two or three balls was enough to declare that here is a batsman of the very highest class. The manner in which he shapes up to the ball, his wonderful footwork, and the ease with which he plays all his strokes surpassed in fact even what we in this country have read of him.' There was no mention of Bradman.

Next day, the tourists went to the Cenotaph where a crowd gathered to mark Gallipoli Day and Woodfull laid a wreath. They attended the Anzac Memorial Service (12) at St. Clement Dane's Church in The Strand, went to Waterman's where each was presented with a pen and pencil, went to the Savoy Hotel for a luncheon by the British Sportsman's Club.

They had another net at Lord's, too, but it was 'unimpressive' in cold, gloomy weather and on sodden practice wickets. McCabe, recovered, batted and bowled but the conditions still didn't allow initial judgements to be made.

The tourists literally went through the motions. Wall bowled at half pace, Hurwood, Hornibrook and Fairfax scarcely bowled at all and the wickets were so lifeless that even Grimmett couldn't make the ball spin. Kippax, however, looked in some sort of form. Walker did some wicket-keeping to Grimmett but Oldfield didn't appear.

Woodfull and Ponsford timed the ball well, Richardson and a'Beckett gave it a belt or two and Bradman didn't stay long. Jackson had a good session, mostly against Grimmett.

On Saturday morning, however much sleep they'd lost to the nocturnal train movements, they had another net at Lord's and this time they attracted a large crowd, many of those from Huddersfield who'd come on the trains for the afternoon's FA Cup final against Arsenal – for which the tourists had tickets. The Yorkshire folk loved their cricket and what better way to spend the morning than sizing up these Australians, especially since they'd only seen four of them before? Lord Plumer and MCC secretary Billy Findlay cast a benevolent eye over it for a while, too.

This net, lasting about an hour and played out under another gloomy sky, was conducted much more intently that the two before it. The tourists looked 'fit and keen. Nothing very serious was, of course, attempted but it was obvious that the men are now getting down to it.' (13) The admission charge, a shilling, proved just right because enough members of the public came to surround the nets but not enough to make viewing difficult.

The batsmen were hitting the ball 'hard, high and often' now.

The Evening News reported:

> *'After Don Bradman, in a bright blue, rather perky-looking inter-State cap which picked him out from the vivid green worn by his colleagues, had made a few preliminary flourishes, Archie Jackson got the entire "gate" to himself. Many of the MCC ground bowlers gathered at the back of Jackson's net, and "Plum" Warner called his young son across to gather hints from Australia's second Trumper. Jackson, with delightful ease and style, brought most of his large repertoire of shots into play, including the scintillating square cut of which we have heard a great deal. Much of his colleagues' bowling he hit for fours – or as near a four as the nets would permit – but Clarence Grimmett, assiduously practising googlies, had him more than once. Grimmett grinned and Jackson nodded his appreciation.'*

(Tebbutt claimed a spectator got Fairfax out twice – bowled, played on – although who the spectator was, and why he bowled, is not clear. Two schoolboys were invited to bowl and were delighted to do it. However, 'on the other side of the practice ground Young England were busy at the schoolboy nets, and great was the delight when one of the boys, an Irish lad, was allowed to bowl a few balls at Alan Fairfax'. **(14)** Whether this was the explanation or even happened on the same day, is not clear.)

Although the wickets were soft, the bowlers found pace off it, especially Wall, Hornibrook and a'Beckett. **(15)**

The Institute of Journalists entertained the team to lunch. Woodfull paid tribute to Anzac Day which, he said 'was remembered not merely because of the landing but because it was a great link between all overseas Dominions and the mother country'. An ashtray had been placed on each table inscribed '*I am here for the Ashes*' and Woodfull said: 'Before we go any further you can take these with you' – which, amidst great laughter, the Australians did. A silent toast was drunk to the Australians who fell at Gallipoli.

On this Saturday morning the Worcester team for the Australians' opening match the following Wednesday was announced, although the Hon. John Coventry, captain of Worcestershire *and* Mayor of Worcester, was ill with a severe cold and couldn't play. The Australians were careful to send Coventry a telegram: 'The Australian team deeply regret your absence from the match, and your illness, and hope you will very soon be leading your team to victory.'

The Cup final made a deep impression. 'We arrived early at Wembley, in time to lunch with the Football Association officials, to join the community singing and to harken to the rousing music of the massed bands,' Richardson remembered.

King George had been recuperating at Bognor Regis from a serious bronchial illness and had now returned to Windsor Castle. Word came to Wembley that, weather permitting, he'd make his first public appearance there. Between songs in the community singing an announcement said the King had left Windsor and 'the great crowd went wild at the news'. (16) When the King arrived, the crowd rose and sang the National Anthem with a fervour which – in his own words – thrilled Bradman in a way he'd not experienced before. (17)

That evening they went to a gala night at the Coliseum, one of London's largest theatres. *The Age* reported that the tourists would 'probably establish a reputation as the shyest team that has visited England. They entered the Coliseum in darkness after the commencement of the First Act, but the watchful audience, to whom the cricketers were a greater attraction than the vaudeville, gave them an ovation. The Australians occupied the royal box, which was draped in green and gold'.

Years later, Bert Oldfield wrote that 'as far back as I can remember, every Australian team has been entertained in a very wonderful fashion by the management of the Coliseum Theatre, London, where usually a special performance in our honour is arranged. Each player is given a suitable souvenir to celebrate the occasion.' (18)

This time it was a thoroughbred Australian terrier. The players and officials assembled on the stage and Tom Webster, the famous cartoonist, made the presentation to Kelly, who accepted it as the team's mascot. Webster suggested the dog be called 'Anzac' and the audience loved that, cheered and cheered. So Anzac it was, and the terrier was christened with ginger beer.

Afterwards they went to a party at the Grosvenor House Hotel, had supper and danced until the early hours. On the Sunday, as was the custom, they rested.

Some time during these initial days in London, Bradman was approached by a literary agent, David Cromb, to write a book about the tour. He pointed out that he could not publish a word until it was over. He could of course write during it for subsequent publication and that is what he did, keeping a diary. People remember seeing him engrossed in doing this.

On the Monday the tourists moved through a more intense, prolonged practice session although Bradman and Kippax were confined to bed with chills. Under more leaden skies, a biting wind and more sodden wickets a'Beckett bowled impressively in front of a small crowd. The shilling admission evidently deterred them now. Richardson played a hard-hitting, light-hearted innings and was bowled three times in a few minutes.

There would be no more light-hearted innings from any of them. The tour was about to get serious.

Chapter Three

Murder in May (Act I)

Worcestershire

WORCESTER HUMMED WITH ANTICIPATION. SOME SIXTY REPORTERS were due and an ordinary County match rarely attracted more than six. Scores of photographers would be coming, too.

The *Worcester Daily Times* noted that 'the primitive Press Box is capable, with the greatest crush, of accommodating only about 14 or 16 so the management are arranging to set apart two or three dozen seats in one of the stands with an improvised desk. The interest in the match has induced members of the Club to pay their subscriptions early. In fact 1,000 have already paid, presumably to profit by the membership privileges at this match.'

The tourists had had to refuse a dinner from Lord Doverdale, Chairman of the Committee, because of pressure of time but they would, however, dine at the Guildhall on the Wednesday.

They left London on Tuesday afternoon and arrived at Shrub Hill Station, Worcester at 7pm although Kippax stayed behind, bed-ridden with a chill. That was improving and he was due to travel to Worcester the following day. Richardson remembered 'the first glance we cast there was at that stately old Cathedral'.

Major Maurice Jewell, acting captain in Coventry's absence, the

Deputy Mayor and many others were on the platform to greet them. The formalities over they went to the Star Hotel. They intended to be up early and Woodfull intended to announce the side early, too.

The Times cricket correspondent Beau Vincent remembered Bradman that evening. 'He was sitting in front of the fireplace in the public writing-room – alone and thinking.' Vincent never forgot that and felt it came to symbolise his approach to the game. The man was 'master of himself, always thinking, always concentrating on what needed doing'.

Wednesday dawned cloudless and the London *Evening Standard* claimed that 'the sun shone down with almost summer-like intensity. On the one side, the River Severn flowed peacefully and the old Cathedral looked down. On the other, Malvern Hills were seen dimly in the distance.'

The fact the ground had been flooded only weeks before seemed difficult to believe, and there had been a succession of floods before that. The fact that someone caught fish where the wicket was laid seemed equally difficult to believe. The tourists didn't recognise the weather as summer or anything approaching it and Bradman said ruefully that, even with the thickest sweater on, the wind 'cut into our very bones'. The flooding meant that the pitch would be spongy and unlike anything the newcomers in the Australian side had ever seen before.

Worcester weren't a strong side although they did have Fred Root, a medium-fast bowler who'd invented leg theory. Against the 1926 Australians, a much more experienced side, he deployed his inswingers on the leg stump for the North of England at Edgbaston, and wrecked the Australians' first innings by taking 7 for 42.

Later, for Worcester he took 4 for 61 in the first innings from 35 overs and conceded only 4 runs from 6 overs in the second. That year he played three Tests.

Root had been playing county cricket since 1910 and, from the 1920s, took 100 wickets in nine straight seasons. He seemed exactly the type of bowler to expose Bradman's faults. Root knew every blade of grass, knew how to exploit the wind off the river and – with his predatory field placing – had imprisoned and defeated a whole generation of batsmen. Country boys with cross bats from far, far away were little lambs especially on a spongy wicket.

The tourists did get to the County Ground early and at 11am had a net. The knowing among the spectators congregrated around the net Bradman batted in and although other nets were being used nobody bothered about them much. 'It was the young Australian wonder batsman all were eager to see.' [(1)] Apart from nets, he had not of course yet batted in England.

What Root would do to Bradman had to wait because Jewell won the toss and batted. People in the stands murmured they wouldn't be seeing Bradman today. Thereby hangs a tale because the match, and the toss, were being filmed. Jewell had a penny and when he spun it Woodfull called 'tails'. The cameraman wasn't satisfied with the shot he got and asked Jewell to spin again. Jewell agreed but insisted it wouldn't count. [(2)]

The tourists left out Ponsford, who had a slight knee injury – he'd been hit on it the previous day having a net – and that showed how dangerously they might be exposed with only the fifteen players. By definition, Walker wouldn't be playing when Oldfield was and Kippax lay abed in London, so Hurwood became the only player genuinely rested.

As the Cathedral clock tolled midday – the peals varied during the day, and played the opening of such tunes as 'Home Sweet Home' and 'The Last Rose of Summer' – Woodfull led the Australians out and Wall prepared to launch the tour. Bradman, having a good look round, saw how delightful the ground was.

Grimmett – small, gnome-like and with a low round-arm action – could make his leg-breaks play havoc with Test sides and Worcester, despite playing the graceful and promising Cyril Walters in mid-order, were not remotely that. They reached 70 for 4 by lunch, and collapsed to 131 all out at 3.30pm. Only Walters approached Grimmett with confidence and after lunch used his feet to hit him on the full. His downfall came when he tried to 'hit a ball from him over a kite which supported a banner recommending the spectators to buy Australian apples, and was deservedly stumped'. [(3)]

Woodfull and Jackson opened the Australian innings and, as they walked out, Root already had his field placed for the leg theory. Woodfull, who'd seen it before, played it comfortably but Jackson had a long, hard look. Then they scored 67 in fifty-five minutes before Jackson hooked a short ball from leg-break bowler George Brook and was caught at short leg. They took tea and when the batsmen emerged from the pavilion the crowd stood in a throng to witness Bradman. [(4)]

Bradman came in, no doubt slowly to let his eyes become accustomed to the light.

'The lush, cushiony Worcester turf was dotted with worm casts, the deposits secreted by worms burrowing in the fertile soil; and even though the roller had broken these down, they left small slippery patches. The cool misty air and prevailing breeze favoured the bowlers, and caused unexpected variations in the flight of the ball.' (5)

Perhaps because he had not batted on an English pitch before, and not played Root before, he started carefully, watching the ball full on to the bat. The reporters who hadn't seen him bat before recorded their first impression: how frequently he played back, how fast his feet moved. He never looked like getting out.

When he was ready he 'at once exposed the poverty of the bowling. At times, brilliant stroke-maker that he is, he must have been puzzled to know where to look for the ball, so lavishly were full pitches mixed up with long hops and other balls for which there is no established form of description. Major Jewell tried all of his team who were known to bowl [. . .] but play soon became little more than a fielding practice.' (6)

At least Root the old pro contained him initially. Root knew his trade and he'd describe the problems leg theory created and how quickly Bradman solved them.

> *'The accurate pitching of the ball, on or about leg stump, cramps the style of the two-eyed batsmen whose feet are almost always together and who can only score runs by "jabbing" the ball, generally behind the wicket and only with what little power the arms can lend to a stroke of that description.*
>
> *'Bradman is an exception. His footwork would do credit to an expert dancer and enables him to make use of his left shoulder. When he first experienced my leg theory [. . .] he was palpably puzzled but eventually he overcame it by his magnificent footwork, and was finally driving inswingers from the leg stump past extra cover.*
>
> *'There is no temerity about Bradman's methods. He does not suspect a trap in a half-volley, long hop or full toss, and his method of defence is to attack. As a bowler I can readily vouch for the efficacy of such a theory. Nothing upsets the average bowler so much as to be hit hard and often. Even the leg theory wilts under punishment, and I have always maintained that if batsmen will "go for it" this attack loses half its terrors.'* (7)

Bradman was playing shots along the ground all round the wicket and some forty minutes before the close began to belt boundaries. His 50 came from a full toss and Arthur Mailey, writing in the Sydney *Sun,* distilled the final half hour: during it '*Bradman did as he liked*'. By the close the Australians made 199 for 1, Woodfull 95 and Bradman – 75 in an hour and a half with eight 4s – travelling fast.

Describing the innings, Warner wrote that Bradman was 'blessed with powerful wrists and a rare eye. He timed the ball beautifully. If not such a stylist as Jackson, he is a most interesting batsman to watch and, like Jackson, makes full use of his nimbleness of foot and when he hits he hits quickly, if one may use the expression.' **(8)**

That evening they went to the Guildhall for the dinner and by now Bradman found himself enchanted by Worcester. You can easily imagine the impact the Guildhall, originally built around 1227 and rebuilt in 1722, had on a young man from a young country. The exterior was brick dressed with stone, there were carved figures of Queen Anne, Charles the first and second, and the interior was 'superb, boasting exceptional period decoration'. **(9)**

The Deputy Mayor greeted them because Coventry wasn't even well enough to attend. He sent a message, however. 'I think this is one of the saddest days of my life. I have been so looking forward to leading the Worcestershire team out to play the Australians, and then in the evening welcoming them at the dinner. Will you convey my regrets to the Australian team and to the others present. I am confident that they will not find another Mayor to play against them on this tour [laughter]. Will you, for me, wish them a pleasant game, a very happy tour, and a successful season [applause].'

The Deputy Mayor (forgetting Sandham's 325) pointed out that R.E. Foster of Worcestershire still held the Test record score and 'if any Australian beat that record, Worcestershire men and England men would be glad to take their hats off to him'. [Hear, hear, applause.] He also said that a clergyman held a record no Australian would beat: during the flooding he had swum across the ground from the pavilion and back again.

Woodfull made *his* speech. Kelly made *his* speech.

Warner, a guest of honour, spoke of Foster's innings because he – Warner – had been captain that day. Nobody said that, having stood for twenty-six years, it might stand for another twenty-six or much, much longer. Who, seated in the Guildhall's ancient splendours, could imagine that the cross-bat country boy listening to these speeches and with no more than 75 runs in England would get to within 33 of it the following month, beat it by 47 the month after that and get to within 55 of it the month after *that.*

He stayed until 9pm and excused himself, wanting to get to bed. It was nothing personal about the dinner, it was business. He told Root that before he left Australia he decided to dedicate himself to cricket and ignore every distraction. The social side, beyond the mandatory 'official' functions, would not be permitted to intrude. So he went to bed.

Next morning frost lay like a skin across the ground at 5am but by breakfast it had gone and the weather turned 'as perfect as the imagination of a poet could think of' (*The Times)* although 'a chilly wind blew clouds across the ground' (*The Sun,* Sydney*).* The crowd was big and would become bigger when the shops closed at midday.

Bradman sought out Root and asked if George Geary turned 'the ball a lot on English wickets?' Geary played for Leicestershire, the Australians' next opponents, and although he was in the middle of his Worcester innings he was already preparing mentally for Leicester. (10)

The wicket played a little faster when Root opened, with his leg theory, and Bradman on-drove him to the boundary although the final ball struck him on the leg.

Woodfull moved serenely to his century in the second over of the day.

The leg theory no longer disturbed Bradman at all. He was quite prepared, as someone noted, to spend half an hour playing himself – but during that time the batsmen added 49. Then Bradman began to apply his power to the strokes against Root and off-break bowler Peter Jackson. He moved into the 90s and on the way punched Jackson through the covers. In the 90s he turned Jackson to the leg-side boundary and, at midday, cut him for 2 to reach a century out of 169 in just under two hours.

Brook came on, went for 10 in his first over and the Australians were travelling at two runs a minute. Bradman scored at will, guiding Root through the leg trap as well as on-driving him. Bradman positively danced from and across the crease and the crowd loved it.

Brook struck by bowling the unbowlable Woodfull for 133, bringing young McCabe in but he went quickly, caught at mid-on by Root off Brook, and Richardson – hatless, as was his custom – set about the bowling while Bradman moved past Woodfull's 133 with two lusty shots. He played a beautiful off-drive from Brook and then a couple of late cuts to reach 150 in three hours.

Richardson was unlucky because Bradman drove a ball hard back at medium-pacer Leslie Wright and it deflected from Wright's finger on to the stumps with Richardson out of his ground.

Fairfax was out almost immediately and the Australians came in to lunch at 380 for 5, Bradman 173 – from the second ball before it, he'd survived an appeal for caught at the wicket off Root when he tried to hit him to the leg-side boundary.

The crowd grew from 1,200 to some 2,500 when play resumed and Worcester bowled tighter. Bradman went into his careful mode again as he reached towards his double century. Root demonstrated how effective the leg theory could be against the rest of the Australians because he dismissed a'Beckett and Oldfield in it.

Bradman took the attack to him, dancing impudently out to hit a boundary and then, poaching a single, he had 200 in three and a quarter hours. He swung Root to the leg-side boundary and became so aggressive that the leg theory fielders were 'moved back to a safer beat'.

Bradman was to break a great deal across this summer – records and reputations – and here was the first example. As it happened, he reached the double century when the Cathedral bells were chiming *Last Rose of Summer.* It should have been *First Rose of Summer.*

Root had tried to tempt Bradman with the leg theory but Bradman, smiling, simply ignored it or plundered it. In this duel all Root could claim was the confident but unsuccessful appeal for a catch behind the wicket just before lunch. Bradman now hit at everything and when he was 215 gave a real chance, smacking a ball back at Brook but it went so hard that it burst through Brook's hands into his stomach and fell to the ground.

He was finally out caught at square leg for 236 going halfway down the wicket to pull Brook. The *Australian Press Association* wrote that 'after punching the bowling to all parts of the field, Bradman attempted a hit which looked like an effort to reach the spire of Worcester Cathedral, but mis-timed. Walters, running back, took a good catch and the fieldsmen joined in the ovation, doubtless with better reason than the spectators.'

Apart from the semi-chance to Brook, this was Bradman's first mis-hit in four hours forty minutes and during that time he'd scored twenty-eight boundaries, seven 3s and fifteen 2s.

The Worcester crowd were impressed and cheered him all the way back from the wicket. *The Times* was impressed too:

> *'Bradman does not lift up his bat straight, but over and over again he makes the stroke in the end absurdly simple by the speed of his footwork, and never once did he make the slightest suggestion of hitting the ball in the air [before 215]. Until he had made 200 Bradman took no undue liberties, but he found time composedly to play almost every stroke which the most greedy spectator could ask to see. His drives, whether straight or square, were equally certain. His cutting was perfect, always with the full blade of the bat coming down on the ball, and his forcing strokes off his right leg were beautifully timed, but the most welcome of all his strokes was his true, honest on-drive.'*

The Guardian's 'Cricketer' – Neville Cardus – had mixed feelings:

> *'After Woodfull's passing the play was Bradman's almost entirely. So busily did he score his runs that I got the impression that he was batting at both ends of the wicket. He drove to the on pugnaciously, wasting not a penn'orth of agility and power. He frequently delighted us with a swift and pretty late cut – the flashing sort that wakens up the slips with a start on a day of sunshine. To a short ball on the off side Bradman would lie back and crack through the covers from his right foot. His batsmanship might be described as thick-set: it is virile not supple, agile rather than flexible. Good honest muscle provides the motive-power; Bradman has not the volatility of mind, the sheer sensibility of Jackson. He is for his age a batsman of extraordinary technical scope and finish, but his style is so to say, democratic: Jackson and Kippax are the pedigree batsmen of the Australian eleven.'*

Getting Bradman into proper focus was not going to be easy, as the initial Cardus impression demonstrates. Woodfull declared at 492 for 8 but the Australians toiled on the third day to dismiss Worcestershire – they did eventually – which seemed to indicate that their batting was powerful but their bowling wasn't.

And Bradman? He was barely into his stride, as George Geary would discover, starting tomorrow.

WORCESTERSHIRE V AUSTRALIANS

Worcester 30 April, 1, 2 May. Australians won by an innings and 165 runs.

WORCESTERSHIRE

*M.F.S. Jewell	c Fairfax	b Grimmett	7	ht wkt	b Hornibrook	10
L. Wright	lbw	b Grimmett	28		run out	18
M. Nichol		run out	8	c Hornibrook	b Grimmett	1
H.H.I.H. Gibbons		not out	31		b Hornibrook	22
W.V. Fox	lbw	b Grimmett	0	c Oldfield	b Grimmett	28
C.F. Walters	st Oldfield	b Grimmett	21		c&b Grimmett	44
C.F. Root	st Oldfield	b Fairfax	9		b Grimmett	48
G.W. Brook		b Fairfax	2		b Grimmett	0
+S.W. Styler		run out	13	lbw	b Hornibrook	1
H.A. Gilbert		b Fairfax	0	absent hurt		
P.F. Jackson	lbw	b Fairfax	0		not out	4
Extras	(b 7, lb 4, nb 1)		12	(b 8, lb 10, w 1, nb 1)		20
Total			131			196

1-16, 2-41, 3-53, 4-53, 5-95, 6-106, 7-111, 8-131, 9-131

1-25, 2-26, 3-41, 4-75, 5-103, 6-187, 7-187, 8-192, 9-196

	O	M	R	W	O	M	R	W
Wall	8	1	21	0	11	5	22	0
a'Beckett	6	4	2	0	11	3	25	0
Grimmett	24	12	38	4	28.3	13	46	5
Hornibrook	7	1	22	0	17	5	30	3
Fairfax	12.3	2	36	4	21	8	45	0
McCabe					3	1	8	0

AUSTRALIANS

*W.M. Woodfull		b Brook	133
A.A. Jackson	c Walters	b Brook	24
D.G. Bradman	c Walters	b Brook	236
S.J. McCabe	c Root	b Brook	15
V.Y. Richardson		run out	24
A.G. Fairfax	c Root	b Jackson	0
E.L. a'Beckett	c Gilbert	b Root	24
+W.A. Oldfield	c Jackson	b Root	4
C.V. Grimmett		not out	15
T.W. Wall		not out	9
Extras	(b 4, lb 2, w 1, nb 1)		8
Total	(8 wkts dec)		492

Dnb: P.M. Hornibrook.

1-67, 2-275, 3-293, 4-366, 5-368, 6-415, 7-426, 8-480

	O	M	R	W
Root	43	9	112	2
Jackson	25	1	105	1
Gilbert	4	0	30	0
Brook	36	1	148	4
Wright	18	1	68	0
Gibbons	2	0	21	0

Leicestershire

They caught the 3pm train to Leicester and next morning were up early again, this time for a look round the city. *The Leicester Mercury* nicely caught their departure for the ground.

> *'Judging from the number of bags containing cricket kit which were moved from the tourists' hotel headquarters to the Aylestone Road Ground this morning, it looked as though the Australians were at least hopeful of outnumbering the men from the huntingshire.*
>
> *'A number of interested spectators watched the kit being loaded on to a couple of hand carts, and as this unusual cavalcade made its way to the ground the interest of many people was aroused, because of the several names famous in the cricket world that could be recognised on the bags.*
>
> *'All told there were 17 bags, all painted with a binding of green and yellow. Those of Alex [sic] Kippax and Archie Jackson came most prominently into the eye because of their unusual shape and size. Each was adorned with four handles, and looked big enough to accommodate a kangaroo. A large mystery box proved to be the medicine chest.'*

Still the English journalists reached to find the proper Bradman focus, a theme which became a torment for many of those doing it. On the morning of the Leicester match *The Evening News* in London carried a column by their cricket correspondent, Harry Carson, who'd covered Worcester.

> *'We saw a lot of Bradman, and for sheer beauty of shot and variety of stroke we should have to go back to the old-timers to find anyone to compare with him. Bradman has a vicious drive past the bowler just a bit too straight for either mid-on or mid-off to cover the stroke, and I am inclined to think this will upset our fields.*
>
> *'We saw [him] get over two hundred runs on a plumb wicket – a really magnificent batting wicket – and it did not require five minutes' watching to know that he is a great batsman on a wicket that suits him. Whether he is as good on turf where the ball is turning cannot be said at present. His footwork is superb: a movement an inch or two either way gives him the position he wants. But he swings his bat out instead of parallel to the stumps – and that may give us a chance.'*

Here again was something approaching consensus: the flaw in the technique could be exploited. No doubt the Leicester players didn't have a chance to read this and in a moment they'd have a chance to find out for themselves.

The Australians reached the ground at 10.45am on the sort of dull, overcast morning they'd become accustomed to in London. Early drizzle had melted into the grey and stopped. Geary, wearing an enormous hat, was there to greet them.

The Leicester players had a net and when the Australians took their turn the crowd swarmed across to see Ponsford, who was among the first in. McCabe's 'extraordinarily powerful off-driving' kept the crowd alert and at a safe distance.

At just before midday Richardson and the Leicestershire captain, John Adrian Frederick March Phillipps de Lisle, went out to toss the coin in front of the pavilion. Richardson lost the toss and Leicester batted, watched by about 2,000 spectators. The grass hadn't recovered from winter [11] and sawdust was needed for the footholds. Rain punctuated the day although the crowd swelled to 5,000. During play Grimmett (7 for 46) reduced Leicestershire to 148 all out and the Australians had an hour to bat.

Jackson went for 4, bowled by Geary, who later – at 35 – had Ponsford lbw. Bradman finished the day with 9 and Kippax 11.

On the strength of this 9, and Worcester, *The Times* wrote: 'It will soon be difficult to know what to say of him. He is clearly a genius in the manner in which he is continually looking for runs, but throughout gives an impression of complete security.'

The Australians spent a quiet weekend, said the weather really was cold and felt a bit stiff after Worcester.

On the Monday morning, mist left enough moisture on the pitch for sawdust to be needed again. Leicester was known for its early morning dew and that might make the pitch difficult for half an hour or so.

In front of 2,000 spectators, Bradman took Geary's first over and ran a leg bye to get the play moving. Geary's leg-spinners kept Bradman on the defensive because they were bowling him outside the leg stump but he pushed his innings into motion again with a couple off Alan Shipman, right-arm fast. A tone had been set: only 9 runs added in the first twenty minutes, 16 in thirty. Bradman looked stiff, snicked one ball through the slips and, next over, was comprehensively beaten – but not dismissed. Geary even beat Bradman who played forward. The spin took the ball past the edge of the bat and past the stumps.

At 77 Horace Snary, right-arm medium-slow, had Kippax caught after Bradman square cut him to the boundary. McCabe came in but Geary 'puzzled' (12) him and struck the leg stump for 2 and Bradman and Richardson were together. Richardson prepared to take the bowling on as he had done at Worcester, Bradman circumspect enough to have spent the first hour and forty minutes scoring 25. The dew meant that the batsmen had to defend and the ball was keeping low.

Five minutes later the Australian 100 came up in two hours five minutes when Bradman delicately leg-glanced Ewart Astill, who could spin the ball from something like medium pace. It made Bradman 40, scored in an hour and forty-five.

Richardson struck a boundary to square leg and four runs later 'there was a mild sensation when Shipman failed to get to a sharp return from Bradman' although there are disputed accounts about whether it was a bump ball or a genuine chance. (13)

He'd lingered long in the 40s but now began to go up the wicket – three full yards to Astill and 'with a flick of the wrists the ball was amongst the crowd' (14) to reach 50 in two and a quarter hours. It was Bradman's first boundary.

Bradman had been so defensive that Astill, accurate and on a length, was able to position a silly mid-on. Emerging from that he repeatedly swept Astill, who was bowling round the wicket and with no slip, then late cut fast-medium bowler Norman Armstrong to the boundary and the crowd of over 4,000 adored that.

The second Australian hundred came up in only an hour and a quarter, Richardson all muscle and ferocious intent. The Australians went in to lunch at 211 (Bradman 82, Richardson 73), the stand worth 131.

After lunch, Snary opened the bowling with the new ball. *The Times* noted that Bradman still looked a bit stiff and that prevented him displaying his full range of strokes. He moved to 90 with a late cut to the boundary off Snary (what one reporter called his favourite 'chop' shot) but might have been run out backing up.

Richardson, who'd started hitting straight 6s, beat Bradman to the century – Bradman on 97 when Richardson got there with a single off Geary. Bradman took three and a half hours to get there, reaching it with a snick on the leg side for 3 from Snary.

Richardson was out immediately and Fairfax, needing an innings after his failure at Worcester, batted circumspectly while Bradman produced a rasping square-cut to the boundary off Geary. With Richardson gone, Bradman clearly felt the need to shift to aggression. He brought up the 300 in four hours forty minutes but slowed and when he tried to play Armstrong's medium pace to the leg side he was struck on the elbow. Play halted for several minutes. He was fine because he reached his 150 soon after, the last 50 scored in two minutes over an hour.

They went in to tea with the Australians on 325 (Bradman 152) and during it the weather suddenly deteriorated. *The Times* described this as 'something like a tornado of wind and rain', but play resumed soon after 5pm and Bradman attacked. In the first over after the resumption he hit Snary for four boundaries from the first five balls, two through mid-on and two through mid-off. One reporter even thought he threatened to become reckless. A voice from the crowd called 'run Bradman out' because that seemed the only way Leicester could do it.

Rain curtailed the day, Bradman on 185 (sixteen 4s) made in five hours seventeen minutes. As he came off he had been at the wicket for three minutes short of ten hours so far in England for once out.

Bradman reflected on how the Leicester wicket had educated him because you couldn't trust it like Sydney with its regular bounce and the ball coming nicely on to the bat. Here you had to watch it all the way.[15]

He understood already that you had to alter your shot selection to accommodate all this. Because the air was heavier, the ball swung more, the lusher grass helped the bowlers and the wickets changed much more during a match than at home. Because the ball was coming at him more slowly, and because he was so small (5ft 8in/173cm), he could play back and deploy the shots he liked so much. He was, he concluded – again already – enjoying himself.[16]

The third day was washed out, the match drawn. During the match a curious thing happened. Some of the Australians – Wall, Walker, Hurwood and Grimmett – had been invited by Leicestershire Aero Club to have a flight from Desford aerodrome. The Australian Board of Control forbade flying and Grimmett said plaintively: 'What's the use of going to the aerodrome if we are not allowed to fly?' He stayed at the hotel. The other three did go and watched Tebbutt have a flight, to which Walker, also plaintively, said: 'In these circumstances it is better to write about cricket than play.'

Bradman now had 421 runs. It was more than seven of the fifteen players would total on the whole tour.

Essex

By now newspapers were paying attention to the phenomenon off the field and reported that three girls waited outside the Australians' hotel in Leicester. A hatless young man went in and someone said: 'Well played.' He smiled and murmured: 'I am lucky.' The girls missed him. Newspapers spoke of 'Bradmanitis' – everyone talking about him – and music halls were making jokes based around him. He was no joking matter.

He didn't play against Essex, on the day after Leicester, at unlovely, unloved Leyton in the anonymous reaches of north London. Tebbutt, describing the weather as icy, said: 'There can be few more desolate spots for cricket when the elements are unkind.' Bradman, spectating, found the weather 'extremely unpleasant'.

Australia, batting first, made only 156 but Hornibrook broke the Essex reply (67) with 6 for 11 and 10,000 were there to see it. Australia declared at 264 for 6 and bowled Essex out again, this time for 146, to win by 207.

Yorkshire

After the match they travelled to Sheffield to play Yorkshire, arriving in the evening.

They 'smiled as they saw porters wrestling with their baggage. The covenant which they have all signed obviously does not limit the party's baggage to 96lbs (43kg) per man. They are a happy set of fellows, judging by the brief glances [our] representative could get of them,' *The Sheffield Daily Telegraph* wrote.

'When he smiles, Woodfull [. . .] does not seem to be the grim, determined batsman he really is. Jackson looks surprisingly young. It seemed incredible that this young man could have won fame as a cricketer. One wondered if he had been a chorister as a boy. It was so easy to picture him in the mind's eye wearing a surplice.

'That the covenant is a sacred thing was soon apparent. A more dignified guardian than the manager, Mr. W.L. Kelly, J.P., of Melbourne could not be found. When he was asked about his impressions of our

LEICESTERSHIRE V AUSTRALIANS

Leicester, 3, 5, 6 May. Drawn.

LEICESTERSHIRE

A.W. Shipman	c Wall	b Grimmett	63
G.L. Berry	c Ponsford	b Grimmett	50
N.F. Armstrong	st Walker	b Grimmett	3
J.C. Bradshaw	lbw	b Grimmett	0
H. Riley		c & b Grimmett	0
A.T. Sharp	st Walker	b Grimmett	5
W.E. Astill	c McCabe	b Wall	7
G. Geary	lbw	b Wall	6
*J.A.F.M.P. de Lisle		not out	2
+T.E. Sidwell	st Walker	b Grimmett	6
H.C. Snary		b Wall	0
Extras	(b 3, lb 3)		6
Total			148

1-103, 2-121, 3-121, 4-121, 5-122,
6-131, 7-133, 8-140, 9-147

	O	M	R	W
Wall	16.5	1	37	3
Hurwood	12	5	18	0
Fairfax	16	4	38	0
Grimmett	25	8	46	7
McCabe	4	2	3	0

AUSTRALIANS

W.H. Ponsford	lbw	b Geary	25
A.A. Jackson		b Geary	4
D.G. Bradman		not out	185
A.F. Kippax	c Sidwell	b Snary	22
S.J. McCabe		b Geary	2
*V.Y. Richardson	c Armstrong	b Geary	100
A.G. Fairfax		not out	21
Extras	(b 2, lb 4)		6
Total	(5 wkts dec)		365

Dnb: C.V. Grimmett, +C.W. Walker, A. Hurwood, T.W. Wall.

1-18, 2-35, 3-77, 4-80, 5-259

	O	M	R	W
Shipman	22	2	59	0
Snary	29	6	89	1
Geary	35	9	85	4
Astill	30	2	99	0
Armstrong	9	2	27	0

> *climate he vouchsafed not a word: the weather has been a trifle "mixed" so as he could hardly have spoken well of it, it was perhaps as well he did not commit himself! Caution is the watchword of the Tourists, if a newspaperman is at hand [. . .] However Mr. Kelly was very courteous. Before he walked off in search of a cup of tea he did permit himself to state that all the players were fit and well but the team would not be selected until this morning.'*

Bradman's first impression of Sheffield was 'frowning, forbidding' – a steel town from the Victorian era – and his first impression of the Bramall Lane pitch that it bore the scars of the recent football season. Sheffield United played there as well.

Bradman was about to confront a strong bowling attack for the first time on the tour. Wilfred Rhodes, one of the greatest of all left-arm slow bowlers, had been playing Test cricket nine years before Bradman was born. George Macauley started as a fast bowler but under the influence of Rhodes reduced that to medium pace and added spin. Bill Bowes was developing into a genuine fast bowler who would soon be playing for England. Emmott Robinson was right-arm medium pace who'd been playing for Yorkshire since 1919.

A crowd of 7,500 watched Yorkshire bat first in sunshine but cloud coming over. Percy Holmes and Herbert Sutcliffe put on 46 before Woodfull summoned Grimmett, who proved mesmeric. He destroyed the innings with 10 for 37 off 22.3 overs.

Rain affected the later part of the day but, at 35, Robinson had Ponsford lbw and that brought Bradman in. *The Sheffield Daily Telegraph* said: 'We saw enough of Bradman to appreciate his supreme confidence in himself. This is another C.G. Macartney in the making.'

Macauley came on and after a couple of balls turned to Bowes. 'I shall get this chap caught and bowled,' he said. [17] Bradman ended the day on 24, Woodfull 37.

The tourists went to the theatre and, back in their hotel afterwards, decided to toast Grimmett. They ordered wine but couldn't find him – he'd gone to bed. On the Sunday, Bradman played golf with the Yorkshire captain, Alan Barber, about 50 miles (80km) from Sheffield. In comparison he found the golf course 'Arcadia'.[18]

The Sydney *Sun* described the Monday as 'yet another winter's day. Rain threatened, and a bitterly cold wind blew across [the] ground, carrying with it the usual share of Sheffield smoke. The ground was very sodden and the wicket bad. The ground, except for the members' stand was almost deserted.' No play was possible before 2.15pm and Bradman had to resume on the slowest wicket he'd met so far.

Robinson, wily, had four men close in on the off side but Bradman, untroubled, simply kept the ball down. The wicket began to cut up and the batsmen were constantly patting it down. Robinson made the ball lift awkwardly. Bowes was soon replaced at the other end by Macauley who bowled without a slip but three short-legs and two men on the leg boundary – leg theory.

Bradman attacked, putting 'astonishing' power into all his strokes. He off-drove Macauley to the boundary – a superb stroke – and drove him there a second time. He late cut Robinson to the boundary, too, and the Australian 100 came up in even time.

At 115, Rhodes replaced Robinson and Bradman described his bowling action as 'a thing of grace'. He was impressed but not intimidated because once he 'laid back to a short-pitched ball and hit it so hard the umpire examined his bat to make sure it contained no mechanical device'.[19]

Woodfull had been on 30 when Bradman came in but now he moved past him and played all the Yorkshire bowlers with such ease that one newspaper suggested he was smiling as he batted. He 'defied' the bowlers to set a field – any field, however deep – which he couldn't penetrate. No spectator missed the 'powerful combination of strength and timing' he used in front of the wicket or the whole square leg area, 'but the strokes which charmed the eye most were those he made behind the wicket. Down the gully he made some delicious late cuts which C.G. Macartney, looking on, must have watched with deep appreciation.' [20]

Nor did any spectator miss the shot Bradman could claim as his own, because he deployed it so frequently and effectively. It was like a 'glance on the off side . . . a deflection made with a quick twist of the wrists which steered the ball through the slips'. [21] It was a business shot, the sort that kept an innings in constant motion, and, as it seems, he was able to place it: if you bowled at him with only one slip you left an unprotected arc wide of that slip; if you bowled at him with two slips he'd glance wider. Even in his innings which became savage assaults the glance was there, too, safe, productive and unendingly irritating to captain and bowler.

Now at Sheffield he scored faster and faster, bringing this judgement from *The Times*: he played 'a beautiful innings, in which he played an even greater variety of strokes than he had done at Worcester or Leicester'.

He hit eight 4s and didn't lift a ball until Macauley caught and bowled him for 78 made in slightly over an hour and a half (out of 107). Macauley had been right about how he'd get him – he just got the wrong day.

Arthur Mailey, writing in the Sydney *Sun,* said: 'It was interesting to watch Bradman's tactics for the first time on an English damp wicket. He disregarded the customary English practice of waiting to pull a short ball on the leg side, but drove terrifically, and guided the ball through the slips to the boundary with remarkable speed considering the slow wicket. His form on such a wicket convinced me of his remarkable ability.'

Australia made 320 (Woodfull 121) but rain ruined the third day.

From Yorkshire, Bradman wrote to Mr. W.H. Williams, vice-president of the Goulburn Cricket Association, that 'no two wickets are the same in England and, compared with ours, they are very treacherous. One simply cannot trust to the pitch of the ball, but what groundwork it is for a young player just starting out!'

He pointed out that playing six days a week, and travelling extensively as well, created a problem for the players in finding time for themselves. No one could doubt, though, that he was having the time of his life, unlike all the bowlers he'd met so far.

Bradman's 499 runs for twice out represented more than a genuine sensation. Great men had trodden this way before but not like this.

Victor Trumper began (1899) with 0 and 3 against Essex, 13 against Surrey, 5 and 64 against an England XI – five innings in his first three matches, total 85. Macartney of the repeated comparison began (1909) with 0 not out against Northamptonshire, 48 not out against Essex, 33 and 5 against Surrey – four innings in his first three matches, total 86.

Woodfull and Ponsford came in 1926. Woodfull began with 19 against the Minor Counties, 201 against Essex and 118 against Surrey – three innings in his first three matches, total 338. (The 201 occupied him four hours and ten minutes, the 118 three hours and forty minutes, and contained one 4.) Ponsford began with 12 against the Minor Counties, 56 against Leicester and 23 against Essex – three innings in his first three matches, total 91.

YORKSHIRE V AUSTRALIANS

Sheffield, 10, 12, 13 May. Drawn.

YORKSHIRE			
P. Holmes		b Grimmett	31
H. Sutcliffe	c Walker	b Grimmett	69
E. Oldroyd	lbw	b Grimmett	2
M. Leyland	st Walker	b Grimmett	9
*A.T. Barber	st Walker	b Grimmett	1
A. Mitchell		b Grimmett	3
E. Robinson	c Bradman	b Grimmett	2
+A. Wood	c Richardson	b Grimmett	17
G.G. Macaulay	st Walker	b Grimmett	1
W. Rhodes		not out	6
W.E. Bowes		b Grimmett	0
Extras	(b 4, lb 9, nb 1)		14
Total			155

1-59, 2-84, 3-120, 4-125, 5-126,
6-130, 7-130, 8-132, 9-155

	O	M	R	W
Wall	16	3	42	0
a'Beckett	12	6	11	0
Hornibrook	12	4	49	0
Grimmett	22.3	8	37	10
McCabe	3	2	2	0

AUSTRALIANS			
*W.M. Woodfull	c Barber	b Macaulay	121
W.H. Ponsford	lbw	b Robinson	6
D.G. Bradman		c & b Macaulay	78
A.F. Kippax	lbw	b Leyland	3
S.J. McCabe	c Oldroyd	b Robinson	16
V.Y. Richardson	c Wood	b Rhodes	45
E.L. a'Beckett	st Wood	b Rhodes	14
C.V. Grimmett		not out	23
+C.W. Walker	c Macaulay	b Leyland	3
T.W. Wall	c Robinson	b Leyland	1
P.M. Hornibrook	st Wood	b Rhodes	6
Extras	(lb 4)		4
Total			320

1-35, 2-142, 3-159, 4-200, 5-243,
6-274, 7-289, 8-296, 9-302

	O	M	R	W
Robinson	28	8	60	2
Bowes	26	7	63	0
Macaulay	28	2	80	2
Rhodes	31.5	5	95	3
Leyland	8	3	18	3

Of these four echoing names, only Woodfull scored heavily and the next highest innings, Ponsford's 56, remains very modest indeed. *These* men were the history and the folklore of the game, *these* innings were what the English audience had seen, *these* were the sort of scores you'd expect from newcomers until Bradman broke history and folklore apart and recreated both of them in his own image in thirteen days between Wednesday 30 April and Monday 12 May.

That was the initial impact and it echoes still among historians but it also brought another dimension, perhaps now or soon after: the beginning of tension within the touring party. That beginning is impossible to position accurately because it does not seem to have happened at any defined moment or had any single catalyst but was something organic, something growing and, given Bradman's unbending character, it became inevitable if he maintained the momentum of these opening three matches.

The dimension was this: nobody could quite decide whether he was one of the boys or was even interested in being one of the lads. Bradman may have wished to be – within reason – solitary, attending only those functions he was obliged to and concentrating without distraction, as he had vowed, on his cricket. That was no longer possible. He had already become a fascination, a curiosity and a celebrity – by Leicester, as we have seen, big enough to be joked about at music halls, famous enough to have girls waiting outside the hotel. Whether he liked it or not, he had made himself public property. The immediate comparison with his team-mates is almost embarrassing to set down, and that can't have helped.

Jackson, who was going to subjugate England with a caress of his bat while the cross-batted country boy stood exposed began with 24 against Worcester, 4 against Leicester, 7 and 27 against Essex in his first three matches – total 62, 16 less than Bradman made at Sheffield alone.

McCabe, young and pumping with potential, began with 15 at Worcester, 2 at Leicester, 5 and 6 against Essex, 16 against Yorkshire. It's inhumane to total them.

Kippax the stylist began with 22 against Leicester, 57 and 42 against Essex, 3 against Yorkshire – total 124.

Only Woodfull stood any sort of comparison: 133 against Worcester, 4 and 54 against Essex and 121 against Yorkshire – four innings in his first three matches, total 312 – but of course he'd been before. He played like a dependable, rock-like pillar around whose broad bat the others could build. Bill Woodfull was many things but he was never going to be a sensation.

The tension Bradman was creating, or would create, is unfathomable because, in that era, obtrusive sports journalism did not exist any more than tabloid revelations or kiss 'n' tell sporting memoirs. What the players really thought, how much understandable jealousy existed, whether there was deep resentment at the extent of his success and how he chose to handle it remain elusive. Tebbutt wrote about 'occasional coldness' between Bradman and the others, about how his 'immense popularity with the public was not echoed by his team-mates'. Tebbutt, doing something very brave in 1930 to broach such subjects, took care to explore them fully, sympathetically and honestly. We shall see, in the matter of Leeds, the unknown benefactor and the £1,000.

What remains beyond dispute is that, after the 236, 185 and 78, nothing could or would be the same again – ever again.

Chapter Four

Murder in May (Act II)

Lancashire

THEY TRAVELLED FROM SHEFFIELD TO LIVERPOOL TO PLAY Lancashire at Aigburth, arriving at the Central Station shortly before 7pm. *The Liverpool Post* reporter sent to cover the arrival joined the growing list of local papermen who waited, notebook and pencil in hand, on a railway platform for them to come into his patch, and get no change out of them at all.

They'd been due at 9pm but because play was washed out caught an earlier train. Kelly was the first to alight, followed by the tanned and fit-looking players. 'All that greeted them were several porters, three Pressmen, a photographer and a special bus. So there was no urgent need for them to finger that curious document of its 36 "Don't . . ." and recite in a muttered tone "I must not . . ."'

The reporter noted that 'the Australians are the super "Hush Hush" team. They have a chance of telephoning from Aigburth to their wives and sweethearts "way under" tomorrow by the courtesy and generosity of Mr. L.D.W. Pearce, a Sydney accountant, who is paying for the call.' The reporter broached this and was met with the reply: 'Mr. Kelly knew about it.' The reporter added that Kelly, 'with his attaché case and military moustache', admitted that he knew of the offer.

When the reporter put other questions to the players they mouthed 'Mr. Kelly knew' and mouthed it 'gracefully and easily as though it were a much rehearsed phrase'.

One porter – obviously from Lancashire – said he fully intended to ask them what they thought of Yorkshire but another porter, catching the mood, said he'd have to ask Mr. Kelly.

Kelly was even reluctant to have the team photographed but finally consented if it was done quickly and 'marshalled them' with the command 'Hurry, please' – and Woodfull did the same. Then they were gone to the North Western Hotel, a massive, heavy, city-centre building in the French Renaissance style with some 300 rooms.

There, Kelly said the team wouldn't be chosen until shortly before the match began, as was their custom, and added he didn't imagine the selection would present a problem. (It rarely did with only the fifteen to select from.) 'If the wicket is on the dead side, as it appears likely to be, Wall will probably stand down.'

Kelly explained the players had no social engagements that evening and were seeing as much of the town as they could. They had however accepted one invitation. *The Liverpool Echo* ran a column 'Bee's Notes On Sports Of The Day' and it said both teams were going to a boxing evening after play on the second day. The column added: 'Above all we shall be interested in the appearance of Don Bradman, the world's top scorer with 452 in 415 minutes in January [. . .] Bradman drives frequently, and short stuff goes to leg with a bang; a bit tentative on the off, they say, but a great batsman for all that. One critic has discerned some crudities, but I don't think we shall be able to see them now. In any case, they are obviously not much use to us.'

Like Yorkshire, Lancashire were a strong, experienced side and, more than that, the tourists faced a match within the match. Ted McDonald, a feared fast bowler with the 1921 Australian side, had long played for Lancashire and felt he had a point or two to prove.

The Australians had a bus to take them, as Bradman estimated, the 7 miles (11km) from the hotel to the ground at Aigburth, a place Tebbutt described as 'close to but detached from the busy, blackened city of Liverpool. The Australians found it hard to believe it was only a club ground.

'Aigburth, with its handsome and yet unobtrusive pavilion, its striped canvas deck chairs placed around the edge of the boundary, and the amenities of open-air tea which make one feel so much more charitable towards the white figures straining out in the middle – you can see them over the edge of the lazily raised cup! – is a place where those who like to see cricket only in good reproductions of its indigenous surroundings would prefer to have more matches played.' (1)

The tourists could now add this very English quaintness to the charm of Worcester, the functionality of Leicester, the wasteland of Leyton and the dark, satanic chimneys of Sheffield. More than all that, it was *warm.*

What they didn't do was open up. 'Their quarters in the pavilion,' *The Liverpool Echo* wrote, 'are screened off from everybody, all intruders being sternly kept out in keeping with the policy of strict privacy which governs the trip. One wonders whether Charles Macartney, who was early on the ground, was able to see the boys.'

Lancashire batted first, evidently to the crowd's disappointment, and Grimmett tormented the middle out of the Lancashire innings with 6 for 57.

The Australians faced an hour and a quarter before the close. Woodfull and Jackson opened and 'it was interesting to see McDonald putting out something of his former pace, as if to show the lads of the Australian team what a real fast bowler still can be'. (2) At 29 he was too quick for Jackson and had him lbw.

Bradman came in and made 9 before, trying to turn a ball to leg, McDonald plucked his leg stump out of the ground. (3) The enormous crowd roared their approval. It was, of course, his first failure. The Australians finished on 83 for 5.

Next morning, *The Liverpool Echo* described the circumstances surrounding the promised phone call to Sydney (at £2 a minute).

> *'As early as 7.30am syncopated piano music was heard in the Australians' quarters on the first-floor of the hotel. Apart from the music, however, there was an air of mystery about the party as eight o'clock, the time when the call should have come through, drew near. Presently Arthur Mailey, the stalwart of former sides, attired in dressing gown and pyjamas, looked out. The "Echo" representative approached. Were the conversations about to begin? No . . . Mailey was looking for a waiter to bring another cup of tea.*
>
> *'A few minutes later [treasurer] Mr. J. A. Howard who had been up and ready since 6am [said] there had been a slight delay; possibly the call*

might come through within a few minutes. Mr. Howard is not an excitable man. Bronzed and slightly grey, he is quiet spoken and eminently sensible, but even he was getting somewhat nervy as the minutes crept on. He was to speak first, to his wife and children. The relatives of the others who were to speak were gathered in his Sydney home 12,000 miles (19,000 km) away.

'Mr. W.L. Kelly, who was to follow Mr. Howard, was also growing a little impatient as he thought of his wife and children. W.A. Oldfield, who was third man in this novel "innings", walked about anxiously because he wanted to hear his wife's voice while Kippax, Archie Jackson, Fairfax and Young Bradman, who in the order named hoped to have three minutes' talk with their mothers, were feeling more thrilled than if they had been waiting to bat in a Test match.

'It was arranged that after the Liverpool calls had been made the line would be switched to London, where the 19-year-old babe of the team, Stanley McCabe, was waiting for a "word with mother".

'Young Archie Jackson came out and walked to the end of the heavily carpeted corridor and back to break the monotony. Don Bradman followed. There was another tinkle and we were all alert again . . . Another false alarm. Gradually the clock neared 9am. Another tinkle . . . At last! Everyone was silent while Mr. Howard took up the phone. Then, his disappointment showing, he approached the waiting Pressmen. "Sorry, but it's all off for today."'

Evidently the Post Office couldn't make the wireless connection with Sydney.

Rain prevented play until 1.45pm. The Australians were quickly dismissed and Lancashire, batting a second time, reached 101 for 5 by the close.

That evening some of the tourists went to the boxing at Liverpool Stadium and Bradman, recognised, was invited into the ring to make a speech. If we can rely on the evidence of a photograph of him doing it, he was not entirely comfortable.

Next morning, they were up early again for another attempt to speak to Sydney but by 8pm became convinced that atmospheric conditions had defeated them. They were wrong, and wronged. A statement from the Postmaster General's office said the call had been 'cancelled at 4.30 yesterday afternoon. The cancellation instructions came from Australia.

If the Australians tried to get through this morning they must have been acting in ignorance of the fact that the calls had been cancelled.' Somebody might have told them.

On this final day, although the Aigburth wicket seemed easier Lancashire were all out for 165. Stumps had been agreed for 4.30pm – the Australians were due to play the MCC at Lord's the following day – and the match died. The Australians lacked the time to make 227 to win and Lancashire lacked the time, on this wicket, to bowl them out.

Richardson, opening, made 39 and Bradman went out to join Jackson. Bradman initially looked as if he wanted to force the pace but settled back into pure defence, and nobody in England had seen that before. Because of his speed, monitoring and smothering every danger, penetrating that defence was more than the *seven* Lancashire bowlers could do. He was 48 not out at the end, Jackson lbw for 40.

As someone said, even watching these two defend was a pleasure.

MCC

The MCC selected an England strength side and the Australians approached it 'with every seriousness and not a little anxiety'. [(4)] They sensed, no doubt, that after their five initial skirmishes they'd find out how good they really were. The MCC team included a young leg-break bowler from Oxford University, Ian Peebles. People spoke of him as a Test prospect and here was a chance to find out how good he really was.

Queues began at seven that Saturday morning. The trains to St. John's Wood were full, the area around the ground alive with people and speculation. The crowd grew to the point where, after lunch, the gates had to be closed.

Woodfull won the toss on a sunny morning – dull and overcast later – and prepared to bat on a wicket which offered no bounce. Chapman, captaining the MCC, emerged without a sweater which, this particular May, made at least one reporter wonder.

Gubby Allen opened the bowling to Woodfull, Maurice Allom to Jackson. Allen's first over consisted of outswingers which Woodfull watched go by. Jackson played mechanically forward to Allom's fifth ball, also an outswinger, and was caught behind.

The 'compact, menacing figure' emerged from the famous old pavilion to a deep groundswell of applause. [(5)] He turned his first ball on to the leg side for a scampered single and this, like the glance through

LANCASHIRE V AUSTRALIANS

Aigburth, Liverpool 14, 15, 16 May. Drawn.

LANCASHIRE

F.B. Watson	c Walker	b Hornibrook	37		b Hornibrook	14
C. Hallows	c Hornibrook	b Grimmett	21		b Fairfax	0
G.E. Tyldesley	lbw	b Grimmett	5	lbw	b Grimmett	28
J. Iddon	lbw	b Grimmett	2	c Bradman	b Hornibrook	3
J.L. Hopwood		b Grimmett	9	c a'Beckett	b Hornibrook	12
E. Paynter		b Grimmett	0		c&b Fairfax	15
*P.T. Eckersley		b Hornibrook	54		c&b Hornibrook	38
F.M. Sibbles		b Fairfax	23		b a'Beckett	9
+G. Duckworth		not out	14		not out	10
R.K. Tyldesley		b Hornibrook	0	c Fairfax	b Grimmett	25
E.A. McDonald	c Hornibrook	b Grimmett	3	c Grimmett	b Hornibrook	1
Extras	(b 8)		8	(b 4, lb 5, nb 1)		10
Total			176			165

1-38, 2-54, 3-60, 4-74, 5-74, 6-92, 7-152, 8-173, 9-173

1-1, 2-39, 3-45, 4-53, 5-70, 6-107, 7-127, 8-133, 9-62

	O	M	R	W	O	M	R	W
Fairfax	17	7	30	1	18	5	24	2
a'Beckett	9	2	15	0	12	7	15	1
Grimmett	32.2	13	57	6	31	10	71	2
Hornibrook	23	8	45	3	26.3	10	38	5
Hurwood	7	1	16	0	5	3	7	0
Bradman	1	0	5	0				

AUSTRALIANS

*W.M. Woodfull		b R Tyldesley	21			
A.A. Jackson	lbw	b McDonald	19	lbw	b Sibbles	40
D.G. Bradman		b McDonald	9		not out	48
A.F. Kippax		not out	40		not out	6
V.Y. Richardson	c Hopwood	b McDonald	0	lbw	b R Tyldesley	39
+C.W. Walker	lbw	b R Tyldesley	4			
A.G. Fairfax	st Duckworth	b Hopwood	18			
E.L. a'Beckett	lbw	b R Tyldesley	3			
C.V. Grimmett	c R Tyldesley	b Hopwood	0			
A. Hurwood	c R Tyldesley	b Hopwood	0			
P.M. Hornibrook		b Hopwood	0			
Extras	(lb 1)		1	(b 1, lb 1, w 2)		4
Total			115	(2 wkts)		137

1-29, 2-49, 3-49, 4-58, 5-63, 6-105, 7-114, 8-115, 9-115

1-67, 2-108

	O	M	R	W	O	M	R	W
McDonald	20	3	51	3	11	1	36	0
Sibbles	14	4	33	0	15	6	18	1
R.K. Tyldesley	14	7	17	3	12	3	19	1
Hopwood	10	4	13	4	13	1	29	0
Iddon					4	0	16	0
Watson					4	0	7	0
E. Tyldesley					1	0	8	0

the slips, was a favoured mechanism; he always wanted to get off the mark immediately, set the innings in motion and often the push to leg was the way he did it.

Allen's first ball broke back, beat the bat and struck Bradman's pads hard in line with the leg stump. It did not disturb him and he began to work the leg side more seriously, once late cutting, too, so that he reached 8 in a few minutes. He was, *The Evening Standard* felt, 'a young man in a hurry.'

Woodfull typically spent twenty minutes over his first single. Bradman looked fallible. After half an hour Allen struck his boot and the ball might have gone anywhere, including the stumps – but in the same over, with a dismissive flick of the wrists, he steered the ball to square leg for the first boundary of the innings.

Peebles came on for Allom and bowled a maiden to Woodfull. Bradman hunted Allen, who had four slips but bowled two balls outside the leg stump. Bradman sent both to the boundary.

At 32 Allen came off for Alex Kennedy's medium-pace inswing. Bradman 'adroitly' turned Peebles to the leg side and then began driving for the first time: one went straight to long on for a single, another past cover point to rattle the boundary at the Mound stand.

After that stroke Bradman went to speak to the umpire and Chapman. His left hand, it seems, had been hit by a fast delivery and he did not resume for several minutes. When he did he played as if nothing had happened, his placing of the ball still perfect, his selection of shots 'intriguing'. *The Evening Standard* concluded: 'He stands for utility.' Utility? What was the proper focus to describe Bradman?

At 12.45pm Australia reached 40 for 1 (Bradman 32).

Cardus reached for the focus. 'Quicksilver was in his bat's blade, he was as cheeky as he was agile. His style laughs at the canons [of orthodoxy], he plays back often with a cross bat, which he holds almost still, allowing the ball to hit it. But that happens only when the ball pitches on a length that renders a dynamic stroke dangerous. To anything like an easy ball Bradman's bat makes rapid and quite voracious thrusts, stabs, and thumps.'[(6)]

The 50 came in fifty-five minutes. Peebles, unafraid of pitching the ball up, was enjoying himself and had an lbw against Woodfull refused. Chapman positioned himself at silly point but Bradman 'obliged him to think again. He *chasséed* down the pitch to the higher-tossed balls and drove them all along the ground wide of mid-off.' (7) Peebles found Bradman's batting a revelation, particularly his 'extraordinary speed of foot' against spinners. He'd 'wait till the ball was well on its way, then dart out to kill the spin'. (8)

The Australians took lunch at 80 (Woodfull 32, Bradman 47) and, soon after it, Bradman attacked Peebles with a pull-drive so hard that no fielder moved and a spectator threw the ball back. It made him 53 in an hour and twenty-five minutes and Peebles wasn't bowling as well as he had done before lunch. Bradman moved to 56 when the hundred came up.

Woodfull finally reached 50 and in the same over Bradman tried to off-drive Allom – the ball appeared a yorker – and dragged it into his stumps. He and Woodfull had put on 119 in an hour and fifty minutes.

The proper focus?

The Times (Vincent): 'Throughout his innings Bradman had obstinately tried to bring off a flat-batted slash at balls outside the off-stump and short of a length. Repeated failure had not discouraged him, but his final attempt dragged the ball down on to his stumps.'

The Observer (Fender): 'Bradman showed fine form, although not the same brilliance as he did in Australia against Chapman's side, and I feel that he has it in his power to be even more dazzling. I was very interested to see that there were no signs yesterday of those periods of almost schoolboy batting which, on occasions, were evident in his first season as a Test player. He seems to have quite got over that without in any way losing any of his greatness.'

The Manchester Guardian (Cardus): 'There was no Macartney' at Lord's 'though some day it is possible that Bradman will remind us of the one and only Figaro of cricket. Bradman did at least play an innings which told of an original and volatile mind. His bat was always making a personal movement, not merely swinging mechanically down the line of the ball. Bradman is not another Macartney or Trumper any more than a virile and healthy little cub is another lion, but with experience he may become in time a master of the unorthodox – and all masters are that.'

In mitigation, these three good men and true could not see tomorrow and consequently had no idea what was coming next. They did not yet understand that they had just had the greatest batsman who ever lived before their very eyes. It did make the focus very, very difficult.

The Australians made 285 and the MCC replied with 258. The Australians batted again in front of 15,000 and Allom bowled Woodfull for 7. Allen made the ball buck and endured the mortification of having Bradman missed by Greville Stevens in the slips. Stevens called out: 'Why don't you bowl at the bloody wicket instead of creating these catches?' And Allen's reply is not recorded. [(9)] Chapman put Stevens on to bowl to make amends and he did, trapping Bradman lbw for 4.

Rain ruined the match, and if the tourists hadn't found out how good they were, they now knew they weren't bad.

Derbyshire

A large crowd gathered at the pretty Chesterfield ground, in a public park, for the match against Derbyshire which began the day after the MCC match. Even an admission charge of two shillings did not deter them. The accommodation was 'simple and adequate, being one long circle of wooden benches supported by thick logs or bricks'. [(10)] In their travelogue, the tourists could add that to the charm of Worcester, the functionality of Leicester, arctic Leyton . . .

Chesterfield must have reminded them of Leyton because the weather resembled, Bradman thought, 'deep winter'. In the dressing room he wore a sweater, a blazer on top and overcoat on top of that while he crouched over a fire. He'd never been so cold in his life.

Grimmett was rested for the first time but Hornibrook took six wickets when Derbyshire batted and Bradman, 'wearing the mantle of Grimmett', [(11)] got the second top scorer, Harry Storer, lbw. Derbyshire were all out for 215. Australia had an hour and twenty minutes to bat, and Ponsford and Jackson negotiated them slowly but safely.

A bitter wind blew on the second day and rain hung in the air. Ponsford and Jackson moved faster now while, no doubt, Bradman hunched in front of the fire. Some light rain fell as play began, making the ball difficult to handle, and Ponsford took full advantage of that. The crowd kept their hands in their pockets but brought them out to applaud when Ponsford dealt with anything short or wide. They'd put on 127 when Jackson – who'd hit two 6s, into a marquee and almost through the pavilion door – was caught at the wicket.

Bradman came in and was twice struck on the unprotected part of the leg by Stan Worthington, who bowled medium-fast. It hurt – the cold didn't help. The *Derby Daily Telegraph* reported: 'Worthington sent a no-ball up to Don Bradman, who was struck on the left thigh by a ball from the same bowler. This temporarily cramped his movement and

MCC V AUSTRALIANS

Lord's, 17, 19, 20 May. Drawn.

AUSTRALIANS

*W.M. Woodfull	c Lee	b Kennedy	52		b Allom	1
A.A. Jackson	c Lyon	b Allom	0	c Hendred	b Stevens	64
D.G. Bradman		b Allom	66	lbw	b Stevens	4
A.F. Kippax		b Peebles	18	c Lyon	b Allen	24
W.H. Ponsford		not out	82	c Duleepsinhji	b Allen	15
V.Y. Richardson	c Hendren	b Kennedy	34	c Duleepsinhji	b Kennedy	5
A.G. Fairfax	lbw	b Allom	1	st Lyon	b Stevens	26
C.V. Grimmett		b Allom	4		b Allen	15
+C.W. Walker	c Lyon	b Allom	0		not out	10
T.W. Wall	lbw	b Kennedy	5		b Allen	2
P.M. Hornibrook	lbw	b Peebles	6		b Peebles	11
Extras	(b 11, lb 6)		17	(b 18, lb 9, w 1, nb 2)		30
Total			285			207

1-0, 2-119, 3-127, 4-167, 5-236, 6-241, 7-245, 8-245, 9-266

1-14, 2-23, 3-80, 4-96, 5-139, 6-147, 7-155, 8-175, 9-177

	O	M	R	W	O	M	R	W
Allen	16	5	38	0	14	6	28	4
Allom	32	11	67	5	12	3	27	1
Peebles	25.3	1	87	2	19	4	48	1
Kennedy	34	13	60	3	10	3	16	1
Stevens	9	2	16	0	24.3	5	64	3

MCC

H.W. Lee	st Walker	b Fairfax	11
+M.D. Lyon	c Richardson	b Fairfax	3
K.S. Duleepsinhji	st Walker	b Hornibrook	92
E.H. Hendren	c Woodfull	b Fairfax	31
D.R. Jardine	lbw	b Wall	25
*A.P.F. Chapman		b Wall	7
G.T.S. Stevens	c Grimmett	b Hornibrook	48
G.O.B. Allen		b Fairfax	3
A.S. Kennedy		b Fairfax	14
M.J.C. Allom		not out	5
I.A.R. Peebles		b Fairfax	3
Extras	(b 11, lb 3, nb 2)		16
Total			258

1-8, 2-31, 3-96, 4-171, 5-175, 6-181, 7-219, 8-233, 9-251

	O	M	R	W
Wall	21	2	66	2
Fairfax	31	5	54	6
Hornibrook	29	11	44	2
Grimmett	26	8	78	0

Worthington unsuccessfully appealed for obstruction. Worthington was again no-balled soon afterwards. Bradman hit a 4 to leg off Harry Storer.'

He was trying to force the pace but his timing wasn't quite right, although once he unleashed a glorious square drive off Worthington. The wind cut at him and he'd remember it 'whistling'. Arthur Mailey thought the cold inhibited his batting.

Ponsford reached a century, rain fell again as lunch neared and the Australians went in to that at 196. Surveying the whole situation Bradman, cold to his bones, felt you needed a 'lively imagination' to believe you were playing cricket at all. Play wasn't resumed until 3.20pm in poor light and again Bradman tried to force the pace.

'Ponsford hit another 4 to send up the 200 and Bradman pulled another round to leg. The scoring was certainly slow now. What was happening was that the Derby close fielding was too good for short runs, and Ponsford and Bradman followed the Australian custom of letting any number of balls go past until exactly the right one came along. This they hit, and hit hard so that boundaries were frequent in the small ring at Chesterfield.' (12)

Bradman was out at 231, caught on the leg side by the wicket-keeper off Worthington for 44.

Ponsford kept on to 131 and the Australians totalled 348. Hornibrook took another six wickets when Derbyshire batted again, and Ponsford and Jackson made the necessary 52 to complete the sort of clinical victory touring sides do against weaker counties.

After the match the team were the guests of the Duke of Devonshire at Chatsworth, the country house outside Stoke-on-Trent. They were shown his collection of antiques, which included a Bible used by King Henry IV. In return, they promised to send the Duke an autographed cricket ball. This was all very apt: England offering her past, Australians offering their present.

Anyway, because they'd beaten Derbyshire inside two days they'd given themselves a day off before they met Surrey at The Oval on the Saturday.

Surrey

The Surrey match carried a particular poignancy because Bradman would meet Fender who had criticised him so trenchantly (see the Introduction). To add to that, on the morning of the match former England captain Archie MacLaren tried to find the proper focus himself.

DERBYSHIRE V AUSTRALIANS

Chesterfield, 21, 22, 23 May. Australians won by 10 wickets.

DERBYSHIRE

G.M. Lee		b Hornibrook	14		b Fairfax	2
H. Storer jnr.	lbw	b Bradman	65	st Oldfield	b Hornibrook	25
A.E. Alderman		b Hornibrook	0		b Hornibrook	38
A.G. Slater	c Fairfax	b Hornibrook	0	c Oldfield	b Wall	0
N.M. Ford	c Bradman	b Wall	33	c Fairfax	b Hornibrook	48
T.S. Worthington	c McCabe	b Wall	79		b Hornibrook	1
L.F. Townsend		b Hornibrook	1		b Wall	38
*G.R. Jackson		b Hornibrook	2		c&b Hornibrook	10
J.M. Hutchinson	c Ponsford	b Hornibrook	0		b Kippax	1
+H. Elliott		not out	12		not out	5
T.B. Mitchell		b Wall	0	c Ponsford	b Hornibrook	0
Extras	(b 6, lb 3)		9	(b 9, lb 4)		13
Total			215			181

1-32, 2-32, 3-34, 4-85, 5-161, 6-162, 7-186, 8-186, 9-215

1-10, 2-45, 3-79, 4-96, 5-98, 6-99, 7-171, 8-171, 9-181

	O	M	R	W	O	M	R	W
Wall	15	0	48	3	9	4	14	2
Fairfax	12	3	23	0	16	5	48	1
Hornibrook	29	10	61	6	28.2	8	82	6
Hurwood	12	4	31	0	7	4	11	0
Bradman	7	1	24	1				
McCabe	7	2	19	0				
Kippax					5	1	13	1

AUSTRALIANS

W.H. Ponsford	c Hutchinson	b Worthington	131	not out	30
A.A. Jackson	c Elliott	b Worthington	63	not out	18
D.G. Bradman	c Elliott	b Worthington	44		
A.F. Kippax	c Elliott	b Mitchell	25		
*V.Y. Richardson		b Townsend	10		
S.J. McCabe	c Hutchinson	b Townsend	5		
A.G. Fairfax		b Mitchell	20		
+W.A. Oldfield		c & b Worthington	14		
A. Hurwood		b Mitchell	15		
P.M. Hornibrook		not out	2		
T.W. Wall	lbw	b Mitchell	0		
Extras	(b 6, lb 5, w 2, nb 6)		19	(lb 3, nb 1)	4
Total			348		52

1-127, 2-231, 3-252, 4-273, 5-281, 6-288, 7-327, 8-337, 9-348

	O	M	R	W	O	M	R	W
Slater	21	9	34	0				
Worthington	38	6	103	4	5	2	9	0
Townsend	37	13	68	2	6	1	11	0
Mitchell	34.5	10	78	4	6	3	3	0
Lee	4	0	22	0				
Storer	7	1	24	0				
Ford					2	0	9	0
Jackson					1.1	0	16	0

In the *Evening Standard* he wrote that Jackson 'is just as easy and graceful as Bradman is demonstrative. The latter undoubtedly models himself on the wonderful Charlie Macartney, who was a law unto himself. Bradman, to me, is too "saucy" too early. This is sure to undo him on our uncertain wickets until he has learnt his lessons. The learning may cost him little or much, according to what he retains and what he cuts out. At present he has no reserve for timing his square cuts. Macartney was never guilty of cutting too hard.'

Whether Bradman read this before play began isn't known but if he did, and if MacLaren was in the Press Box he, like Fender, could be made to suffer, Fender physically and mentally, MacLaren just mentally.

Bradman felt he had a 'particularly personal reason for looking forward' to the match because Fender, 'besides being a great captain of a great county, is also a leading critic', and if Bradman hadn't misunderstood him, Fender 'did not think too highly of my batting during the last series of Tests in Australia. I am not at all susceptible to criticism, but I need not make any secret of the fact that I was filled with a quiet determination to do well at The Oval.' (13)

This miserable May, the outfield was rain-soaked and the weather cold, dark, almost forbidding. It gave a wicket which lacked pace all day. Inside the pavilion and the players' dressing rooms fires were lit.

Woodfull won the toss and batted but . . . the stumps were wrong. They were a larger experimental kind and had been pitched by mistake. Smaller, normal ones were brought out. Jackson simply couldn't find form. In the eleventh over Allom made a ball rear outside the off stump and Jackson tried to cut it but was caught at the wicket. The light was poor, no more than half-light, really.

Bradman nibbled at Allom's first ball as it moved away outside the off stump but didn't touch it. He nibbled at the second but got away with that, too. Then he turned Allom to the square leg boundary and everyone could see that *he* could see perfectly well even in the half-light.(14)

Fender, fielding in the slips, awaited his turn or his fate. He wore 'a queer, loose garment beloved of the cartoonists, who describe it as a "nightshirt sweater"'. (15) Mailey in Sydney's *The Sun* pointed out how critical Fender had been of Bradman and how, now, he set a field to try and block Bradman's strokes. Bradman, however, 'forced openings in all directions'. When the score reached 26 Eric Stroud, a medium-pacer with a jerking action, bowled and Bradman played him into the on side for 3.

Fender replaced Allom and effortlessly Bradman glanced him to the fine leg boundary. The light improved and the sun tried to get through the cloud while Bradman glanced Fender again, but very fine, demonstrating 'what a master he is with the least opportunity to that part of the field'. (16) Fender, scheming outside the off-stump, couldn't stop Bradman playing it to leg; like everybody else, Bradman's speed was too much for him. Bradman was deciding line and length, not Fender.

Fender changed the bowling but a single to each batsman brought the 50 up in an hour although the tempo did not increase to lunch, which the Australians took at 63 (Woodfull 28, Bradman 25.)

The crowd grew to about 9,000 in the afternoon and the weather improved again. Woodfull and Bradman resumed quietly before Bradman late cut to towards the boundary but the fielder cut it off. He was under way again and 19 were added off 10 overs before, at 37, he gave a chance to the slips. It sailed through and on to the boundary. He prepared to accelerate, building on the solid morning's foundation.

He wielded his off side glance against medium-pacer Eric Stroud, 'chopping' them through the slips to Sandham at fine leg. From the first Sandham moved fast enough to save a couple of runs but Bradman, placing the second at a finer angle and hitting the ball slightly harder, beat him completely. Sandham stood and smiled. Was Bradman toying with him? It looked like that. The Australians reached 100 (Bradman 48, Woodfull 42) and in the same over Bradman swept to the square leg boundary for his own 50 out of 93 in an hour and twenty-five minutes.

At 109 one medium-pacer, Thomas Shepherd, replaced another, Bert Lock, and Bradman greeted this by savagely pulling a short-pitched ball then played a square cut so hard that poor old Sandham, only a yard or two from the ball's trajectory, couldn't get near it. Woodfull was being left behind; at 124 Fender put himself on and Woodfull moved to 50. It had taken him two hours and twenty minutes, Bradman then 66. In the next Fender over, Woodfull was caught by Shepherd one-handed at first slip.

Warner, reaching for the proper focus, wrote: 'It is not easy for a captain to stop a Bradman from scoring fast when well set, and though a pavilion critic hesitates to criticise so astute a captain as the Surrey leader [Fender] it struck me that more might have been done to "block the exits", and particularly Bradman's hook strokes. The bowlers were simply helpless against this amazing young cricketer.' (17)

The crowd grew to 12,000.

Bradman, now partnered by Richardson, bestrode the afternoon – particularly since Richardson didn't time the ball well when he first came in. Richardson survived, while Bradman, 'prancing from one end to the other, was scoring almost when and how he liked. Any ball, however, which he did not consider fit to be scored from he played in the most correct manner of defence.' (18) He even played the hook, something unusual on faster Australian wickets but entirely possible here because a batsman had more time to get into position.

He plundered 12 from an Allom over to move into the 90s and a pull took him to 99 but he was content to play out the rest of the over. Nine minutes later he drove Lock for a single and had his hundred. It had taken two hours twenty-five minutes and in the hour and a half since lunch he'd made 70. It was no more than a prelude.

With Richardson into his stride, playing forcing shots at either side of the wicket, 'Fender repeatedly changed the bowling but Bradman continued more freely, and was especially severe on Stroud. Bradman, by pulling him for a magnificent 4, made the partnership worth a 100 in under an hour.' (19) At tea he'd made 142 out of 234, Richardson 32.

He resumed aggressively after tea, driving Fender to the boundary before Richardson was caught at square leg off Allom. They'd put on 113 in seventy-seven minutes.

Artful Fender twice had Bradman in difficulty and was bowling well enough to trap Ponsford lbw. McCabe lasted but a moment – caught by Fender off Allom – but Fairfax steadied it down and watched. Bradman made 51 while he made 4, and reached his 200 out of 289 in three and three quarter hours. This second hundred took eighty-five minutes. He kept punching the Surrey attack until it buckled.

At 207 Bradman faced Allom and lifted a ball for the first time but Stroud at forward short leg dropped it.

Fairfax plodded on and of his century partnership with Bradman he made only 22. Whenever he had strike Cockney voices called out: 'Hurry up, Guv'nor.' He didn't. Bradman, showing signs of weariness, slowed towards the close although he still had the energy to try and run a fifth to the one big hit Fairfax made. Fairfax sent him back.

He surpassed the Worcester innings with a clinical back cut and punched a couple of boundaries past cover point – the last a tremendous shot from a leg break by Robert Gregory – before rain ended play five minutes early.

Bradman finished with 252 out of 379, Fairfax 28, and Fender was left contemplating figures of 2 for 75 from 21 overs. The crowd came on to the pitch as Bradman made his way back and were so enthusiastic that the police had difficulty creating a passage through them.

'Bradman modestly travelled home in a tube train,' the *Australian Press Association* wrote, 'but took a long time to reach the station through the crowds of admirers, especially boys, some of whom fought to catch the same train, refusing to leave the carriage until the hero got out at St. Pancras. Then Bradman, who drinks tea for breakfast, lunch and dinner, celebrated his triumph in the same beverage, before going to the theatre where Fender entertained the Surrey and Australian teams.'

The Daily Express put everything concisely in a headline: 'BRADMAN, THE BATTING WONDER'.

The proper focus remained as problematical as it had before play began, and the presence of Macartney in England, as well as memories of what Macartney had done in England, didn't help. Bradman was being incessantly compared to him, as we've seen.

Vincent in *The Times* even tried to get away from the comparison. 'For long periods Bradman was making strokes which at first sight might appear impertinent, but he effected them without the suggestion of risk. It is unproductive to compare him with C.G. Macartney, but like that great master he has a tendency to squat down low when he is playing many of his attacking strokes, and one cannot help feeling that he has to a great extent moulded his style upon that of Macartney. Whether he yet has the gift of shattering first-class bowling on a really difficult wicket remains to be seen.'

Tebbutt wrote that the MacLaren article in the *Evening Standard* 'provided Bradman much amusement, especially the statements that Bradman is "saucy too early, cuts too hard, and had modelled his style on Macartney" [. . .] Bradman has seen Macartney bat only once.'

That evening Tebbutt dined with Bradman and when the article was produced Bradman retorted: 'I hope he was at The Oval today.'

Tebbutt tackled him about MacLaren's accusation of cutting too hard.

'Of course I cut hard, the harder the better,' Bradman said. 'How do you expect the ball to travel if you don't hit it?'

Bradman assured Tebbutt that he had certainly not modelled himself on Macartney. [20]

What he had done was come across the horizon like a missile and detonated, sending reverberations in all directions. He had now scored 922 runs and been dismissed a mere six times, giving him an average of 153. The 922 had taken him slightly over twenty-one hours, which meant that, on all wickets and against all bowling so far, he was averaging 43 runs an hour himself.

Perhaps comparison was the only way to find the proper focus, the only way to try to make Bradman explicable, and that led to Macartney, medium height, also pugnacious, also a slayer of England bowling since 1907. *Wisden* described Macartney as 'daring and confident' and said 'he possessed a quickness of eye, hand and foot, a perfection of timing which made him a menace to the best of bowlers'. Just like Bradman, in fact.

Macartney's career finished in 1926–27; Bradman's began in 1927–28. Both were from New South Wales and to assume Bradman had been weaned on Macartney must have seemed entirely natural. Cricket lovers treasure continuity anyway, because it constantly takes them so smoothly on the journey to the beloved past.

What you can't know, unless you ask the man himself, is quite how much of anyone they have seen. Who knew whether Bradman watched several seasons of State matches as a little lad lost in the crowd or never went once? There is no suggestion that the comparers – *The Times,* Cardus, MacLaren, Fender or anyone else – went to ask him, not least, presumably, because personal interviews were virtually unknown (and strictly discouraged by this tour management on top of that). A thousand newspaper reports and whole tour books appeared quite naturally without a single quotation from anybody.

So, the comparers felt, Bradman came across the horizon and, in the detonation, proved himself to be Macartney mark II, or a clone, or a disciple, or an imitation or another version of the same thing. This endured for the first month of the tour and lingered a while after that but at some undefined point Bradman emerged entirely on his own in the eyes of others. As the tour progressed the comparison was made less and less often and ultimately Bradman's achievements swept *all* comparisons aside.

This miserable May, rain washed out the remaining two days of the Surrey match.

Bradman insisted he wasn't 'gloating' about the 252 not out, but 'I did feel that if this innings had not put me on my feet as far as Mr. Fender was concerned, I at least felt satisfied and had learned a good deal about an English wicket'. (21) Ouch.

In *The Observer* Fender wrote he felt the Australians were 'a little below par' at The Oval. After a day in the field:

> *'I came away with the impression that they were, and have been for the past few matches, showing their best. That they have no reserve of power other than that which they have already shown us. Bradman made a huge score, and made it in a manner on which no one could cast any aspersions, but it was the things he did not do which impressed me most, and the same may be said of Woodfull and Richardson, as well as Fairfax. Jackson, Ponsford and McCabe did not stay long enough to permit any particular impression to be gathered.*
>
> *'Of those who made runs, however, one had a very curious feeling, considering the circumstances, and that was that, despite their large total, they were not so very fearsome after all. One never got the impression of Bradman, for instance, that it mattered little what one bowled to him he would take runs where and when he liked. He made most of his runs off bad balls, delivered by bowlers who are not really among the strongest in the country. He seldom, if ever, forced runs off a good ball, and certainly never gave one the impression as Macartney used to do, that one simply did not know where to bowl to him to stop him.*
>
> *'Bradman had one outstanding merit, however, which marks him out among the majority of present-day batsmen, and that is that when he receives a ball a trifle short or a little too far up, he is certain in his ability to make four runs off it, while there are many today who would take fewer off the same ball. He is outstanding in that, but not by any means so severe on the good length ball. I can quite well visualize that the bowlers of a Test side would be well able to keep him under control, and in a way in which Charlie Macartney, for instance, would never have permitted them to do. I do not wish in any way to detract, or attempt to do so, from his wonderful displays so far, but I feel that he could, and probably will, be controlled by a Test team of bowlers in a way in which he has never hitherto been controlled.'*

Again being fair, Fender couldn't see tomorrow but if he could have done he wouldn't have written what he just had.

Subsequently Fender defended his earlier criticism by saying that a 'lot of people in 1928–29 shared my reservations, initially, though they did not make them publicly known. Bradman had this marvellous pull stroke but fundamentally he did not play as straight regularly as some of us thought would be necessary to combat the variable bounce on English wickets. I genuinely thought this would be his undoing and I was not alone; some of the English players agreed with me. The fact that Bradman made so many runs in England, of course, showed what a fine player he was and my first thoughts were proved badly wrong.' (22)

Yes, there was that, there was certainly that.

SURREY V AUSTRALIANS

Kennington Oval, 24, 26, 27 May. Drawn.

AUSTRALIANS

*W.M. Woodfull	c Shepherd	b Fender	50
A.A. Jackson	c Brooks	b Allom	9
D.G. Bradman		not out	252
V.Y. Richardson	c Stroud	b Allom	32
W.H. Ponsford	lbw	b Fender	1
S.J. McCabe	c Fender	b Allom	2
A.G. Fairfax		not out	28
Extras	(b 3, lb 1, w 1)		5
Total			379

Dnb: +W.A. Oldfield, P.M. Hornibrook, T.W. Wall, C.V. Grimmett.

1-11, 2-127, 3-240, 4-243, 5-250

	O	M	R	W
Allom	34	8	74	3
Lock	22	5	73	0
Stroud	16	1	66	0
Fender	21	1	75	2
Shepherd	20	5	46	0
Gregory	10.4	1	40	0

Surrey: *P.G.H. Fender, M.J.C. Allom, D.R. Jardine, E.G. Stroud, J.B. Hobbs, A. Sandham, A. Ducat, T.F. Shepherd, R.J. Gregory, +E.W.J. Brooks, H.C. Lock.

Oxford University

The 78 runs needed to make 1,000 by the end of May preoccupied Bradman because no Australian had ever done it and, he reasoned, he might never get the chance again. Oxford University ought to have provided the ideal opportunity because their bowling attack wasn't particularly strong and the one man who might have got amongst them, Peebles, had a strained shoulder. After their initial meeting at Lord's, Bradman would take this further opportunity of studying him carefully, for present and future reference because he felt sure they'd be meeting again.

The match was played at Christ Church College Ground for the most pragmatic of reasons. You couldn't take gate money at their traditional home, The Parks, and a crowd of between 4,000 and 4,500 came. Various English reporters described the weather as summery, to which Bradman said cryptically that, although it was a merciful relief after Leyton, seven Australians still needed sweaters. Kelly said later that all the players wore two pairs of socks, two shirts and heavy sweaters.

'The sun came out at Oxford,' Tebbutt wrote. 'There cricket was as it ought to be, even though University culture had not been equal to the task of placing the scoring-board in sight of the Press marquee. The breeze stirred the tall poplars, shouts and bursts of blank pistol reports drifted up from the river where the crowds on the paths followed the racing rowers, and out on the field young men from the University were pitting their immature talent in the quadrennial match against the Australians. A quiet, enjoyable, almost dreamy match. Who could be energetic in the Oxford air?'

Woodfull won the toss and, on an easy wicket – Peebles described it as 'beautiful' – Ponsford and McCabe opened. Ponsford took strike against Charles Hill-Wood, 'a rather fast left-hander with an extraordinary action of delivering the ball with his head down'. (23)

They put on 96 in the hour and a half before lunch (McCabe 47, Ponsford 46). McCabe began to blossom in his range of stroke play as confidence finally came to him, although Peebles might have had him stumped when he was on 24. After lunch McCabe was bowled by Monty Garland-Wells, right-arm medium, for 91 with a ball which kept low. The crowd had grown by several hundred in anticipation of Bradman and when he appeared they gave him a big ovation.

He announced himself by hooking a delivery from Hill-Wood which rose head high but might have played on in the next over. Peebles, despite his strain, was soon on but, as Warner noted in dismay, 'with three short legs, a mid-on, *and no man out either at square leg or in the long field*'. [Warner's italics] Ponsford and Bradman helped themselves to 18 from two Peebles overs although Ponsford, now on 83, was missed at the wicket.

Peebles now bowled two no-balls. Bradman was caught off the first but made a 'prodigious short-arm stroke for 6' off the second. (24) It was his first of the tour. He'd based his concept of batsmanship on keeping the ball on the ground and regarded 6s as a sort of aberration violating basic principles.

This was, however, Ponsford's day, as Bradman himself acknowledged. It was not Peebles's because he went off for treatment to the strain – the Australian masseur was most obliging – and didn't bowl another ball before tea.

With the Australian total at 253 Bradman played on to a ball from Garland-Wells which gathered pace off the wicket, came back quickly and kept low. The *Oxford Mail* headline called out starkly: 'DON BRADMAN FAILS'. He'd made 32 and consoled himself that on this wicket the University ought to be able to make the Australians bat again, giving him another chance at the 1,000, now a tantalising 46 away.

While he waited he savoured ancient, enchanting Oxford to the full. It seems to have had the same sort of effect on him as Worcester and he delighted in watching the pageant of some rowing, the colourful crowds on the tow-path, the cheering, everything. (25)

Peebles, meanwhile, went to the Pembroke Ball, 'not meaning to have a very late night'. As he left, in a friend's car, they offered 'a lady a lift home. This she accepted with alacrity which was not surprising when it turned out that she lived, not in Oxford, but in London. Gallantry prevailed.' Peebles got back early in the morning still of course wearing white tie and tails, knowing full well that 'absence without leave was a serious offence'. He encountered a Don – a professor, not Bradman! – who murmured: 'Been to see the Pope?' and said no more.

Woodfull declared at 406 for 2 at the end of the first day and the University folded for 124, Peebles second top scorer with 22 including a boundary from a Grimmett full toss, a delivery so rare that Peebles remembered it fifty years later. (26)

The University followed on and folded again. Even Bradman bowled, taking a couple of wickets and being hit for 6 by Peebles, who did *not* remember it fifty years later – which tells you all you need to know about the respective merits of Grimmett's and Bradman's bowling.

During the match Peebles went to a dinner party where he and two other undergraduates entertained Macartney, Grimmett and Oldfield. Peebles noted that, almost without trying, Macartney became the dominant presence.

Hampshire

Winning in two days gave the tourists another free day on the Friday. Bradman had a game of golf in the morning and drove a Buick through the New Forest (an experience he'd remember as beautiful) to Southampton where, on the Saturday, they'd play Hampshire. He arrived at the 'sumptuous' South Western Hotel at 8.15pm.

Saturday was 31 May, the last day of the month and the final chance to make the 1,000. It would be a day of inherent, building drama under heavy cloud and played out on a pitch slightly moist from early morning rain, making the outfield slow. The Australians travelled to the ground by taxi.

When Woodfull and the Hampshire captain, Lord Tennyson, emerged from the pavilion to toss, some 5,000 people were already in the ground. That reflected the gathering fascination with Bradman and what he might do next. More would come during the day.

Tennyson won the toss and chose to bat. At that moment – an easy wicket, rain constantly threatening – Bradman's chance seemed to be gone. George Brown, an experienced player governed by moods, and Alexander Hosie opened. Brown was clearly in the mood: he square drove Fairfax to the boundary and in the same over pulled him full into the members' enclosure for 6. Hampshire scored at a run a minute for the first twenty minutes and Brown made 30 of the first 33. The 50 came up in thirty-five minutes (Brown 42).

Bradman watched Brown and reflected ruefully that 'by failing at Oxford I had allowed the golden opportunity to slip'.

Hosie went at 60, driving Grimmett back over his head to Wall who leapt up at full stretch, parried the ball and snaffled it as it came down.

Brown reached 56 and Geoffrey Lowndes, who'd come in for Hosie, played a ball wide of Bradman at deep extra cover. Bradman started to run towards the ball as it came off the bat but, instead of gathering it cleanly betrayed one of his own principles and used his foot. He 'over-ran' the ball and Brown, seeing this, embarked on a second run. [27]

OXFORD UNIVERSITY V AUSTRALIANS

Oxford, 28, 29 May. Australians won by an innings and 158 runs.

AUSTRALIANS

S.J. McCabe	b Garland-Wells	91
W.H. Ponsford	not out	220
D.G. Bradman	b Garland-Wells	32
A.F. Kippax	not out	56
Extras	(b 3, lb 2, w 1, nb 1)	7
Total	(2 wkts dec)	406

Dnb: *W.M. Woodfull, V.Y. Richardson, A.G. Fairfax, C.V. Grimmett, +C.W. Walker, T.W. Wall, A. Hurwood.

1-172, 2-253

	O	M	R	W
Hill-Wood	25	2	75	0
Nevinson	23	3	72	0
Peebles	22	3	71	0
Garland-Wells	25	4	99	2
Melville	6	1	45	0
Moore	3	0	12	0
Kingsley	5	1	25	0

OXFORD UNIVERSITY

P.G.T. Kingsley		b Wall	0	c Fairfax	b Grimmett	10
*D.N. Moore	lbw	b Grimmett	34		b Wall	1
Nawab of Pataudi	c McCabe	b Wall	22	st Walker	b Grimmett	9
A. Melville	c Walker	b Fairfax	10	c Hurwood	b Wall	22
N.M. Ford		b Grimmett	7		c&b Wall	31
I.S. Akers-Douglas	st Walker	b Grimmett	7		b Wall	6
H.M. Garland-Wells	st Walker	b Grimmett	3		b Bradman	8
C.K.H. Hill-Wood	c Richardson	b Hurwood	11	c Richardson	b Fairfax	12
I.A.R. Peebles		not out	22		b McCabe	11
+J.F.N. Mayhew		b Hurwood	0		b Bradman	0
J.H. Nevinson		b Grimmett	0		not out	7
Extras	(b 4, lb 2, nb 2)		8	(b 2, lb 3, nb 2)		7
Total			124			124

1-0, 2-30, 3-72, 4-72, 5-87, 6-88, 7-101, 8-123, 9-123

1-10, 2-14, 3-25, 4-74, 5-80, 6-83, 7-100, 8-106, 9-117

	O	M	R	W	O	M	R	W
Wall	8	2	26	2	16	4	29	4
Hurwood	8	2	27	2	5	1	20	0
Grimmett	21.3	5	48	5	18	7	31	2
Fairfax	12	6	15	1	12	6	13	1
Bradman					5	1	19	2
McCabe					1.1	0	5	1

Bradman, fully fifty yards away, prepared to throw to the end Brown was running for. 'Practically broadside' to the wicket he aimed, threw and struck the middle stump. He described it as the greatest 'fluke' of all time but it was much more than that. 100 to 1 might now = 1,000.

Grimmett wove his web (7 for 39 off 20.4 overs) and Hampshire were all out for 151 at half past three. Woodfull signalled Bradman to open with Jackson, giving him ample time to get the 46. Woodfull, Bradman noted, was as keen on Bradman getting them as *he* was. The crowd had grown to 7,000 but the heavy cloud threatened rain at any moment.

Bradman took strike and played a maiden to Jackson. Jackson faced Lofty Herman, right-arm fast-medium, and tried to hook a short ball. It went to forward short-leg and he was caught. This gave Bradman a profound 'fright' because 'I must confess I was more anxious than I had ever been. I felt the occasion and the special circumstances very much indeed – in fact, I was never more disturbed in my mind about getting runs.' [28]

Ponsford came in and he and Bradman batted carefully despite the fact that the bowling troubled neither. Bradman did accelerate in one Herman over, twice late cutting him to the boundary because third man was positioned too square.

Ponsford matched Bradman's scoring rate and at 40 Herman came off. The 50 came up in even time and at tea Bradman had 28, Ponsford 27. Enough drizzle began falling to bring the tarpaulin covers out but they were soon carted away.

Bradman thought *the weather has baulked me* as he gazed out on the desolate scene. The 18 he needed were impossibly far away but just then the drizzle stopped completely. It had been a 'heartbreaking delay of a quarter of an hour'. Play resumed at 5pm, the crowd now 9,000.

Bradman hooked Jack Newman for 3 but in the same over – at 62 – Ponsford played outside a ball and was bowled. Kippax came in.

Bradman had only one thought: *I must get the runs as quickly as I can before the weather breaks again.* The rain had made the wicket the most difficult he'd yet encountered in England. The crowd fell silent whenever he faced the bowling and once Stuart Boyes got a ball clean through him to an audible groan from the crowd but it missed the stumps. He stole a single here, a single there and moved into a glorious off-drive from Boyes to the boundary. He needed 7 more. The weather broke again but rain now, not drizzle.

Tennyson signalled they'd bowl one more over regardless and walked over to Newman. He'd been playing for Hampshire since 1906, making runs and plying his right-arm medium deliveries. Bradman did not know what Tennyson said to Newman but he could guess, and Newman knew what he was doing.

In the rain Newman bowled a head-high full toss on the leg side and Bradman pulled it to the boundary. Newman bowled a long hop and Bradman pulled that to the boundary, too. The crowed rushed the ground 'cheering wildly' (29) and the players sprinted to the shelter of the pavilion.

He had made 1,001 since he took guard against Worcester exactly one calendar month and one day before.

The Sports Echo in Southampton said that if Newman bowled the long hop 'intentionally it was a sporting action; if the ball – wet and slippery from the rain – slipped out of his hand, then Fate, after toying with Bradman all day, must have relented.'

Bradman had no doubts he reached the 1,000 because of Grimmett's bowling and the sportsmanship of Woodfull, Tennyson and Newman. Tennyson remembered that 'we played on in pouring rain to let him get them. Bradman appreciated such a sporting action at the time.' (30)

Only four other men had done it: W.G. Grace in 1895 (1,016 runs), Hammond in 1927 (1,028), Charlie Hallows of Lancashire in 1928 (1,000) and Tom Hayward of Surrey in 1900 (1,074). Bradman was delighted and gratified when he received telegrams of congratulation from Hammond and Hallows.

The tourists spent the Sunday at Lepe, an area of outstanding natural beauty on the coast not far from Southampton, as guests of Lord Henry Forster, a former Governor-General – the seventh – of Australia. He'd played first-class cricket and been President of the MCC.

On the Monday Bradman was surprised by how well the wicket had recovered from its drenching, although at moments it proved venemous. He felt released and celebrated by driving the final ball of Newman's uncompleted over to the boundary to reach 50. The crowd of 5,000 were to be treated to a profound exhibition.

The Australian 100 came up in an hour and a half although when he'd made 52 Bradman played a ball from Newman near – but not within reach – of Boyes at short leg.

After a mini collapse – Kippax out for 20, Woodfull soon stumped –

Bradman and McCabe came together. This was not necessarily good news for the Hampshire bowlers. McCabe attacked immediately and his first 24 runs were all boundaries. Bradman went with him so that in sixty-five minutes they scored 141. At one point Bradman hit Boyes 'firm-footed' for 6 on the leg side and Tennyson couldn't set a field to him. His century took him two hours fifteen minutes.

McCabe battered his way to 65 and by then Bradman was past 150, the last 50 in even time. With McCabe gone, bowled middle stump by Lowndes, the tail offered limited resistance. At 157 Bradman thought he'd been caught and set off for the pavilion but it was a bump ball. He batted on as wickets fell and was last man out, caught in the slips trying to steer Boyes on to the leg side. His innings lasted four hours and contained the 6 as well as twenty-six 4s.

Grimmett took care of the second Hampshire innings as he'd taken care of the first, and the tourists journeyed back to London to meet Middlesex, June here at last and the First Test in Nottingham two weeks away.

HAMPSHIRE V AUSTRALIANS

Southampton, 31 May, 2 June. Australians won by an innings and 8 runs.

HAMPSHIRE

+G. Brown		run out	56	c Hornibrook	b Grimmett	47
A.L. Hosie	c Wall	b Grimmett	12		c&b Grimmett	24
W.G.L.F. Lowndes	c Woodfull	b Hornibrook	5	c Bradman	b Hornibrook	1
C.P. Mead	c McCabe	b Grimmett	0	c Fairfax	b Hornibrook	0
J.A. Newman	c Fairfax	b Grimmett	10		b Grimmett	18
A.S. Kennedy		b Grimmett	5	c Hornibrook	b Grimmett	8
T.O. Jameson	c Oldfield	b Grimmett	27		b Hornibrook	19
*Lord Tennyson	c Jackson	b Wall	15		b Grimmett	24
W.C.L. Creese	lbw	b Grimmett	9	c Bradman	b Grimmett	10
G.S. Boyes		not out	4	st Oldfield	b Grimmett	15
O.W. Herman	c Hornibrook	b Grimmett	3		not out	0
Extras	(lb 5)		5	(b 4, lb 3, nb 2)		9
Total			151			175

1-60, 2-73, 3-74, 4-76, 5-90, 6-104, 7-133, 8-143, 9-147

1-50, 2-57, 3-57, 4-83, 5-97, 6-100, 7-143, 8-155, 9-159

	O	M	R	W	O	M	R	W
Wall	9	1	36	1	12	1	39	0
Fairfax	7	1	22	0	4	0	20	0
Hornibrook	18	2	49	1	22	5	51	3
Grimmett	20.4	4	39	7	29.3	5	56	7

AUSTRALIANS

D.G. Bradman	c Mead	b Boyes	191
A.A. Jackson	c Boyes	b Herman	0
W.H. Ponsford		b Newman	29
A.F. Kippax	c Kennedy	b Boyes	20
*W.M. Woodfull	st Brown	b Boyes	4
S.J. McCabe		b Lowndes	65
A.G. Fairfax	c Hosie	b Boyes	14
+W.A. Oldfield	lbw	b Kennedy	1
C.V. Grimmett	c Brown	b Boyes	1
T.W. Wall	lbw	b Boyes	0
P.M. Hornibrook		not out	0
Extras	(b 4, lb 2, w 1, nb 2)		9
Total			334

1-0, 2-62, 3-123, 4-135, 5-276, 6-319, 7-320, 8-321, 9-321

	O	M	R	W
Kennedy	30	5	89	1
Herman	9	1	47	1
Newman	18	3	80	1
Boyes	26	4	90	6
Creese	2	0	13	0
Lowndes	3	0	6	1

Chapter Five

8 and 131

IT COULD NOT GO ON, AND THE NATURE OF CRICKET DECREED that. Batting is the only sporting activity where the competitor must play as if he can't afford a single mistake. He may give a catch which is dropped and he may get a lucky decision from the umpire but he can't count on either of those. In a single innings match, by definition, there won't be a second innings for him, and even in a two-innings match he can't count on batting twice.

Sprinters are allowed false starts, baseball batters have their three strikes, and in everything else – tennis and golf, rugby and football, all forms of racing and so on – you can recover. No batsman thinks like that; they spend their whole careers one ball away from extinction or, using the tennis analogy, every ball is potentially match point. This makes batting permanently precarious and large scores important because they have been constructed in spite of that, but even Bradman was bound to make some mistakes on – forgive the phrase – the law of averages.

By mid-May he'd scored over 550 runs. By mid-June that would be 224 in five innings. In other words he made five mistakes and they brought his progress round the length and breadth of olde Englande to some sort of recognisable, explicable, comprehensible proportions.

The 224 were scored against Middlesex, Cambridge University – where in theory a run festival beckoned – and the First Test at Nottingham.

Middlesex

Grimmett and Hornibrook cut through the Middlesex first innings and a total of 103 looked what it was, paltry, despite the fact that Middlesex were a strong bowling side.

Allen trapped Ponsford lbw for 5 with the total at only 13. Bradman didn't like the pitch although – the tactic – he glanced his first ball from middle and leg for 3. Vincent in *The Times,* reflecting on this stroke, said: 'Bradman is one of the great batsmen who seem to have the whole of their stroke practically over and done with before the ball is more than halfway down the pitch.'

He took most of the bowling and made 35 in three quarters of an hour from 57 deliveries. Jack Hearne bowled medium pace and could make the ball break viciously from the off – essentially orthodox off-breaks at speed. Round the wicket, he pitched one outside the off-stump and Bradman sprang out to meet it but was beaten by its pace off the wicket. The ball turned enough to strike the leg stump. He'd looked comfortable before that but insisted he didn't *feel* comfortable.

Jackson still found runs elusive (out for 14) but Kippax redeemed the whole Australian effort with 102 and that meant a lead of 167. The Middlesex reply to that was grouped around Patsy Hendren's 138 (the first century to be hit against the tourists) so that the Australians needed 121 to win.

Ponsford rifled 10 before he was bowled but Bradman, who still didn't like the wicket and still didn't feel comfortable, again seemed to be batting well though not so impressively as the first innings. He couldn't get his timing quite right and with the total at 45 Greville Stevens produced a slow yorker. Bradman hit over the top of it. In the end Fairfax and Richardson guided the Australians home.

Cambridge University

They stayed at the University Arms Hotel with a view on to Parker's Piece, the broad public parkland which the town authorities bought from Trinity College in 1613, a century and a half before Cook charted the Australian coast.

Fenner's, the delightful and scenic home of Cambridge University's cricket team, was only a couple of streets away. The Cambridge captain, Welshman John Morgan, won the toss and batted on a perfect day in front of a crowd of 4,000. No doubt the Australians were more relaxed

MIDDLESEX V AUSTRALIANS

Lord's, 4, 5, 6 June. Australians won by 5 wickets.

MIDDLESEX

G.T.S. Stevens	c Hurwood	b Hornibrook	22	st Richardson	b Grimmett	18
H.W. Lee		b Hornibrook	26	lbw	b Hurwood	2
J.W. Hearne	c Hurwood	b Hornibrook	11	lbw	b McCabe	21
E.H. Hendren	c Richardson	b Grimmett	17	c Richardson	b Hornibrook	138
G.O.B. Allen		b Hornibrook	4	lbw	b Hornibrook	18
*N.E. Haig	c Richardson	b Hornibrook	0	lbw	b Grimmett	6
H.J. Enthoven		not out	15	c Richardson	b Fairfax	38
G.C. Newman	c Fairfax	b Grimmett	0		b Grimmett	5
E.G. Canning	b Hornibrook		7	c Hurwood	b Hornibrook	4
F.J. Durston	c McCabe	b Grimmett	0		b Hornibrook	10
+W.F.F. Price	b Hornibrook	0			not out	0
Extras	(lb 1)		1	(b 13, lb 9, w1, nb 4)		27
Total			103			287

1-48, 2-53, 3-68, 4-78, 5-80, 6-82, 7-82, 8-97, 9-98

1-10, 2-38, 3-58, 4-142, 5-153, 6-254, 7-271, 8-275, 9-283

	O	M	R	W	O	M	R	W
Fairfax	9	1	20	0	27	11	41	1
Hurwood	2	0	4	0	13	6	30	1
Hornibrook	27.1	9	42	7	27.4	7	60	4
Grimmett	26	10	36	3	33	7	81	3
McCabe					18	6	48	1

AUSTRALIANS

W.H. Ponsford	lbw	b Allen	5		b Haig	10
A.A. Jackson	c Canning	b Stevens	14	lbw	b Hearne	26
D.G. Bradman		b Hearne	35		b Stevens	18
A.F. Kippax	lbw	b Allen	102		not out	17
*V.Y. Richardson	lbw	b Hearne	1	c Newman	b Stevens	11
S.J. McCabe	c Lee	b Allen	31	c Allen	b Stevens	18
A.G. Fairfax		b Lee	34		not out	13
C.V. Grimmett		b Allen	21			
A. Hurwood		b Allen	1			
+C.W. Walker		not out	5			
P.M. Hornibrook	lbw		b Allen		4	
Extras	(b 9, lb 6, nb 2)		17	(b 2, lb 4, w 2)		8
Total			270	(5 wkts)		121

1-13, 2-58, 3-68, 4-72, 5-137, 6-229, 7-245, 8-247, 9-266

1-16, 2-45, 3-65, 4-83, 5-85

	O	M	R	W	O	M	R	W
Allen	37.1	8	77	6	7.4	3	19	0
Haig	13	3	24	0	11	3	18	1
Durston	15	3	27	0				
Stevens	23	2	70	1	17	1	47	3
Hearne	25	10	34	2	13	3	27	1
Lee	3	2	1	1				
Enthoven	7	3	20	0				
Newman					1	0	2	0

in their approach than usual because Bradman bowled eleven overs and took three wickets – including two very promising bats, Tim Killick (who wore glasses for the first time – Bradman judged him one of the best young players in England) and Roger Human, an all-rounder from Newcastle-upon-Tyne.

Woodfull settled to a distant double hundred when the Australians batted. Ponsford went early and Bradman was 'subdued'. He concentrated on gathering runs on the leg side before, at 32, edging a very wide ball from Human to Threlfall Baines, a South African, in the slips. The Australians finished this first day on 179 for 2.

On the Sunday at 10.30am they motored out to be lunch guests of Viscount and Lady Downe at Hillington Hall near King's Lynn, a journey of some two hours on the country roads. The hall was a typically imposing country house of the kind the Australians were coming to know so well and Downe, related to previous MCC Presidents, knew his cricket. Hillington was very close to Sandringham and at 2.30pm Downe took the Australians there to meet the King and Queen. Bradman wrote of 'great joy' and a 'momentous' occasion. The Australians were made to feel 'entirely at home. The absence of anything in the nature of formality put us at our ease immediately. The King showed the liveliest interest in our tour.' The Royals chatted to the tourists for about half an hour and the King congratulated Bradman.

Tebbutt records how the Australians relaxed when the King called Downe 'Jack' and, as they walked in the grounds, espied the Queen coming towards them. 'Here comes the Queen. I must introduce you boys to her.' They asked if they could take photographs and the King said: 'Fire away! Take as many as you like!' The Queen said she'd like copies of them.

The King asked Walker how old he was, then McCabe who replied: '19.'

'I wish I was 19 again,' the King said.

He commented that the weather reminded him of Adelaide and when he said that the Australians cheered.

Bradman remembered, in a rush of impressions, the gardens, the museum, the stables and the church where royalty went. This was St. Mary Magdalene, dating in its present form from the 16th century. Bradman was impressed by the solid silver altar and Bible of precious stones.

The importance of this Royal visit was both profound and sincere. Tebbutt wrote quite naturally about how such visits gave a 'heightened regard for the Throne, and the more real understanding of the hold of its occupant upon his people, cannot fail to act as a binding element'.

Word of their presence must have spread, because when they left in the motorcade for Hillington Hall and afternoon tea a crowd had gathered in an 'avenue' and as the motorcade passed down it they cheered. They got back to Cambridge and had dinner at 8.45pm.

At Fenner's on the Monday, Woodfull went to the double hundred out of 504 for 8 declared, and the University were tumbled out for 225 – Bradman another three wickets, including Human again, caught by Ponsford. The match ended in cold weather with a fine drizzle falling. Somehow the English summer stayed coy as a maiden wherever the tourists approached her.

That was the Tuesday and the First Test would begin on the Friday. They motored to London and caught the train to Bath. There they motored the 12 miles (19km) to Downside School for two days' privacy, gentle rest and some net practice, although Bradman stayed in London as the guest of Alf Stevens, once mayor of Bowral and captain of the cricket club there, and his English wife. They happened to be in England. a'Beckett, ill, stayed in London and was expected to have a net at Lord's.

Downside represented sanctuary – police even guarded the cricket field when the Australians practised, keeping the public away and a barbed wire fence had been put in place. If the players had gone to London or Nottingham they risked being buffeted by invitations and autograph hunters. They arrived without pomp and ceremony, and the 340 pupils cheered them. Within a short while they were in the swimming pool and, after that, they played billiards and snooker. They insisted on sleeping in the dormitories.

'Though Jackson batted attractively towards the end of his latest innings, he is clearly not in the best of health,' the *Australian Press Association* reported. 'He looks rather wan. Muscular rheumatism was the official diagnosis of his illness at Cambridge.' [(1)]

Next day the Australians did practice – the headmaster had even hired fast bowlers from Gloucestershire and Devon. The *Australian Press Association* reported: 'The police have used barbed wire to keep the crowds away from the playing ground, only the college boys and the Downside Abbey monks being admitted.'

CAMBRIDGE UNIVERSITY V AUSTRALIANS

Cambridge, 7, 9, 10 June. Australians won by an innings and 134 runs.

CAMBRIDGE UNIVERSITY

G.D. Kemp-Welch		b McCabe	20		b Hurwood	2
A. Ratcliffe	c Hornibrook	b Hurwood	4		b McCabe	5
E.T. Killick	c Wall	b Bradman	48		b Bradman	44
G.C. Grant	c Hurwood	b McCabe	12	lbw	b Bradman	10
*+J.T. Morgan		run out	0	c Oldfield	b McCabe	14
T.W.T. Baines	lbw	b Bradman	12		b McCabe	8
H.R.W. Butterworth	c Hurwood	b McCabe	10		b McCabe	8
H.R.C. Human		b Bradman	0	c Ponsford	b Bradman	47
F.R. Brown	c Hurwood	b McCabe	10	c McCabe	b Hurwood	52
W.H. Webster		not out	10		b Wall	24
A.H. Fabian	c Oldfield	b Wall	8		not out	1
Extras	(b 3, lb 6, w 2)		11	(b 7, lb 3)		10
Total			145			225

1-9, 2-35, 3-57, 4-57, 5-91, 6-112, 7-116, 8-116, 9-127

1-3, 2-20, 3-42, 4-64, 5-78, 6-99, 7-99, 8-184, 9-221

	O	M	R	W	O	M	R	W
Wall	17.3	3	47	1	10.2	3	54	1
Hurwood	6	2	9	1	10	1	20	2
Hornibrook	11	4	18	0	6	1	13	0
McCabe	11	2	25	4	20	3	60	4
Bradman	11	1	35	3	17	3	68	3

AUSTRALIANS

*W.M. Woodfull	c Fabian	b Webster	216
W.H. Ponsford		b Kemp-Welch	7
D.G. Bradman	c Baines	b Human	32
S.J. McCabe		run out	96
V.Y. Richardson	c Kemp-Welch	b Human	34
A.A. Jackson		run out	25
W.A. Oldfield	c Human	b Webster	28
P.M. Hornibrook		b Human	6
T.W. Wall		not out	9
A. Hurwood		not out	8
Extras	(b 24, lb 8, w 7, nb 4)		43
Total (8 wkts dec)			504

Dnb: +C.W. Walker.

1-13, 2-79, 3-253, 4-348, 5-424, 6-473, 7-480, 8-489

	O	M	R	W
Kemp-Welch	30	3	100	1
Human	35	3	106	3
Fabian	26	4	104	0
Brown	31	5	72	0
Webster	21	8	45	2
Grant	1	0	13	0
Butterworth	2	0	21	0

The boys helped in the practice, were enthralled when Grimmett demonstrated the googly and very impressed when Fairfax bowled at a single stump and hit it repeatedly. They were not however allowed to ask for autographs. The head boy presented Woodfull with a silver cigarette case on behalf of the school (Woodfull didn't smoke) and Woodfull said: 'After knocking about hotels so long I cannot tell you how much we appreciate the peace and quiet of Downside. We are looking forward to a great victory in the First Test and, of course, you boys won't want us to win.'

First Test – Trent Bridge

On the Thursday in Nottingham, groundsman Walter Marshall patted the pitch and said: 'There are hundreds of runs in that, and if England win the toss I can see the Australians having a tiring day in the field tomorrow.' Someone asked what would happen if Australia won the toss. 'Don't say that, but if they do I shall feel guilty for preparing such a wicket. There is not going to be enough rain to give a worm a drink, but if there is it won't hurt the wicket because it will be effectively covered.'

Some social engagements were already in place. The Duke and Duchess of Portland were to entertain both teams at Welbeck Abbey near Worksop on the Sunday. That same morning, Plum Warner was due to make a special broadcast to Australia on the match, bringing the cricket alive to the audience there. It had never been done before. There was a radiotelephone link which allowed Australian commentators to listen to the English commentary on matches and then broadcast it as if they were doing it. This became hugely popular, especially because Bradman was scoring so heavily. The radiotelephone was quite different; on the Sunday Australia would be getting authentic Warner direct and unfiltered.

The tourists arrived at Nottingham LMS station at 6.36pm from Downside on this Thursday evening. A crowd estimated at 3,000 had made their way to the station and the stationmaster, one H. Briggs, greeted them. The players were all but mobbed. As they struggled through the crowd Herbert Sutcliffe, who'd arrived a few moments earlier and was ascending some steps towards the exit, saw Woodfull and waved to him. Woodfull smiled, waved and doffed his cap.

The crowd naturally recognised the Australian captain when he emerged and from the depths of the crowd a voice with a thick Nottinghamshire accent called out: 'Good owd Woodfull.' Four cars had been placed at their disposal, decorated red, white, blue and green and named St. George, St. David, St. Andrew and St. Patrick. The convoy headed towards the Black Boy, an old hotel close by the Town Hall. A crowd waited there, too, and cheered each of the four cars as it arrived.

The Town Hall clock chimed during the night as well as the day and Woodfull quickly approached the local authorities to have it silenced between 11pm and 7am during the Test.

The English team stayed at the Victoria Hotel in Beeston although Harold Larwood had his own car and commuted from the family home in Nuncargate, a small mining community just north of Nottingham. Hundred of schoolboys played a game called 'spot 'em' at the station all the day as the English players came in from various parts of the country. They didn't see Chapman. He drove and didn't arrive until 10.15pm.

The *Nottingham Evening News* reported that 'great interest was displayed in the electrically-controlled scoreboard in the course of erection near the Queen's Statue on Beastmarket-hill. Hundreds of people congregated to watch the workmen putting the finishing touches to the board, which will indicate every run scored.'

On the Friday the first spectators – two young men – arrived at Trent Bridge at dawn. One had walked from Leicester and he said: 'I lost my job three months ago but I made up my mind to see this match and so yesterday I started walking. I arrived here about 2 o'clock this morning and joined my pal who lives in Nottingham.' (2)

The *Nottingham Evening News* sent reporters to see what the teams were doing in the hours before the match began.

'The English team were early astir today. A.P.F. Chapman, who is accompanied by his wife (the sister of T.C. Lowry, another famous cricketer), was down to breakfast soon after eight o'clock, and he was quickly followed by White, Robins and Tate. Eggs and bacon, the traditional English breakfast, was the stock order and the cricketers fell to their meal as if without a thought of the great ordeal before them.

'They did not talk much, and when they did it was about anything but cricket. White told Chapman about his crop of hay down in Somerset, Tate was full of Brighton's good season, and Patsy Hendren explained at great length how he nearly missed his train from London last night.

'Not far away at the Black Boy the Australians were having their breakfasts. They were a dour company, hugging their secrets close to their

hearts. When asked if the team had been finally selected Mr. Kelly looked blankly at the questioner. "Team," he said, as if he had never heard the word, "there is plenty of time yet. The best team that we can put out, that will be our team."

'Then he attacked vigorously a large plate of eggs and bacon. As with the English team, that seemed to be the most popular dish with all the Australians, with the exception of Grimmett. He was content with grapefruit and some toast with marmalade.'

The turnstiles opened at 9am. Ominous grey cloud loomed but as the people began to go into the ground the sun broke through.

An old gentleman passed five small boys looking longingly at the gates. The gentleman paused and turned back. He and the boys 'went into committee'. (3) The boys turned their pockets out and between them had 6s 9d but they needed 12s 6d to get in. 'Follow me,' he said, and in they went. By 9.30am long queues snaked back along the Radcliffe Road, mostly men in hats either wearing raincoats or with them folded over their arms. The queue in the Bridgford Road had many women in it.

At 10am the England players slipped quietly from the Victoria Hotel but 'there was nothing in the nature of a send-off. A small group of enthusiasts assembled to see them leave but not a cheer was raised. Someone murmured that it was typical of us English folk to make more fuss over the Australians than over our own men.' (4)

Chapman and Sutcliffe emerged and began signing autographs so they were soon surrounded. Sutcliffe then got into a taxi by himself. Hobbs and Duckworth shared one, and so did Duleepsinhji and Robins. A 'happy trio' – Hendred, White and Tate – shared another.

A large crowd gathered outside the Black Boy, and they cheered and clapped when they saw the Australians coming out towards their four-car motorcade.

England left out Duleepsinhji but still fielded a side of many strengths and great experience. Hobbs and Sutcliffe by now formed an opening partnership of legend, Hammond bestrode the 1928–29 series, Frank Woolley had been making elegant runs since before the First War, Hendren was the Cockney who'd just taken 138 off the Australians for Middlesex, cherubic Chapman represented the uninhibited amateur, Tate was a masterful medium-pace bowler (who'd advised Bradman at the end of the 1928–29 series, don't forget), Larwood was the fastest bowler in the world and on his home ground, Robins bowled penetrating leg breaks, Dick Tyldesley had taken 3 for 17 for Lancashire against the Australians and Duckworth was an experienced wicket-keeper.

The Australian side selected itself because, of the fifteen, a'Beckett hadn't recovered and there were doubts about Jackson and Hurwood. Once Oldfield was selected as wicket-keeper, deputy Walker had no place – and that was the team.

Woodfull called heads but it landed tails and Chapman said: '*We'll bat.*' At 11.30am, Hobbs and Sutcliffe came out and began an opening partnership of 53 followed not only by the 15,763 inside Trent Bridge but many thousands at the Exchange Square watching the electronic scoreboard. This 'second' crowd grew so large that a man with a megaphone asked the crowd to keep the pavements and roadway clear.

Once Fairfax had Sutcliffe caught by Hornibrook, mesmeric Grimmett seduced Hammond lbw for 8, had Woolley stumped for a duck and Hendren bowled for 5. That was 4 for 71 but Chapman breezed to 52 and England reached 241 for 8 (Robins 28 not out) at the close.

Crowds gathered outside both hotels before play on the Saturday – more outside the Black Boy than there had been the previous morning, although they were quieter. Grimmett emerged early – evidently he had an appointment before the game – and went off all but unnoticed. The main body of the team were applauded again when they appeared.

The England players had been up at eight and some went for a stroll. Chapman emerged with 'a small bag and a light mackintosh – hoping perhaps to be mistaken for a commercial traveller – but he was readily recognised by the admiring crowd. The crowd surged round his car and the police had some little difficulty in finding a way out for him.' (5)

The electronic scoreboard was banned by the police as a danger to traffic and pedestrians.

Rain fell during the night so that play didn't resume until 2.15pm, and while the crowd waited they drank beer and minerals at a rate of 5,000 an hour (local papers notice details like this because they make compelling headlines). When play resumed England added 29.

By now the sun, which had came through the cloud at about 1pm, was drying the wicket and Australia faced a nasty session. The clouds had gone and a breeze stirred. Woodfull ordered the light roller and changed the order, moving Fairfax up to three and Bradman down to four presumably with the idea that the wicket might improve and, if Bradman could be saved for that, he'd score heavily.

At 2.59pm Larwood opened the bowling from the Radcliffe Road end and Woodfull took a single from the second ball. Ponsford played the over out and Woodfull took guard against Tate from the Pavilion end. Tate, who spread sawdust on the crease to secure his footholds, knew what to do in conditions like these and bowled Woodfull a maiden.

Ponsford scored a single from the first ball of Larwood's second over and Woodfull played the other five safely enough. This was tight cricket. Ponsford scored a couple from Tate's second over and Larwood bowled a maiden to Woodfull: 4 overs, 4 runs. The second ball of Tate's next over to Ponsford bowled him behind his legs: 4 for 1 after fifteen long minutes. Fairfax played out the remainder of the over but the cricket tightened. Larwood bowled a maiden to Woodfull, Tate bowled a maiden to Fairfax before each batsman took a single from Larwood.

As was custom, Larwood dealt in five-over, dramatically fast bursts and he'd done that. Tyldesley replaced Tate, and that allowed Tate to replace Larwood at the Radcliffe Road end – again custom. Tyldesley bowled a maiden to Fairfax and Woodfull faced Tate. He played the second ball into the gully where Chapman caught it two-handed: 6 for 2.

At 3.30pm Bradman came to a Test crease for the first time in England. No doubt he came slowly, letting his eyes adjust to the light. No doubt he carefully scanned genial, masterful Maurice Tate waiting at the end of his run. Tate was too old at 35, some said. He didn't look too old now.

'Two walking steps, falling into six accelerating running strides and – mid-way between the fifth and sixth – the body rocked easily back. The left arm was thrown up, the ball held in the back-slung right hand [. . .] then, with the final leap, came the full rhythmic swing of those heavy shoulders: he delivered at the highest point of the vertical swing.' (6) That was Tate and it was what Bradman faced now.

Bradman took a single from the first ball – the tactic: a quickly-timed glance – and Fairfax played out the over with 2 from the final ball.

Bradman faced Tyldesley and didn't score from the first three balls. What happened next represented a glimpse of the future because Bradman attacked Tyldesley with consecutive 2s and a single from the final ball to keep the strike. Whether Bradman sensed Tyldesley might be the weakest link in the England bowling and hitting him off would destabilise the English attack; whether Tyldesley just bowled badly for the second half of the over; or whether Bradman's speed enabled him to launch the attack is not clear now.

What remains clear is that after this over the cricket tightened again once Bradman had taken a single from Tate's first ball. Fairfax played out the over. Tyldesley bowled a maiden to Bradman, who was visibly uncomfortable against him – and Tate. Tate bowled a maiden to Fairfax.

Tyldesley bowled four balls from which Bradman didn't score. He edged the fifth and Duckworth may have touched it – a slight deflection – as it went towards tall, angular Woolley at first slip standing close. Woolley couldn't hold it and they ran a sharp single.

That took Bradman up to the other end to face Tate and he didn't score from the first three balls. Tate was famous for something approaching an optical illusion: that his deliveries speeded up *after* they'd hit the ground. The truth must have been that somehow they lost less speed than other bowlers. The fourth ball beat Bradman for pace – which is a way of saying speed off the wicket and, in the context of Bradman in 1930, an extraordinary achievement. He played across it, the ball kept low and he managed to touch it before it hit the middle and off stumps.

During his eighteen minutes at the crease he'd faced twenty-two balls and given the chance as well as being comprehensively bowled. Was Fender right after all? This Test attack had certainly controlled him and Australia at 16 for 3 were in deep trouble. Kippax and Richardson gave the innings some sort of backbone and they ended this second day 140 for 8.

Nottinghamshire put a room at Warner's disposal and he made his radio broadcast at the close of play, albeit that the time in Sydney was 4.20am. He'd made a sheaf of notes and Sir Henry (Shrimp) Leveson-Gower, MCC stalwart and – as we shall see – a leading figure in the Scarborough Cricket Festival, handed them to him as he spoke. Warner was 'very frightened at the start' but calmed himself by thinking it was just like making a speech. The news agency Reuters, in a message datelined Sydney, said: 'The Australian Broadcasting Company relayed Mr. P. F. Warner's talk on the First Test match to all states. Mr. Warner spoke for twenty minutes and gave a full description of the match, which came through clearly and was much appreciated by listeners-in.'

We can only wonder what he said about Bradman, and we can only wonder what the Australian domestic reaction was. After the thousand runs in May the 8 didn't even represent a cameo but an ominous disaster.

Welbeck Abbey was a historic pile in landscaped woodland with an eccentric history. One owner had a labyrinth of tunnels dug and a subterranean ballroom to accommodate 2,000 dancers. It wasn't used. In London the owner 'always travelled in a closed carriage; maintained a shuttered box at the Opera and kept the curtains permanently drawn at the windows of his substantial town house'. The present incumbent who welcomed the Australians was not, however, eccentric. No doubt the Australians passed a pleasant day because they were getting used to historic piles.

They were all out for 144 on Monday morning, a deficit of 126, but they restricted England's second innings to 302 so the match resolved itself into a great simplicity: Australia needed 429 to win with fifty-three minutes of this third day left and all the fourth.

Woodfull and Ponsford began at 5.37pm, Woodfull on strike against the Larwood burst. The second delivery went for 4 byes, Woodfull took a single from the fourth and Ponsford played out the over.

What was Bradman thinking? Two-fold pressure bore down on him: his first innings, so uncomfortable and uncertain and brief, *did* suggest he might have real difficulties at this level against a Test attack. Plundering Worcestershire, flaying Fender round The Oval, hammering compliant Hampshire weren't the same thing. He still had all the real proving to do and it would have to be done knowing Australia's chance of winning rested on him. Woodfull might bring stability, Ponsford was always greedy for big runs, McCabe might enchant with his daring, Richardson bludgeon some runs, Kippax charm everybody – but 429? That was Bradman territory. Did he feel self-doubt as he watched Woodfull calmly play out the second over to Tate? Did he *ever* feel self-doubt? Maybe it is instructive that in *Don Bradman's Book* he doesn't mention his first innings, although you don't want to make too much of that and, surveying the 429, he used words like 'formidable' but 'optimistic'.

The batting order had been returned to normal, Bradman in next and no thoughts of a night watchman.

Larwood worked up to his full speed from that feline, predatory run-up and sometimes he pitched awkwardly short. Woodfull played him serenely but Ponsford, shuffling across his stumps, got some 'horrible' balls and 'somehow contrived to get out of the way of them'. [8]

In Larwood's second over Ponsford managed a single and Woodfull picked up a couple. Then Ponsford played a maiden to Tate, Woodfull a maiden to Larwood. This was tight cricket again, tense moments and meagre pickings. Ponsford eked out a single, Woodfull took one, Ponsford eked out one from Tate's third over, took another from the first ball of Larwood's fourth over bringing, at 12, Woodfull to the stike.

Larwood produced an explosive bouncer to Woodfull and followed it with one which drew a loose, almost lazy stroke from Woodfull. Chapman in the gully caught it. That was 5.55pm, leaving a difficult and potentially fatal thirty-five minutes.

The pavilion at Trent Bridge, like the others at England's Test grounds, might have been a citadel guarding its Victorian past, the walls hung with old masters. As Woodfull set off for the pavilion Bradman would have left the dressing room on the first floor, descended the staircase, made his way along a corridor where some of the old masters hung and come out down the concrete steps between the ranks of seated members to the pitch.

He must have walked slowly because Bill Ferguson, scoring for Australia, records him in at 5.58pm, a full three minutes after Woodfull's dismissal. Hammond remembered Bradman 'looked sourly towards the gully as he came in, and no more chances were let fly in that direction, or anywhere else'. [9]

He took guard [10] and Larwood ran in to bowl the final ball of the over. It, too, was short – head high – and Bradman cut it over Chapman for a single. He'd begun, he'd begun immediately and he'd begun uncharacteristically. Cutting over people's heads was what he normally didn't do at all, even across his long, major innings. Nerves? Misjudgement? Or did he see, all in the moment, easy pickings?

He reverted to his own orthodoxy: a safe single from the second ball of Tate's next over and then Ponsford hit directly into Hendren's hands at silly short leg – and Hendren spilled it. Bradman took a single from the first ball of Larwood's next over and Ponsford 'prettily' [11] square cut the fifth for 2. Bradman took a single from the first ball of Tate's next over and Ponsford square cut the last to the boundary. They were establishing a pattern, prising open the tightening grip – although Bradman had yet to hit a boundary in a Test match in England.

The Larwood burst completed, Robins came on and both batsmen hunted runs. It became a session of psychologies, Bradman emerging from other people's doubts and beginning to dictate Chapman's tactics. The first Robins over yielded a 2 and a single to Bradman, a single to Ponsford and another single to Bradman. He looked brisk and worked the leg side with consummate ease before he finally did reach the boundary off Tate. That took Australia to 30.

Robins's next over cost 4 and Bradman took another boundary from Tate. Robins's third over cost 8, four singles and a lovely Ponsford straight drive. By now both batsmen, sensing Robins was vulnerable, were applying the psychology by going down the wicket to good length balls.

They couldn't do that with Tate and Bradman was lucky when he edged him through the slips for a couple at 6.20pm to bring up the 50. It had taken only forty-three minutes and he was batting 'as if it were the middle of the afternoon rather than that dangerous last half hour'. (12)

Tyldesley came on for Robins, the first psychological blow struck. From this moment Chapman would be reluctant to bowl Robins. Bradman extended the psychology with an immediate assault on Tyldesley, pulling the first and last balls of the over to the boundary.

Larwood ought to have come on for a final burst but mysteriously did not. Instead Ponsford played a maiden to Tate and Bradman, facing the last over of the day, played a maiden to Tyldesley. Australia closed on 60 for 1, Ponsford 21, Bradman 31 made in the thirty-two minutes.

They needed 369 more but had the whole of Tuesday to get them and they had Bradman. The 369 translated to around a run a ball and surveying it Bradman felt sure it could be done.

One journalist found Larwood pale and drawn, although a member of the Nottinghamshire team said he was fine. He wasn't. He drove back to Nuncargate but felt so ill he had difficulty actually maintaining control of the car. When he reached home he went to bed and during the night became semi-delirious. His wife heard him murmuring: 'Oh, I can't play today.' They sent for a doctor, who diagnosed acute gastritis and ordered him to remain in bed.

In the morning, Larwood's father Robert visited the house and then journeyed to the Victoria Hotel in Beeston to inform Chapman. Then he described to the local papers how Larwood had told him 'he did not know how he managed to stay on the field during the last half hour of play. He suffered great pain in the stomach. He could hardly see the stumps. He was heartbroken when I left him at home.'

When a journalist asked Chapman about it he replied, typically: 'Isn't it a nuisance?' It was, and not least because Tate might hold the key to the whole match but the Australians could grind him physically so that he'd have to be rested. Hammond would be steady but Bradman and Ponsford could – and surely would – re-apply the psychology to Robins and extend it to Tyldesley. The match could be taken away from England very, very quickly. Tate would be strike bowler, match-winner and workhorse all at the same time, and most of the time.

There'd been gentle overnight rain but the pitch still looked good. The crowd would be no more than 11,500 on this working day, bringing the total attendance to 77,591.

Play began at 11.02am, Hammond bowling from the Pavilion end to Ponsford who flicked a single to leg from his second delivery. Bradman didn't score from the remaining four balls. Tate bowled from the Radcliffe Road end and Ponsford flicked the third ball towards the boundary but Robins restricted it to 2.

Bradman tapped a single through the slips – the off-side glance – from the first ball of Hammond's second over and his innings was in motion again. The batsmen traded singles: Ponsford – a heavy-set man but nimble – from the second ball, Bradman the third, Ponsford the last to keep the strike. Ponsford edged Tate's fourth ball past Hammond in the slips to the boundary.

The play seemed to be feeling for a shape and a direction, and Bradman compounded that impression because in a maiden over Hammond beat him outside the off stump and had an lbw appeal refused.

Just like the previous evening, the cricket tightened. Ponsford played a maiden to Tate and across the following two overs only Bradman scored: a single, from Hammond. He played a maiden from Tate and by now the crowd were cheering because they saw Tate's genuinely heroic qualities. In build, temperament and attitude he resembled a yeoman.

'It was obvious from the very first ball bowled that Australia had fully realised the position and knew that Tate was the key to the game,' Fender wrote. 'Bradman and Ponsford made no stroke at all to the Sussex man, concentrating entirely on defence, with an occasional single to leg or to third man as the opportunity offered.'

Australia reached 72 for 1. Warner wrote [(13)] that the batsmen 'began in a manner which led one to imagine that they had no idea of victory'. The *Evening Standard* felt 'the Australians were not running risks. It appeared to me that the batsmen had said to themselves: "We have the whole day to get the runs; we are not in a hurry; above all things we shall wait for the opportunity and wear out the diminished attack of England; we will keep our wickets up and the runs will come in good time."' The *Nottingham Evening News* wrote that Hammond 'swung the ball to the off and kept such a good length that Ponsford and Bradman seemed content to save the game rather than force the pace'.

The next few minutes confirmed these Press Box impressions. Ponsford took a single from Hammond and the next Tate over yielded two singles before Bradman played a maiden to Hammond. Two more singles, one to each batsman, from Tate brought the Australians to 77. That was 11.32am. The 17 added so far had taken twelve overs, and Bradman made only 5 of them. The 1.30pm lunch interval seemed a long, long way away and so did the target, now 352.

Tyldesley came on for Hammond and found a length immediately. Bradman played a maiden, simply patting each ball down a couple of yards in front of him. Both batsmen dealt in singles and the next five overs yielded seven of them, Tate at his best and so good Bradman showed him more respect than he'd shown any bowler on the tour so far. Chapman brought the field up, tightening the cricket further, although the fielders were reduced to spectators. Bradman and Ponsford killed virtually every ball, showing no interest in hitting them.

Bradman 'hung out a tentative bat' to Tyldesley's 'slow and speculative deliveries,' the *Evening Standard* wrote. 'This subjugation of Bradman was most interesting. He was not a bit like the man who scored a thousand runs before some of our cricketers were awake and unlimbered. Over after over passed for an unbroken succession of singles. Of course, the bowling was very exact. The Australians were expected to earn what they got.'

Something amazing was happening, however, no matter how much this was not evident in the Press Box. Bradman, still completely unproven on an English Test wicket, saw his innings unfolding on two distinct timescales: the necessarily immediate lockstep of ball-by-ball but, overall, spread over the *day*. It seems certain he wasn't asking himself *where will we be at lunch?* but *where will we be after tea?*

He patted a spot on the pitch with his bat and that provoked a question: how long would the wicket last?

Tyldesley produced a murmur of excitement when the last delivery of his fourth over kept low enough to beat Duckworth and scurry to the boundary for 4 byes.

Next over Ponsford gathered a couple from Tate with a square cut which Duleepsinhji (substituting for Larwood) cut off before it reached the boundary, Bradman took a single from Tyldesley and Ponsford a single, too, bringing him to face Tate. That was 11.52am.

The sixth ball fizzed off the pitch, keeping 'viciously' low, into the middle and leg stumps – much as Tate got Bradman in the first innings – and the middle stump was plucked out of the ground to a great shout of acclaim and relief. Bradman paid tribute to it as among the very best he'd witnessed Tate produce. [(14)] Duckworth caught the stump and brandished it as if it had been the ball.

Ponsford's 39 took him two hours thirty-three minutes, 118 balls and three 4s. Australia, at 93 for 2, still needed 336. Bradman had made 42. He was content to steer Tyldesley through the slips when he safely could, content to play his favoured leg glances whenever possible.

Kippax might have been run out immediately: Bradman on-drove Hammond to Sydney Copley, a young Nottinghamshire substitute for Sutcliffe, who'd hurt his hand. Bradman called: 'Yes!' and Kippax, thinking the ball would beat Copley, began to run but Bradman shouted for him to get back. Copley, with only one stump to aim at, threw it down – Kippax narrowly home. Bradman took a single from the last ball, and a single from Tate next over.

Both batsmen took singles from Tyldesley, the scoreboard ticking evenly but slowly: Australia 97 for 2. Tate bowled a maiden to Kippax. Bradman took 2 and a single from Tyldesley's eighth over to bring the Australian hundred up. That was 12.05pm and it had taken an hour and fifty-eight minutes.

Hammond relieved Tate, who'd bowled twelve straight overs in seventy minutes and needed a rest. From Hammond's second ball Bradman cut a single to reach 50 in an hour and thirty-eight minutes. He was loudly applauded although, as the *Evening Standard* noted, 'he was playing a great game but was not the light-hearted boy who makes runs as if they were the easiest thing in the world. Bradman today was the spirit of watchfulness. His bat was rarely raised three inches above the ground. He played back to nine balls out of ten as if every ball was watched on to the bat.' That was 12.07pm.

Kippax survived a tremendous shout from Tate and Duckworth for lbw, an appeal which made Bradman smile. At 12.30pm, ninety minutes into the day, still only a single boundary had been scored off the bat, Ponsford's, in the fourth over.

Bradman accelerated gently by 'artistic placings' on both sides of the wicket [(15)] but took nine overs to move through the 50s. Hammond bowled line and length, making the ball leave the bat, and play fell into a pattern: the first four balls of an over would be met by the resolute defence, a scampered single – or 2 – taken from the remaining balls. The fielders were still so close that these runs had to be run hard.

Tyldesley, turning the ball, beat both of the batsmen at least once and had them playing dangerous snicks through the slips. However, Kippax pushed a delivery from Tyldesley to the on side for 2 and struck the next ball with a flick of the wrist to the square leg boundary. He'd run no more than two or three paces up the wicket when the umpire signalled 4.

Bradman moved to 60 with a 2 from Hammond but, at that score and in the next over, he edged Tyldesley towards Hammond at slip. Duckworth grabbed at it and, exultant, appealed but couldn't hold the ball – and neither could Hammond.

Tyldesley toiled on and might have had Kippax but the ball curled wide of Hammond at slip. Kippax square cut Hammond but Duleepsinhji, to loud applause, prevented the boundary and they ran 3.

The clouds were coming back across the ground, rain hung in the air and the pitch was ever dustier. Australia looked vulnerable.

At 137 Chapman decided he must use Robins – like Tate, Tyldesley had toiled for seventy minutes – and summoned him from the deep. Bradman was 68 and took 2 from the third Robins delivery. They ran a leg bye from the next and Kippax off-drove the fifth to the boundary, the biggest shot of the day, a 'tremendous' strike of the ball between mid-off and extra-cover.

Hammond conceded a single but Robins threatened to be costly: Kippax took a single from the first delivery of his second over, then Bradman 2 and 1 – 10 off two overs – and the single brought up the 150. That was 12.50pm.

Inadvertently, the Robins leg breaks were loosening the match up but, however costly, he might conjure a wicket ball at any moment. Walter Robins was firmly in the great tradition of leg-break bowlers in that he could win or lose you the match, with very little in between. Bradman took a single from Hammond and they ran a leg bye, Hammond struck Kippax on the knee and it hurt.

Kippax now faced Robins. The third ball was a leg-break which turned. Kippax tried to cut it but it went to Hammond who caught it. Robins had conjured the wicket ball. Kippax batted for an hour and three minutes, faced 80 deliveries and scored 23. At 152 for 3, the Australian target receded. That was 12.57pm.

McCabe came in and by the time he'd taken guard it was 12.59pm so he had a potentially awkward thirty-one minutes to survive or impose himself before lunch. McCabe didn't waste any time announcing which it would be. He struck the final ball of the over hard to the leg side boundary.

Tate came on for Hammond, perhaps to ram the advantage home, settle the match. After Richardson, next, there was dour Fairfax and the tail. Bradman played a careful maiden to Tate. McCabe was having none of that and prepared to pull and drive Robins whenever he could. He struck the first ball of the next Robins over to the boundary, took a single from the fourth, Bradman a single from the fifth, McCabe a single from the sixth – 7 off the over to make Australia 163.

When Bradman made 75 Robins almost bowled him but he still took a single and McCabe smacked two boundaries in the same over. Two overs later Bradman played a leg glide from Robins to move to 79, the top score in the match and again loudly applauded. He genuinely felt he was capable of bringing the game round to Australia (and hoped that didn't sound boastful). [(16)]

Four overs remained before lunch and all at once the Australians were busy.Tate conceded a single to McCabe, a 2 and a single to Bradman. They applied the psychology to Robins, no doubt to make Chapman contemplate the long afternoon with profound misgivings: Bradman a single, McCabe a single, Bradman 2 and a single, McCabe a boundary – 9 off the over.

Tate bowled to Bradman who took a single from the second ball and McCabe a single from the third, leaving Bradman to play out the over before they turned and came off for lunch with Australia 198 for 3 (Bradman 88, McCabe 32).

The lunch interval lasted until 2.15pm, leaving two and a quarter hours to tea and a further hour and three quarters between tea and the close, so that 240 minutes remained to get 230. Without Larwood, and with Robins shipping punishment at an alarming rate, the McCabe assault tilted the match. Bradman hadn't hit a boundary in the morning session and that had to be ominous. What happened when he did?

At slightly after 2.15pm Tate opened the bowling and from the third delivery Bradman played a graceful leg glide for 2, making Australia 200 in three hours twenty-six minutes, virtually even time and, despite the early defence, just the right rate to win it. This, surely, is what the extraordinary 21-year-old had seen even as he patted the bowling back down the pitch as if it didn't interest him. He was thinking in that second dimension of time, the whole *day,* and here it was stretching before him, two thirds remaining to be fully exploited.

Hammond bowled from the other end, took the new ball and McCabe had a single to get moving early. The wicket was beginning to crumble at one end, the end Hammond bowled to.

McCabe was impetuous. He took a single from the first ball of Tate's next over, Bradman a single from the second, McCabe another single from the third and then he attacked Hammond with a boundary and a 2 so that within four overs of Lunch Australia moved to 210 – 219 to win.

Bradman prepared to work a patient path through the 90s and, with McCabe in this mood, he could afford to. After the McCabe assault on Hammond, Tate bowled Bradman a maiden.

McCabe took a single from Hammond, a single from Tate and so did Bradman, giving him the strike against Hammond who made one ball rear head high and another beat him. That, too, was a maiden so that of the 27 balls he'd received since lunch he scored 4 runs from three of them. This was not the boy who massacred May but a careful, responsible adult using his bat like a guiding hand.

Chapman constantly consulted Hobbs for advice, and needed to. At 95 Bradman square drove Hammond to the boundary – his first of the day – and two overs later square drove Hammond again. Chapman misfielded it and they ran Bradman's 52nd single to complete his century in three hours thirty-five minutes.

That was 2.50pm. He'd been in the 90s for slightly more than half an hour.

A few moments later he took a single from Tate, leaving McCabe to play the final three balls of the over. McCabe was on 49, made in seventy minutes and adorned by seven boundaries. He pumped the second ball to mid-on where young Copley, swallow-diving, caught it magnificently. That was 2.54pm.

At 229 for 4, Australia needed 200 in 195 minutes. McCabe had kept them up with the rate but much more importantly Bradman was still there. While he waited for Richardson to come to the crease he surveyed the situation and concluded Australia could still win – even though Tate was making the ball swing.

Richardson, so frequently bellicose with a bat, would take twenty-five minutes to get off the mark. Tyldesley came on for Hammond and Bradman took a single from him, took a single from Tate and now attacked Tyldesley, pulling and driving him to the boundary. Here was the psychology again because if Chapman couldn't trust Robins and couldn't risk Tyldesley, he could only turn to Hammond and Tate – who'd already bowled nine straight overs since lunch.

Tate summoned a maiden to Richardson. Now Bradman increased the pressure with a fresh assault on Tyldesley. He took a couple from the first ball of the over, sent the third to the leg side boundary and straight drove the next to the pavilion boundary, making him 119 and Australia 247 – 182 to win.

Tate summoned another maiden to Richardson and Tyldesley managed one to Bradman. Richardson finally did get off the mark with a 2 from Tate. Robins came on for Tate and Bradman took a single from the fifth ball, making Australia 250 – 179 to get in 174 minutes. That was 3.21pm.

Hammond came on for Tate and Bradman bustled, the change in tempo very evident. He hit Hammond for two boundaries in the over, took a single from Robins, a single from Hammond, a single from Robins again. Richardson, now into his stride, hit Robins to the boundary and took a single, bringing Australia to 267 – the target down to 162 – and Bradman back on to strike. It was 3.33pm.

The sixth ball was, as Bradman described it, 'ordinary-looking' and on the off side. He read it as a leg-break and judged it would miss the stumps. He felt safe enough in his judgement to move in front of the wicket and hold his bat away from the ball. Richardson read the ball right – a googly – and watched in horror. Instead of spinning harmlessly away it twisted back *and* bounced low. Bradman had his bat hoisted high when it struck the off-stump. According to Richardson, Bradman subsequently claimed that he picked it but 'as I moved across to play it my bat got caught in my pad'. (17)

Neither version altered the truth that Bradman had been bowled although Bradman blamed himself for this terrible error, which he surely wouldn't have done if he'd picked the googly and got his bat caught. He'd been batting for four hours eighteen minutes for his 131, facing 287 deliveries. In the end he'd hit ten boundaries. The crowd cheered him all the way back to the pavilion, hats and handkerchiefs waving.

The googly reduced Australia to 267 for 5 and, with Bradman gone, the whole match tilted back. Richardson made a brave 29 before Tyldesley trapped him lbw, Tate had Fairfax caught and the tail faded away. England won by 93 runs. The crowd gathered in front of the pavilion and called for Chapman. When he appeared they called for Bradman who, it seems, was reluctant to appear – because he didn't for several minutes. When he did the crowd gave him an 'unroarious reception'. (18)

As Bradman left the ground people acclaimed him, and a crowd acclaimed him again when he emerged from The Black Boy to go to Nottingham Station for the train to London.

His innings would become significant for three reasons. The most obvious was that he could make runs against a Test attack in England. Larwood's absence obviously simplified that but he'd done it all the same, and no rational judge could doubt that he would do it again, with or without Larwood.

The second came from the journalists in the Press Box, writing at the time and in their tour books afterwards. Unanimous they felt that while Bradman remained Australia would win and once he was out Australia would lose. This may seem obvious, too, but their descriptions conveyed a sense of how central Bradman had become. The country boy advised by Tate – of all people – to alter his technique or flounder in England had achieved this central position, this *stature,* in only six weeks.

The third significance lay in the nature of the innings itself. He took more than an hour to make the 19 runs he needed for his 50 as the final morning unfolded. At one point during this he scored 14 singles. He did not hit a boundary on the final day until he'd reached 95 and even so spent that half hour negotiating the 90s. He knew he didn't have to hurry. He had all the strokes, extraordinary speed of footwork, a gargantuan appetite, absolute confidence, a nimble brain and a love of playing shots some of which were, truth to tell, just plain cheeky. He had something more: patience and genuine tactical acumen built on a rock of a defence. Even the shot which dismissed him was in no way rash. He was trying to play safe and just got it wrong.

Moreover, on Tuesday 17 June 1930 he demonstrated that he had a quality above and beyond all of this. He had self-denial. It was not good news for Maurice Tate's theory and it was about to get much, much worse.

ENGLAND V AUSTRALIA – THE FIRST TEST

Nottingham 13, 14, 16, 17 June. England won by 93 runs.

ENGLAND						
J.B. Hobbs	c Richardson	b McCabe	78	st Oldfield	b Grimmett	74
H. Sutcliffe	c Hornibrook	b Fairfax	29	rtd hurt		58
W.R. Hammond	lbw	b Grimmett	8	lbw	b Grimmett	4
F.E. Woolley	st Oldfield	b Grimmett	0		b Wall	5
E.H. Hendren		b Grimmett	5	c Richardson	b Wall	72
*A.P.F. Chapman	c Ponsford	b Hornibrook	52		b Wall	29
H. Larwood		b Grimmett	18		b Grimmett	7
R.W.V. Robins		not out	50		b McCabe	4
M.W. Tate		b Grimmett	13	c Kippax	b Grimmett	24
R.K. Tyldesley	c Fairfax	b Wall	1		b Grimmett	5
+G. Duckworth	lbw	b Fairfax	4		not out	14
Extras	(b 4, lb 7, nb 1)		12	(b 5, lb 1)		6
Total			270			302

1-53, 2-63, 3-63, 4-71, 5-153, 6-188, 7-218, 8-241, 9-242

1-125, 2-137, 3-147, 4-211, 5-250, 6-260, 7-283, 8-283, 9-302

	O	M	R	W	O	M	R	W
Wall	17	4	47	1	26	4	67	3
Fairfax	21.4	5	51	2	15	4	58	0
Grimmett	32	6	107	5	30	4	94	5
Hornibrook	12	3	30	1	11	4	35	0
McCabe	7	3	23	1	14	3	42	1

AUSTRALIA						
*W.M. Woodfull	c Chapman	b Tate	2	c Chapman	b Larwood	4
W.H. Ponsford		b Tate	3		b Tate	39
A.G. Fairfax	c Hobbs	b Robins	14	c Robins	b Tate	14
D.G. Bradman		b Tate	8		b Robins	131
A.F. Kippax		not out	64	c Hammond	b Robins	23
S.J. McCabe	c Hammond	b Robins	4	c sub	b Tate	49
V.Y. Richardson		b Tyldesley	37	lbw	b Tyldesley	29
+W.A. Oldfield	c Duckworth	b Robins	4	c Hammond	b Tyldesley	11
C.V. Grimmett	st Duckworth	b Robins	0	c Hammond	b Tyldesley	0
P.M. Hornibrook	lbw	b Larwood	0	c Duckworth	b Robins	5
T.W. Wall		b Tyldesley	0		not out	8
Extras	(b 4, lb 4)		8	(b 17, lb 5)		22
Total			144			335

1-4, 2-6, 3-16, 4-57, 5-61, 6-105, 7-134, 8-140, 9-141

1-12, 2-93, 3-152, 4-229, 5-267, 6-296, 7-316, 8-322, 9-324

	O	M	R	W	O	M	R	W
Larwood	15	8	12	1	5	1	9	1
Tate	19	8	20	3	50	20	69	3
Tyldesley	21	8	53	2	35	10	77	3
Robins	17	4	51	4	17.2	1	81	3
Hammond					29	5	74	0
Woolley					3	1	3	0

Chapter Six

254 and 1

THE TOUR ITINERARY WAS ARDUOUS, ALMOST REMORSELESS. THE Australians travelled from Nottingham to London to play Surrey, then were due to meet Lancashire at Old Trafford before returning for the Second Test at Lord's. Between Trent Bridge and Old Trafford they'd play every day, with only the Wednesday and Thursday off before the Test.

Surrey

Fender was playing for Surrey, which, given the subterranean current flowing between him and Bradman, ought to have spiced the match again but the weather came back to taunt the tourists as it had done so often in May. When play began at 12pm Surrey batted but between then and 3.30pm, when a heavy downpour drowned the day, they made only 140 for 5. a'Beckett was finally well enough to play but Grimmett spun his web (6 for 24) so that on the second day Australia went out to chase down Surrey's 162.

Woodfull and Fairfax opened and showed a distrust of the pitch by taking half an hour to make 16, although the heavy roller had been used. After lunch Woodfull began to hit more freely, twice driving straight to the boundary. Fairfax loosened up, too, and Fender – overpitching – received punishment. Fairfax had been in for two and a quarter hours for 36 when he tried to hook a straight ball from the medium pace of Thomas Shepherd and was lbw.

Bradman followed his tactic and took runs to leg from his first ball, a 2. He made three more runs when he, too, tried to hook Shepherd and was caught at forward short leg. It lasted ten minutes and wasn't even a cameo.

Woodfull eventually made 141, Hobbs a wonderful 146 not out when Surrey batted again – Bradman delighted in watching how he played Grimmett – and the match wandered to a draw. Noises off . . .

From his hotel bedroom, Richardson was able to get a connection to Australia and spoke to his wife, son and brother.

The *Sydney Morning Herald* carried this paragraph (no doubt from Tebbutt): 'As a result of the newspapers publishing photographs of the Australian cricketers wearing hats while conversing with the King and Queen at Sandringham on June 7, the team manager Mr. Kelly and Woodfull have received letters of protest from many quarters. Mr. Kelly requests the Australian Press Association to state that the players retained their hats at the King's request after they had been introduced to their Majesties.'

Lancashire

Bradman described Old Trafford as the finest ground in England and the only one which might stand comparison with Sydney. Ted McDonald couldn't play because he was suffering from water on the knee and at one stage play was interrupted by water on the pitch. Yes, the taunting again.

a'Beckett hurt his leg at The Oval where Walker was hit on the shoulder; Ponsford took a blow from Larwood at Trent Bridge and wasn't completely fit, and Grimmett was rested. The other eleven played. *The Times* commented that the Australians 'generally bore the look of a collection of players who are playing themselves into the team before the big event' at Lord's.

Woodfull won the toss and opened with Jackson on a tame pitch. Woodfull was stumped for 27 (itself a news event) with the total at 59 and Bradman began confidently, late cutting and pulling two boundaries before he slowed. They went off for bad light and rain.

Jackson was bowled by pace man Gordon Hodgson. Bradman treated the slow left arms of Jack Iddon and the left-arm mediums of Len

SURREY V AUSTRALIANS

The Oval, 18, 19, 20 June. Drawn.

SURREY

J.B. Hobbs	st Walker	b Grimmett	19		not out	146
A. Sandham	c Fairfax	b Hurwood	29	lbw	b Grimmett	10
H.T. Barling	c Walker	b Grimmett	0	c Woodfull	b Wall	13
T.F. Shepherd	c McCabe	b a'Beckett	56		not out	65
E.F. Wilson		b Hurwood	9			
R.J. Gregory	c Fairfax	b Grimmett	16			
*P.G.H. Fender	c Fairfax	b Grimmett	11			
H.G. Baldwin	c Woodfull	b Fairfax	0			
H.A. Peach		c & b Grimmett	7			
M.J.C. Allom		not out	5			
+E.W.J. Brooks	c Kippax	b Grimmett	4			
Extras	(lb 5, nb 1)		6	(b 7, lb 7, w 1)		15
Total			162	(2 wkts)		249

1-34, 2-34, 3-65, 4-117, 5-117, 6-140, 7-145, 8-147, 9-154 — 1-18, 2-67

	O	M	R	W	O	M	R	W
Wall	8	1	19	0	12	5	18	1
a'Beckett	18	6	41	1	7	1	24	0
Grimmett	21.3	10	24	6	13	3	35	1
Fairfax	10	2	26	1	12	1	38	0
McCabe	5	0	17	0	15	3	35	0
Hurwood	13	5	29	2	18	5	48	0
Bradman					6	0	31	0
Kippax					3	1	5	0

AUSTRALIANS

*W.M. Woodfull	c Wilson	b Shepherd	141
A.G. Fairfax	lbw	b Shepherd	36
D.G. Bradman	c Allom	b Shepherd	5
A.F. Kippax		c & b Peach	36
S.J. McCabe		b Shepherd	42
A.A. Jackson		not out	37
E.L. a'Beckett		not out	67
Extras	(b 18, lb 6)		24
Total	(5 wkts dec)		388

Dnb: +C.W. Walker, A. Hurwood, C.V. Grimmett, T.W. Wall.

1-115, 2-127, 3-205, 4-281, 5-284

	O	M	R	W
Allom	27	2	66	0
Peach	32	16	66	1
Fender	29	6	93	0
Gregory	28	6	74	0
Shepherd	27	6	65	4

Hopwood with almost exaggerated care. He was missed at the wicket when he'd made 33 and gave another chance two runs later: Frank Sibbles at slip didn't move fast enough. Eventually Duckworth caught him on the leg side from a Sibbles off-break for 38.

The Australians made 427, Lancashire 259 and, the game all but dead, the Australians batted a second time. Richardson opened with McCabe and went for 12, which left enough time for Bradman to make an undefeated 23. Warner described the match as 'in many ways' the 'most unsatisfactory of the tour' and Bradman himself conceded it was dull.

There's an irony here because what happened, or more properly what failed to happen, at Old Trafford did not represent either the mood or the capabilities of the Australians. They were about to make one of the most dramatic collective gestures in Test cricket history, constructed around one of the most dramatic individual gestures.

We are in the land of giants, and one of them was a genius.

Second Test – Lord's

The Second Test, which began at Lord's on a fine, warm Friday, was initially quite normal. Sutcliffe and Larwood were unfit and Tyldesley dropped. That brought in Duleepsinhji, Allen and JC 'Farmer' White of Somerset, a selector and mature purveyor of left-arm spin for his fifteenth (and final) Test. Fourteen of them came after his thirty-seventh birthday. He'd toured with Chapman in 1928–29, dismissing Bradman at Brisbane and taking 13 wickets at Adelaide (Bradman not among them) from 124.5 overs. Scoring runs against White was like visiting your dentist, a necessary but painful experience.

Woodfull wrongly called heads and Chapman chose to bat. Woolley opened with Hobbs, who was soon caught behind off Fairfax. Woolley played a lovely, elegant innings as if he was distilling the craftsmanship of a lifetime, Hammond made 38 but young Duleepsinhji – slender, wan, instinctively graceful – created a masterpiece of 173 in just under five hours. England finished the day on 405 for 9.

At 11am next morning Duckworth indulged in some lively hitting to reach 18 and White made 23. The England total, 425, represented normality.

Woodfull and Ponsford began the reply at 11.35am. Allen had three slips and Chapman at backward point. He began with a maiden, Ponsford took a single from the last ball of Tate's first over, into the

LANCASHIRE V AUSTRALIANS

Old Trafford, 21, 23, 24 June. Drawn.

AUSTRALIANS

*W.M. Woodfull	st Duckworth	b Sibbles	27			
A.A. Jackson	b Hodgson		52			
D.G. Bradman	c Duckworth	b Sibbles	38		not out	23
A.F. Kippax	st Duckworth	b Hopwood	120			
S.J. McCabe	c Duckworth	b Hodgson	34		not out	36
V.Y. Richardson	c R Tyldesley	b Hodgson	13	c Eckersley	b Hodgson	12
A.G. Fairfax	st Duckworth	b R. Tyldesley	63			
+W.A. Oldfield		not out	34			
A. Hurwood	c Taylor	b Hopwood	9			
T.W. Wall	lbw	b R. Tyldesley	0			
P.M. Hornibrook		b Sibbles	20			
Extras	(b 4, lb 13)		17	(b 8)		8
Total			427	(1 wkt)		79

1-59, 2-103, 3-144, 4-202, 5-230, 6-354, 7-364, 8-387, 9-388 — 1-17

	O	M	R	W	O	M	R	W
Hodgson	37	7	97	3	3	1	6	1
Sibbles	50	6	89	3	2	0	13	0
R.K. Tyldesley	38	8	87	2				
Hopwood	43	11	92	2				
Watson	4	1	10	0	1	0	3	0
Iddon	16	4	35	0				
Eckersley					2	0	12	0
Duckworth					2	0	13	0
Hallows					2	0	15	0
G.E. Tyldesley					1	0	9	0

LANCASHIRE

F.B. Watson	c Oldfield	b Hornibrook	74
C. Hallows	c Woodfull	b Wall	42
G.E. Tyldesley		b Fairfax	48
J. Iddon		run out	20
J.L. Hopwood		b Fairfax	40
M.L. Taylor		b Wall	1
*P.T. Eckersley		b Wall	11
F.M. Sibbles	c Hurwood	b Fairfax	9
+G. Duckworth		b Wall	1
R.K. Tyldesley	c Hurwood	b Fairfax	3
G. Hodgson		not out	0
Extras	(b 3, lb 5, nb 2)		10
Total			259

1-110, 2-125, 3-165, 4-231, 5-234, 6-234, 7-243, 8-244, 9-259

	O	M	R	W
Wall	28	3	92	4
Fairfax	15.1	5	29	4
Hornibrook	33	16	52	1
Hurwood	11	2	17	0
McCabe	9	2	35	0
Bradman	9	4	24	0

covers and only just got home before Hobbs threw down the wicket. Ponsford now faced Allen's second over. During it Allen hit him three times on the body. The Australian openers settled and slowly massaged the score to 96 at lunch (Woodfull 35, Ponsford 59). After it, with 31,000 inside the ground, they pressed on until 3.10pm when they'd reached 162, Ponsford 81. At this point play halted so that the players could be presented to the King.

White bowled the first over after the visit from the Nursery End and Ponsford mis-hit the fifth delivery to Hammond at slip. His dismissal became known as the 'King's wicket'.

Bradman had the greatest stage in the world, Lord's in perfect summer weather on a Saturday, the old historic ground absolutely full and the crowd eager to savour him. It was 3.29pm.

He began by dancing far up the wicket to his first ball from White and impertinently drove it to long-off, danced *so* far up the wicket that when he'd 'finished the stroke he was close enough to see the look of astonishment on the bowler's face. Nobody had dreamed in England then of using their feet with impunity to J.C. White.' (1)

You can, especially with hindsight, read all manner of things into this one delivery, not least that it was premeditated. Bradman was surely making a statement: *I am master in this house already.* It was surely worth more than the single it brought.

Wilfred Rhodes, who surely *read* batsmen as well as anyone ever to play the game, gives the context which allowed Bradman to do it.

> *'First, judgment is all-important, but except for the fortunate few who seem gifted with it right from the start, judgment is the result of experience. Judgment is backed up by accuracy of eye and quickness of foot. The wonderful and untiring eye of Donald Bradman and his brilliant footwork, together with his superb self-confidence, made it possible for him to accomplish the record-breaking performances he began on his first visit to England. Bradman can go straight to the wicket and start scoring at once, and all the time he is batting he looks like continuing to score at the same even but rapid pace.'* (2)

Hammond bowled from the Pavilion end rather than Tate, and Bradman pulled the final ball to the boundary. The pace of the pitch, he'd remember, was exactly to his liking.

Woodfull played a maiden to White, Bradman a maiden to Hammond and then a great onslaught threatened, Bradman dancing like an executioner and, always in the background, Woodfull heavy with runs. The batsmen bustled. From White, they both took a single and Woodfull a 3. From Hammond, a single each. From White, a Bradman single before Woodfull on-drove the final ball to the boundary.

Hammond was putting in a good spell of defensive bowling but this meant, of necessity, a single slip. Hammond 'sent down a fast, good-length ball which broke back viciously at the top of the off and middle stumps. Bradman met it with an orthodox-looking back stroke which had the effect of a late cut. The ball flew, and was clearly meant to fly, wide of the solitary slip and fine enough to beat the deep third man.' (3)

Bradman stole a single from the final delivery to keep the strike. Twice in White's next over he scored boundaries and White could do nothing because Bradman moved too fast to be contained. Later White made an astonishing statement: 'Bradman was so fast he could have made every ball I bowled into a full toss if he'd cared to'. At 3.46pm, seventeen minutes into the innings, he'd already reached 21.

Sandham went into the Australian dressing room and said he was thinking of sending for the Prince of Wales to get Bradman out – a repeat of the King's wicket – and, if that didn't work, he'd send for the whole Royal family.

Woodfull profited from Bradman beginning to break up the England attack and bustled again – a 2 and a single from Hammond – but Bradman stole a single from the final delivery to keep the strike again. He cut White to the boundary, making the Australians 200, and stole another single. The crowd were silent except for the Australian section, who greeted each run with something approaching rapture.

Allen took the new ball and Bradman feasted on it with a pull to the boundary, a 2 and a single from the final delivery. Tate came on to have the new ball, too, but they took three singles from him and Bradman, greedy, feasted on Allen again, pulling the first ball to the boundary, taking 2 from the next and a single from the fourth. Here was the psychology of destruction, because Allen's selection had been criticised and he wasn't bowling well. Chapman would take him off after only one more over.

At 3.59pm, thirty minutes into the innings, Bradman had already reached 43. He and Woodfull exchanged the strike with singles for a couple of overs and he glanced Tate for 2. At 4.11pm he glanced Tate for 2 again, giving him his 50 out of 66 in forty-six minutes.

In the five remaining overs before tea he was relatively subdued (three singles) while Woodfull prospered to the extent of adding 11, including a boundary from the final Hammond over. During this he reached his 100. At 4.30pm, tea, Australia were 244 for 1 (Woodfull 105, Bradman 54 in an hour and a minute).

An analogy with Trent Bridge is too tempting. There Bradman attacked before close of play on the Monday but, under the imperative of occupying the crease to win the match on the Tuesday, defended. When the players did come back out at Lord's at 4.50pm to resume, he'd respond to this different imperative by continuing the attack. *This* was not good news for Maurice Tate *or* miser White *or* Woolley – put on in desperation – *or* Hammond *or* Robins, the slayer at Trent Bridge, *or* enthusiastic Gubby Allen. Worse, so far Bradman had not lifted a ball off the ground never mind actually made a mistake.

The 54 runs in the hour before tea suggested a masterpiece. The 100 minutes after it would *be* a masterpiece.

Bradman and Woodfull re-established the tempo immediately with a single from each ball of Robins's over. As *The Sunday Times* reported, the batsmen 'experienced no difficulty in playing themselves in again when they returned to the field. Woodfull was content to proceed at an average pace while Bradman soon began again to hit away in brilliant and forceful fashion.'

Woodfull took a single from Tate, a 4 from Robins and now Bradman was into his stride. Runs seemed everywhere: a 4 and two singles in a Tate over. At 4.58pm he'd moved from 54 to 63 in eight minutes since tea.

He took a single from Robins. Tate somehow managed a maiden to him and it drew echoing applause – as loud as any on this long afternoon – as if something amazing had happened. It had. Next Bradman moved into position to cut a dangerous ball from Tate and several thousand in the crowd appealed for a catch at the wicket – but he'd checked his stroke and let the ball go. That was amazing, too, because he'd done it faster than the crowd could see. By now the whole England attack lay at his mercy.

Tate bowled a maiden to Woodfull (which wasn't the same thing, of course, and doesn't seem to have been given anything more than traditionally polite applause). Woodfull continued in the background, hitting Robins to the boundary. Bradman, on 68, took a 2 and a single from Tate. At 5.13pm he'd moved from 54 to 71 in twenty-three minutes since tea.

He attacked a new over from Robins. He didn't score off the first ball, delicately glanced the second for 4, savagely pulled the third for 4 and savagely pulled the last for 4 – 12 off the over. It was more psychology of destruction being applied here as it had been at Trent Bridge. Robins might produce the unplayable ball, because all who trade in leg breaks can do that, but it might be prohibitively expensive.

At 5.16pm, twenty-six minutes after tea, Bradman had moved to 83. At 5.24pm, three overs later, he turned Tate neatly for a single to bring up the 300 (Woodfull 127, Bradman 88). An hour and six minutes of play remained and at this rate – they'd put on 56 in thirty-four minutes – they'd be at England's 425. Chapman's dilemma was sharply defined because he had to try and husband his resources and simultaneously prevent them being butchered. He replaced Robins with White.

Bradman went smoothly into the 90s with a boundary from White. At 5.27pm he'd moved to 93 in thirty-seven minutes since tea. He ran a single from White to keep the strike, took a couple and a single from Tate's next over: 96.

Now White again. Bradman ran a single from the second ball but Woodfull returned the strike with a single from the fourth and Bradman hit the fifth for a couple: 99.

Now Hammond on for Tate – to disconcert Bradman, contain him in the hope of a mistake, or just a routine bowling change? Tate had bowled eight straight overs since tea. Bradman didn't score from the first three Hammond balls, cut the fourth for a single. It was 5.35pm and he had his 100. He'd moved from 54 to it in three quarters of an hour since tea. He'd only been at the crease an hour and forty-six minutes – Woodfull over three hours for just 29 more. Australia were now in a massively strong position and it was getting stronger by the minute.

Bradman mauled White with two boundaries and a single, took 2 from Hammond. At 5.41pm, fifty-one minutes since tea, he'd moved to 111.

White came off. Warner wrote that Bradman 'made any ball the length he cared to make it. No Macartney, no Hobbs, could have been more nimble of foot. Indeed, I think he is the quickest batsman on his feet I have ever seen. He did what he liked with White, the most accurate of bowlers.'

In the spell White bowled four overs and this is what Bradman did to the nineteen deliveries he faced:

Single, 0, single

Boundary, 0000, single

0, single, two, 0

Boundary, 00, boundary, 0, single

That meant he'd scored from nine of the nineteen. White had doggedly tried to keep to a length and it's hard to imagine what else he could have done. The problem was that, in this mood, length did not exist to Bradman.

Bradman took a couple from a Hammond over – Hammond steady, unobtrusive, simply toiling – and Woolley, who bowled slow left arm, came on. The crowd roared with delight when, preparing to bowl to Bradman, he directed Chapman to go and field in the deep. Woolley, born 1887, was scarcely in the first flush of youth and scarely a front-line bowler any more. He had five men on the boundary and, impish and cheeky, Braman and Woodfull responded by taking singles in the wide open spaces these fielders left from the first four balls. The crowd were laughing. Woodfull restored a sense of decorum by hitting the last ball to the boundary.

Despite this Chapman kept Woolley on for another five overs. Chapman simply lacked the resources to close the game down and perhaps nobody could have done that, any captain or any bowler.

At 5.57pm Bradman had moved to 124 in sixty-seven minutes since tea. At one point he turned and smashed a long hop so viciously that the square leg umpire ducked for his life. Woolley's spell cost 35 and when he came off Australia were 370, Bradman 139. He faced twenty-three balls from Woolley:

Single, single

Single, single, 2 byes

Single, 0000

Boundary, 0, single, single

Boundary, 0, single

Two, 0, two, two, 0, 0

Only nine did not yield runs and Bradman scored 22, not counting the byes. Chapman might have remonstrated *What have I to lose by putting Woolley on?* and now he had the answer to that: the match.

Hammond bowled a maiden to Woodfull amidst all this and, the over before Woolley was taken off, Bradman clipped Hammond for 3 and took a single from the last ball of the over. At 6.05pm he'd moved from 133 in seventy-five minuts since tea.

Chapman made a double change, Allen for Hammond and Robins for Woolley. Allen lacked penetration all day – leaving Woolley aside, he seemed the least likely to take a wicket – and although Robins bowled tighter than he had done at Trent Bridge runs came from every delivery of his first over: three singles to Woodfull, a single, a 2 and a single to Bradman.

At 6.10pm Bradman had moved to 144 in eighty minutes since tea and Australia were 382.

Allen contained Woodfull to a couple but two singles from Robins brought Bradman to 146. Another single from Allen and then a pretty cut to the boundary and he had 151. It was greeted by a tremendous cheer. At 6.20pm he'd moved to 151 in ninety minutes since tea.

To the first delivery of the next Robins over, a leg break, Woodfull went forward and missed. Duckworth fumbled but Woodfull, assuming he'd be stumped, had already set off. He'd made 155, Australia 393 for 2.

Kippax came in and hit Robins to the boundary, took a single, Bradman took one, Kippax took another. The remorseless psychology of destruction *must* have made Chapman gaze at the clock to see how much of the day remained, how much more of this there would be. Time for one more Allen over. Robins had bowled three overs in his spell, and only four balls weren't scored off.

Kippax faced Allen and took a single from the fifth ball – no thought of protecting Bradman for the morrow – and in a final flourish, like a gesture of temporary farewell, Bradham hit the last for 3 to make him 155 in two hours forty-one minutes and Australia 404 for 2.

The 31,000 seem to have sensed they were in the presence of immortality and the people in the Press Box fumbled for words to frame it. 'Masterly to a degree,' wrote *The Daily Telegraph*; 'fierce punishment,' wrote *The Sunday Times*; 'It is necessary to use the language of superlatives,' wrote *The Times.*

'Bradman literally flayed the bowling,' wrote the *Australian Press Association.*

'Bradman showed a fine appreciation of the situation. It was an occasion made to measure for a batsman of his type to swing the fortunes of the

game. More passive resistance would have achieved only negative results but Bradman's dazzling effort thoroughly demoralised the bowling. It quickly changed the Australian position from an uphill fight to a bold and threatening challenge. While Woodfull kept up his end only scoring when runs could be made without risk, Bradman pounded the bowling into helplessness. Admittedly he treated Tate with more respect than the others, but this was only a matter of degree. He never showed the least difficulty in tapping, glancing and cutting delicate singles and twos. He attacked White, Robins, Woolley and Hammond impartially, punishing all with full-blooded drives and perfectly-timed pulls. Bradman plays so many grand innings, each of which seems more brilliant than the last, that it is difficult to pronounce which is really his greatest feat, but today's exhibition is bound to go down in history as a cricketing classic.'

No doubt he went back to the hotel at St. Pancras and celebrated with a nice cup of tea before contemplating what he'd do on Sunday, the rest day.

The magnitude of what Bradman was achieving, the magnetism he was exercising, are not easy to recapture from 1930 when the great British public lived without an endless daily diet of events being projected at them from screens in the corner of their living rooms, and without an endless progression of figurines being paraded across those same screens; when there wasn't so much sport, and it wasn't devalued because it was so incessant; when Hitler was three years from power and nuclear weapons unimagined. Britain was a hard place – it had always been that – but more socially structured and quieter. Celebrities were much bigger because, in the public's imagination, the competition around them was much smaller.

The Australian newspapers carried action photographs of the Tests but that posed a number of problems. They had 'stock' library material on all the players and frequently used them. Sometimes the captions were artfully constructed to suggest they might be current. Sydney's *The Sun* did manage some 'live' same-day coverage, explaining that the images were 'reproduced by a combination of telegraphy and photography'. Others papers don't seem to have had this facility and contented themselves with action pictures from the previous Test or even the Test before that.

To the ordinary citizen in both countries, the world was itself more remote, more passive, less intrusive and when a Bradman came across the horizon and detonated, the impact was commensurately greater. That said, the Australian newspapers present a remarkable spectacle, the cricket frequently the main story on the front page and match reports running to many column inches. *The Sun* fielded a reporter who described the play, and Mailey and former Australian captain Monty Noble to provide expert comments. Allied with the radio commentaries, however unauthentic, the Australian public was getting the full Bradman effect. So were the British.

The queue for Monday's play began at ten on Sunday *evening.* The gates opened at 9am and by then the queue had grown to between 7,000 and 8,000. They passed through the turnstiles in three quarters of an hour. They all knew that they might witness a special kind of history: feats never seen or even imagined before. *Everything* seemed possible and during the summer there was serious talk of Bradman making 500 in an innings.

The *Evening News* reported that one man fainted in the queue, and evidently that hadn't happened so far in 1930 – presumably in a cricket queue, anyway. The day was hot and getting hotter.

Bradman had a net.

The spectators sat under brilliant sunshine and were soon taking their jackets off, knotting handkerchiefs over the heads. Mercifully a breeze blew.

Woodfull ordered the heavy roller and towards the start of play at 11am the crowd was 12,000, slightly over a third full. It was a hot morning with a little heat haze and the crowd waited 'in a fever of enthusiasm'.

Tate opened the bowling from the Nursery end, Sandham fielding for Hobbs who'd got caught in the traffic. Bradman played the sixth delivery to square leg for a couple and the scoreboard clicked into life again. It had a lot more clicking to do, not least because that first over suggested the wicket remained placid.

Allen bowled from the Pavilion end and knowing eyes in the Press Box watched for any sign of the ball lifting or kicking but it didn't although Sydney's *The Sun* described it as 'fiery'. Allen bowled a maiden to Kippax.

After four balls of his second over Tate took the new ball. He beat Bradman – and raised his hands; Chapman prevented runs with some fine fielding in the gully. That, too, was a maiden.

Bradman now prepared to demonstrate his tactical maturity by assessing that consolidation was more important than another attack because Australia, 19 runs behind and with eight wickets in hand, could remove any chance of England winning and still give themselves enough time to bowl them out.

Hobbs trotted on and waved – apology? – to Chapman while Sandham trotted off.

Bradman contented himself with a couple to leg from the fifth delivery of Tate's third over and quite deliberately this astonishing young man had decided to set a different tempo to Saturday. In the next seven overs he scored a 2, a single and a single (Kippax a 3, a 2, three singles, a 2 and a single). Tate bowled an immaculate length, mixing in the occasional slower ball to try and tempt Bradman into a glance – part of a deliberate plot because when Tate bowled them Duckworth moved on to the leg side in case a catch came. Bradman tried to attack Allen and twice Chapman at backward point stopped powerful drives which would have gone to the boundary.

Robins came on and Kippax took a single from the fifth ball but Bradman – perhaps the psychology, perhaps because the ball was a plain long hop – pulled the sixth viciously to square leg where Woolley managed to stop it with his foot. At 11.35am Australia had advanced from 404 to 425, eminently respectable, obviously ominous for Chapman because the sides were now level, but still within the register of a normal Test match.

Tate came on at Allen's end and Bradman hooked a boundary, and he and Kippax chipped five from Robins, bringing Bradman to 171. Tate bowled a maiden to Kippax, and three singles came from Robins – the last of them a cut which took Bradman to 173, equalling Duleepsinhji.

The third ball of Tate's next over was the first he'd bowled short. Bradman unleashed a glorious square cut and the crowd saluted the highest score in the match lustily. Still Bradman showed his self-restraint again and Tate bowled him a maiden at 11.52am, Australia 443 so they'd made 39 in the morning.

Kippax took a 5 from Robins (4 overthrows), who also bowled a wide in the same over before Bradman took a single from the final delivery: 7 off the over, a rate Chapman couldn't afford to be sustained.

Bradman moved through the 180s, punctuated by a boundary off Tate although one ball fizzed past his bat but didn't hit anything, much to Tate's disgust. The old pro scratched his head, a favourite mannerism when fate denied him.

Chapman positioned Duleepsinhji near Woolley on the square-leg boundary to try and prevent Bradman hammering 4s there but, in a game within a game, Bradman chipped 2s instead. In another game within a game, Tate brought Hendren up to silly mid-on to try and catch Bradman who'd cannily steer the ball just wide of him.

He reached 191 with an edge off Hammond through the slips. Two overs later he played 'his first really bad stroke, when he tried to turn Hammond to leg. He got the ball on the bottom of his bat, and dragged it to the off within inches of his stumps.' (4) It went through the slips for 3 and he was past the 193 scored by Warren Bardsley for Australia at Lord's in 1926, until that moment the highest Test score at Lord's by anyone. The shot for 3 was variously described as a cut or inadvertent – one source (5) said he mis-read the ball, trying to play it to leg but it 'turned the other way'. Whatever, it was certainly the *first* shot which went where Bradman did not intend it to go. That is the most eloquent testament you can get about an innings spanning two days, almost four hours and approaching 200 runs.

Bradman tightenened the pressure on Robins with three 2s in an over to reach 200 although even when Robins bowled long hops on the leg side, he restrained himself from the potential danger of lashing them. That was at 12.15pm. He had been at the crease for three hours fifty-four minutes.

The scene, the *Evening News* reported, 'was amazing. The crowd cheered him again and again. Bradman, nearly dancing, waved his cap to them. One of the Australian contingent picked up the ball from the boundary and kissed it before throwing it back to Chapman.' (Since the stroke which took him to 200 was a 2, you'd have to wonder about that.) The cheering went on and on, people standing waving their hats and handkerchiefs, obliging Bradman to stand bareheaded – holding his cap in his hand – for some minutes, apart from the traditional formality of shaking hands with Kippax and most of the England team who gathered round to congratulate him.

Chapman, fearful of what Bradman was doing to Robins, replaced him with White and in the subsequent half an hour Bradman made only six and Kippax 11. *The Times* 'noticed with some sinking of heart that Chapman showed no interest in standing at silly mid-off for him. The inference was that [. . .] something of guile, possibly a deceptive trick of flight, was lacking from White's bowling. Both batsmen played him in the right way by running him down with three quick steps, and driving him with straight bats.' The crowd, perhaps ironically, barracked Bradman whenever he failed to score from a ball. Mailey in the Sydney *Sun* noted that Chapman was determined to slow the game down, which is why Hammond and White had such a long spell.

During this, at 12.30pm, drinks were brought out which – cryptically – the Sydney *Sun* pointed out was 'an experience the Australians had not previously encountered on this tour'. It had been far too cold for that.

Bradman played White with such immediate ease, although he was scoring so lightly from him and having to play at every ball, that someone in the Press Box felt he could score another 200.

Hammond, bowling to the Nursery End where the wicket was beginning to wear, made some balls lift nastily and once rapped Bradman on the fingers. Hammond slowed the scoring to the point where a barracker called out to Bradman, surely in irony: 'Wake up!'

At 12.53pm, Bradman scored a couple from the third ball of Hammond's tenth over and cut the final ball for 2, making Australia 500 and his own total 210.

He took a single from White, another from Hammond to reach 212, beating the highest score ever made in a Test match in England, Murdoch's 211 at The Oval in 1884. Some of the Australians present were well aware of this and waved their hats as well as applauding, but the rest of the crowd seemed unaware. Old Ebor wrote chastising them in *The Yorkshire Evening Post*: 'There was only a faint cheer, and from this one gathers that the Australian enthusiasts are not as well posted up in the achievements of their giants of the past as they might be.' At 1pm, they'd added 108, Bradman 59 of them.

Bradman on-drove White to the boundary with what was described as vicious power. That made him 221. After a single from Tate, Bradman faced White again and drove him so hard that Hobbs earned applause for stopping it. He placed the next ball so precisely between Hobbs and Chapman in the covers that the crowd turned towards the boundary but Allen, sprinting, used his foot and saved two runs. By now 'even Bradman's classic versatility and Kippax's fine glances failed to arouse the crowd, which was completely stunned by England's bad plight'. (6)

Five more overs remained to lunch, and Kippax and Bradman both scored boundaries. Australia went in at 544 for 2 (Bradman 231, Kippax 65). The crowd grew to 25,000 when play resumed and many sat in shirt sleeves, something Tebbutt thought so astonishing he mentioned it in despatches.

White bowled the first over from the Nursery End to Kippax, who took a step forward to the third ball and square cut it to the Mound Stand boundary. Bradman took a single from Tate's opening delivery, Kippax square cut a single from the third and that made Australia 550.

White, unusually, couldn't maintain a proper length, and Bradman – already in motion as the ball arched towards him – met a ball on the half-volley and smacked it to the boundary 'at an astonishing pace'. (7) That made him 238. He'd go down the wicket to White repeatedly but couldn't penetrate the field again.

The batsmen settled and in the next seven overs, from 2.22pm to 2.39pm, scored only 10, all in singles and including a bye. A moment later Bradman pulled White majestically to the square-leg boundary, and with such naked power that the umpire ducked for his life again. Bradman cover drove the third for a single to reach his own 250 in five hours thirty-five minutes.

He was now only 38 runs from Foster's record and it was very much in his mind, not least because Foster set it at Sydney and he felt someone from Sydney should break it.

In Tate's next over Kippax took a single, they ran a leg bye and Kippax played out the over. Bradman faced White. He went down the wicket and drove the ball to the boundary between square leg and mid-on. 'The crowd laughed when a rotund constable ran out and laboriously threw the ball back.' (8)

Bradman didn't score from the next two and he'd record how he'd very deliberately tried to keep every ball down. (9) He was about to make a fatal exception. He went down the wicket again to the fourth ball, a loose one, he'd say, and he thought he'd 'slashed' it well wide of Chapman. The ball sailed to one side of extra cover but Chapman, jumping and with his arm outstretched, caught it. 'Bradman didn't quite get to the pitch of an off ball,' *The Times* said, 'and hit it apparently within reach of the fieldsman's right hand. But there was less pace on the ball than the stroke had indicated, and Chapman' – running in – 'had to take it at the extreme of his telescopic reach' – and at the second time. Bradman described the catch as 'unbelievable' and said he reflected ruefully that you didn't play shots like that with Chapman anywhere around.

In his 254 he'd hit twenty-five 4s and put on 192 with Kippax in three hours three minutes. His innings lasted five hours forty-one minutes.

The innings unfolded in three phases, establishing mental and physical domination before tea on the Saturday, flaying the bowling from tea to the close, consolidating on this on Monday. Warner wrote that he 'was the champion batsman of the world', and used the word genius. 'Even from the ring one can see that he possesses small and exceptionally neat feet, and so young is he that many a boy still in the nursery – indeed, many an unborn bowler – is destined to suffer at his hands.' **(10)**

Fender wrote that Bradman had shown a 'perfect defence to all bowlers when they looked at all likely to be dangerous, and with that defence he had mixed as devastating a punishing power as could be credited to any player now in the game'. Fender added:

> *'The most remarkable thing about his play was the extreme severity with which he dealt with any ball off which he wished to score, and what was so impressive was the way in which almost anything off which he wished to make an attacking stroke was hit with speed and certainty to the boundary without ever leaving the ground. Bradman has not seemed a super-man in his batting except in this respect. He either made a defensive stroke, off which sometimes a run or two came, to third man or to long leg, or he hit the ball with such ferocity and accuracy, that it was four.'* **(11)**

At 2.48pm this London afternoon, the proper focus was becoming less and less elusive. In fact, after the five hours forty-one minutes it was becoming harder and harder to miss. Nobody talked of Macartney.

Australia continued to 729, Woodfull declared and England needed 304 to avoid an innings defeat. Chapman made a heroic 121 on the final day so that Australia had to bat again to make 72. They experienced an earth tremor which threatened to develop into a full earthquake.

They began at 3.46pm. Woodfull quickly entrenched himself, and when Robins came on after seven overs at 4.03pm – Chapman risking everything: win or bust – he'd only scored a single. Ponsford took a single from the first ball, Woodfull didn't score from the second and might have been out to the third. He hit a difficult, low chance wide of Duleepsinhji at mid-on. They ran one. Robins bowled Ponsford for 14 with the fourth ball.

Just like the run feast in May, it could not go on, and the nature of cricket decreed that. The dictum that batting is the only sporting activity where the competitor must play as if he can't afford one mistake was about to assert itself. Bradman pulled the fifth ball for a single and Woodfull didn't score from the sixth.

The over seemed to distill Robins; he'd bowled at three different batsmen, conceded three scoring strokes and taken a wicket.

Bradman faced Tate. He didn't score from the first ball which went to Chapman who fielded it. The second was wide enough to cut. He did cut, hard and low – the way he said the shot should be played, the harder the better – but it flew to Chapman in the gully who caught it. Australia were 17 for 2 and it hadn't gone on: Bradman's first innings safe in cricketing history, his second lasting three balls and comprising a single and a mistake.

Five runs later Duckworth caught Kippax off Robins. Woodfull and McCabe steered them home.

In the midst of the Test, newspapers reported that Bradman's family origins had been traced to a village called Withersfield on the Suffolk-Cambridge border. His grandfather's parents were buried in the parish churchyard, his grandfather emigrated and at one point the family had been known as Bradnam. A Mrs. Tilbrook evidently claimed to be Bradman's second cousin although many others were trying to prove connections like that, too. But Bradnam? It didn't sounded right then and it doesn't sound right now.

ENGLAND V AUSTRALIA – THE SECOND TEST

Lord's, 27, 28, 30 June, 1 July. Australia won by 7 wickets.

ENGLAND

J.B. Hobbs	c Oldfield	b Fairfax	1		b Grimmett	19
F.E. Woolley	c Wall	b Fairfax	41	ht wkt	b Grimmett	28
W.R. Hammond		b Grimmett	38	c Fairfax	b Grimmett	32
K.S. Duleepsinhji	c Bradman	b Grimmett	173	c Oldfield	b Hornibrook	48
E.H. Hendren	c McCabe	b Fairfax	48	c Richardson	b Grimmett	9
*A.P.F. Chapman	c Oldfield	b Wall	11	c Oldfield	b Fairfax	121
G.O.B. Allen		b Fairfax	3	lbw	b Grimmett	57
M.W. Tate	c McCabe	b Wall	54	c Ponsford	b Grimmett	10
R.W.V. Robins	c Oldfield	b Hornibrook	5		not out	11
J.C. White		not out	23		run out	10
+G. Duckworth	c Oldfield	b Wall	18	lbw	b Fairfax	0
Extras	(b 2, lb 7, nb 1)		10	(b 16, lb 13, w 1)		30
Total			425			375

1-13, 2-53, 3-105, 4-209, 5-236, 6-239, 7-337, 8-363, 9-387

1-45, 2-58, 3-129, 4-141, 5-147, 6-272, 7-329, 8-354, 9-372

	O	M	R	W	O	M	R	W
Wall	29.4	2	118	3	25	2	80	0
Fairfax	31	6	101	4	12.4	2	37	2
Grimmett	33	4	105	2	53	13	167	6
Hornibrook	26	6	62	1	22	6	49	1
McCabe	9	1	29	0	3	1	11	0
Bradman					1	0	1	0

AUSTRALIA

*W.M. Woodfull	st Duckworth	b Robins	155		not out	26
W.H. Ponsford	c Hammond	b White	81		b Robins	14
D.G. Bradman	c Chapman	b White	254	c Chapman	b Tate	1
A.F. Kippax		b White	83	c Duckworth	b Robins	3
S.J. McCabe	c Woolley	b Hammond	44		not out	25
V.Y. Richardson	c Hobbs	b Tate	30			
+W.A. Oldfield		not out	43			
A.G. Fairfax		not out	20			
Extras	(b 6, lb 8, w 5)		19	(b 1, lb 2)		3
Total	(6 wkts dec)		729			72

Dnb: C.V. Grimmett, P.M. Hornibrook, T.W. Wall.

1-162, 2-393, 3-585, 4-588, 5-643, 6-672

1-16, 2-17, 3-22

	O	M	R	W	O	M	R	W
Allen	34	7	115	0				
Tate	64	16	148	1	13	6	21	1
White	51	7	158	3	2	0	8	0
Robins	42	1	172	1	9	1	34	2
Hammond	35	8	82	1	4.2	1	6	0
Woolley	6	0	35	0				

Chapter Seven

334

THE SECOND TEST ENDED ON TUESDAY 1 JULY. THAT EVENING THE Australians went to Bradford to play Yorkshire over three days. They travelled all night because the Test hadn't finished until five in the evening.

From Bradford they'd go to Trent Bridge for three days against Nottinghamshire, when Bradman would be rested, and then enjoy three days off before the Third Test at Leeds on Friday 11 July.

Yorkshire

Bradman felt some of the players were suffering a reaction from Lord's. In sunny weather at Bradford a large crowd watched Woodfull win the toss and bat. He was out caught behind in the second over, Australia 4 for 1. Bradman was given a tremendous ovation as he walked out. He made a single but then 'went back in front of his wicket to push a well-pitched up ball from Emmott Robinson down the pitch, but the ball did not swing out as he expected and Bradman, playing outside it, was palpably leg before wicket'. (1)

The Australians made 302 (Ponsford's 143), Grimmett got among Yorkshire twice and the match was won by ten wickets.

Sydney's *The Sun,* however, wrote under a front-page headline 'TIRED OUT', datelined Bradford, Thursday: 'Don Bradman is almost certain to be rested from the Nottingham match, which will begin on Saturday. The young batsman looks jaded and spiritless, which is quite understandable, considering that so far he has been rested from only one match of the tour. Today he was not himself in the field against Yorkshire, and missed a fairly easy catch.'

While the team travelled to Nottingham, where they'd draw with Nottinghamshire, Bradman had a proper look round London, sailed up the Thames as far as Richmond and went to Wimbledon to watch fellow Australian Jack Crawford, one of the leading players of the day, and his American partner Elizabeth Ryan win the mixed doubles final.

Third Test – Headingley

The rest of the Australians travelled from Nottingham to Leeds on the Wednesday, giving them precious time before the Test began on the Friday. They enjoyed 'a thoroughly lazy time [. . .] Within certain well defined limits their daily programme has been go-as-you-please, but there is a long list of taboos and formal social occasions are among them. Leeds would probably have fêted them in accord with the generous instincts of the city, but tactful intimation has been given that receptions and the like are not welcome just now.' (2)

Some of the players, including Woodfull, Ponsford, a'Beckett and Walker, had a net at Headingley and Woodfull 'delighted the spectators by inviting them to field. The Australians gave them plenty of work to do, and some of the impromptu fieldsmen were very active, picking up balls neatly. Needless to say, the Australians indulged in some big hitting, and the civilian field had to stop many hot drives. There was much laughter when "unbowlable" Woodfull had his leg stump knocked out of the ground by a'Beckett.' (3)

There was no net on the Thursday. 'Obviously there is anxiety to avoid any suspicion of staleness among the players, and to turn them out today completely refreshed by rest. A few of them, including Ponsford, Hornibrook, a'Beckett, Wall and Walker enjoyed a round of golf at Sand Moor yesterday morning, while others strolled round the city. In the afternoon a party went for a motor run into the dales and in the evening they saw the gliding exhibition at Beamsley Beacon, and some went to a cinema.' (4) Both teams stayed at the Queen's Hotel.

The Yorkshire Evening News reported that if the Australians

YORKSHIRE V AUSTRALIANS

Bradford, 2, 3, 4 July. Australians won by 10 wickets.

AUSTRALIANS

*W.M. Woodfull	c Wood	b Dennis	3		
W.H. Ponsford		c & b Hall	143		
D.G. Bradman	lbw	b Robinson	1		
S.J. McCabe	c Macaulay	b Hall	40		
A.A. Jackson	lbw	b Macaulay	46		
V.Y. Richardson	c Dennis	b Robinson	3		
E.L. a'Beckett		not out	30	not out	6
C.V. Grimmett		c & b Hall	1		
A. Hurwood	c A.T. Barber	b Rhodes	4		
P.M. Hornibrook	c Mitchell	b Rhodes	10		
+C.W. Walker	st Wood	b Rhodes	6	not out	1
Extras	(b 4, lb 7, w 1, nb 3)		15		
Total			302		7

1-4, 2-11, 3-63, 4-201, 5-218,
6-248, 7-260, 8-272, 9-292

	O	M	R	W	O	M	R	W
Robinson	21	5	69	2	0.1	0	2	0
Dennis	13	6	25	1				
Macaulay	32	10	58	1				
Hall	24	6	61	3	1	0	5	0
Rhodes	25.3	8	49	3				
Leyland	10	1	25	0				

YORKSHIRE

P. Holmes	c Richardson	b Hornibrook	13		b Hurwood	8
A. Mitchell	c a'Beckett	b Grimmett	5		b Hurwood	2
*A.T. Barber	c a'Beckett	b Grimmett	6		b McCabe	10
M. Leyland	c Hornibrook	b Grimmett	17	c Ponsford	b Hurwood	5
W. Barber	c Walker	b a'Beckett	21	c Bradman	b Grimmett	42
E. Robinson	lbw	b Grimmett	1	c Ponsford	b Grimmett	9
W. Rhodes		b a'Beckett	35		c&b Grimmett	17
F. Dennis		b Grimmett	23	c Bradman	b Grimmett	25
+A. Wood		not out	11	c McCabe	b Hurwood	0
G.G. Macaulay	lbw	b a'Beckett	6		not out	18
C.H. Hall		c & b Grimmett	0	c a'Beckett	b Grimmett	5
Extras	(b 6, lb 2)		8	(b 17, lb 3)		20
Total			146			161

1-18, 2-18, 3-38, 4-43, 5-47,
6-95, 7-116, 8-134, 9-143

1-12, 2-24, 3-35, 4-77, 5-79,
6-91, 7-118, 8-119, 9-147

	O	M	R	W	O	M	R	W
a'Beckett	19	1	42	3	4	1	4	0
Hurwood	4	3	1	0	21	12	35	4
Grimmett	28.5	5	75	6	19.4	4	58	5
Hornibrook	14	5	20	1	8	2	16	0
McCabe					13	3	28	1

'had any cares at all they have a happy way of not showing it. They go about in an easy and leisurely manner when they are not concerned with serious cricket, and they are not averse to snatching an extra hour in bed. [. . .] As 10 o'clock was approaching this morning [Thursday] only a handful had made their way to the breakfast room. Though there is nothing secretive about their movements, they are men of few words. They smiled appreciatively to the morning greetings of newly made acquaintances in the hotel, but even the "nice day, isn't it?" which many people uttered brought forth no comment.

'Only Mr. Kelly the manager indulges in informative statements and we shall have to wait until he arrives later in the day – he is not expected until the evening – for any official declaration on his part. Don Bradman, too, has yet to arrive in the city. No doubt he will make his appearance at the same time as Mr. Kelly.

'One thing is certain: the Aussies have made themselves popular in their own unassuming way with all with whom they have been in contact – including the staff of the hotel. The rumours about the Colonials being "faddy" with their food and requiring special dishes have proved to be a mere myth. "They cause us less concern than the average visitor," said one who helps to look after their needs. "They like a good steak, like any of us, but one thing they insist upon is grapefruit."'

That afternoon only Woodfull remained in the hotel, handling correspondence.

When Kelly did arrive he assured a reporter that Bradman was fit and well and would be coming on a later train. Presumably Kelly didn't know Bradman was out there somewhere having set off for Leeds driving in a Singer car. The journey proved an adventure but he enjoyed it. Another adventure altogether was about to begin.

Poor Fairfax had been taken to a Nottingham nursing home with boils and an abcess needed lancing. He wouldn't be playing again for ten days. 'Otherwise,' Kelly said, 'everything is all right. We are all happy and looking forward to tomorrow.'

A *Yorkshire Evening Post* reporter was struck by how reticent the Australians were to say anything. 'You meet Mr. Ponsford and say: "Good morning, Mr. Ponsford, and what are you going to do today?" Mr. Ponsford is as cautious as if it were Larwood who was bowling – and almost as quickly is he gone.' Wall was the same but Woodfull answered questions politely, revealing nothing at all.

The England players arrived during the day and so did Bradman. There were so many players and others in the hotel that, as Bradman said, you were constantly encountering cricket celebrities. (5) One newspaper estimated, apart from the players, there were at least fifty other notable Australians in the hotel and it felt more like Melbourne Cup day.

England made three changes: Leyland for Hendren, Geary for Robins and Larwood, fit again, for Allen.

That evening a little rain fell. At six the next morning the sun was shining from a cloudless sky. The gates opened at 9am and 3,000 people moved quickly in to the ground. More and more came and an hour before the start they numbered some 10,000 with room for many, many more because the boundary had been shortened by six yards. A white line and a cord round the field marked this. (6) The Australians arrived in a fleet of cars, Chapman arrived by himself and when the crowd saw him they shouted: "Good luck!"

From about 10.30am the 'ground was in a constant buzz'. (7)

Shortly before 11am Chapman and Hobbs emerged from the pavilion and walked to the wicket amidst cheering and the clicking of cameras. They inspected it carefully and returned. Some moments later Woodfull and Bradman did the same – 'more cheers, and much pointing of fingers at the boy prodigy, whose famous smile was eagerly recognised'. (8) They didn't stay long: 'After a glance at the wicket the two went to the side of the field near the Winter Shed for a little practice. Sutcliffe and Leyland followed suit.' (9)

At 11.15am Chapman emerged from the pavilion and Woodfull broke off practice to join him. Chapman spun his half-sovereign in front of assorted film and Press cameras, Woodfull called 'heads' and it came down – heads. Woodfull, smiling, said: 'We'll bat'. Chapman smiled more expansively and signalled with a thumbs down.

There was still some space on the popular side for more spectators and Headingley's absolute capacity might be reached during the day. A 'strangely quiet' crowd, now rising towards 20,000, watched Chapman lead England out in the sunshine but with a cross wind, while Woodfull and Jackson – Ponsford out with gastritis – got a bigger cheer, especially from the many Australians.

Fender, peering from the Press Box, was filing a 'running' story –

describing play in short takes for London's *Star*. His first despatch was at 11.30am and began with some canvassing he had done about the state of the pitch. He'd received general assurance that it would last to the final day although, as he peered, he nursed doubts. It had, he thought, 'many bad patches'. He intended to watch the wicket closely.

The *Yorkshire Telegraph & Star* reporter expressed surprise 'to see the many bare patches. The wicket looked like a batsman's dream of paradise [. . .] firm and well knit.' The *Nottingham Journal* reporter said the wicket 'looked brown and parched but it was easy paced'.

11.30am: Woodfull took strike to Larwood from the Kirkstall Lane end, giving him the help of the cross wind – a raking wind which during the day would force spectators to stamp their feet for warmth and turn their coat collars up despite the sunshine. Larwood had three slips and a gully standing a long way back, a cover and mid-off and mid-on as he bowled down the hill.

Woodfull scored a single to fine leg from the second ball and Jackson played his first ball in a Test in England to point for no run. He scored a single to the right of cover point from the last, bringing him down to face Tate and he spooned the fifth ball – it swung in to him – feebly to Larwood at short leg, who caught it knee-high. It was an easy chance but the crowd roared all the same.

11.38am: Bradman, cap firmly on, [(10)] 'sauntered to the wicket as if he was going to the net for a practice. He is a cool customer, this young cricketing genius from an Australian village.' [(11)]

A degree of mystery surrounds his first ball. Tate subsequently insisted he beat Bradman and it went just past the off stump while Duckworth, sure it would hit, roared in triumph. Contemporary reports don't mention this. For example, the *Bradford Telegraph & Argus* wrote: 'The remaining delivery of Tate's opening over was played with great care by Bradman, who came in amid a storm of cheers.' The *Sun*, Sydney, said he played it 'not too comfortably'. What remains certain is that Bradman did not score from it. [(12)]

Larwood had already reached some sort of speed although Hammond says he was 'still obviously unwell and could not send them down with the old familiar hiss'. [(13)] Woodfull nicked the first ball of Larwood's second over past Hammond at second slip – Hammond almost touched it – to the boundary.

Then, the ball hitting the middle of the bat, Bradman got to work.

He safely glanced Tate for a brisk 2 to square leg, a stroke which had Leyland sprinting over the ground to pick smartly up. Bradman 2 at 11.43am.

In the next Tate over, sixth of the innings, Bradman drove almost straight to the sightscreen, the timing perfect, 'a carpet drive'. (14) Tate seemed to beat him next ball, striking his pads, and appealed. Fender noted that 'the wicket, in the opening overs at any rate, was playing perfectly, not a ball in the first six overs getting stump high'. Bradman 6 at 11.49am.

Bradman confirmed the Fender diagnosis because he found the wicket comfortable to play on and felt 'at home' immediately. (15) Moreover, he was adopting a distinctive method of selecting the ball which would yield runs or making no attempt to score. Woodfull took a single from Larwood, Bradman 2 past point and a single to mid-on to keep the strike. Bradman 9 at 11.53am.

He took a single from Tate past point. Bradman 10 at 11.54am. That had been made in sixteen minutes, a measured prelude with one boundary adorning it. His eyes must have been fully adjusted to the excellent light now, his taut, trim body loose now, the short boundary constantly beckoning. Within a moment he closed the prelude and opened the way to the monumental.

Larwood prepared to bowl his fifth over, the last of the initial burst. Relying on speed, he positioned only three men in front of the bat, Hobbs in the covers, Tyldesley at mid-off and Tate at forward short-leg. In this mood Bradman could see there were runs everywhere, especially the wide-open spaces.

A reporter doing a colour piece for London's *Evening News* said Bradman 'stands at the wicket his square shoulders curiously hunched. He watches Larwood running his long, lithe run towards him – abruptly he has moved and his bat has swung, and the red ball is speeding across the grass.'

That might have been the first ball of this over. Bradman laid back and off-drove it for a beautiful boundary, his wrists seemingly made of steel. (16) He 'twisted' the third to the long leg boundary and turned the next for 2 to the same place. That could have been a boundary, too, but Sutcliffe ran urgently from fine leg to cut it off. Bradman scampered a single from the fifth ball – a drive into the covers which went straight to Tyldesley or it would have been another boundary – to retain the strike.

He 'did not leave us long to wait to find out his intentions', the *Evening Standard* wrote.

> *'They were strictly tactical and wholly honourable. He conceived the idea of chastising Larwood and, if possible, "knocking him off". He drove the fast bowler to long-off, a virile clout, turned the next ball but one to the rails on the square-leg side and, using the same strokes again, completed 11 in the over. At once Larwood pulled on his sweater. Bradman's strokes were splendid and he was away for the runs almost as soon as the ball had left the bat. This man always seems to know exactly what he is doing. There is no note of hesitation about his batsmanship, which is aggressive without effort.'*

Bradman 21 at 12pm.

Geary replaced Larwood and his first ball was almost a wide. Bradman managed to reach it and whacked it but Chapman made a reflex stop. Geary kept Bradman quiet for the next four balls but he punched the last past Larwood at mid-on to the boundary – no other fielder for forty yards; those wide-open spaces.

Fender criticised Geary for opening with 'a bad over' and criticised him for an abnormal field setting: only one slip, Hammond, and the extra man – Larwood – at mid wicket (instead of second slip) for Bradman's favourite pull. Bradman played precisely that shot 'along the ground clean through Larwood'. Whether Fender judged that no mid-wicket could staunch the flow of runs there, and so he might as well have been in the slips, is unclear. Bradman 25 at 12.01pm.

As if to emphasise the dual structure of the innings, Tate came on at the other end and bowled a maiden to Woodfull, 8 – although Geary managed to do the same to Bradman, something which Fender describes as a 'great achievement'. It wouldn't happen again for nearly an hour.

Woodfull took a single on the leg side from Tate, played a maiden to Geary. Bradman took a single through the slips – the on-side glance? – from Tate and Woodfull a single, too, in a seven-ball over. Bradman 26 at 12.12pm.

Geary, finding some spin, bowled another maiden to Woodfull.

Bradman, facing Tate, saw a ball that took his fancy. This was a half-volley outside the off stump. There was a tap – a sparkling stroke behind point – and the ball was at the boundary before Leyland could do anything about it. Bradman 30 at 12.16pm.

Woodfull took a single from Geary and Bradman played the ball inadvertently – off the edge. He twisted his head: *Where did that go?* It had gone through the slips and they ran 3. Leaving aside the disputed first ball of his innings and the one which struck his pads, this was his first real mistake, and even then one reporter (17) described it as an orthodox late cut. Duleepsinhji fielded the ball so well that the third run became dangerous. Bradman 33 at 12.19pm.

The edge gave him the strike and he struck Tate to mid-on for 2 then fed his favourite place – past point – for a single. Bradman 36 at 12.22pm.

Woodfull negotiated the final delivery without scoring so Bradman had the strike again when Chapman replaced Tate with Tyldesley. Bradman applied the psychology of destruction to Robins at Trent Bridge, Robins and White at Lord's. Tyldesley would get it now and in full measure. Bradman went for him from the first ball, a full toss which he sprang out to hammer past mid-off to the boundary like a gunshot.

Australia reached 50 at just under a run a minute.

Bradman sprang out and drove the third ball to the mid-off boundary and tucked a single there from the fifth. The two boundaries in the over had travelled with nice symmetry either side of the sightscreen and both were struck with such power that Hammond, positioned in front of it, had no time to move the few yards to either side to stop them.

'By going out to meet Tyldesley four times in his first over,' Fender concluded, Bradman 'showed that he was not going to let him get a length if he could help it. Woodfull, seeing the trend of events, was quite happy to let Bradman have all the bowling, and took a sharp single whenever he could to let his partner get on with the good work.' Although he was 'scoring so fast and appeared to be hitting the ball so hard, he was making what are for him normal strokes, pulls and late cuts, without taking any risks whatever'. (18)

Bradman 45 at 12.25pm.

Geary changed to the Kirkstall Lane end and Bradman took a single through the slip area from the first ball. Woodfull returned the strike to him and he played 'a crisp cut full of charm' (19) through a gaping gap in the slips to the boundary.

Bradman 50 at 12.28pm, made in even time. He did it by 'brilliant cricket, his timing of the ball being so perfect and his quickness of foot so supreme that he seemed able to force any ball, however good a length it might be. He allowed the bowler very little margin of inaccuracy. You had to pitch on the proverbial sixpence [20] to keep him quiet.' [21]

The Bradford Telegraph & Argus emphasised Warner's point. Bradman's footwork was 'wonderful and whether he went out to the slow bowler to hit at the pitch of the ball or drew back his timing was always perfect, and the stroke always aggressive in character. No one was able to keep Bradman quiet because he never permitted an English bowler to send down a good length ball. If it was normally pitched at a good length Bradman went out to it and made it into a half-volley, so quick and accurate was he with his footwork.'

The *Sun,* Sydney, reinforced these opinions. 'It must be said, with all respect to Macartney, that Bradman was now overshadowing him. He was getting the strike uncannily, and no ball seemed to be too good to score from.'

Woodfull took 2 from Tyldesley and Bradman savaged two bad balls from Geary, making a nonsense of Geary's field; Sutcliffe, Hammond and Leyland pulled back to try and guard the boundary. Bradman indulged himself in 'the first impudent stroke' when he created 'an amazing hook only just wide of mid-on from a ball outside the off-stump' [22] – a long hop which went just in front of square leg – and square cut the next to the boundary. Both shots travelled at ferocious speed, making those three fielders on the boundary into impotent spectators. He finished the over with the off-glance for a single. Bradman 59 at 12.32pm.

Chapman looked worried because he'd made three bowling changes in ten minutes and although this slowed the scoring rate a little it hadn't looked likely to produce a wicket.

Bradman steered Tyldesley's first ball into the mid-on area for 2, cut the fourth to the boundary and took a single past slip to keep the strike. 'The smallness of the ground, the shortness of the boundary and the slope as the ball races for the ropes helped him to reap a rich harvest for his skill,' the *Evening Standard* wrote. 'His talent touched the scene with animation because the fielders were seldom at rest, and the ball was flying off Bradman's bat like sparks from a Catherine wheel.'

Bradman 66 at 12.35pm, made in fifty-seven minutes out of 81, Woodfull 14.

Tate came on for Geary. 'Bradman let his natural abilities have full play, and never allowed the bad start [Jackson's dismissal] to cramp him,' *The Yorkshire Evening News* wrote. 'There was real joy in this youngster's batting. Frequent bowling changes made no difference to him. He dominated the situation, driving, cutting or hooking with apparently no effort.'

Bradman glanced Tate's fifth ball to the boundary with delightful ease, almost taking the ball off his toes. Bradman 70 at 12.37pm.

Woodfull hadn't faced a ball for three overs but took a single from Geary, who'd switched ends, Bradman another from the fourth ball to mid-on. Woodfull played out the over. Bradman 71 at 12.39pm.

He cut Tyldesley's first delivery past slip for a single, Woodfull took one from the fifth ball, Bradman cut a single past slip to keep the strike. Were these the off-side glances? Maybe . . . Bradman 73 at 12.42pm.

He steered Geary to square leg for 2 and steered him there again for a single. Bradman 76 at 12.45pm. He struck Tyldesley's third ball to the cover boundary. Bradman 80 at 12.47pm.

Woodfull took a single from Geary's fourth ball, Bradman a single on the leg side from the next. Fender noted that Bradman's runs were virtually all coming from cuts and pulls, mingled with placing an occasional shot on the leg side, as he'd just done. (23) Bradman 81 at 12.50pm.

He slowed, although whether the bowling or the situation steadied him is not clear. Lunch wasn't until 1.30pm, giving him forty minutes to make the remaining 19 for a century, and that in turn would make him only the third batsman in Test match history to do it before lunch. Trumper (Manchester, 1902) was the first and Macartney (Leeds, 1926) the second. Whether Bradman nursed any personal ambitions to equal, then eclipse, Macartney after all the unfavourable comparisons is not clear either. Perhaps he slowed because he could slow and still make it.

At 81, Tyldesley bowled him a maiden. He reached urgently forward to one of these Tyldesley deliveries and sent it low towards Hobbs at cover. Hobbs dived, grasped it but couldn't hold it. The crowd made a deep murmuring noise because they assumed Hobbs had missed a chance – they hadn't noticed it was a bump ball and Bradman had hit it hard into the ground. The maiden received loud applause – a compliment to Bradman.

Woodfull took a single from the first ball of Geary's next over and Bradman cut past slip for 2. Bradman 83 at 12.54pm.

They ran a leg bye to give Bradman the strike against Tyldesley and he promptly struck the ball to square leg – a short-arm pull – with such ferocity that it beat Sutcliffe at short leg and Duleepsinhji, full on the boundary, only had time to put his right hand down. Even then he couldn't stop it. Bradman 87 at 12.56pm.

From Geary, both batsmen took singles, Bradman's through point. Bradman 88 at 12.59pm.

Tyldesley bowled another maiden to Bradman – to a thunder of applause – and he'd scored from only eleven of the previous thirty-one balls. This slowing against Tyldesley and Geary happened suddenly and, to many in the crowd and Press Box, inexplicably. That did not disturb a central truth and *The Times* expressed it in plain language. 'At 1pm the English bowlers bore every appearance of hoping that a batsman would get out, rather than suspecting that they would get him out.'

Hammond replaced Geary, who'd been on since midday, and Woodfull hit the final ball to the cover boundary, taking him to 23.

Tyldesley stayed on and Bradman turned him into the leg side for a single but Woodfull poached a single from the final delivery to keep the strike. Bradman 89 at 1.05pm.

Woodfull took a single from Hammond's fifth delivery and Bradman a single past point, keeping the strike. Bradman 90 at 1.07pm, made in eighty-nine minutes. The journey through the 80s lasted twenty-one minutes.

Chapman used orthodox tactics, bringing Larwood back for a four-over burst. Some in the crowd thought Bradman was caught at third slip by Geary, falling over, and cheered but he'd played the ball down. Then Bradman steered the last ball past point for a single. He was treating Larwood's fastest deliveries with some caution but obviously manoeuvring the strike so he'd equal Trumper and Macartney. The single kept him the strike. Bradman 91 at 1.10pm.

He faced Hammond and made a mistake, mis-hitting over Geary's head in the slips. They ran 2. He followed that with a single past point from the final ball, keeping the strike. Woodfull had not faced a ball for three overs again. Bradman 94 at 1.13pm.

He faced Larwood and forced the first ball – a hook – to the mid-on boundary. He lashed 'wildly' at the next, 'which just shaved the stump'. (24) He pulled the fifth in front of square leg to the boundary and the whole ground erupted. The applause went on and on, round after round, and he acknowledged it with a 'jerky salute'. (25) At one moment, cap held in his right hand, bat leant against his pads he stood quite still smiling broadly. His hair, parted to one side, was perfectly in place. He looked terrifyingly young. Duckworth ambled back from the stumps to resume his position, hands like flippers in the heavy dark gloves beating out applause as he went.

Bradman 102 at 1.17pm in one hour thirty-nine minutes out of 127 with sixteen boundaries. (Trumper one hour forty-eight minutes, Macartney one hour forty-three).

In the thirteen minutes to lunch Woodfull made two singles and a 2, Bradman a single past point and in the final over, from Hammond, 2 to mid-on, making him 105 out of 136. As he walked back to the pavilion the crowd cheered him.

During the lunch interval the *Evening Standard* reporter went round questioning people to see if they had seen Bradman give a semblance of a chance and, unanimously, they had not. 'His display was perfect and as icily cold as perfection usually is.' During the lunch interval, too, cloud moved across the ground.

The crowd grew after lunch – 17,928 had paid (£1,669 4s). Booked seats realised £1,260. Chapman led England out down a narrow corridor through the standing members, Tyldesley so broad that he virtually filled it as he came. Bradman, wearing no cap now, looked fresh and very eager, and rotund, roly-poly Tyldesley would soon find out all about that. The crowd settled into the afternoon sunshine.

At 2.18pm Larwood resumed from the Kirkstall Lane end to Woodfull who took a single, and Bradman one on the leg side from the final delivery. Bradman 106 at 2.21pm.

Chapman put Geary on, not Tate or Hammond, to try and restrain Bradman immediately but he square cut the fifth ball, a half-volley on the off-stump, to the boundary, a glorious stroke and struck down so hard that it bounced over Chapman's head at point – although one report (*The Yorkshire Evening* Post) describes it as a cover drive. Tactically and psychologically this was a significant moment because Chapman moved Hobbs back from his traditional cover point to the boundary. Perhaps, already, Chapman feared for the afternoon and what Bradman would do between now and tea at 4.30, a lifetime away. Bradman 110 at 2.22pm.

Larwood reached full pace, faster than he'd been in the morning but his control not so tight. He had three slips and a backward point.

Woodfull played a single into the off side and Bradman sent the ball past Hammond's left hand in the slips. In the Press Box, opinion divided over whether this was a snick or a most delicate late cut, the division itself a testament to Bradman's speed. It sped through the slips for 4. He did make a genuine mistake to the next ball, sending it over the slips, and they ran one. *The Yorkshire Evening News* didn't commit itself to a view on the first snick-or-cut, simply pointing out that 'in each case the ball flew perilously close to the fieldsmen, but neither Duleepsinhji nor Hammond could get to it'. Woodfull straight drove the final ball for 3 to bring up Australia's 150. Bradman 115 at 2.26pm. Woodfull hit Geary to the square-leg boundary.

At 2.29pm, eleven minutes after the resumption, Larwood prepared to bowl his third over of the burst and Bradman prepared to take him on. Here again was a game within a game, Larwood bowling wide of the off stump to try and entice Bradman there – and give a catch. Bradman flicked at the second ball but edged it – again – through the slips just wide of Hammond to the boundary, sent the third past point for 2, *placed* the fourth through the slips past Hammond for a boundary again, sent the fifth towards square leg for 2. A mystery remains about such overs: did Larwood simply bowl badly or was Bradman extending the psychology to him? Bradman 127 at 2.32pm, so that in fourteen minutes 22 had been added.

Woodfull and Bradman both took singles from Geary's next over, Bradman into his happy hunting ground around point although Geary found a 'spot' on the wicket and aimed to try and hit it. Bradman 128 at 2.34pm.

He worked the slips area for a single from the first delivery of Larwood's fourth over and, although Woodfull played the over out, Chapman took Larwood off and brought Tate on to try and exercise some sort of control. During this long and lengthening afternoon Larwood would bowl only four more overs. Bradman 129 at 2.37pm.

Geary was steadier, confining Bradman to a single towards mid-on. He'd found a good length and Bradman would find himself playing Geary into the covers as the likeliest way of taking regular runs from him. More than that, Geary was consistent. Bradman 130 at 2.38pm, so that in twenty minutes he'd added 25.

Tate couldn't exercise the control, at least immediately. Bradman worked the cover point area for a single from the first delivery – a cut –

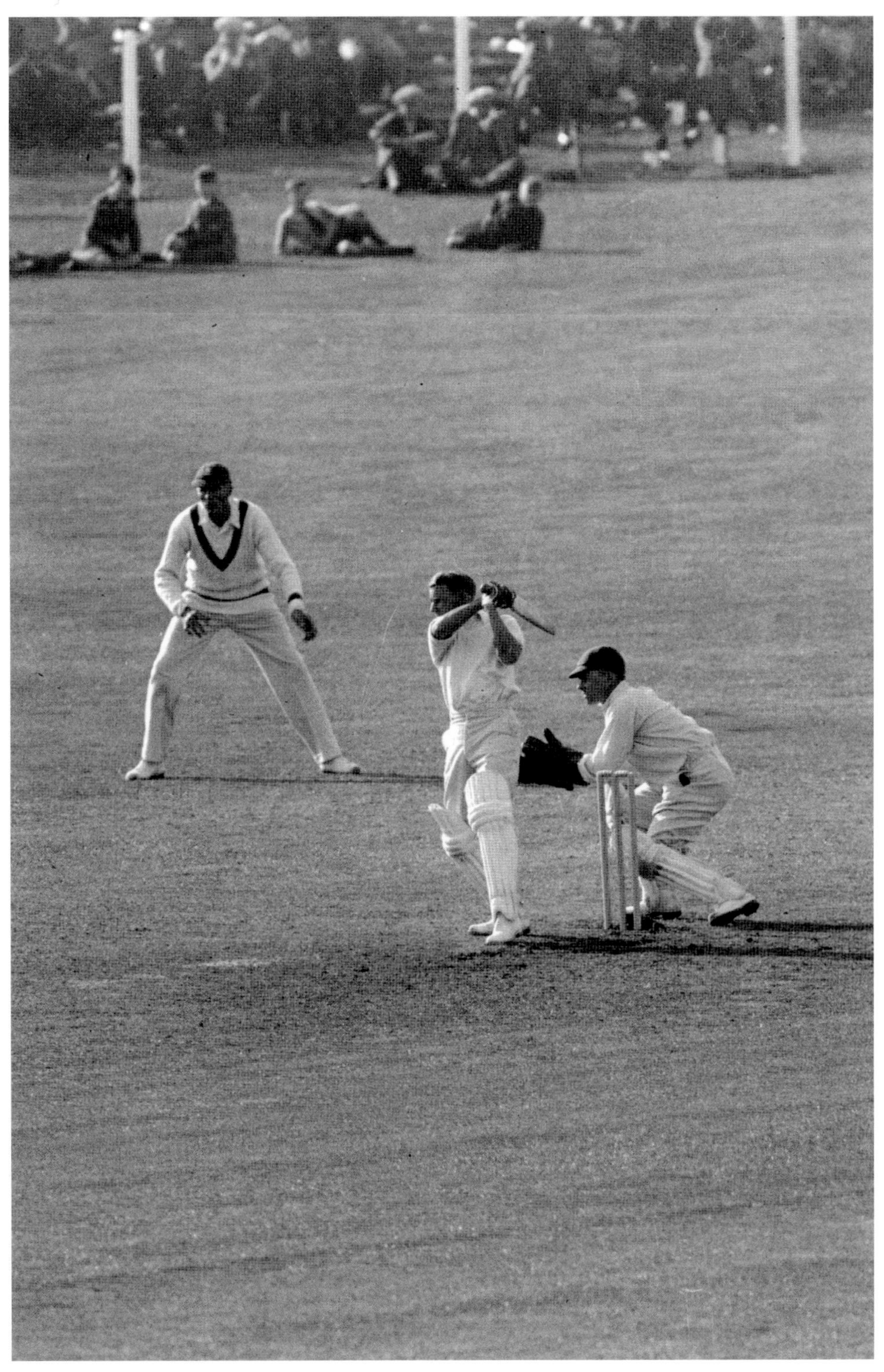

The immortal innings in the Third Test at Leeds. The shadows lengthen and Bradman, still fresh, plunders the bowling of Maurice Tate on his way to 309 not out at the close. (Press Association)

WHAT AUSTRALIA WAS READING . . .

RECEPTION AT KALGOORLIE.

KALGOORLIE, March 20.—The members of the Australian test team, who are travelling to Perth, en route for England, were enthusiastically received when they arrived in Kalgoorlie this afternoon by the Great Western express. crowds of people assembling at the railway station to welcome them. At a civic reception in the Town Hall, the Mayor of Kalgoorlie (Mr. B. Leslie) expressed the confidence of the people of the Eastern Goldfields in the capabilities of the team. and hoped the Ashes would be secured. He said that he regretted that they could not stay longer in the town, but hoped when they returned they would be able to play a match against a local team.

The Mayor of Boulder (Mr. F. W. Coath), who supported Mr. Leslie's remarks, said that he was satisfied that no body of sportsmen did so much for the prestige of Australia as the test teams.

West Australian, 21 March.

TEAM LEAVES FREMANTLE

ENTHUSIASTIC FAREWELL.

FREMANTLE, Monday.

Members of the Australian Eleven sailed from Fremantle this evening on the liner Orford. As the vessel moved into midstream to commence her voyage to London the crowd on the Quay sent cheer after cheer across the water.

With few exceptions, all the players were grouped within a few yards of one another on the two decks, and the wharf below that vantage point was black with people. The players were on the vessel earlier than was anticipated, but not too early to defeat the object of a handful of enthusiasts, who gave them each a cheer as they passed aboard. Woodfull, Richardson, Ponsford, Hornibrook, Jackson, Bradman, McCabe, Hurwood, and a'Beckett arrived practically simultaneously. Wall followed, and the last to go aboard was C. Grimmett, who walked slowly up the gangway, as if trying to think out a new curly one.

Sydney Morning Herald, 25 March.

AUSTRALIAN CRICKETERS.

Snowballing in Switzerland.

[From the Special Representative of the Australian Press Association.]

LUCERNE, 20th April.

The Australian cricketers, who a few days ago were sweltering in the tropics, to-day rejoiced in snowballing on the summit of Montrigi, 6000 feet above sea level. The manager (Mr. W. L. Kelly) and the treasurer (Mr. Howard) went to Interlaken, but the players proceeded to Lake Vitznau, ascended the cog-wheel railway to the peak, and bathed in brilliant sunshine. The team saw some magnificent panoramas in Lake Lucerne during respites in the snowball battles, which were waged with an unlimited supply of ammunition, even press representatives coming in for a share of good-natured bombardment.

The Age, 22 April.

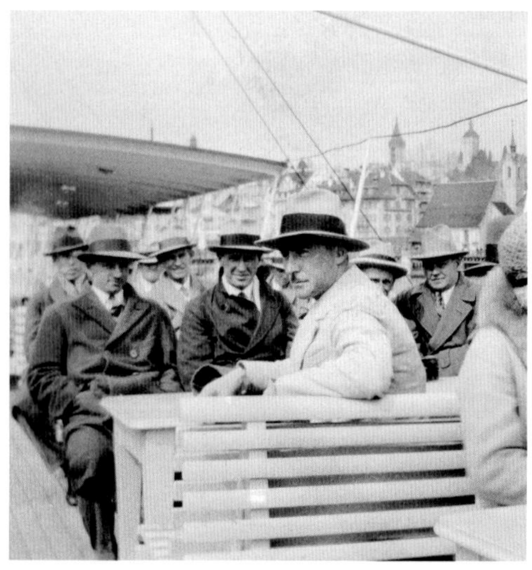

The Australians take a boat across Lake Lucerne en route to England. Bradman is extreme left next to Alan Kippax, Vic Richardson turning towards the camera. (Getty Images)

THE AUSTRALIAN TEAM.

ARRIVAL IN PARIS.

A Rush for the Folies Bergere

PARIS, 21st April.

On arriving in Paris, though travel weary after the journey from Lucerne, the Australian cricketers lost no time in seeing the Folies Bergere, the most renowned music hall in Paris. They were vastly amused by a timely skit on British tourists in Paris, which reminded them of their own language difficulties since their arrival in Europe. Judging by the applause awarded the items given in English, 50 per cent. of the audience were English or American.

The Age, 23 April.

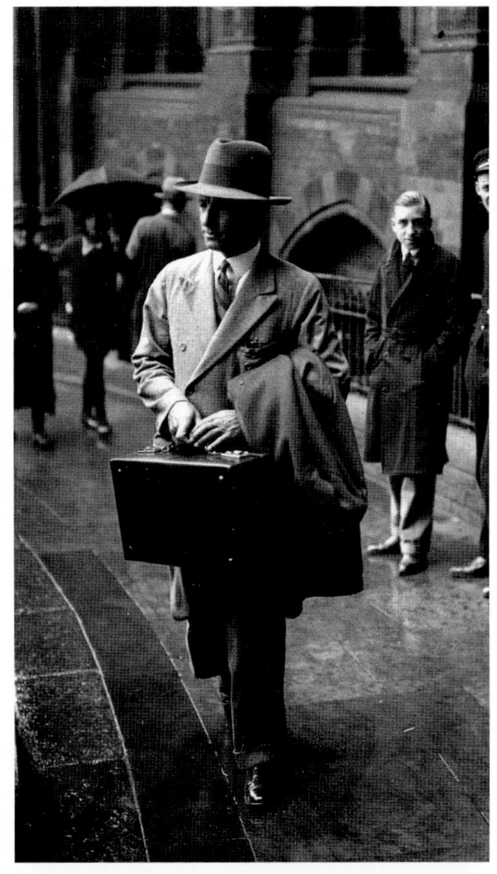

Right: More polite, more restrained times. Bradman arrives at Paddington Station in London distinctly unmobbed en route to Bristol and the tied match against Gloucestershire. (Getty Images)

Bradman with Bill and Ethel Sykes (although on the next tour.) William Sykes & Sons of Horbury Bridge near Wakefield were famous bat makers and Bradman used one during his career. (Courtesy Charles Day)

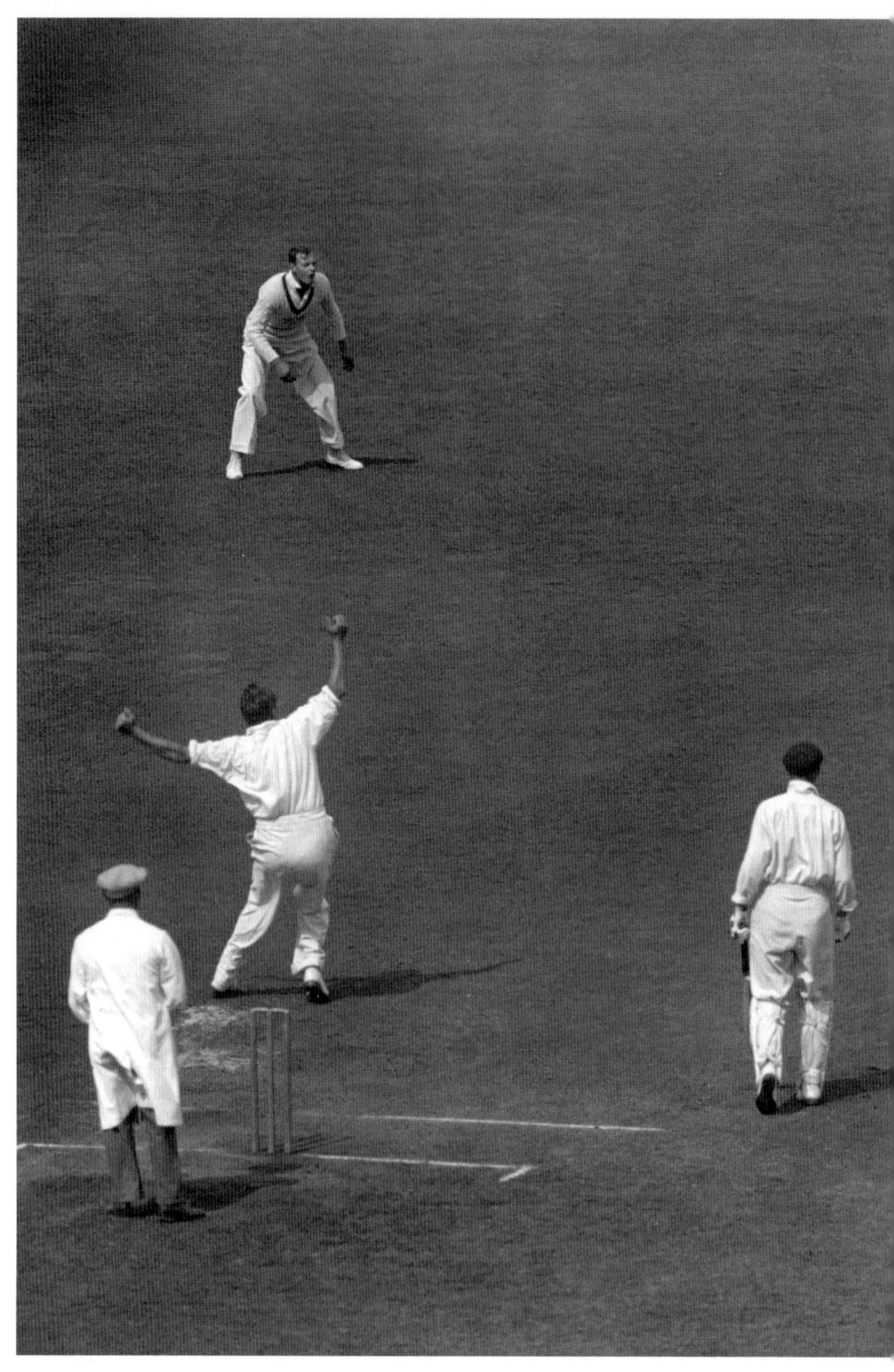

Moment of agony for Tate – arms outstretched – as wicket-keeper George Duckworth misses Bradman on 154 at The Oval. (Press Association)

THE EVENING STANDARD.

Test Team Wives Cancel 'Phone Calls

Australian Cricketers Wait in Vain from 6 a.m. for Sydney to 'Phone :: Did Not Know Call Was Cancelled.

THE Australian cricketers at Liverpool are wondering whether another clause has been added to their 36-clause contract.

The new clause would read "An Australian cricketer on tour may not talk to his wife over the new Anglo-Australian telephone service."

For the second morning in succession five Australian cricketers got out of bed at 6.0 a.m. in their Liverpool hotel.

For two hours they waited in vain for Sydney to ring them up.

Now the Australians are trying to solve a mystery.

At 8.0 a.m. they were convinced that atmospherics had robbed them of their chances of speaking over the Anglo-Australian 'phone.

But the new department in London, which deals with these calls, says "No."

An official of the department said:—

"The Australians could not have been trying to get through to Australia because they had not booked the calls."

An official statement from the Postmaster-general's Department says:—

"The calls were cancelled at 4.30 yesterday afternoon. The cancellation instructions came from Australia. If the Australians tried to get through this morning they must have been acting in ignorance of the fact that the calls have been cancelled."

Apparently the Australian cricketers had not been advised of this fact.

It is understood that a further attempt will be made from London on June 26.

The way the world was: bigger and more distant.

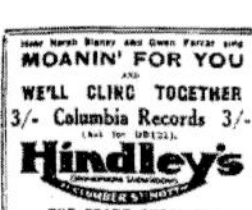

Nottingham Evening News — LATE EXTRA

No. 15,906 TELEPHONE 3211 (12 LINES). TUESDAY, 17 JUNE, 1930 PRICE ONE PENNY.

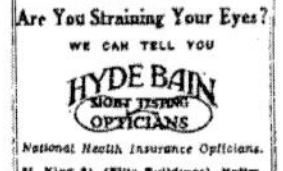

AUSTRALIAN RECORD-BREAKER'S THIRD CENTURY IN TESTS

BRADMAN HITS A CENTURY AND EQUALS MACLAREN'S TRENT BRIDGE FEAT.

D. G. BRADMAN.

AUSTRALIANS HOLD THEIR OWN IN A RACE WITH THE CLOCK: GREAT STRUGGLE FOR MASTERY.

BRILLIANT SWALLOW-DIVE CATCH BY COPLEY DISMISSES THE DASHING M^cCABE.

PONSFORD FINELY BOWLED BY A TATE "SPECIAL"

Bradman 131, First Test.

THE SYDNEY MORNING HERALD, TUESDAY, JULY 1, 1930.

COLOSSAL SCORING.

Bradman's Triumph at Lord's.

SEVERAL RECORDS BROKEN.

Highest Aggregate Exceeded.

LONDON, June 30.

In glorious weather, reminiscent of Australia, the second test match was continued to-day at Lord's.

At tea-time Woodfull declared, with the score at 729 for six wickets. The previous highest test aggregate is 636.

Bradman and Kippax carried on the batting which closed on Saturday with two wickets down for 404 runs, though they were not so brilliant as on the second day.

Bradman made 254 runs, the second highest score ever made in test cricket.

Before lunch he had broken two major records. He passed the previous highest score made by an Australian in a test match (W. L. Murdoch's 211 at the Oval in 1884), and became the highest individual scorer in test cricket in England.

The record individual score for a test match is 287, made by R. E. Foster at Sydney in 1903.

The mid-day weather forecast indicated a possibility of thunderstorms in the evening.

Bradman 254, Second Test.

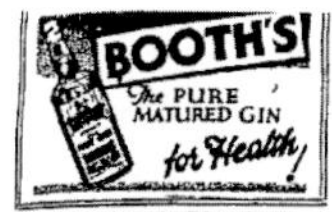

The Star
LONDON, FRIDAY, JULY 11, 1930.
No. 13147.
INDEPENDENT OF THE NEWSPAPER TRUSTS.
ONE PENNY.
6·30

BRADMAN'S 105 BEFORE LUNCH.

BOY WONDER BATSMAN EQUALS ANOTHER RECORD.

Australia Soon Lose Jackson But Bradman Alters The Tale.

PONSFORD NOT PLAYING.

Chapman's Lucky Coin Fails Him At Last.

AUSTRALIA 136 FOR 1. BRADMAN 105 NOT OUT.

Bradman, on his way to 334, Third Test.

NET SALES LARGER THAN THOSE OF ANY OTHER NEWSPAPER IN AUSTRALIA

THE SUN

No. 6149 SYDNEY : SATURDAY, JULY 26, 1930 PRICE 1d 'Phone: B.O. 333

UNSETTLED

Dramatic Duel: Mystery-bowler Peebles and Bradman

QUEER WICKET

CHAMPION FALLS TO NEW ATTACK

PONSFORD'S GREAT INNINGS

TAIL STIFFENS AFTER COLLAPSE SEEMED IMMINENT

("Sun" Special)

MANCHESTER, Friday.

There were many dramatic features in to-day's opening play in the fourth Test at the Old Trafford ground.

Woodfull and Ponsford, the latter giving his finest exhibition of the tour, stayed together till the score reached 107, but Bradman, who followed his captain, fell a victim to England's bowling "find," Peebles, when he had made only 14.

Ponsford, McCabe and Richardson all went within 20 minutes before tea, while only 8 runs were scored.

A remarkable display was given by Kippax, whose innings is described "as an extraordinary mixture of hard hitting and missing the ball." He should have been out a dozen times, but he made 51.

Stumps were drawn with seven wickets down for 275, Fairfax and Grimmett having made an unexpectedly stubborn stand.

Bradman 14, Fourth Test.

ANOTHER BRADMAN CENTURY.

BOY WONDER AGAIN TRANSFORMS GAME.

Bradman's Fourth Test Century Of The Present Tour.

NEAR ENGLAND'S TOTAL.

Third Wicket For Peebles: Good Catch By Wyatt.

AUSTRALIA 371 FOR 3 (Bradman not out 112)—Lunch.

Don Bradman, the " wonder boy " batsman—whose life story is being told exclusively in " The Star "—made his fourth century in the present Test series in the timeless final match at the Oval to-day, and greatly helped to place Australia in a formidable position.

Bradman, on his way to 232, Fifth Test.

WINNERS OF ASHES RETURN

CRICKETERS LIONISED IN ADELAIDE

CIVIC RECEPTION: LUNCHEON AT OVAL

W. M. Woodfull

The Australian cricketers reached the Outer Harbor on Saturday morning, and were feted throughout the whole of short time spent in Adelaide. With the exception of the four South Australians, the players rejoined the Oronsay in the afternoon and resumed the journey to the eastern States.

V. Y. Richardson

The Advertiser, Adelaide, 3 November.

DON BRADMAN.

Famous Cricketer Comes Home.

RECEPTION AT BOWRAL.

BOWRAL, Tuesday.

Don Bradman was accorded a civic reception on his arrival here this afternoon. A large crowd was present, and the band played "Our Don Bradman" as the famous cricketer, accompanied by his father, mother, sister, and brother, walked to the dais in the Corbett Gardens, which was occupied by a large number of civic representatives. Speeches of welcome were made by the Mayor (Alderman Sheaffe), Alderman South, acting-president of the Moss Vale and Southern Districts Cricket Association, and Alderman A. Westbrook, Bradman's former employer. Alderman Westbrook said that Bradman had come back the same carefree, unassuming, clear-eyed boy that he was when he went away eight months ago. Bradman replied briefly. He spoke of the team's wonderful experiences and of their welcomes, adding that, although some of the welcomes had been attended by greater numbers, none had been appreciated more than the one accorded him that day, because he was aware of its sincerity. He hoped to return to Bowral before long and renew old acquaintances.

Ten police were necessary to control the crowd.

Sydney Morning Herald, 5 November.

Bradman toured England another three times – 1934,1938 and 1948 – and became a giant equalled only by W.G. Grace himself. Here he leads the Australians out for the last time on English soil, at Scarborough. (Author's collection)

and Woodfull took a single from the third. Bradman superbly square cut the fifth to the boundary and steered the last to square leg. Bradman 136 at 2.42pm.

Geary kept his line and length, restricting Bradman to a single to point and Woodfull couldn't manage even that. Bradman 137 at 2.44pm.

Now Tate did establish some control and he, too, restricted Bradman to a single on the leg side. A voice in the crowd shouted: 'Put Leyland on!' but Chapman was poised to replace Tate with Hammond after a spell of only two overs. Like Geary, Hammond might be able to exercise a restraining influence. This single gave Bradman his 1,000th Test run, all scored against England. Bradman 138 at 2.47pm.

Woodfull drove Geary to the boundary and Hammond moved into a spell of sustained aggression although he couldn't stop Bradman feeding square leg for a single from his first ball. Woodfull played out the over. Bradman 139 at 2.52pm.

He fed square leg again from Geary with 2 from the first ball but the second produced a genuine sensation. He played too soon and poked it towards mid-on. It was safe because it didn't go near Tate, fielding there, but the crowd murmured 'Oh!' – one source describes this as a great, instinctive, communal gasp – that he lifted the ball at all in front of the wicket. The ball reared and Bradman 'feebly poked it up inches short of Tate'. (26) He placed a single to square leg from the third ball but Woodfull took one from the last and would face Hammond. Bradman 142 at 2.54pm, so that in thirty-six minutes he'd added 37.

Woodfull took a single from the final ball of that over and played out a maiden to Geary.

Bradman played out a maiden to Hammond and Woodfull didn't score from the first four balls of Geary's next over; more than five minutes without a run. Woodfull took a single from the fifth, however, and kept the strike. He didn't score off Hammond's first two balls and tried to turn the third but was bowled off his pads.

That was 3.05pm, Australia 194 for 2. The second wicket added 192 in two hours thirty-nine minutes. Woodfull had been slow, content with pushes and prods – he'd struck no more than four boundaries – but that wasn't the point. He wasn't even a foil for Bradman, really, but the dependable leader who kept the background safe so Bradman could exploit the foreground. Clearly he saw that Bradman might have saved or won Trent Bridge but, by Lord's, had become a match winner. Here

Woodfull, watching from the other end, had been given conclusive evidence. One of the most endearing of Woodfull's traits was that, as far as one can tell, he never said or did anything – even once – in his career to elbow himself into the foreground.

Kippax came in but wasn't comfortable at first and Geary conjured another maiden to Bradman.

Kippax got off the mark against Hammond and Bradman took 3 past mid-on. Bradman 145 at 3.10pm, his first run for an astonishing sixteen minutes. Carefully he moved towards the 150, steering Geary past point for 2 to bring up the Australian 200.

Bradman 147 at 3.14pm.

The new ball was available for Larwood and Tate. Larwood took it and Kippax played a maiden although he looked vulnerable and might have been bowled twice.

Bradman did nothing with the first ball of Tate's over but cover drove the second to the boundary. Bradman 151 at 3.19pm, so that in an hour and a minute he'd added 46. He'd been at the crease for ten minutes short of three hours and *The Yorkshire Post* tried to capture the overall mood:

> *'It was Bradman, Bradman all the way. It is almost impossible to describe his innings, because it was all of a piece. Any one period of it was just like any other. There was no crescendo, and very certainly no diminuendo; it was as eternal and spontaneous and delightful as a Bach fugue.*
>
> *'Once we had put aside partisanship, with the philosophical reflection that he might as well make the runs as the others, we could give ourselves up to pure enjoyment. He showed us every stroke [. . .] There were some magnificent shots through the covers that the fieldsman hardly moved for, while the spectators did what was necessary. By way of contrast there were some most delectable shots to the on, craftily placed to beat an astutely-stationed fielder, in spite of his efforts.'*

Larwood bowled a maiden to Kippax.

Bradman accelerated against Tate: a leg-side deflection for 2 – Leyland cut off the boundary – which took him past the ubiqutous Macartney and his 151 in 1926, making Bradman the highest scorer at Leeds in the Ashes series; a forcing shot past Sutcliffe at mid-off to the boundary, a 'really cheeky single' (27) to mid-on – Tate so physically subdued that they sprinted the single while he fielded the ball.

Here, or hereabouts, Bradman was tormenting Tyldesley by placing the ball near him and making Tyldesley run. Whether Bradman did this as a deliberate ploy to exhaust the weighty Lancashire bowler, to amuse himself or whether it just happened that way is lost for ever; but Tyldesley did some running, all right. 'The spectators laughed at Dick Tyldesley when the burly Lancastrian had to chase the ball but he stopped some pretty hot shots close in when the ball came within reasonable reach.' **(28)**

Bradman 158 at 3.26pm. He had the strike and worked Larwood to mid-on for a single, Kippax taking a single from the last ball. Bradman 159 at 3.27pm.

Tate bowled a maiden to Kippax and Bradman belted the first ball of Larwood's next over to the boundary, steered a single through the slips – and Kippax took a boundary, too, so that after nearly half an hour he was finding his rhythm. Bradman 164 at 3.33pm, so that in seventy minutes he'd added 59.

He dealt roughly with Hammond, a boundary and a single, both into the off side. Bradman 169 at 3.34pm.

By now runs flowed from Tate, a single to Bradman to mid-off, a single to Kippax on the leg side, a 2 to Bradman past point, another 2 to square leg. He was busy as a terrier, fast between the wickets.

'Old Ebor' wrote in *The Yorkshire Evening Post:* 'On the boundaries, Leyland, Sutcliffe and Duleepsinhji have been very active, though I have noted that Bradman generally placed his 4s out of reach of any of them. The pace of the outfield was very great. I have never seen the ball travel more quickly, especially on the slopes towards the members' stand and pavilion.'

Bradman 174 at 3.39pm.

Kippax took a single from Hammond and Bradman pounded a boundary past mid-on. Chapman had drawn his field back to try to save boundaries and Hobbs, at the age of 48, faced a long walk from cover to very deep extra cover when the overs ended but Chapman, Leyland and Duleepsinhji were walking a long way, too. Bradman 178 at 3.43pm.

Kippak took a single from Tate and Bradman 2, again to mid-on. Bradman 180 at 3.45pm so that in eighty-six minutes he'd added 75. He'd moved from 159 in thirteen minutes. Hammond was bowling as well as any of the others but barely a ball got past the bat to Duckworth, who was having the equivalent of an afternoon off. The innings just went on and on.

Hammond could find maidens against Kippax, and did.

Tyldesley came on for Tate and, as someone ironically remarked, probably enjoyed this because while he was bowling he couldn't be in the deep puffing after the drives Bradman taunted him with for so long. Bradman hammered Tyldesley's first ball to the mid-on boundary and Tyldesley watched it, watched somebody else in vain pursuit. The third ball is itself historical. Bradman went up the wicket but this once couldn't dictate the length and changed his mind. He turned and as he fell on to his knee cut the ball for a single *from the middle of the bat.* It wasn't so much that he had time to do this, more that he was operating in a different time zone.

The *Nottingham Journal* caught the moment. Bradman's innings 'was just easy batting all round the wicket by a cricketer who seemed to know what every ball was doing and how he intended to play it as soon as it had left the bowler's hand'. The cut as he fell demonstrates perfectly his 'mobility of eye, hand and foot'.

Bradman 185 at 3.50pm.

Kippax hit Hammond to the mid-on boundary. Bradman steered a single from Tyldesley, again working the favoured mid-on route. Bradman 186 at 3.54pm.

Chapman summoned Leyland from the deep to bowl his left-arm orthodox spin, which Fender called a grave error because Chapman ought to have been either trying to pressure or restrict Bradman with his 200 so close. Leyland was in no sense a Test match bowler and the great cheer from the Yorkshire crowd wasn't going to conceal that. His initial over developed into a shambles even with four men in the deep. Bradman hooked the first two balls for 2 into the mid-on area, didn't score from the third, hooked full tosses to the on-side boundary from the fourth and fifth and worked a single to the on-side from the last. Every shot had been played along the ground. Bradman 199 at 3.58pm.

He faced Tyldesley and did nothing with the first ball. He played back to the next and was so quick he almost seemed to wait for it to reach him. He prodded it gently and defensively into the on-side and turned away; a clear separation between the strokes not intended to produce runs and those which were. He faced Tyldesley's third ball, went back on to the stumps and guided it – a caress – into the business area past point. No fielder stood there, an acre of ground open to him. He trotted the single.

Bradman 200 at 4pm, so that in two hours two minutes he'd added 95. Only 66 runs came at the other end, or 67 if you count the one bye. No man had ever made two Test double centuries before, never mind in consecutive matches, and that was partly the wonder of it. Before the clock reached 4pm on this Friday afternoon, a double century defined a whole career, proclaiming that only five batsman had been capable of such a feat. That they'd only achieved it once did not diminish the sense of wonder and awe it had been done at all. Australia and England had been playing Tests against each other since 1876 and, as we've seen, Hammond made his 251 in 1928, Murdoch his 211 in 1884, Gregory his 201 in 1894–95, Foster his 287 in 1903–04, Ryder his 201 in 1924–25. That was all until Lord's. Now this. Nor could anyone doubt that far from defining his whole career this represented a beginning. Bradman teemed with runs, against everyone everywhere.

He took a single to point from the second ball of Leyland's next over, Kippax a single, Bradman another single to mid-on. The Australian innings was a compound of savagery and systematic accumulation, mounting and mounting. Bradman 202 at 4.03pm.

At last he made another mistake, lofting Tyldesley's first ball towards mid-on but Tate, fielding there, was 'curiously slow' **(29)** to set off. He ran backwards but couldn't reach the ball and perhaps, after so much bowling, was just plain tired. Kippax took a single and Bradman struck a boundary though mid-on.

Bradman 207 at 4.05pm. Since lunch he'd made 102 and become the first player to score a Test century before lunch and another before tea, with plenty of time in the afternoon session to score more. The session of a Test lasted two hours (11.30am to 1.30pm), the afternoon session two hours ten minutes (2.20pm to 4.30pm), extending Bradman's possibilities.

Chapman persisted with Leyland and both batsmen took two singles. Bradman 209 at 4.08pm. Tyldesley toiled on, and from him Bradman took a single with the off-glance. Bradman 210 at 4.10pm, so that in a hundred and twelve minutes he'd added 105.

He was eking out singles now and, if he safely negotiated the twenty minutes to tea, *every* significant individual Test record came into view, his own 254 at Lord's as the highest by an Australian, Foster's 287 which he coveted so much and ultimately Sandham's 325.

He off-glanced Leyland for a single. Bradman 211 at 4.12pm.

He played a maiden to Tyldesley, who looked the only bowler with the control to contain him in any serious way. Kippax took a 2 and a single from Leyland, a single from Tyldesley's next over. Bradman worked a single to mid-on and Kippax played the over out. Bradman 212 at 4.18pm.

He contented himself with a single past point from the final ball of Leyland's over. Bradman 213 at 4.20pm.

He contented himself with another single past point from the fourth ball of Tyldesley's over, ten minutes to tea. Bradman 214 at 4.22pm.

Leyland's bowling remained a tempting target and Bradman seems to have had no thoughts of safety through docility to tea. He hammered the second ball to the mid-on boundary and positioned the fourth into the covers for a single, an area he hardly raided for singles during the entire innings. Bradman 219 at 4.25pm.

Kippax nipped a single to keep the strike and played out a maiden to Tyldesley. That gave Bradman the strike and he completed his afternoon by stroking Leyland into the off side for a single. Bradman 220 at 4.29pm, so that in two hours thirteen minutes he'd added 115. The whole innings had lasted four hours three minutes. At moments in the last half hour before tea, however, he'd looked tired. Kippax struck a boundary two balls later and the Australians took tea at 305 for 2.

The 220 represented the highest score anyone had ever made in a Test match by tea on any day. More worrying for Chapman, Bradman looked fresh and hungry for more, a lot more, after his cup of tea had refreshed the tiredness out of him. He looked limitless. He said [(30)] that he started to think seriously about Foster and the 287 at tea. The crowd still grew by the minute and reached 25,000 when the players emerged. No doubt they were thinking about Foster and the 287, too. Bradman resolved to ration himself to safe scoring strokes.

At 4.50pm Larwood opened the bowling to Bradman who cut the third ball to the boundary and pulled the last for 3. Bradman 227 at 4.54pm.

Tyldesley bowled from the other end. They ran a bye from the third ball and Kippax took a single to keep the strike from the last.

Larwood couldn't contain either of them: Kippax a single, Bradman a single past point, Kippax a single from the fourth, Bradman a single into the covers, Kippax a single. Bradman 229 at 4.59pm.

From Tyldesley, Kippax took a single and Bradman another when he placed the ball into the mid-off area. Bradman 230 at 5.01pm, so that in eleven minutes he'd added 10. He turned Larwood's fifth ball to the square-leg boundary, the timing perfect. Bradman 234 at 5.04pm.

Kippax took a single from Tyldesley, Bradman another to mid-off. The Australian innings remained a compound of savagery and systematic accumulation, mounting and mounting, and nothing could stop it. Bradman 235 at 5.07pm.

He plundered Larwood to the mid-off boundary from the first ball of the over, picked up a couple to mid-on from the fifth. Bradman 241 at 5.11pm, so that in twenty minutes he'd added 21.

After tea Bradman 'kept up the wonderful form which he had shown from the first ball bowled him', Warner wrote. 'He had a stroke for every ball, and he went on his way serenely. To call him a run-getting machine, as he has been called, is a poor compliment; that rather implies that the runs are ground out with a roar and a clash and a clatter, while in fact he makes his runs easily and smoothly and naturally, with the mark of genius throughout. He is never in flurries or in any apparent hurry, and yet runs come from his bat as bullets from a machine-gun; there has never been a batsman who in match after match has claimed such a huge proportion of the runs scored.' [(31)] The 241 was out of 332, and of this third wicket partnership he'd made 99 of the 141.

Kippax, all lissom grace, was creating a beautiful innings of delicacy and sophistication at a steady rate. He took a single from Tyldesley, Bradman a single past point, Kippax 3 from the final ball. Bradman 242 at 5.14pm.

Tate came on for Larwood. Bradman had given Larwood another pounding and now he did the same to Tate. Initially, however, Kippax took a single from the fourth ball of Tate's opening over, retaining the strike.

In the next over from Tyldesley they took two singles each, Bradman retaining the strike. Bradman at 244 at 5.19pm.

He did pound Tate, pumping the third ball to the mid-on boundary and 3 to the same place from the last. Was it now that Duckworth called out: 'Maurice, you said in Australia you'd get Don out in England. What about trying?'

'You'd better try yourself, Ducky, I've had enough.' (32)

Bradman 251 at 5.21pm, so that in thirty-one minutes he'd added 31 and maintained exquisitely the run-a-minute ratio. His whole innings had taken four hours thirty-five minutes.

He took a single from Tyldesley to mid-on, 2 from the final ball. Bradman 254 at 5.24pm. He'd now equalled his score at Lord's and, sending the fifth ball of Tate's next over scurrying to square leg for 2, went past it. Bradman 256 at 5.26pm. The comparison: Lord's took five hours thirty-nine minutes, this work-in-progress not yet five hours. No announcement was made but the crowd were perfectly well aware he'd gone past his Lord's total and gave him a warm cheer.

Tyldesley was now shipping heavy punishment, and it would have been even heavier but Kippax couldn't find the gaps in the field. He took a single, Bradman another into the covers from the next ball and the systematic accumulation went on. Bradman 257 at 5.28pm.

He cut a single past slip but Kippax took a 2 and a single to keep the strike. Bradman 258 at 5.29pm.

Kippax played a maiden to Tyldesley. Bradman cut Tate for 2, cut him again for a single from the last ball.

Bradman 261 at 5.34pm so that in forty-four minutes he'd added 41, slipping slightly behind the ratio. In the same time Kippax added 23 so the cumulative run rate was 65 in the forty-four minutes, created without risk and under great control. The England attack wasn't being blasted or dismembered but remorselessly crushed, minute by minute. The close of play wasn't until 6.30pm . . .

Bradman took a single to mid-off from Tyldesley's fourth ball, Kippax a couple from the last ball. Bradman 262 at 5.36pm.

Sometime around here someone in the crowd shouted: 'Put Duckworth on!' Chapman ignored that and signalled Geary to replace Tate. Bradman hammered the first ball to the mid-off boundary, hammered the third to the mid-off boundary, too. Geary bowled without a slip and spread three fielders in a distant, protective arc: one behind the bowler on the boundary, a long-on and long-off. Bradman 270 at 5.39pm, so that in forty-nine minutes he'd added 50, the two boundaries lifting him above the ratio again.

Tyldesley toiled on, Kippax a single, Bradman a single into the covers to keep the strike. Tyldesley shared the philosophy of so many slow bowlers in that he'd usually be content if batsmen hit him – it would lead them to fatal error. Now he was forced to set the same field as Geary. Only Tate was able to maintain a normal field.

Bradman 271 at 5.41pm.

He took 2 to mid-on from the second ball of Geary's next over but appeared to touch a ball to Duckworth and Duckworth, impossibly intoxicated, appealed as he dropped it. Bradman, showing no sign of being unnerved, took a rare single to cover from the fifth ball. Bradman 274 at 5.44pm.

Leyland replaced Tyldesley but Bradman contented himself with a single to mid-off from the fourth ball. Kippax, however, clipped the last through point to the boundary. Bradman 275 at 5.47pm.

Geary toiled on. Bradman worked a single to square leg, Kippax a single, Bradman 2 past slip from the final ball. Bradman 278 at 5.49pm.

The systematic accumulation ticked on: Kippax a single from Leyland and Bradman played out the last four balls; Kippax a single from Geary and Bradman a single past slip. Kippax played the last two balls, giving Bradman the strike. Bradman 279 at 5.53pm.

He played the first ball of Leyland's next over towards mid-off and they ran the single. Bradman 280 at 5.55pm, so that in sixty-five minutes he'd added 60, falling a little further behind the nominal ratio although Kippax was scoring more freely now.

Kippax didn't score from the next four balls but took a single from the last to bring Australia's 400 up from 124 overs in five hours nineteen minutes, and that was the real ratio in the context of the match. Spread over the whole day to here they averaged 1.2 runs a minute, 3.2 runs an over.

The crowd fell silent because they sensed within a few moments they'd see Foster's bastion, secure since December 1903, stormed and conquered. You could feel the tension right round the ground.

Larwood took the new ball and even with it could only afford one slip and a gully because he needed to reinforce the covers and deep square leg. Kippax took a single from the third ball, Bradman a square cut for 3 from the fifth. Bradman 283 at 6pm.

Tate shared the new ball. Bradman hooking him cleanly and decisively to the mid-on boundary, bringing him level with Foster to a mighty roar of applause. That was 6.02pm.

He did not linger because it wasn't that kind of innings and he wasn't that kind of man. From the next ball he hooked a single and Leeds surrendered completely to him. It touched him deeply. The game halted. The acclaim couldn't have been greater if it had all happened at Sydney. He hoisted his bat high while this rolling thunder of applause went on and on. The enthusiasm was so intense play couldn't be resumed until it finally softened back into silence.

Bradman's 288 took five hours fourteen minutes, Foster's 287 six hours nine minutes. Such comparisons can never be accurate, or perhaps fair, but Bradman had almost beaten the 287 at Lord's, was now past it and not out. In context Bradman reached the bastion very, very quickly and conquered it the moment after that. The 287 represented the climax of Foster's career and, in the whole Ashes series, a climactic event. Bradman could continue at the nominal ratio to . . . who knew where? He was 21; England faced another two *decades* of this. Quietly, so far in the background, stood Andrew Sandham and his 325. Nobody seemed to see or remember him. We shall see. Kippax rounded the over off with a boundary and a 2.

Bradman sent Larwood to the mid-off boundary with a rasping, crackling drive and placed the next ball past slip for a single, the innings continuing in its normal way. Bradman 293 at 6.05pm, so that in seventy-five minutes he'd added 73, just about back on the ratio.

At last Tate's persistence was rewarded because Kippax cut a ball high to Chapman near point, and he caught it: Australia 423 for 3. Kippax and Bradman put on 229 in two hours forty-three minutes.

Bradman lay down, stretched fully out and buried his face in the grass – instant rest and recuperation – while young McCabe strode to the wicket. It was the only sign in the whole evening session of tiredness.

They ran a bye, and McCabe took a single from Larwood's first ball. Bradman took one to cover from the next. Was a little legend born from this ball? They sprinted so fast that McCabe said: 'Steady on, you'll exhaust me!' Perhaps Bradman, deep into the fifth hour of such sprints inside his marathon, smiled. Perhaps McCabe said it for effect and the fielders laughed. They needed one. McCabe played out the over, during which they ran 4 byes. Was *that* when the mini-legend was born . . . ?

Bradman 294 at 6.13pm. He struck Tate to the cover boundary and played out the over. Bradman 298 at 6.15pm.

Hammond came on and McCabe attacked, two boundaries from the first two balls, and they ran a leg bye. Bradman pushed the fourth ball past slip – the off-glance? Bradman 299 at 6.20pm.

He worked the first ball of Tate's next over into the leg side for a single. Bradman 300 at 6.22pm, so that in ninety-two minutes he'd added 80, the ratio gone from him. He'd been at the crease for five hours thirty-six minutes. No man, of course, had scored a triple century in an Ashes Test before and all at once Foster's 287 must have seemed in the past in every sense.

McCabe took 2 before they ran another leg bye, Bradman a single on the leg side. Bradman 301 at 6.26pm.

Tate prepared to bowl the final over of the day and might reasonably have assumed that Bradman, satiated and playing for tomorrow, would defend. He cut the second ball to the boundary and, triumphantly, off-drove the fifth there, too.

A moment later they walked off, Bradman looking perfectly fresh. A policeman in a bell-shaped helmet came out to try and hold the crowd back. Bradman, bare headed – his hair perfectly parted, not a hair out of place – moved past this policeman. He sleeves were rolled up and neatly folded at the elbows. He held the bat in his right hand, the batting gloves in the left. He smiled, and it looked the smile of deepest satisfaction. Behind him McCabe, wearing the baggy green cap, followed and further away Tyldesley applauded. These three cricketers cast elongated shadows across the pitch as they came. It was evening, and such an evening as cricket has rarely seen. When they reached the members' enclosure another policeman led them through a narrow human corridor, hands slapping Bradman's back and shoulders as he went.

Australia were 458 for 3, Bradman 309 and McCabe 12. The off-drive gave him 2,000 runs for the season, the youngest batsman to have achieved that. In this session of a hundred and thirty-two minutes he'd added 89. During the day he'd hit forty-two boundaries and lifted the ball no more than two or three times.

Several newspapers wrote freely about how he had broken the Test record for a highest score, making no mention of Sandham.

Bradman said he must cable home because of course 'they will want to hear about this'. He added: 'My feet are awfully tired, but I could have gone on if it hadn't been the close. I did not know I was so near Foster's record until Kippax told me. I am very happy to have beaten the record, but happier still to think that Australia is in such a good position.' [(33)]

Even today (1 January 2009) only Hammond has reached 300 in a Test quicker – four hours forty-eight minutes, England v New Zealand at Auckland in 1932–33 – than Bradman's five hours thirty-six. He remains the fastest to 200 – three hours thirty-four against the three hours thirty-seven of Nathan J. Astle, New Zealand v England at Christchurch in 2001–02. Bradman's 105 by lunch remained the biggest innings in a Test before lunch until Majid Khan (108*) beat it for Pakistan against New Zealand at Karachi in 1976–77.

R.E. Foster was dead but one of his brothers, Basil – who'd played for Middlesex and Worcestershire – sent a telegram to Bradman congratulating him. [34]

Mailey happened to be sitting in the pavilion and, when Larwood was bowling ineffectively at Bradman, Warner said to Lord Hawke bowling at Bradman was about the same as throwing stones at the rock of Gibraltar. Perhaps that captures the innings best of all.

An hour after play ended, three men arrived at the Kirkstall Lane end fully intending to see the following day's play. They were two brothers from Newcastle who had come down by bus and a man from Nottingham, F. Stone, who evidently had seen the Test there and been delighted by Bradman's batting. When he read in the evening paper of what Bradman was doing 'I decided there and then to set off for Leeds'. He put on his raincoat and hat and did set off.

The *Sun,* Sydney, reported that 'tonight is Bradman night. Nobody and nothing else is talked about at the Queen's Hotel. Groups sit around toasting Bradman and discussing today's epic, but Bradman unobtrusively dined in the grill room. He made so many records that two escaped almost unnoticed – his 2,000 in England, which he reached off the last ball of the day, and his 1,000 in Tests. Bradman is resting tonight, hoping to add another hundred tomorrow, thereby passing the highest first-class score in England.'

This Friday was a cold night and 'I could not get to sleep for it. The brothers and I passed the time away by taking strolls up and down the lane.' A man and his wife arrived at midnight and bedded down. They slept until 6am when the bells of nearby St. Michael's Church rang out. They woke to another cloudless sky, bright sunshine and a little breeze. They had breakfast: a thermos flask of tea, ham sandwiches and fruit. As they ate, people began to arrive and by 7am well over 1,000 waited for the gates to open. The queue in St. Michael's Lane stretched a couple of hundred yards and by 9am had 800 in it. A reporter was surprised to note how many were women. By 9.30am at least 5,000 people were in the ground.

A huge crowd gathered at the Wellington Station entrance of the Queen's Hotel for a glimpse of Bradman as he left for the ground but he slipped out another way and most never did see him. He seems to have emerged from a side or rear entrance because a *Yorkshire Evening Post* photographer took a picture of him coming down four shallow steps with a couple of people around him. He wore a suit and hat, waistcoat, collar and tie, and he could have passed for a businessman. Someone middle-aged advanced towards him holding out a bat for signature but he wasn't having any of that.

They saw the England players, some being given lifts by players who had cars. Hammond and Hendren travelled together.

At 10.30am, at least 13,000 were inside Headingley and more coming the whole time. Excited schoolboys sat in the grass. As the 11am resumption neared, outside Headingley 'hundreds of enthusiasts were rushing about and perspiring freely, mounted police were busily engaged in dealing with the multitude of cars, and huge queues stretched from each and every entrance. There was clamour and bustle everywhere. The turnstiles clicked furiously but could not cope with the rush, and at one time in this road alone [St. Michael's] there was anything up to 2,000 spectators seeking admission.' [35] In modern parlance it was Brad-mania.

Woodfull ordered the light roller.

Under brilliant sunshine, 18,000–20,000 were inside when 'the England team strolled on to the field and were followed more briskly by Bradman and McCabe'. Bradman was smiling broadly as he came through the corridor of members who'd spilt out on to the pitch, McCabe close behind. They applauded both batsmen who were now out on to the pitch itself and moving past an arc of twelve cameramen. [36]

The dominant topic of conversation was *how far can Bradman go?* He recorded [37] how people thought *he* thought he might get 500 and added that he wasn't thinking like that at all. He also recorded how, just before he resumed the innings, a telegram was handed to him saying 'Your house is on fire and your girl wants you' – presumably a crude attempt to destabilise him. If that's what it was it didn't work. When he appeared the crowd gave him a great ovation spiced by an overwhelming sense of anticipation.

The crowd must have been growing quickly because it would reach 33,000. At 11am, Larwood opened the bowling to McCabe from the

Kirkstall Lane end, and McCabe announced immediately that he was going to chase runs. He cut the second ball square for 2 and hooked the next, a bad length, behind square leg to the boundary – but cocked the last one up. It didn't go near a fielder. The wicket looked slightly faster than the Friday – Bradman described it as much faster – but even Larwood couldn't get the ball to rise. It looked ominous already because McCabe felt able to hit Larwood rather than just play him or indeed play himself in.

Bradman made an immediate announcement, too. He played defensively to Tate's first ball but drove the second, a long hop, to the cover point boundary without leaving the crease. Tate had a sort of umbrella field: slip, gully and point to one side, short square leg (Larwood) and orthodox mid-on (Tyldesley) to the other. Bradman stood motionless as Tate ran up to bowl the fourth ball. It was a good length but he had already gone on to the back foot, creating space to on-drive it with complete economy of movement, the stroke more a controlled flick. The ball was struck so square that it only just went past Larwood, who, as the other bowler, didn't give chase. Tyldesley, moving with surprising speed, did but they ran three eager runs. The *Evening Standard* commented wrily that 'it is Bradman's delight to pick Tyldesley out in the field and make him run'. Tate, the willing workhorse, simply couldn't find pace off this wicket and had only one slip – Larwood only two. Bradman 316 at 11.06am.

That kept him the strike and he took a single from the first ball of Larwood's next over. McCabe didn't score from the remaining five. Bradman 317 at 11.08am.

A devastating thought crossed the mind of the *Nottingham Journal* reporter. Bradman, fresh, not in the least weary from the previous day, was playing himself in for a fourth hundred.

Tate bowled a maiden to Bradman to loud cheering and McCabe took on Larwood: two boundaries, a hook past square leg, a drive through mid-off which poor Tyldesley tried to field by using his feet. ('Tyldesley at mid-off could not bend quickly enough.' [38] Perhaps that amused the crowd, and perhaps it didn't because it meant 22 runs had been added in thirteen minutes. What Chapman and the England team thought is not recorded but they can only have contemplated the rest of the day with mounting horror. Bradman would kill you over a long period of time, McCabe might kill you quickly. Now it was happening simultaneously.

Bradman took a single from Tate to mid-on, and from a slower ball McCabe sent a perfect off-drive to the boundary. It seemed to fizz. Bradman 318 at 11.17am.

He took a single to mid-on from the first ball of Larwood's next over but McCabe tried to drive the second – Bradman described it as unplayable – and was bowled leg stump. Australia were 486 for 4.

Richardson came in and late cut his first ball for a single. Bradman turned the next ball off his toes to the square leg boundary 'with that peculiar short-arm stroke of his' **(39)** and it travelled so quickly it skipped across into the spectators – an unusual shot because it was pitched well up and on the middle stump. The next ball went clean through him but didn't hit the stumps. Bradman 323 at 11.23am, so that in twenty-three minutes he'd added 14.

Tate bowled to Richardson who tried to on-drive him but spooned a catch to Larwood at short leg, making Australia 491 for 5. a'Beckett played out the over. Bradman took a single past slip – the off-glance? – from the first ball of Larwood's next over and a'Beckett got off the mark with a 2. Bradman 324 at 11.28am.

He cut Tate's second ball for 2 – 'a lovely, light cut' **(40)** which might have gone to the boundary but Duleepsinhji headed it off. That made Australia 496, the highest Test score ever made at Headingley, beating the 494 of 1926. He had now beaten Sandham and become beyond dispute the highest scorer in a Test innings, but no contemporary account seems to mention this. Perhaps a clue lies in *Wisden.* In the winter of 1929–30 the MCC sent out two teams, one via Australia to New Zealand where they played a four-match series, each called a Test. The other party, to the West Indies, also played a four-match series, but these *Wisden* called Representative Matches. No doubt in 1930, and specifically at Leeds, they weren't counted as Test records.

Whatever, Bradman pummelled the last ball of this Tate over straight to the sightscreen, another perfect stroke and only the third he'd placed there in the entire innings. It flew to the boundary 'at tremendous speed' **(41)** and struck the sightscreen with a thump so loud the whole ground heard it. No fielder could have got near, or did. Bradman 330 at 11.33am, so that in thirty-three minutes he'd added 21.

a'Beckett looked uncomfortable against Larwood and although he cut him to the boundary an inswinger almost bowled him.

Bradman faced Tate. He latecut the second ball to the boundary and tried the same stroke to the fifth but it had width. He missed. Tate, seeing perhaps sudden weakness and opportunity – a few moments before, Bradman had slashed at Larwood – bowled what seemed to be an identical delivery. It wasn't. It was tighter. 'Not in the whole innings did I have a ball from Tate like the last one,' Bradman would say. [42] 'My intention was to drive it hard between mid-on and the bowler. I stepped back so as to hit it hard but the ball came in [. . .] My bat was at a certain angle to make the stroke I intended, and the result was that the ball was only touched as it passed into Duckworth's hands.' Duckworth caught it to an animal roar from what was now a packed crowd. Duckworth's appeal was so loud that one reporter felt sure it must have been heard in the city centre.

Bradman 334 at 11.39am, so that in forty minutes he'd added 25. He'd been at the crease six hours twenty-three minutes, scoring his runs at 52 an hour without hitting a 6. The forty-six boundaries had been enough.

As he turned towards the pavilion the noise went on and on. *The Times* described it as an 'uproar' which could likely be heard as far afield as Sheffield while 'Bradman, quite composedly, ambled back to the pavilion'. He did this slowly, and he was smiling. The impression in the Press Box was that he was savouring the moment. *The Yorkshire Evening News* reported that he 'seemed deeply touched by this ovation, because suddenly his usual bright sunny smile vanished, momentarily suggesting that a lump had come into his throat'. The *Nottingham Journal* wrote that he 'walked calmly back to the pavilion like a man modestly proud of his achievement.'

A 14-year-old was in that crowd, watching intently. He was called Leonard Hutton and he'd get past the 334 to another uproar eight years later. By then, as we have seen, Hammond would be past it, too, although against weak New Zealand which gave it a Sandham context: a record but not really *the* record.

Bradman's dismissal made Australia 508 for 6. a'Beckett and Grimmett indulged themselves in some hitting to take the score to 566 and England closed the day on 212 for 5.

By this stage Brad-mania swept Australia, too. The *Sun,* Sydney, quoted many former cricketers who expressed awe and one official said Bradman's club, St. George, had cabled him to take it easy because they were sending him so many cables of congratulation it was affecting their finances.

'Most excited of all the cricket fans in Sydney last night was the family of Mr. and Mrs. Frank Cush, of Kogarah, where Don Bradman lives when he is in Sydney. Mr. Cush listened in 'til stumps were drawn, and Miss Murray, Neville Cush and a neighbor, Mr. Primrose, grew more and more excited as Don's wonderful score kept mounting. "It was gorgeous! Why, it only seems a couple of days ago that Don was showing the boys how to play in the backyard," said Mrs Cush.'

The *Sun* sent a reporter out to 'the little bungalow in Glebe-street, Bowral' to interview his parents. George Bradman said he'd describe his son's batting as 'a freak. There is no other term which adequately describes it.' Mrs. Bradman explained that she was kept busy answering cables and letters of congratulations and if her son broke any more records she didn't know how she'd handle the quantity.

The players – they were at the same hotel, remember – evidently saw little of each other on the Sunday rest day. 'The Australians were late risers, having breakfast served in bed. In the afternoon motor trips were taken in the surrounding countryside. Tate was the only English player to stay in the hotel, and he spent the morning describing Bradman's innings with graphic features to friends in the lounge.' (43)

Before play resumed on the Monday, an *Evening Standard* reporter called Clyde Foster went to the Queen's Hotel to try and interview Bradman. Tebbutt of the *Australian Press Association* was there and perhaps smoothed the way because, despite the restrictions on talking to the Press, Bradman spoke without formality in his room.

Foster wrote that Bradman began with an amazing confession. 'I never train. I just live like anybody else. Perhaps I may say that I do nothing to put myself out of condition. And I do not smoke. I don't drink. I eat what I like and ask no questions. I sleep soundly and – well, is not that just what might be said of every other young fellow who plays games?'

Foster suggested he'd modelled himself on Trumper, Grace [!] and the ubiquitous Macartney. Bradman replied: 'Sorry to say it but – no! I had seen only two days of a first-class fixture before I found myself playing in one.'

Foster made Bradman laugh by recounting that he'd heard a man in the street in Leeds say: 'There don't seem to be nowt of him but w'en 'e gets at 't bowling he fairly thrashes it, don't 'e?'

Foster wondered what Bradman weighed and ventured nearer 9st than 10. Bradman pointed out it was nearer 11 than 10, and just then Foster noticed how wide his shoulders were, accounting for the weight. He reminded Bradman that his wrists had been likened to steel but Bradman shrugged that off by rolling up his sleeves. The three men indulged in an arm-wrestling contest. Tebbutt won, Foster came second and Bradman third. Bradman reckoned that if you compared his wrists with those of Hobbs or Tate theirs would be twice as big.

So Foster wondered what the secret was. 'I am trying all the time to find out what is in the bowler's mind as he delivers the ball. It is a constant battle, one man against another – I to hit him and he to beat me.'

Foster mentioned that Bradman seemed to be able to bat for hours without lifting the ball and the crowds were commenting on that. Bradman explained that if he hit into the air but mis-hit it the consequences could be serious but if he mis-hit along the ground he'd be safe. He pointed out that on the whole tour so far he'd hit only two 6s, at Oxford and against Hampshire.

The talk over, Foster left but noticed a queue of boys waiting to try and get Bradman's autograph.

Rain on this third day gave England a chance of saving the match. They followed on and finished at 95 for 3 although Bradman cleverly ran Hobbs out. Grimmett was bowling and Bradman fielded deep enough to suggest quick singles could be taken to him. Hobbs played one there and set off but Bradman had come five yards closer.

The series remained alive at 1-1 with two Tests to play.

The *Nottingham Journal* reporter reflected that the Test

> *'will be enshrined in* Wisden *as Bradman's match. Twenty years hence [. . .] there will have been many fresh records made to eclipse it statistically but my impression of it is not in the least statistical. He made his runs so regularly and easily that his centuries seemed no longer than bright twenties by a care-free hitter.*
>
> *'The preachers – and there are many of them here early and late – have already fastened on Bradman as a pulpit homily on the merit of non-drinking and non-smoking. His feat has extended the interest in cricket among classes hitherto unversed in its technique or legend. Here in Leeds Bradmanism has been all pervasive. Hotels, shops, trams and music-halls have echoed and re-echoed his name.'*

By now news reached the English Press that Bradman was a private in the Illawarra Regiment and when he got home he'd be considered for promotion before studying for a commission. There was also talk of a public testimonial for him in Sydney.

The question, however, was what would Bradman do next in England. Before anyone could know the answer to that, something completely unexpected, and eventually controversial, happened.

ENGLAND V AUSTRALIA – THIRD TEST

Leeds, 11, 12, 14, 15 July. Drawn.

AUSTRALIA

*W.M. Woodfull	b Hammond		50
A.A. Jackson	c Larwood	b Tate	1
D.G. Bradman	c Duckworth	b Tate	334
A.F. Kippax	c Chapman	b Tate	77
S.J. McCabe		b Larwood	30
V.Y. Richardson	c Larwood	b Tate	1
E.L. a'Beckett	c Chapman	b Geary	29
+W.A. Oldfield	c Hobbs	b Tate	2
C.V. Grimmett	c Duckworth	b Tyldesley	24
T.W. Wall		b Tyldesley	3
P.M. Hornibrook		not out	1
Extras	(b 5, lb 8, w 1)		14
Total			566

1-2, 2-194, 3-423, 4-486, 5-491,
6-508, 7-519, 8-544, 9-565

	O	M	R	W
Larwood	33	3	139	1
Tate	39	9	124	5
Geary	35	10	95	1
Tyldesley	33	5	104	2
Hammond	17	3	46	1
Leyland	11	0	44	0

ENGLAND

J.B. Hobbs	c a'Beckett	b Grimmett	29		run out	13
H. Sutcliffe	c Hornibrook	b Grimmett	32		not out	28
W.R. Hammond	c Oldfield	b McCabe	113	c Oldfield	b Grimmett	35
K.S. Duleepsinhji	b Hornibrook		35	c Grimmett	b Hornibrook	10
M. Leyland	c Kippax	b Wall	44		not out	1
G. Geary		run out	0			
+G. Duckworth	c Oldfield	b a'Beckett	33			
*A.P.F. Chapman		b Grimmett	45			
M.W. Tate	c Jackson	b Grimmett	22			
H. Larwood		not out	10			
R.K. Tyldesley	c Hornibrook	b Grimmett	6			
Extras	(b 9, lb 10, nb 3)		22	(lb 8)		8
Total			391	(3 wkts)		95

1-53, 2-64, 3-123, 4-206, 5-206,
6-289, 7-319, 8-370, 9-375

1-24, 2-72, 3-94

	O	M	R	W	O	M	R	W
Wall	40	12	70	1	10	3	20	0
a'Beckett	28	8	47	1	11	4	19	0
Grimmett	56.2	16	135	5	17	3	33	1
Hornibrook	41	7	94	1	11.5	5	14	1
McCabe	10	4	23	1	2	1	1	0

Chapter Eight

14

WHEN ENGLAND BATTED AT LEEDS, REPLYING TO AUSTRALIA'S 566, Sutcliffe was second out for 21 with the total at 64. As Sutcliffe went off the Australian twelfth man, Hurwood, came on with a telegram which he gave to Bradman. It read: '*Kindly convey my congratulations to Bradman. Tell him I wish him to accept £1,000 as a token of my admiration of his performance.* [signed] *Arthur Whitelaw.*' Because the telegram had been delivered to the Australian dressing room during play Kelly replied to it. '*Bradman on field. Kindly accept deepest gratitude on his behalf. Wonderful generosity.*'

Whitelaw, *The Sydney Morning Herald* reported under a London dateline:

> *'Is a member of the firm of Fleming and Whitelaw, and has lived in London for six years. He owes his fortune to a patent soapmaking process, and is well known in Australian circles here for his generosity and sportsmanship. He is an admirable bridge player, and resides at Mansion Apartments, Portland-place. He said: "I am an Australian born and bred. I thought Bradman's performance merited such recognition as it would be useful to a young fellow on the threshold of his career. Boxers get more for far less important achievements. We must encourage our cricketers in every possible way, since cricket is the greatest of all games. This is not so*

much a gift as a mark of appreciation on behalf of Australians."

'Mr. Whitelaw, who has given this tangible retort to tales of Australian depression, is a grey-haired middle-aged man, of tall and well-knit figure with twinkling blue eyes and considerable charm of manner. He pointed to a large photograph of the Australian team. He admitted he had not yet met any of them, but had seen them play at Lord's. He was a keen cricketer himself when young.'

Bradman says that when he was given the telegram he assumed it was a practical joke but Woodfull assured him it wasn't and he almost felt in a dream as he resumed his fielding place on the boundary on the leg side. [(1)] Bradman makes no further comment except to say that when he was in London again the first thing he'd do was thank Whitelaw.

Tebbutt, reflecting in his book at the end of the tour, wrote that had Whitelaw known 'the situation prevalent in the Australian camp, I think he would have taken different steps to recognise the merit of this amazing youngster.' Specifically, Bradman's team-mates did not 'begrudge' Bradman the £1,000 but they did for the 'rather less than human way he took success'.

Tebbutt suggested Bradman might have 'basked in the sunshine of his team-mates' admiration and shown some human joy in achievement. And when to sporting success is added the manna of a small fortune, the inclination towards even the mildest of "celebrations" ought to be irresistible. But not with Bradman. I believe he spent that night of triumph alone in his room, playing the phonograph! As one of the Australians said to me later: "He is not one of us." That did not worry Bradman. There was no open breach, he was content to lead a life aloof, and Mr. Kelly lacked the firmness to take the situation in hand before it got beyond him.'

The £1,000 was £400 more than the players were receiving for the whole tour. Bradman did make more mention of this [(2)] when he explained that he'd never seen such an amount ever before. He'd never met Whitelaw.

Bradman added two things: 'Returning to my hotel that night, I was so bewildered I had practically no dinner, and went to bed immediately.'

'Young and inexperienced boys are unaccustomed to such publicity, and in my efforts to dodge the limelight at that time I fear I was very often misunderstood.'

As Tebbutt points out, the other members of the team needed Bradman but he needed them, too. The difference, however, was becoming more pronounced every day: they were dispensable, he wasn't. Like supremely gifted practitioners of any sport – or anything else, for that matter – he was able to meet the world in his own way because the world needed him so badly.

The Yorkshire Evening News wrote that

> *'while most of the Australian cricketers went to a theatre in Leeds [. . .] Bradman pleaded that he was too tired to go out, but really it was an attack of shyness that had overcome him, so he hid himself in his hotel, modestly writing letters home telling his people of the mammoth innings that has electrified the cricket world. At the same time, he was receiving cables of congratulations from his admirers down under and messages from all over this country. Undying fame had come to him in a day, but had left no mark on him. He was still an unassuming, rather shy boy with fair hair and keen blue eyes. He neither smokes nor drinks because he believes it would impair his physical fitness, and so, his letters finished, he went off to bed before 11 for a well-earned sleep in preparation for the renewal of his battle.'*

Several people have defended – or rather given reasons why – Bradman behaved as he did on that evening at the Queen's Hotel, Leeds. When he made hundreds he preferred to spend quiet hours with himself and, in 1930, may well have spent some of them writing. He wrote home every week and he was contracted to write *Don Bradman's Book,* to be published by Hutchinson at the end of the tour. He took that seriously and wrote as he went along.

Irving Rosenwater, in his compendious and authoritative *Sir Donald Bradman: A Biography*, argues that listening to music and writing 'was precisely the relaxation he required, best suited to his temperament. Beer-drinking, not one of his habits at any time, would have been his *last* desire. "Was I expected to parade the streets of Leeds?" asked Sir Donald in his autobiography.'

This is quite extraordinary as well as revealing. Nobody, so far as I am aware, has ever suggested Bradman indulge in beer drinking or parade himself that evening, nor had he any need to. Every other member of that team knew his character, habits and customs *but* he had made a triple century and he *was* getting £1,000. Just this once he might have allowed the good of the team to over-ride his own wishes, gone to the bar and bought the whole lot of them whatever they wanted to drink. He might have stayed half an hour and made a point of saying *no man is an island* before excusing himself. He was entitled to quiet, privacy and rest. But he was becoming an island.

As I've said, the tensions within the team are impossible to gauge now that all the players are gone, and the memoirs they left behind don't venture near such sensitive terrain. Did it affect morale? Did Bradman find himself batting with team-mates who resented him? Was there whispering and muttering and cabals? Those who could tell us are silent as tombstones now although, as we shall see in a moment, *The Sun*, Sydney, had something to say.

Scottish XI

Between Headingley and the Fourth Test at Old Trafford, the tourists had what to them must have seemed a pleasant break. They were due to play Scotland over two days at Edinburgh, a Scottish XI over two days in Glasgow and Durham over two days at Sunderland. The pleasant break became an enforced break.

Rain restricted the first day at Edinburgh to a couple of hours, Scotland making 129 for 3. The rain washed the second day away completely. Bradman did however manage to see the Scottish War Memorial at Edinburgh Castle although mist cloaked Princes Street and he could barely make it out. The tourists also enjoyed a day's golf at Gleneagles.

In Glasgow rain lurked and fell, too. Scotland made 140 for 6 on the first day and declared overnight so a crowd of 5,000 could see the Australians. They were to see them, all right.

Tebbutt reported that the wicket was damp and easy, the bowling 'mediocre'. Ponsford went early, to which *The Glasgow Herald* added: 'A new wicket had been prepared beside the one that had suffered so badly on Saturday, but although the ground was drying all day in the sun and wind, the effects of the heavy rain were still apparent both on the wicket and in the outfield.' (3)

Bradman appeared wearing a sweater. He began his innings immediately with the tactic, a safe single into the on-side. Then the bowler appealed for lbw, much to the consternation of the crowd who didn't want Bradman out. The appeal was turned down.

Woodfull and Bradman batted confidently without forcing the pace against keen fielding – so keen many runs were cut off – and put on 50 in fifty-five minutes. Then, some half an hour before lunch, Bradman delighted the crowd, driving and pulling with real aggression, and scored twice as fast as Woodfull although one local reporter was impressed by how he played a completely dead bat to balls he didn't intend to score from. The bowling wasn't on a length and one slow bowler, over-pitching, was literally pulled to pieces. In two hours Bradman had a century and, in the final over before lunch, kept the fielders busy.

'It has been said that Bradman is not gracious in execution, but if he lacks the effortless ease of a Woolley, who has only to caress the ball with his bat to send it racing to the boundary, Bradman has tremendous power in his shoulders, and his eye is so good and his feet so quick that he can change his mind in the middle of a stroke and make another,' *The Glasgow Herald* wrote. 'The power in his shoulders was best seen when he was lying back to slash Baxter and Ackroyd through the covers, and his timing was revealed in the way he turned the ball to leg.'

After lunch the crowd grew to 6,000, the sun shone and Woodfull and Bradman 'gave a slogging exhibition, scoring at a great rate'. (4) When the new ball was taken Bradman hooked it to the boundary and hit the next out of the ground, only his third 6 of the tour. He tried another big hit at the ball after that and was bowled. His 140 had taken two hours twenty-five minutes and apart from the 6 contained nineteen 4s. It was his eighth century on the tour.

He described the 6 in terms of wanting to entertain the crowd and, delightfully, that it represented something of a lapse from his usual self-discipline to belt their fast bowler clean out of the Glasgow ground.

The Durham match, the only one against a second-class county, was completely washed out. Why Durham? In 1926 the Australians had gone there and proved such an attraction that the gates had to be closed with 22,000 inside. Bradman wasn't due to play – he has a 'slight disposition' (upset stomach) – and went straight to Manchester instead. There Australia were meeting England at speedway and the Australians asked Bradman along to watch. He had to decline because he had a prior engagement outside Manchester but otherwise said he'd have been delighted to accept.

Under a 'Sunderland, Tuesday' dateline, *The Sun,* Sydney, discreetly explored the dominant position Bradman had assumed in relation to the touring party.

A SCOTTISH XI V AUSTRALIANS

Glasgow, 19, 20 July. Drawn.

A SCOTTISH XI

J. Kerr		b Hornibrook	25
B.W.G. Atkinson		c & b Hornibrook	23
A.K. McTavish	c Bradman	b Hornibrook	10
G.W.A. Alexandor	c Hornibrook	b Wall	8
W. Nicholson		b Hurwood	22
B.R. Todd	c Woodfull	b Kippax	34
Ackroyd		not out	12
Extras			6
Total	(6 wkts dec)		140

Dnb: A.D. Baxter, D.A. Bompas, Preston, and T. Watson.

	O	M	R	W
Hornibrook	24	9	40	3
a'Beckett	3	1	2	0
Wall	11	2	17	1
McCabe	10	1	32	0
Kippax	5.5	5	1	1
Hurwood	22	4	42	1

AUSTRALIANS

W.M. Woodfull	c Kerr	b Preston	65
W.H. Ponsford		b Baxter	6
D.G. Bradman		b Baxter	140
A.F. Kippax	lbw	b Watson	0
S. McCabe		b Baxter	1
A.A. Jackson		not out	52
E.L. a'Beckett	st Bompas	b Todd	43
A. Hurwood	lbw	b Watson	3
P.M. Hornibrook		b Preston	8
C.W. Walker	c Kerr	b Baxter	0
T. Wall		not out	2
Extras			17
Total	(9 wkts)		337

	O	M	R	W
Baxter	35	8	89	4
Preston	40	7	94	2
Ackroyd	16	4	45	0
Watson	20	3	47	2
Todd	8	0	45	1

'Don Bradman is becoming a real problem to Woodfull, the Australian selectors, and his team-mates.

'His fame is such that the public regard him as the star turn to such an extent that even Grimmett has to play second fiddle, while the rest of the team are merely scene shifters and supers.

'Some teams are so anxious to see Bradman that they willingly send in Australia to bat just to watch him. This is unparalleled.

'A typical example of his popularity, one of many, was shown to-day. Five elderly gentlemen came 150 miles (240km) this morning to see him play against Durham. But they were doomed to disappointment. More than likely they will see neither Bradman nor cricket.

'Bradman was not chosen to play, in view of the closeness of the Test, and three days' continuance and heavy rain rain resulted in the ground to-day being under water. There is only a faint hope of play to-morrow.

'Bradman has hardly had a moment to himself since his arrival in England. He has played in almost every match, but obviously he must be rested sometimes. However, his omission perplexes towns almost to the extent of offending them. Local newspapers' placards invariably announce that Bradman is playing or is not playing, and a constant stream of callers come to the hotel on various pretexts seeking Bradman.

'It is common for someone to say "My Aunt or Uncle saw him in Australia. I would like to meet him."

'Bradman continues to receive a postbag that would be the envy of any film fan. One hears all sorts of rumours about proposals of marriage, weird offers and requests, but Bradman in the presence of pressmen gives infinitely less chances than in the field.'

Fourth Test – Old Trafford

After Sunderland the Australians travelled to Manchester and manager Kelly, approached by the Press on the eve of the Test, dismissed stories that Bradman was unwell. 'I do not know where these stories come from.'

By now he'd brought something approaching panic to the England selectors. They dropped Larwood for Stan Nichols, the Essex fast bowler; they dropped Tyldesley and Geary for Robins and Peebles – two leg spinners, of course, with all the problematic elements that brought.

Peebles has recorded how he embarked for Manchester 'in a do-or-die but slightly nervous frame of mind [. . .] Apart from normal anxieties of a newcomer making a first appearance against Australia there was the uneasy reflection that at that stage Bradman had batted five times against England and made just 728 runs.' When Peebles arrived he heard that the selectors, reflecting on the perils of both Robins and Peebles, had added Tom Goddard of Gloucestershire, a tall, phlegmatic man who bowled off-breaks reliably and could really spin the ball on helpful wickets.

Peebles was surprised Robins had been picked in the first place because, evidently, he'd had a blazing row with Leveson-Gower, chairman of the selectors, at Lord's over a run-out. Peebles assumed Robins had shouted his way out of the series. In fact he wasn't picked for Manchester, although whether the row had anything to do with that Peebles did not know. That night Peebles confessed to Arthur Mailey that he'd probably be very nervous when he bowled to Bradman. His nerves can't have been helped by a newspaper headline: 'BRADMAN, MEET MR. PEEBLES!'

At 10.45am Chapman, Leveson-Gower and Hobbs inspected the wicket, conferred and soon after an announcement was made that Goddard would play. Woodfull inspected the wicket alone. On an overcast morning he won the toss – Bradman felt he'd have preferred to lose it – and batted on a soft, slightly deadened wicket. Bradman described it as damp, and the outfield slow.

Woodfull and Ponsford opened in front of 30,000 people and plodded to 30 in fifty-five minutes before Chapman signalled for Peebles to come on from the practice ground end. By then the ground looked piebald with patches of sawdust here and there – Chapman even had his own to help his fielding.

When Peebles had marked out his run and waited, Chapman setting the field, Hobbs trotted over from cover to reassure Peebles the way to do it was consider this just another cricket match. Fender, watching from the Press Box, thought Peebles started 'rather shakily' and gave away easy runs before he settled. Peebles himself thought this first bowl in Test cricket produced 'nothing unusual'. Fender didn't agree. Peebles, he pointed out, 'had Woodfull in difficulties several times' although Ponsford played him better. Peebles, Fender concluded, might have got 'a wicket many times before lunch'. Goddard could find nothing in the wicket but at least Peebles had beaten the bat. Australia went into lunch at 75, Woodfull 37 and Ponsford 30.

Peebles and Tate opened the bowling when play resumed and in half an hour the score moved to 106. Then Woodfull was caught behind off Tate and Bradman appeared to prolonged applause.

Peebles would remember how slowly Bradman made his way to the wicket, again letting his eyes get used to the light, and it leant 'a dramatic air to his entry.' (6) A contemporary account (7) says that 'the crowd rose and gave an amazingly noisy cheer. He was cheered all the way to the wicket, and in view of his slow walk that means that the crowd cheered for a long time.'

He hooked the first ball to the short leg area for a single and Ponsford played out the over. Bradman 1.

He took guard and prepared to face Peebles. 'We must both have been aware that this encounter had very much the air of a personal duel,' Peebles wrote. Bradman had seen him at Lord's for the MCC and Oxford but these were only brief glimpses and perhaps Peebles's mysteries of leg break and googly remained – mysterious. Peebles put it pointedly: the unfamiliarity 'might deceive him'. More than this, Peebles knew the Press had been writing he'd been picked specifically to get Bradman. As the *Evening Standard* said, also pointedly: 'Peebles was put into the team with the sole object of getting Bradman out.'

He prepared to bowl him a googly immediately. As he ran in he felt the 'tremendous tension' in the whole ground. The ball pitched outside the off-stump. Bradman, reading it as a leg break, moved fully across the wicket and hoisted his bat out of the way while he tried to pad it. In an astonishing moment Peebles could see all three stumps. The ball spun back *behind* Bradman and went just over the middle stump. Duckworth, unsighted by Bradman's body, let it go for 4 byes. Peebles thought *If we'd been using the bigger, experimental stumps the ball would have hit?*

This one ball was the most revealing in the series because it demonstrated that implacable, remorseless Bradman did have a potentially fatal weakness. He'd confess it himself: for the first time in his life he faced a bowler he couldn't pick. Peebles reflected much later that 'although Bradman was already much too shrewd a tactician to show it, this hazardous start may well have disconcerted him'.

He almost played on to the second Peebles ball after aiming it into the covers but hitting it on to the leg side. The third, striking his pads, almost bowled him. He survived the fourth and managed to take a single to mid-on from the fifth, the first time the ball hadn't taken the edge of the bat. Peebles thought *He's made several mistakes, he's clearly ill at ease.* He 'wore a worried look for the first time in weeks'. (8) *The Sun,* Sydney, reporter wrote: 'I have never seen Bradman so unhappy.' Bradman 2.

He watched Peebles as closely as he could – the hand coming over, the ball coming out – and simply couldn't pick him. (9) Peebles sensed that Bradman certainly couldn't pick the googly.

The batsmen conferred, their conversation lost now but presumably assessing the tactical advantage of Ponsford taking Peebles, Bradman taking Tate. The English fielders must have read this into it because they'd do all they could to keep Bradman facing Peebles.

Ponsford took a single towards square leg from the final ball of this Peebles over, keeping the strike. He, Peebles felt, played these conditions and this sort of bowling best among the Australians. Ponsford seemed 'unpeturbed'. Ponsford, Fender concluded, 'tried to protect' Bradman 'as far as he could'.

Ponsford took a single from the final ball of Tate's next over, keeping the strike, but clearly wasn't trying to protect Bradman *that* much because he took a single from the second ball of the following Peebles over. Bradman managed to get the next ball to the leg side and they ran a single. Bradman 3.

Ponsford played out the over so Bradman faced the more familiar and comforting girth of Tate. Tate beat him with a ball which turned in, Bradman trying to square drive. The ball just cleared the bails. He took 3 from a fine flick to mid-on from the third ball but Ponsford took a single from the fifth. Bradman played at the sixth and Tate appealed for a catch behind the wicket – then 'placed his hand over his mouth, but the word had escaped'. (10) Duckworth didn't appeal and anyway dropped the ball. Bradman 6.

Ponsford faced Peebles and took a single from the first ball again. Bradman got the next one past the slips for 2 and pushed the fifth to mid-on for a single. Ponsford took a single from the sixth and played out a maiden to Tate. Bradman 9.

He faced Peebles and took a single from the first ball, Ponsford a single from the second. From either the third or fourth, Bradman 'came down the wicket to drive a leg-break past extra cover, but failed to get to the pitch of it'. (11) He snicked what Peebles considered an easy chance to Hammond who, diving at first slip, got his right hand to the chance – it was travelling low down – but amazingly couldn't hold it. The next ball beat Bradman. Peebles thought *Having survived it's inevitable*

Bradman will emerge from this nightmare, find his form and make a mountain of runs again. The crowd cheered Peebles for an over which, they felt, had teased him. Bradman 10.

Ponsford faced Tate and took a single from the fourth ball. Bradman played out the over. Ponsford faced Peebles and took a single from the fifth ball. Bradman got a full toss and effortlessly pulled it to the boundary. Peebles thought *That can only have increased his confidence.* Bradman 14.

Ponsford faced Tate and hit a boundary. It let Peebles in against Bradman again. He tried to come down the wicket, made to off-drive the third ball, spinning ferociously, but edged it to second slip where Duleepsinhji caught it. The roar which this drew from the 30,000, Peebles estimated, lasted a full minute. Chapman was so delighted he pretended to kiss Duleepsinhji.

Reflecting, Peebles reasoned that 'for the first time in his life' Bradman found himself on a 'slow' soft English wicket'. This was the opposite to everything he'd been reared on in Australia and, initially, would always be a problem. Peebles concluded: 'Curiously enough it was the one type of pitch upon which Don never looked at ease, presumably because he didn't really apply himself to what, for him, was a rare and not very important matter.'

This seems unlikely because getting out was always a very important matter to Bradman, and certainly afterwards he discussed Peebles with Woodfull, Ponsford and Kippax. They told him they had 'difficulty' picking the googly, which of course is not the same thing as being unable to pick it. Bradman remained puzzled at his inability.

Australia reached 275 for 7 at the close and totalled 345 the next day. England replied with 221 for 5 but rain drowned almost all the third day and all the fourth.

He'd had two failures in Test innings, the 8 at Trent Bridge before the 131, the 1 at Lord's after the 254. Old Trafford was the only Test of the five where he just failed.

Somerset

They went to play Somerset, staying at the Castle Hotel, Taunton, which Tebbutt described as delightful, 'the height of modern comfort in surroundings of antiquity, where the Australians revelled in the Somerset air and West Country cream prodigious in quantity and of the quality of a schoolboy's dream'. [(12)]

ENGLAND V AUSTRALIA – FOURTH TEST

Manchester, 25, 26, 28, 29 July. Drawn.

AUSTRALIA

*W.M. Woodfull	c Duckworth	b Tate	54
W.H. Ponsford		b Hammond	83
D.G. Bradman	c Duleepsinhji	b Peebles	14
A.F. Kippax	c Chapman	b Nichols	51
S.J. McCabe	lbw	b Peebles	4
V.Y. Richardson		b Hammond	1
A.G. Fairfax	lbw	b Goddard	49
+W.A. Oldfield		b Nichols	2
C.V. Grimmett	c Sutcliffe	b Peebles	50
P.M. Hornibrook	c Duleepsinhji	b Goddard	3
T.W. Wall		not out	1
Extras	(b 23, lb 3, nb 7)		33
Total			345

1-106, 2-138, 3-184, 4-189, 5-190,
6-239, 7-243, 8-330, 9-338

	O	M	R	W
Nichols	21	5	33	2
Tate	30	11	39	1
Goddard	32.1	14	49	2
Peebles	55	9	150	3
Leyland	8	2	17	0
Hammond	21	6	24	2

ENGLAND

J.B. Hobbs	c Oldfield	b Wall	31
H. Sutcliffe	c Bradman	b Wall	74
W.R. Hammond		b Wall	3
K.S. Duleepsinhji	c Hornibrook	b McCabe	54
M. Leyland		b McCabe	35
*A.P.F. Chapman	c Grimmett	b Hornibrook	1
M.W. Tate	c Ponsford	b McCabe	15
M.S. Nichols		not out	7
I.A.R. Peebles	c Richardson	b McCabe	6
+G. Duckworth		not out	0
Extras	(b 13, lb 12)		25
Total	(8 wkts)		251

Dnb: T.W.J. Goddard.

1-108, 2-115, 3-119, 4-192, 5-199,
6-222, 7-237, 8-247

	O	M	R	W
Wall	33	9	70	3
Fairfax	13	5	15	0
Grimmett	19	2	59	0
Hornibrook	26	9	41	1
McCabe	17	3	41	4

The ground at Taunton was delightful, too, although under an overcast sky and on an easy wicket, Somerset collapsed to 121 all out in front of a large crowd. The prospect of Bradman, the anticipation of Bradman, filled grounds now.

The Australians began their reply at 3.35pm. Ponsford was soon bowled and Bradman came in to partner Jackson and began his innings with a mis-hit which almost went into the stumps.

Neither batsmen, however, mastered the attack and George Hunt, right-arm fast-medium, bowled four consecutive maidens to Bradman so that he took twenty minutes to get off the mark and scored only 3 in twenty-five minutes. Bradman's 'listlessness depressed the expectant crowd'. (13) At tea, taken at 4.30pm, the score had reached only 28. They remained cautious – and slow – after tea, provoking the crowd to barrack Bradman. It had not happened on the tour before. People were no longer content with hundreds from him, they wanted miracles, too.

White came on at 42 (Bradman 21 in an hour, Jackson 14) and Bradman showed him the respect he hadn't done at Lord's. He did however pull him to the boundary after tea but then almost played on. He went to his 50 out of 85 in a hundred minutes. They accelerated towards the end so that Bradman had 71 and Jackson 57 at the close.

Next day both men played in true character, Bradman attacking and Jackson matching him. Jackson struck three boundaries in the first ten minutes and they added 30 in twenty minutes. *The Times* reported: 'Each batsman was giving a typical exhibition: Jackson of wristwork, timing and grace, in which superb cutting and clear driving were the chief strokes; Bradman of timing as correct but, for the rest, of more all-round methods.'

Both batsmen slowed as they neared their centuries but Bradman made his first, after three hours five minutes. He was caught and bowled for 117 by Archibald (Tom) Young, a slow right-arm bowler. He'd batted for three hours thirty-five minutes and hit thirteen 4s. Jackson made 118, the only century he'd ever make in England.

Grimmett (7 for 33) paralysed the second Somerset innings.

Glamorgan

The match against Glamorgan at Swansea began on a Saturday but rain restricted the crowd to 3,000, with potentially dire financial consequences, and play did not begin until four in the afternoon.

SOMERSET V AUSTRALIANS

Taunton 30, 31 July. Australians won by an innings and 58 runs.

SOMERSET

A. Young		b a'Beckett	4	lbw	b Grimmett	17
E.F. Longrigg	c McCabe	b a'Beckett	0	c Richardson	b a'Beckett	1
R.A. Ingle		run out	2		run out	5
F.S. Lee	c Walker	b Hurwood	0		b Grimmett	0
*J.C. White	lbw	b Grimmett	38	c Hornibrook	b Grimmett	12
C.C.C. Case	c Hornibrook	b Hurwood	5		not out	20
L.C. Hawkins	c Jackson	b Grimmett	11	st Walker	b Grimmett	0
A.W. Wellard		b McCabe	38	c Hornibrook	b Grimmett	17
J.W. Lee	c Woodfull	b McCabe	11	c Hornibrook	b Grimmett	0
G.E. Hunt	c Hornibrook	b Grimmett	12		b McCabe	0
+A.G. Marshall		not out	0	c Bradman	b Grimmett	3
Extras		0		(lb 6)		6
Total			121			81

1-1, 2-4, 3-5, 4-10, 5-30, 6-60, 7-60, 8-108, 9-121

1-17, 2-23, 3-23, 4-26, 5-43, 6-43, 7-69, 8-69, 9-74

	O	M	R	W	O	M	R	W
a'Beckett	15	4	22	2	9	4	16	1
Hurwood	18	3	42	2	5	1	8	0
McCabe	11	7	19	2	9	1	15	1
Grimmett	13.1	3	38	3	15.4	4	33	7
Hornibrook					3	1	3	0

AUSTRALIANS

W.H. Ponsford		b Hunt	8
A.A. Jackson	c J.W. Lee	b Young	118
D.G. Bradman		c & b Young	117
S.J. McCabe		c & b Young	1
V.Y. Richardsonc Hunt		b Young	27
*W.M. Woodfull		c & b White	30
E.L. a'Beckett	c Young	b White	24
C.V. Grimmett	c Young	b White	16
A. Hurwoodhit wicket		b Young	10
P.M. Hornibrook		not out	4
+C.W. Walker	c Wellard	b White	0
Extras	(b 1, lb 4)		5
Total			360

1-13, 2-244, 3-245, 4-248, 5-277, 6-313, 7-332, 8-356, 9-356

	O	M	R	W
Wellard	22	3	66	0
Hunt	38	13	91	1
J.W. Lee	19	8	37	0
White	30.4	8	91	4
Young	34	12	70	5

Richardson captained the Australians and was intrigued to hear, for the first time in his life, loudspeakers announcing each incoming batsman. Since virtually all scoreboards in England gave only a batsman's number, and the crowd had never seen most of the Australians before, unless a spectator had a scorecard to consult he wouldn't know. Bradman's photograph had been in so many newspapers he was familiar but – Hurwood or Walker or Wall?

On a dead pitch Ponsford and Jackson made 93 before Ponsford was bowled by Dai Davies and Bradman came in.

Davies (14) claimed many years later that the first ball he bowled Bradman 'shaved' his off stump and the wicket-keeper, Trevor Every, was so sure it must bowl Bradman that he made no attempt to take it. Davies believed he could get Bradman out and was 'absolutely flabbergasted' when the captain, Maurice Turnbull, took him off. Davies protested but Turnbull explained that for financial reasons Glamorgan *needed* Bradman to be not out so that a big crowd would pay to watch him on the August Bank Holiday Monday.

When only 2 had been added, Jackson went caught at fine short leg. The *South Wales Daily Post* reported:

> *'Only two and a half hours play was possible, but during that time we had the opportunity of studying the methods of the wonder batsman of Australia, Don Bradman. As was the case when Jack Hobbs was here, the crowd did not see him in the light in which they had pictured him. There was nothing aggressive about his methods but he was timing the ball splendidly, getting the ball in the middle of the bat and keeping it well on the carpet. On a pitch rendered lifeless by heavy rain Bradman plodded along with studied restraint and did what everybody who desired an interesting position to be created for today [Monday] wanted him to do by remaining unbeaten.'*

Bradman finished this Saturday 27 not out (McCabe 28 – they'd added 54 in forty-five minutes). The Welsh would be coming to see for themselves on the Monday.

That day *The Star* began serialisation of Bradman's life story and, understandably, they went for it big, leading their front page, 'BRADMAN'S OWN STORY'. There were four decks of headlines under this and then a paragraph set in italic bold:

> *'I was never coached: I was never told how to hold a bat. I was my own teacher . . . Style, as style, I have never studied; my batting is dedicated and fashioned by the need of the moment.'*

Eight meaty paragraphs, the width of two columns for maximum impact, had been set out under this, giving in the third person a précis of what readers would get on page 2 where Bradman's own words were. They began: 'When thirteen years of age I set out upon the greatest adventure of my young and crowded life because then it was that I beheld the Sydney ground and saw for the first time first-class cricket.'

In thirty paragraphs Bradman recounted his early life, and would continue to do so in the instalments to come so that there would be one on the morning of the Fifth Test at The Oval, no bad thing for a London newspaper to be carrying.

At Swansea 20,000 came to watch him resume on the Monday. Davies gave the figure at 25,000 and pointed out that it enabled Glamorgan to finish in surplus for the first time since the Australians came in 1926. People might no longer be content with hundreds from Bradman, they might want the miracles, too, but here was another dimension. The *presence* of Bradman was assuming major financial proportions – at Swansea, amidst the rain, enough to keep a whole county afloat. That rain, on Sunday night, cleared and the pitch recovered so well that play began on time.

Bradman and McCabe continued though neither looked completely comfortable. They put on 101 for the third wicket in ninety minutes but Frank Ryan – left-arm spinner, *bon viveur,* extrovert and possessor of a fierce temper – moved into a devastating spell. He had McCabe caught, Richardson stumped and bowled Bradman who played back but was beaten by the pace off the pitch. Ryan finished with 6 for 76 and the Australians made 245.

Grimmett cut deep into the Glamorgan first innings, restricting them to 99 and the Australians batted again for ten minutes of the Monday.

Next morning a swirl of controversy moved gently round them because, evidently, manager Kelly was reported as saying that when Ryan bowled Bradman it was the first time he'd been bowled on the tour. This led to a trawl through the matches already played: Bradman bowled by McDonald of Lancashire; Allom of the MCC in the match after that; Garland-Wells of Oxford University; Hearne and Stevens of

Middlesex . . . The correspondent of the *Post* set off to investigate and Kelly explained that what he meant was Bradman 'had not been so completely bowled as in this match'.

Heavy overnight rain restricted play on the final day and it resumed under a fierce sun, expected to bake the wicket into awkwardness. Jackson was caught at square leg for 11 but Ponsford forced the pace while Bradman played back a lot, watching the turning ball carefully. They took the score to 71 at lunch when Richardson declared, inviting Glamorgan to make 218 to win in two and three quarter hours. They started carefully then went for them but Grimmett was always there, nagging, probing, exploiting. William Bates made 73 and Turnbull 52 so that for a time Glamorgan might have won but Grimmett had them both and Glamorgan finished on 197 for 7, 21 short.

Only England, at Trent Bridge, had beaten the Australians so far.

During the stay in South Wales the Australians visited the Eisteddfod at Llanelly. The beginning of the *South Wales Daily Post* story is worth quoting verbatim:

> *'Don Bradman was the great thrill of the children's concert which, following custom, closed the first day of the National Eisteddfod. The choir of 1,000 school children gave one yell of delight when they realised that the Australians were on the platform. Here was a mere boy who had captured the imagination of England, and received the welcome that the Eisteddfod reserves for the Royal Family and Mr. Lloyd George!* **NOTE GEORGE**. *One look at the smiling modesty of the young man enjoying the welcome was enough to explain the popularity of the wonder batsman. It was Don Bradman who thanked the audience for the magnificent reception given to the team, and the memorable evening they were sure to have.'*

Bradman wasn't due to play against Warwickshire at Edgbaston and rain destroyed the match, anyway, allowing only two and a half hours of play. The Warwickshire captain, Bob Wyatt, won the toss and batted. The county made 102 for 3 (Wyatt 22 not out) and that was that.

Bradman made a film, and although an extensive amount of footage had been shot it was cut to 10 minutes when it was shown in Australia. It may be that he took the free days to do it – the film was certainly made before the Fifth Test. In it he demonstrated his technique and talked about teamwork. Strictly speaking, making a film did not violate

GLAMORGAN V AUSTRALIANS

Swansea, 2, 4, 5 August. Drawn.

AUSTRALIANS

W.H. Ponsford		b D Davies	53		not out	35
A.A. Jackson	c Hills	b Mercer	39	c Clay	b D. Davies	11
D.G. Bradman		b Ryan	58		not out	19
S.J. McCabe	c D. Davies	b Ryan	53			
*V.Y. Richardson	st Every	b Ryan	3			
A.G. Fairfax	c D. Davies	b Ryan	8			
E.L. a'Beckett		not out	18			
C.V. Grimmett	c D. Davies	b Ryan	0			
T.W. Wall	c Turnbull	b Ryan	2			
A. Hurwood	lbw	b Mercer	0			
+C.W. Walker		b Mercer	1			
Extras	(b 1, lb 6, nb 3)		10	(b 4, lb 2)		6
Total			245	(1 wkt dec)		71

1-93, 2-95, 3-196, 4-208, 5-215, 6-232, 7-232, 8-233, 9-240 | 1-27

	O	M	R	W	O	M	R	W
Mercer	32.3	7	70	3	3	0	15	0
D.E. Davies	6	0	31	0				
Clay	16	3	35	0	10	2	28	0
Ryan	34	3	76	6	4	1	13	0
D. Davies	11	3	23	1	4	1	9	1

GLAMORGAN

W.E. Bates	c Fairfax	b Wall	7	st Walker	b Grimmett	73
A.H. Dyson		b Grimmett	25	c Wall	b Grimmett	20
*M.J.L. Turnbull		b Wall	3		b Grimmett	52
D. Davies		b Fairfax	26		not out	7
J.T. Bell	lbw	b Grimmett	3		b Wall	6
J.J. Hills		not out	21		b Hurwood	7
D.E. Davies		run out	6		not out	1
J.C. Clay	c Bradman	b Grimmett	1		b Wall	15
J. Mercer	c Richardson	b a'Beckett	0	c a'Beckett	b Grimmett	7
+T. Every		b a'Beckett	1			
F.P. Ryan	c Richardson	b Grimmett	2			
Extras		(lb 3, nb 1)	4	(b 8, lb 1)		9
Total			99	(7 wkts)		197

1-14, 2-28, 3-47, 4-58, 5-70, 6-79, 7-86, 8-86, 9-88 | 1-37, 2-59, 3-152, 4-163, 5-177, 6-185, 7-195

	O	M	R	W	O	M	R	W
Wall	11	3	24	2	10	2	23	2
Fairfax	11	1	32	1	12	2	49	0
a'Beckett	8	5	5	2	5	1	12	0
Grimmett	16.3	4	34	4				
Hurwood					6	1	14	0
McCabe					4	0	14	0

Clause 11 of the agreement with the Board the players had signed:

> *'Neither the manager, Executive, treasurer, nor any player shall accept employment as a newspaper correspondent or do any work for, or in connection with, any newspaper or any broadcasting; and no member of the team other than the manager shall directly or indirectly in any capacity whatsoever communicate with Press nor give any information concerning matters connected with the tour to the Press or any member, servant or agent thereof.'*

Whether it violated the spirit of the agreement was another matter.

Northamptonshire

He did play at Northampton in what developed into an extraordinary match, although it began quite normally. This damp August, Northamptonshire batted and, on a shortened day, made 249. Next day, the Monday, the Australians confronted a rain-affected wicket – Bradman called it a sticky – against two bowlers who knew all about exploiting that: Vallance Jupp (right-arm off-breaks) and Albert Thomas (right-arm medium).

Woodfull opened with Jackson but Thomas, making the ball leave the bat, proved an immediate problem and each run became precious. With the total 15 Jackson played too soon at him and spooned a caught and bowled. Evidently Thomas had been promised £5 if he could get Bradman out first ball and almost bowled him.

The pitch constricted Bradman, and Jupp, who had been giving it 'some approving and benevolent glances', [(15)] put himself on. Suddenly 249 seemed an eternity away and, although Bradman sent an over-pitched ball from Jupp to the boundary, both batsmen concentrated on survival. That meant killing the spin of each ball.

They were 48 at lunch but, after adding 3, Bradman played on to Jupp who then cut through the rest of the innings. Australia, all out 93, followed on.

On the final day, the Tuesday, *The Star* published the eighth instalment of Bradman's story. He wrote revealingly of an incident in the previous series after he'd failed at Adelaide. A friend recounted how he'd met someone who said: 'No wonder Don Bradman failed in Adelaide. Success in the Test match in Melbourne evidently turned his head, and he was scarcely sober all the time he was in Adelaide. How could he make runs in that condition?'

Bradman pointed out to readers of *The Star* that 'throughout my life I have been a strict teetotaller, and can honestly say I have never had a drink in my life.'

The revealing aspect was that people were mouthing unfounded rumours, or outright fiction, about him and he'd have to live with that. It was an early price of fame, and an early lesson about it. When he reached England he was two years older and two years more experienced in living with it.

In each *Star* instalment, incidentally, he took good care to stay clear of the present tour so that he was not, he felt, in breach of the contract he had signed with the Australian Board for the tour. The thoughts of manager Kelly on this were not recorded – yet.

The pitch was improving and on this final day Woodfull and Jackson put on 91 before Jackson was caught and bowled by leg-break bowler Arthur Cox.

The Times wrote that

> *'Bradman then joined Woodfull, and any spectator who did not know the state of the match would immediately have guessed that the match was at its crisis. Thomas and Jupp, who once completely beat Woodfull only to see the ball go for four byes, bowled an unconscionable number of maiden overs, but neither of them could produce that ball which does enough to beat the most severely defensive strokes.*
>
> *'The difference between Woodfull and Bradman as batsmen was perfectly illustrated by the fact that Woodfull was the same batsman on a true as he had been on the Monday on a treacherous wicket. Bradman, who, against the turning ball on Monday had been speculative and uncertain, became the assured breaker of records. The conclusion would seem to be that Woodfull has reserves of technique which are at the moment beyond the reach of Bradman. Bradman yesterday, however, batted extremely well and a controlled stroke off Jupp, which brought him two runs to mid-wicket, and a drive past extra cover for 3 in the same over, show how thoroughly he appreciated the fact that the ball was coming on to the bat.'*

He dispatched a poor-length ball from Thomas to the mid-wicket boundary but soon after went down the wicket to Cox and was caught at wide mid-on. He'd made 35.

Woodfull went slowly on to 116, Richardson battered 116 and the Australians batted the match out, to some criticism, although Bradman wondered what else they could have done.

The England selectors, meanwhile, were about to convulse all England.

NORTHAMPTONSHIRE V AUSTRALIANS

Northampton, 9, 11, 12 August. Drawn.

NORTHAMPTONSHIRE

C.N. Woolley		b a'Beckett	12
A.H. Bakewell	c Jackson	b Hurwood	84
A.P.R. Hawtin	c Wall	b Hornibrook	2
J.E. Timms	c Richardson	b Wall	78
*V.W.C. Jupp	c Walker	b Hurwood	15
A.G. Liddell		b Hornibrook	4
A.L. Cox		b Wall	10
A.D.G. Matthews	hit wicket	b Hornibrook	19
+B.W. Bellamy		not out	10
E.F. Towell		b Hornibrook	2
A.E. Thomas		run out	0
Extras	(b 3, lb 9, nb 1)		13
Total			249

1-28, 2-31, 3-146, 4-166, 5-181,
6-208, 7-213, 8-247, 9-249

	O	M	R	W
Wall	18	2	53	2
Fairfax	16	5	30	0
a'Beckett	20	9	29	1
Hornibrook	26	11	45	4
Bradman	8	2	31	0
Hurwood	24	8	48	2

AUSTRALIANS

*W.M. Woodfull		b Jupp	15	c Bellamy	b Towell	116
A.A. Jackson	c&b Thomas		9		c&b Cox	52
D.G. Bradman		b Jupp	22	c Hawtin	b Cox	35
A.G. Fairfax		b Jupp	1	c Bellemy	b Timms	1
A.F. Kippax		b Thomas	10	c Cox	b Jupp	20
V.Y. Richardson	c Bellamy	b Thomas	7	c Jupp	b Towell	116
E.L. a'Beckett	c Bakewell	b Matthews	13		c&b Matthews	22
A. Hurwood	st Bellamy	b Jupp	2		b Jupp	12
P.M. Hornibrook		b Jupp	2		not out	16
T.W. Wall	lbw	b Jupp	3			
+C.W. Walker		not out	0			
Extras	(b 7, lb 2)		9	(b 10, lb 2, w 1, nb 2)		15
Total			93	(8 wkts)		405

1-15, 2-51, 3-52, 4-59, 5-65,
6-79, 7-84, 8-84, 9-88

1-91, 2-106, 3-172, 4-211,
5-300, 6-314, 7-385, 8-405

	O	M	R	W	O	M	R	W
Thomas	29	14	29	3	25	12	32	0
Matthews	10	3	18	1	35.5	5	83	1
Jupp	23.4	10	32	6	21	5	47	2
Towell	3	0	5	0	24	4	84	2
Cox					28	2	87	2
Liddell					12	3	36	0
Timms					5	1	21	1

Chapter Nine

232

AT CHELTENHAM'S GENTEEL CRICKET GROUND GLOUCESTERSHIRE were playing Warwickshire. The match began on Saturday 9 August, the day the Australians found trouble up at Northampton.

Warwickshire batted and Charlie Parker, an old hand who had been on the Gloucester ground staff in 1903 (recommended by W.G. Grace), mesmerised them with his beautiful left-arm spinners. He took 5 for 53 in a total of 120 all out and, replying, Gloucester made 144 for 7. Bob Wyatt, plying his right-arm medium deliveries, had a couple of them including Hammond for 39.

On the Sunday they rested, of course, Hammond no doubt distantly contemplating the Fifth Test at The Oval starting in six days. Because the series stood at 1-1 the Test was to be timeless and therefore the decider however long it took.

On that Sunday, Leveson-Gower wrote a letter to Wyatt:

8, Northwick House,
St. John's Wood Road, X. W.8.
August 10th, 1930

Personal and Private.

My dear Bob,

The Selection Committee at a meeting held today have asked me to let you know that they would like you to captain England against Australia at The

Oval next Saturday. We must have a meeting on Tuesday as soon as you can get to London to definitely select the side – because you, as captain, have the casting vote in the selection of the side if the other members cannot agree.

I see you are playing at Weston-super-Mare on Wednesday – don't you think under the circumstances it would be a good thing for you to have a rest? You can then come to London on Tuesday and take matters easy. We shall probably meet at the Sports Club, St. James's Square – when I hope you will join me at dinner there at 7.45. Keep this to yourself at present as we do not intend to publish the side till we have seen you.

My best congratulations,
Yours very sincerely,
Shrimp. (1)

Chapman had been dropped and it would provoke a convulsion. He'd taken over the captaincy at The Oval in 1926 when England won the Ashes back for the first time since the war and, as we have seen, gone to Australia in 1928–29 and won 4-1.

Leveson-Gower's letter was delivered to Wyatt on the Monday. He had no idea it was going to happen and when he'd read it his mind 'whizzed round'. He found concentration difficult when play resumed.

Gloucestershire made 201, Parker mesmerised Warwickshire a second time (9 for 44) and Gloucestershire made the 29 runs for victory comfortably enough. There was talk that Parker might be picked for The Oval, but there was talk that all manner of other bowlers might be, too, including the aged Sydney Barnes – he was 57 and now slaying batsmen in their dozens for Staffordshire as he had slayed Australians before the First War. The imperative had become finding *anyone* to defeat Bradman.

Wyatt must have sensed the convulsion and sensed it was gathering round him. He judged Chapman hadn't done too badly so far in 1930 and, anyway, there was something of the eternal schoolboy in Chapman's smile, his gait, his cat-like reactions fielding close, the way he smote the ball and devil take the hindmost. He had been the right stuff but cavaliers were no longer enough against Bradman; the future belonged to tacticians. He would kill a generation of bowlers. He had just killed his first captain.

Bradman professed astonishment at the decision and said it boosted the Australians. (2)

On the Tuesday, Wyatt took the train from Cheltenham to Paddington for the Selection Committee meeting and when he arrived was amazed to find 'fifteen Pressmen' on the platform waiting for him. (3) They seemed to know. 'As soon as they saw me they swept down on me and surrounded me, peppering me with questions. I couldn't think what had happened, as Leveson-Gower had told me that the team wouldn't be announced until after they'd seen me; but apparently there had been a leak. However, I was determined not to be a part of it.' (4) Wyatt fended them off.

The Star led their front page with

'TEST CAPTAINCY SURPRISE.

CHAPMAN MAY BE OUT OF TEAM.

WYATT AS PROBABLE LEADER.'

The story underneath cited unattributed sources and suggested that Chapman wouldn't even be picked as a player at the Selectors' Meeting that afternoon. Approached at Hastings, where Kent were playing Sussex, Chapman said he hadn't been told of any decision and consequently could not comment. Tate however did comment obliquely: 'I am not allowed to say anything at present but if I am not chosen to play I will tell you my opinion.'

Apart from Wyatt, the Selectors picked twelve: Hobbs, Sutcliffe, William (Dodger) Whysall, Duleepsinhji, Hammond, Leyland, Tate, Larwood, Duckworth, Peebles, Parker and young Kent wicket-keeper/batsman Leslie Ames.

Wyatt woke next morning to find his replacing of Chapman universally derided. 'The more staid newspapers were a trifle more restrained in their comments, but not altogether so.' It meant that The Oval would be an ordeal.

The Australians had a vigorous practice session on the Thursday although a gale blew. Richardson batted in a bowler hat, giving an impression of burlesque while Bradman, McCabe and Woodfull 'indulged in some hard hitting'. (5)

Fifth Test – The Oval

Wyatt started well by winning the toss and deciding to bat. Hobbs and Sutcliffe had a good wicket to bat on and made 68 for the first wicket before Hobbs was out. Sutcliffe painstakingly constructed one of his major innings and Wyatt held the middle order together so that England reached 316 for 5 at the close. On the Monday they were all out for 405 and, in reply, Woodfull and Ponsford put on 159 by tea. Ponsford (110) was unwell, however, and Peebles' third ball after tea bowled him.

The light was bad and thunder threatened from beyond heavy cloud. As Bradman made his way to the wicket sharp rain fell and all the players scampered off while both ends were covered. Play began again at 5.12pm and Peebles had his over to finish. Wyatt remembered that 'if Peebles hadn't been bowling I should have put him on anyway, because of Bradman's failure against him at Manchester'. (6)

Bradman cut the first ball for a single and Woodfull played out the remaining two so that Bradman took guard against Tate. He steered the first ball on to the leg side for a couple but the next two 'baffled' him.

Woodfull took a single from the next Peebles over but they went off for bad light at 5.23pm, resuming at 5.40pm. Now Bradman faced Peebles with two short legs and he treated the last five balls of the over warily. He 'looked quite definitely anxious when he first started playing Peebles', Wyatt remembered. (7)

Woodfull played a maiden to Tate.

Bradman continued to watch Peebles warily, taking 2 and a single with neat, safe taps which penetrated the leg trap. He played Tate to mid-off for a single and Woodfull drove to the cover boundary, Wyatt in furious and futile pursuit.

Bradman sprang out to the third Peebles ball of the next over and struck it into the square leg region for 2.

Woodfull played out a maiden to Tate.

Bradman took a single to mid-off from Peebles. Facing Tate, he glanced the first ball for 2 and the next for a single. Woodfull, however, cut a single from the next ball to retain the strike and took a single from Peebles. Bradman lifted Peebles *over* the heads of the leg trap and they ran 3.

Hammond came on for Tate and conceded a bye so the batsmen crossed but Woodfull took a single to keep the strike. He faced Peebles and off-drove him to the boundary. The next two balls beat him and he just touched the fourth – caught behind by Duckworth. That made Australia 190 for 2 and Kippax got himself off the mark immediately with a single.

Kippax took all but three balls of the next three overs – and played some typically elegant leg glances – before Bradman stole a single from the first ball of a Peebles over to bring the 200 up. He was then on 17.

Larwood came on for Hammond for the final ten minutes of the day and that loosened the scoring: Bradman cut his first ball for 2, cut his fourth past point for a single, Kippax took one from the next ball, Bradman another cut from the last.

Peebles leaked runs, too: a couple of singles and a 2 from Bradman, a single from Kippax so that Bradman faced the final over, from Larwood. He scored a single past slip – the off-glance? – Kippax scored a single and Bradman rounded the day off by working a single to the leg side. He'd made 27 in an hour (Kippax 11) and, at 215 for 2, Australia looked to be moving to a position of great strength.

At eleven next morning, cool and under heavy cloud, a strong south-westerly breeze raked across the ground. The wicket looked as if it remained in excellent condition – 'a bit bare but is expected still to be firm'. (8) There'd been dew which might give variation of bounce early on.

Fender, peering through his spectacles, wrote: 'The wind was stronger and blowing from a slightly different angle. It will still not help the English bowlers because it is blowing almost straight across the wicket, but I think it will probably be better for them than was the case yesterday. There was no sign of any alteration in the wicket, but we shall know more about that when we have seen a few overs bowled.'

Tate opened from the Pavilion End bowling into the wind. Bradman took a single into the on side from the second ball, Kippax a single from the fourth, Bradman 3 driven past mid-off from the fifth, Kippax a single to keep the strike from the sixth. They'd scored from four of the six balls. The two batsmen 'started off just for all the world as though they had never left the wickets', Fender wrote. (9) 'They did not hurry, there was no need for them to do so, but none the less they progressed quietly and confidently.'

That was evident from this first over and, in a timeless Test, eternity stretched before them. What psychological effect that had on the bowling attack is not difficult to guess, especially since confirmation came as Larwood bowled: Kippax a single from the second ball, Bradman a single to square leg from the third and from the fifth Larwood was called for over-stepping. One of the singles, the *Evening Standard* commented acerbically, hadn't been 'really earned. There was slackness in the field.'

Tate began his second over with the new ball and Bradman cut the first fine for 2 then played the remaining five by keeping his bat out of the way whenever he could, although he had a moment of alarm when one swung in and struck him on the foot.

They ran 3 from a Larwood no-ball – over-stepping again – and Wyatt, sprinting, cut the ball off before it reached the square-leg boundary. Bradman faced Larwood and the breeze blowing across the wicket seemed to concern him. He took a single on the leg side, another from Tate's next over.

Larwood must have been bowling loosely because, after Bradman had taken a single past point, Kippax scored a couple. Larwood then bowled a full-toss shoulder high on the leg side which streaked to the boundary – the first of the day. It was a 'shockingly bad ball'. (10)

Bradman worked the favoured area past point for a single from Tate's first ball, Kippax took a single from the next and Bradman exquisitely late cut the fourth, 'beautiful, wristy' (11) – or luckily snicked it (12) – to the boundary at the Vauxhall End. The ball 'flew' across the grass. That made him 42.

At 11.30am Fender wrote that runs were coming mostly in singles and added how surprised he was that, although Larwood appeared to be at full speed, the batsmen had a remarkable amount of time to play him. 'Kippax seemed thoroughly at home. He scored neat singles with delicate on-side strokes. Bradman was also timing well, his back-play delicate.' (13)

Kippax took a single from Larwood's second ball and Bradman cut the fourth for 2.

Peebles came on for Tate at the Pavilion End, enabling Tate to switch ends and use the breeze to make the ball swing. Kippax 'prettily' turned the first Peebles ball for 2 and on-drove the second, a full toss, to the boundary making Australia 250 in four hours five minutes. England's 405 was becoming more and more vulnerable.

Bradman took a single from the last ball of Tate's over but suddenly Peebles found a length. He baffled Bradman with his first ball and the second, a googly, beat him as Bradman padded up to it. Duckworth's shout for lbw 'was heard all over the ground'. (14) Bradman might have touched it. He didn't score from any of the remaining four balls and the first maiden of the day drew loud applause from the crowd of 20,000. There was more when Tate bowled a maiden to Kippax.

The Sun, Sydney, wrote that Peebles seemed to be trying to hatch a 'deep-seated plot' to get Bradman: the square-leg umpire crossed to point so that Wyatt and Larwood could field at short leg. Bradman responded by 'viciously' lifting Peebles to the square-leg boundary and, two balls later, placed a single safely to mid-off to reach 50. It took an hour and thirty-nine minutes – 'quite slow for a young man who is usually in such a hurry' (15) – but, as Fender had already pointed out, there was no hurry. Peebles even added a third short leg and put a man on the square-leg boundary. Mailey, himself a leg-break bowler, observed that this was an entirely new theory, it surprised the Australians and Peebles now bowled either straight or the googly. Leg breaks would take the ball from leg to off, making the trap useless. (16)

Hammond came on at the Vauxhall end for Tate, who had a foot problem and went off for treatment. Hammond bowled a maiden to Bradman.

Peebles looked more dangerous although he leaked runs in his fourth over: a single from the first ball to Kippax, a 2 to mid-on and a single to cover for Bradman. At some point during these four balls Peebles said to Wyatt that he'd rather have him fielding at extra cover than forward short leg. Wyatt replied: 'Let's talk about that at the end of the over.' Next ball Kippax hit the ball so hard – more drive than push – it looked a boundary but Wyatt, close to the bat, made a yard, stretched out his right hand and caught it, arm fully outstretched. Kippax made 28 out of 73, Australia 263 for 3. That was 11.43am and Peebles was bowling well.

Jackson came in and drove the final ball between mid-off and cover. He set off but Hobbs had long made that territory his own and, underarm, flung the ball at the bowler's end to where Jackson was running. Hobbs just missed the stumps – the ball was deflected by the bowler's rough – and, because neither Peebles nor anybody else had had time to back up, it went for an overthrow.

Hammond bowled a maiden to Bradman who proceeded quietly because the turning point of the game might have been reached. Hammond commanded respect and although some people in the Press Box felt he was bowling too much down the leg side Fender, watching closely, disagreed. Hammond bowled straight.

Both batsmen were able to glance him from the stumps to fine leg. Fender read that as a commentary on how true the wicket was playing and how confident the batsmen were that it would play true. Peebles and

Hammond made the batsmen dig for runs in marked contrast to earlier in the innings. Fender conjured a single word for Bradman: subdued.

Jackson struggled against Peebles, who flighted the ball into the breeze. Peebles sent a rasping googly just past the leg stump and they ran a bye. Bradman worked a single past point, Jackson another and Bradman positioned the last ball for a single into the square-leg area.

He took a single past point from the first ball of Hammond's next over and Jackson a single from the last, bringing him to Peebles again. He took a single from the first ball, Bradman a single from the third – the point area again – but another googly beat Jackson, just missed the leg stump and went for 4 byes. The *Evening Standard* noted that Peebles made the ball 'wriggle about until both Jackson and Duckworth were beaten. They did not know where the ball would go with its twisting and turning.'

The *Evening Standard* also had a sketch writer at The Oval and he wrote: 'Jackson, who makes a careful survey of the field before he bats, did not like Peebles [he] looked, indeed, rather indignant at some of the deliveries which were served personally on him as if they were writs. You would think, as he looked this way and that before facing the bowler, that he was surely intending to send the next ball on a terrific flight, but his scoring was rather slow.'

Warner noted how uncomfortable Jackson looked. 'Over and over again he was hit on the legs by Peebles, making no attempt to play he ball.'

Bradman and Jackson took singles from the first two balls of Hammond's next over and Bradman played the over out. This was survival cricket to a staple diet of singles but, because in that era overs were bowled so quickly, the scoreboard ticked over at more than a run a minute.

Peebles beat Jackson again and the ball went for a bye before Bradman took 2 to square leg, making him 60. Jackson continued nervously even against Hammond, who beat and almost bowled him; the ball went for four more byes.

Still Bradman proceeded cautiously, a single from Peebles before Jackson unburdened himself with a boundary to mid-on, then Bradman worked Hammond to leg for a couple. He had taken half an hour to move from his 50 to 63.

Peebles bowled a maiden to Jackson. The game quietened, neither batsman inclined or interested in chasing runs.

Bradman took a single from Hammond and so did Jackson but Jackson kept the strike as Leyland came on for Peebles with Australia on 299. Bradman brought up the 300, in ten minutes under five hours, when he on-drove Hammond for 3. That was at 12.20pm, so Bradman and Jackson added 37 in exactly even time.

Would Bradman try and savage Leyland as he'd done at Leeds? Not immediately. He was playing a different kind of innings and contented himself with a single to mid-on – a charming off-drive – from the fourth ball, leaving Jackson to play out the over. Jackson seemed to be surviving entirely to give Bradman a platform for runs, but Bradman was taking them carefully and mostly one at a time although, after a single from Hammond, he played a fierce straight drive from Leyland to the boundary and another charming drive which Peebles restricted to a single.

The Australians, Fender wrote, were holding firm and avoiding any form of risk because the loss of a wicket now would be serious.

A single square of the wicket took Bradman to 75 (Jackson 13) and brought him back to Leyland. He did apply a little savagery, straight-driving the third ball to the pavilion fence and late cutting the last for 3. 'It was clear that Leyland,' the *Evening Standard* said, 'could bowl a decent ball but Bradman's quick judgement picked out those which would be profitable, and he drove again for 4 – this time to the off – and scored a 3 past short slip, who ought to have saved the runs but he was too slow of movement.' The culprit was not named.

In the next over Bradman gave his first chance. Hammond had been bowling just outside the off stump forcing the batsmen to play at the ball and making them vulnerable if it did anything. Bradman snicked one which went low and Duckworth couldn't hold it.

Jackson took a single from Leyland and Bradman played out the over. Hammond bowled a maiden to Jackson.

Tate came on for Leyland at 320 and Bradman hit the ball hard enough into the mid-off area to run 3. Jackson took a single to keep the strike. After Jackson played out a maiden to Hammond, Bradman cut Tate for a single and, next over, straight-drove Hammond to the boundary to move into the 90s. He had a single from the next ball and a single from the first ball of Tate's next over. Because Bradman looked so secure when he rationed his run-getting, and because the singles seemed so preordained and unremarkable, he could present an optical illusion and many witnesses have attested to this: he seemed to be chugging slowly along and when you glanced at the scoreboard you saw he was pushing the innings along at a very respectable rate.

Overall, Wyatt would remember: 'As his long innings dragged on we tried every dodge we could think of to dislodge him. I tried to stop him scoring by blocking the exits and putting a deep extra cover. I discussed ways and means of getting him out with Jack Hobbs and with the bowlers, but nothing could be done. At one point I suggested to Tate that he should send down a ball a little shorter but rather faster than usual so that Bradman, in attempting a cut, might mis-time it. This he did, but it was one of the catches that Duckworth dropped.' (17)

Larwood replaced Hammond for the traditional pre-lunch burst of pace but Bradman cut him for 2 and a single to go to 95. Peebles replaced Tate in a clear attempt to unsettle Bradman as he eyed the century. Bradman was not unsettled. He hooked him for a single, Jackson took one and Bradman worked him square again: 97.

Now Larwood, and a single past slip: 98. Jackson played out the over. Now Peebles, and a single from the first ball past slip: 99. Jackson hit the final ball to the boundary.

Now Larwood, and Bradman late cut the first ball beautifully to the pavilion fence. It was 1.05pm and he'd been batting for three hours five minutes. At Trent Bridge, playing even more cautiously, he'd taken three hours and thirty-five; in the carnage at Lord's an hour and forty-six; in the overwhelming initial assault at Leeds an hour and thirty-nine. Here, then, was another distinctive type of innings, tailored to suit the state of the match; here was the self-denial again. It is what great batsmen do quite naturally. 'Bradman, playing with more caution than in the second and third Tests, exploited most of his favourite shots, but, though perfectly confident, he was a little subdued owing to the need for reinforcing Australia's position. It was more like the innings he played in the first Test, when Australia was trying to force a draw. He scored nearly all his runs behind the wicket, and only occasionally jumped out for characteristic drives. It was a fine display, and yet another exhibition of Bradman's adaptability.' (18)

The real key would be revealed at lunch.

The crowd cheered for a full minute and made 'co-eee' noises.

Peebles conjured a maiden to Jackson, they took singles from Larwood, Jackson had 2 from Peebles and Bradman laid into Tate – brought back for Larwood already. He worked him into the on side for a couple and then 3. Still he kept the scoreboard clicking and so, now, did Jackson: Bradman a single square from Peebles, Jackson a single to keep the strike; Jackson a single from Tate, Bradman another past point.

Bradman faced the final over before lunch, from Peebles, and took a single to mid-off. Jackson suddenly opened up with boundaries off consecutive balls: an off-drive and a timed pull. They ran two leg byes from the second-last ball, Jackson survived the last and Australia went in to lunch at 371 for 3 (Bradman 112, Jackson 33). The key? However much Bradman had been dragging, or seeming to drag, 156 runs had been added in the one hundred and fifty minutes of morning play. The crowd called out 'co-eee' again as he came back to the pavilion.

During lunch the Prince of Wales arrived and both teams were presented to him. He said to Bradman: 'How do you do it?' but nobody heard what Bradman replied. A downpour at 2pm lasted quarter of an hour but left pools of water all over the pitch. After an inspection at 2.40pm play resumed at 3pm, the crowd now 30,000.

The pitch did not seem to have been affected although Tate used sawdust freely before he bowled the first over to Bradman, who cut the first ball for a single to set the scoreboard clicking for the afternoon. Both batsmen played themselves in circumspectly: Bradman another single past slip, from Larwood, Bradman a single from Tate in the point area. That was the third over and so far Jackson had faced thirteen balls without scoring.

When Bradman took his fourth single since lunch – in the point area from Larwood – Jackson at last got moving by late-cutting the final ball for 3. However, facing Tate, he took a single from the third ball but, contemplating a second, slipped and fell. Maybe the wicket had been affected.

Bradman sent the first ball of Larwood's next over past the slip area for 3, Jackson played out the over and, against Tate, Bradman played his first bad shot. To the second ball of the over he mis-timed a cut and the ball sailed between Duleepsinhji and Peebles for 2. Bradman was then 122 and very, very lucky. Tate had just moved Peebles from where the ball went. Bradman played out the over and at some point a ball beat him but went over the bails.

Peebles came on for Larwood and bowled Jackson a maiden.

Tate stayed on and Bradman took a single to mid-on, took another from Peebles, another from Tate so that in four overs Jackson had played thirteen balls without scoring – again. He'd made only 4 since lunch. Tate was making the ball snap and snarl.

Bradman might have been caught and bowled by Peebles, who slipped trying to get to the ball. The next beat him completely and then he took a single on the leg side. Jackson played the next two balls without scoring but gloriously on-drove the last to the boundary. They kept the scoreboard clicking: Bradman and Jackson singles in the next Tate over, Jackson a single and Bradman 2 – on the leg side – from Peebles before Hammond replaced Tate.

Hammond found immediate life in the wicket. His first ball reared over Jackson's head, the second reared, too, and Jackson weaved his head out of the way. The third struck him so hard on the left arm that, in obvious pain, he winced as he made to play at the fourth ball. It went for 4 byes to bring the 400 up. That was 3.50pm, and play was held up for several minutes while Jackson recovered. The light was deteriorating and they appealed successfully against it at 3.55pm. A thunderstorm threatened and strong wind dragged rain over. At 4.25pm it rained, heavy and fierce, bouncing on the covers and running off them. The crowd scattered, seeking cover.

The full significance of what Hammond had just done was not, understandably, appreciated and significantly Larwood makes no mention of it in his book *Bodyline?* where he describes exactly how and when that – bodyline – came into being. The wicket was lively, Hammond drew life from it and Jackson looked very vulnerable, as any batsman might have done. If the wicket played like that again, and Larwood achieved full speed, wouldn't that be interesting?

They inspected at 5.30pm and again at 5.45pm, the sun now out. Woodfull naturally didn't want to risk playing again but Wyatt felt the wicket might help the bowlers and did. The umpires made the extraordinary decision to come out at 6.25pm and play the final five minutes. No public announcement was made and when word spread many people thought it was a joke. *The Times* commented loftily: 'It was not clear to which of the teams their decision was the most obnoxious.'

The 5,000 who'd stayed cheered when the covers were removed at 6.20pm and Bradman and Jackson made their way to the wicket very, very slowly. Play resumed at 6.22pm.

Jackson played out the final two balls of the uncompleted Hammond over and Bradman faced Peebles, cut a single past point from the fourth ball. It meant he faced the final over, from Hammond, and left all the balls alone except one. He'd remember being barracked for that! (19) Australia finished on 403 for 3, Bradman 130 and Jackson 43. Bradman had so far batted four hours and twenty-eight minutes and taken Australia to within 2 of the England total.

The morning session of Wednesday, 20 August would seem to anyone glancing at the scorecard as ordinary. Although Jackson was out, Bradman remained at the crease at lunch and far beyond 200 just as Australia were far beyond England. In fact, everything changed but the scorecard didn't say that and neither did the scoreboard.

No rain fell overnight and when the England players emerged in sunshine – some cloud about – they all studied the pitch carefully. The groundsman said it would misbehave.

Fender sent the first report of the day to *The Star* at 11am, beginning with the observation that as far as he knew little or no rain fell overnight. That meant the wicket had had since 5pm the previous day to dry itself out. Fender felt England might still win but they needed quick wickets. He judged this unlikely unless the wicket did misbehave.

Bradman and Jackson came to the wicket much more quickly than they had the night before and were loudly cheered. Ironic cheers?

Again the scorecard, necessarily numerical and therefore arid, is misleading because in front of a disappointing crowd of 15,000 – one report suggests 8,000 – Wyatt opened the bowling with Peebles and Hammond in the hope that they might exploit any dampness in the wicket. Peebles began from the Pavilion End with a maiden to Jackson, turning the ball but only slowly. Chapman was saving Larwood for the new ball, due when Australia reached 420.

To an audible gasp Bradman pushed at Hammond's first ball but completely mis-timed it and sent it looping to Hammond's right in the direction of mid-wicket but it fell short of Whysall there and not even Hammond, who hadn't followed through after the delivery, could make the catch. Bradman got his innings moving by cutting the third ball for a single and Jackson played out the over. Both batsmen spent time patting the pitch down with their bats but the benign pitch was the opposite of the funny one Fender wanted.

Bradman played the first four balls of Peebles's next over safely enough and cut the fifth past point – the business stroke to establish and maintain the rhythm of his innings – but Jackson hesitated, went all at once and only just reached safety before Hammond threw the middle stump down. Jackson took a single from the final ball, making Australia 406 – and now ahead of England's 405.

Jackson took a single from Hammond and they ran a leg bye, keeping Bradman on strike. Hammond concentrated on bowling short and in line with the off-stump, making the batsmen play at every ball.

They moved cautiously again, as if this was a continuation rather than a new beginning, because the basic structural demands remained unaltered. Australia would spend the day batting England out of the match and each run, mostly singles, represented another small ratchet towards that.

Against Peebles, Bradman worked the point area again and Jackson took a single. Fender found the first few overs very interesting. Even from the Press Box he could see the ball was biting but it wasn't doing that enough to let Peebles turn the ball sharply.

Wyatt brought Leyland on for Hammond – Fender suspected, and later confirmed, that the thinking was Leyland might find turn in the wicket's dampness although Fender further suspected that the Australians were not unhappy to see Leyland rather than Larwood coming at them. Fender, peering through his spectacles, wrote: 'I am afraid, with my knowledge of The Oval wicket, that I should have been far more inclined to try a fast bowler at one end at least to see what happened.'

Jackson played a maiden to Leyland who, like Peebles, *was* finding slow turn. Bradman worked Peebles past point – all the runs he'd added had come from there – and Jackson took a 2 and a single to keep the strike. He played another maiden to Leyland.

Bradman played Peebles you-know-where, Jackson played out the over and now Bradman faced Leyland. He cut the second ball between Hobbs at cover and Larwood at deep extra cover so hard that neither man could stop it reaching the boundary. It was the first boundary of the day. He steered the fifth into the mid-off area and, next over, glanced Peebles towards square leg for 2 then, two balls later, glanced him so hard that it left Sutcliffe helpless on the edge of the boundary. That made him 146.

At 11.30am Fender reported that Leyland was bowling well and making the batsmen defend, although Fender wanted a burst from one of the pace bowlers. He assumed Wyatt was waiting for the new ball some 10 runs away.

Jackson did concentrate entirely on defence and played a maiden to Leyland. Now, at 11.35am, just as Tate prepared to bowl instead of Peebles, a shower stopped play. The players headed towards the pavilion but before they got there the shower stopped and they turned round, to loud applause. Bradman kept the score moving by turning Tate's first ball for 2.

Leyland, who'd been bowling round the wicket, went to the orthodox side and bowled Jackson another maiden. Tate responded with a maiden to Bradman and Leyland another to Jackson. No run had been scored for 23 balls but Bradman broke that, and reached 150, with a neatly placed leg glance. Australia were 430.

Next over Jackson drove Leyland for an all-run 4 and he had his 50 in three hours fifteen minutes.

Bradman delightfully late cut Tate to the Vauxhall end boundary but pushed the next and Duckworth just failed to get to it. The ball after that, swinging and leaping off the pitch, beat Bradman.

At last Jackson broke loose against Leyland with two 2s and a single from one over. The *Evening Standard* wrote that his belated success was the more gratifying because 'throughout this trip he has been genial and cheerful in spite of his lack of success'.

Tate took the new ball and Jackson had a single from it. Wyatt consulted Hobbs about whether Larwood or Hammond should share the new ball with Tate. Hammond got it because he could make it swerve but Jackson elegantly turned him for 2.

Bradman faced Tate, who set an attacking field and was clearly quite prepared to risk runs if he could turn the match with a wicket – especially Bradman's. Tate had three slips, a gully, deep third man and only two fielders on the leg side. Bradman turned the first ball to square leg where Sutcliffe on the boundary stopped it using his foot. They ran 3.

Bradman had a single from the third ball of Hammond's next over.

Tate looked dangerous because he was making the ball rise but Bradman deflected the first ball for 2 and straight-drove the fourth for 2. He'd made 162, past Sutcliffe for the highest score in the match. He late-cut the final ball for a single.

Hammond was making the ball kick from a good length but Bradman took two singles through the slips – the off-glance? – and Jackson one from the next over. Both batsmen looked comfortable and

Bradman had 165, taking his aggregate beyond Hammond's record of 905 in 1928–29.

Larwood replaced Tate and there was confusion over a run from the first ball – Jackson almost run out. Bradman pulled the second to the boundary and played out the over. Hammond bowled a maiden to Jackson.

Bradman faced Larwood and square-cut the third ball, a full toss, for 2, making the partnership worth 200 in 230 minutes (Jackson 62). Bradman effortlessly drove the final ball to the off-side boundary.

Jackson late-cut Hammond to the pavilion fence but now, quite suddenly, everything changed. Hammond made the next ball lift enough to rap Jackson painfully on the fingers. Larwood reached full speed and, as Wyatt said many years later, his voice lost in a kind of awe: 'Few people who didn't see Larwood can visualise how quick he really was.'

Unlike Hammond, Larwood couldn't make the ball rear from a length but if he bowled short and at full speed he was physically very dangerous. As *The Times* commented with a touch of sarcasm, when Larwood took over from Tate 'neither batsman was anxious to run a sharp single in order to secure the privilege of playing him'.

The first ball of Larwood's third over reared past the tip of Bradman's nose. The second struck him 'a fairly heavy blow' [(20)] on the right side of the chest and almost laid him out. [(21)] He threw his bat down, looked in great pain and needed some moments to recover.

Very few individual deliveries have changed cricket. This one might have done. In the next minutes he faced only fourteen more balls from Larwood but legend and folklore have been woven into them so that they have become far more than fourteen balls.

Peebles would remember the batsmen having 'a roughish time' against Larwood. 'Thinking how easily they had cruised along the previous day, one marvelled at how little it took to affect the balance between batsman and bowler. Don's consummate skill saved him from injury but Archie Jackson took some nasty knocks, despite his ill-health, unflinchingly.' [(22)]

Larwood would remember the ball 'popping'. Jackson, he'd write, 'stood up to me, getting pinked once or twice in the process, and he never flinched. With Bradman it was different. It was because of that difference that I determined, then and there, that if I was again honoured with an invitation to go to Australia I would not forget that difference.' [23]

Bradman took a single on the leg side from the fifth ball of that third Larwood over and this is the sequence after it: eight overs in a famous or notorious period of play. Bradman described it, in a truly wonderful piece of understatement, as 'a very trying time'. [24]

[0 = a ball the batsman did not score from. Read across then down.]

Hammond Bradman 0221 Jackson 00

Larwood Bradman 1 Jackson 001 Bradman 1
Jackson 0

Hammond Bradman 000000

Larwood Jackson 000000

Wyatt Bradman 3

(Bradman lifted this ball to the on-side and when they'd finished running they'd equalled the Australian fourth wicket record of 221 set by Syd Gregory and Albert Trott at Lord's in 1896.)

Jackson 04000

(Jackson turned that second ball to the square-leg boundary to beat the record.)

Larwood Bradman 40201 Jackson 0

(The boundary in this over was played to a rising ball but Bradman 'contrived to play it by snick or by glove behind the wicket'.) [25]

Wyatt Bradman 01 Jackson 0000

Larwood Bradman 21 Jackson 01 Bradman 01

The contemporary accounts are imprecise and sometimes contradictory although the overview is plain. These are the words of the reporters who were there:

The Times: *'After one or two shortish balls had flown head high, Bradman definitely declined to stand up to him [Larwood]. He retired to short-leg and sparred dangerously at the rising balls. He either missed them completely or knocked them down safely to third man.'*

The *Australian Press Association* recorded how *some of Larwood's deliveries were head high and how, at one point, Bradman almost played on to him. 'Jackson was elegant and attractive, dealing nicely with the rising balls until he dropped his bat in pain when he was hit hard on the left hip by a ball from Larwood just after receiving another nasty knock from Hammond. Larwood [. . .] sent the next ball whizzing past Jackson. Duckworth appealed for a catch.'*

Warner: *Bradman 'received a very nasty blow under the heart from a fast ball from Larwood when he had made 175 – and for an over or two he seemed inclined to draw away from Larwood, who was bowling at top speed and making the ball rise awkwardly at this period – but he quickly recovered his confidence and made some fine strokes to leg off the rising ball on his body.'* (26)

Fender: *'I think it would only be fair to say that during this period, with both bowlers making the ball lift as they did, it was only the ability of the batsmen rising superior to the circumstances, especially facing Hammond, which enabled Australia to weather a period which might otherwise have cost them several wickets.*

'Jackson seemed to run into most of the heavy weather, but he did extremely well, standing up to it and getting well over the ball on all occasions, and although taking some hard knocks, not flinching in the slightest degree. One ball from Larwood pitching on the stumps, but very short, turned in quickly on Bradman and hit him in the chest, and during the following overs there was a very marked difference in the manner in which the two batsmen faced the bowling. Bradman retreated more often than not towards square leg, though Jackson never gave an inch.' (27)

The Sun, Sydney: *'The bowlers actually were rattling the batsmen, who were more engaged in keeping the ball from their bodies than scoring. Larwood continued to send down these wretched balls, and while he may only be legitimately taking advantage of a bad spot, the game had certainly degenerated into a maiming match.'*

Larwood, like a shark, had scented blood during the fourteen balls. As he'd say, bodyline had been born and nobody but he knew it. Nor did the matter end there because, as *The Sun,* Sydney said: 'Larwood continued his terrifying deliveries and Bradman cleverly changed his methods by drawing away slightly to leg, taking the bat over his shoulder, and banging the ball square.' This was precisely the solution he'd attempt in Australia two years later to combat bodyline.

The wicket, however, mysteriously improved as quickly as it had become venomous. At 12.55pm, Bradman turned a Wyatt long hop to the leg-side boundary to move to 202' scored in six hours twenty-three minutes. In the same over Wyatt beat him with a leg-break.

Jackson took a single from Peebles. It brought him back to face Wyatt. He tried to drive and Sutcliffe caught him at extra cover. He'd made 73 (Bradman 203) and Australia were 506 for 4. He'd never play against England again.

McCabe came in prepared to do some instant damage. Before that, Peebles bowled to Bradman who cut the first ball to the boundary, ran 2 to the mid-on area and took a single there from the fourth. McCabe hit the first he received to the leg boundary.

Bradman loosened now, struck Peebles to the boundary and took a single to leg from the final ball; took a single to mid-on from the first ball of the next Peebles over, and McCabe retained the strike with a single from the last.

They were bustling along, McCabe threatening to cut loose. They ran a leg bye to Wyatt, Bradman worked the ball past mid-on for 3, and McCabe attacked the last two balls: a boundary through cover point, 2 to square leg. In four overs they'd added 28.

Peebles couldn't find a length and Bradman punished him freely, taking a boundary and a single through the cover point area. That made him 224.

Tate came on for Wyatt, and Larwood would come on for Peebles, in a pre-lunch assault. Bradman took a single from Tate's first ball, McCabe a couple; Bradman a single from Larwood's first ball, 2 to square leg from Tate's next – the last before lunch. Australia went in at 551 for 4 (Bradman 228, McCabe 18). During lunch Mailey came upon Jackson who smiled and said he'd been hit on the jaw, shoulder, elbow, wrist, ribs and hip.

McCabe had strike after lunch and, facing Larwood, took a single from the fourth ball, Bradman a single to square leg from the next, McCabe square cutting the final, short ball to the boundary. Tate stayed on at the other end and Bradman played him for 2 into the mid-on area.

McCabe announced what he intended to do: a single from Larwood over the slips, a square-cut boundary and single from Tate, a boundary through the slips from Larwood so that in three overs Bradman faced a single ball, from Larwood. Now, against Tate, he took a single through point and McCabe played the over out.

Larwood bowled at Bradman and he flicked the third ball which Duckworth caught. Australia were 570 and he'd made 232 in seven hours eighteen minutes. The dismissal was controversial in that the ball may not have hit his bat but brushed his sleeve.

Fender wrote of 'circumstances which caused a certain number to think that the decision had been a mistaken one. The batsman himself indicated very clearly at the time that he did not think he had touched the ball, but one or two of the fielders thought that the square-cut stroke which he had made at it had got a contact – and the umpire agreed with them.' (28)

The Times wrote that Bradman was 'a trifle late with a defensive stroke'.

Warner judged the innings remarkable. Bradman's defence, he insisted, reached perfection and his late cut reached that exalted state, too. He said he'd never seen a batsman play it more safely. Bradman 'played all the on-side strokes, and every now and again he drove cleanly past cover point. He never, however, drove straight. As always with him in his big innings, he hardly ever lifted the ball off the ground. He gave the impression of being very alert because he ran not only his own runs and those of his partner but even byes and leg byes at top speed.' (29)

The *Australian Press Association* wrote: 'He did not employ his characteristic severe drives as much as usual, preferring cuts, glances and delicate pushes for singles to hard hitting.'

He walked slowly from the wicket to a great storm of applause, many of the crowd on their feet. His head was bent and once he gazed over his shoulder to the scoreboard and shook his head. What that gesture meant nobody knows now: dissent at the decision or, as Mailey suspected, reproaching himself for not scoring enough? Mailey confidently wrote that there could no longer be any doubts about Bradman's abilities on all wickets and he must now be regarded as the greatest batsman of all time.

He'd made 974 Test runs from his seven innings, averaging 139.14. It is still, as I write these words (January 2009), a supreme achievement in Test match cricket despite the enormous proliferation of countries and matches since. Hammond's 905 in 1928–29 remains second and Mark Taylor (Australia v England 1989) third on 839.

The rest of the Fifth Test at The Oval in August 1930 is easily told. Australia pressed on to 695, a day was lost to rain and then Hornibrook (7 for 92) bowled England out for 251. Such a result had been anticipated for *days* and here it finally was. Australia regained The Ashes and, astonishingly, with one of the weakest bowling sides they'd ever sent to England. Grimmett was a genuinely great bowler and of the 76 Test wickets in 1930 he took 29, the rest spread among five others.

Grimmett enabled Australia to win. Bradman made sure they won.

I've been working with these things and thinking about them for more than forty years. It's a complicated subject because the fascination of greatness, comparative greatness and how you make the equations of greatness, involve ephemeral evidence, opinion, unprovables and comparisons which can't really be made. Try Bradman versus Ali.

Seventy-nine years later (when I am writing this) I cannot say if the 974 is the greatest sporting achievement of all time because, under the complication of the subject, nobody can. It did however expand the possibilities of cricket and, as we've just seen, seventy-nine years later nobody has improved on it.

The third ball from Larwood to Duckworth had all the simplicities and complications of every other cricket ball ever bowled. When it was bowled, and when Bradman set off towards the old Victorian edifice which was a pavilion after it had been bowled, nothing would be the same again; or has been.

Gloucestershire

Cricket tours then were proper tours and the Australians still had six matches to play, taking them from the West Country to the south and North Sea coasts. The first match was against Gloucestershire, and it ought to have been innocuous. It wasn't.

The Fifth Test finished on the Friday and the Australians were up early to catch the train to Bristol for a 2pm start. Bradman records how quiet they were on the journey. They'd put everything into the Test and

ENGLAND V AUSTRALIA – THE FIFTH TEST

The Oval, 16, 18, 19, 20, 21, 22 August. Australia won by an innings and 39 runs.

ENGLAND

J.B. Hobbs	c Kippax	b Wall	47		b Fairfax	9
H. Sutcliffe	c Oldfield	b Fairfax	161	c Fairfax	b Hornibrook	54
W.W. Whysall	lbw	b Wall	13	c Hornibrook	b Grimmett	10
K.S. Duleepsinhji	c Fairfax	b Grimmett	50	c Kippax	b Hornibrook	46
W.R. Hammond		b McCabe	13	c Fairfax	b Hornibrook	60
M. Leyland		b Grimmett	3		b Hornibrook	20
*R.E.S. Wyatt	c Oldfield	b Fairfax	64		b Hornibrook	7
M.W. Tate	st Oldfield	b Grimmett	10		run out	0
H. Larwood	lbw	b Grimmett	19	c McCabe	b Hornibrook	9
+G. Duckworth		b Fairfax	3		b Hornibrook	15
I.A.R. Peebles		not out	3		not out	0
Extras	(lb 17, nb 2)		19	(b 16, lb 3, nb 2)		21
Total			405			251

1-68, 2-97, 3-162, 4-190, 5-197, 6-367, 7-379, 8-379, 9-391

1-17, 2-37, 3-118, 4-135, 5-189, 6-207, 7-208, 8-220, 9-248

	O	M	R	W	O	M	R	W
Wall	37	6	96	2	12	2	25	0
Fairfax	31	9	52	3	10	3	21	1
Grimmett	66.2	18	135	4	43	12	90	1
McCabe	22	4	49	1	3	1	2	0
Hornibrook	15	1	54	0	31.2	9	92	7

AUSTRALIA

*W.M. Woodfull	c Duckworth	b Peebles	54
W.H. Ponsford		b Peebles	110
D.G. Bradman	c Duckworth	b Larwood	232
A.F. Kippax	c Wyatt	b Peebles	28
A.A. Jackson	c Sutcliffe	b Wyatt	73
S.J. McCabe	c Duckworth	b Hammond	54
A.G. Fairfax		not out	53
+W.A. Oldfield	c Larwood	b Peebles	34
C.V. Grimmett	lbw	b Peebles	6
T.W. Wall	lbw	b Peebles	0
P.M. Hornibrook	c Duckworth	b Tate	7
Extras	(b 22, lb 18, nb 4)		44
Total			695

1-159, 2-190, 3-263, 4-506, 5-570, 6-594, 7-670, 8-684, 9-684

	O	M	R	W
Larwood	48	6	132	1
Tate	65.1	12	153	1
Peebles	71	8	204	6
Wyatt	14	1	58	1
Hammond	42	12	70	1
Leyland	16	7	34	0

they were plain tired. They'd tried to have the match put back until the Monday but the only concession they received was the 2pm start. They were, Richardson records, (30) 'bedraggled and weary' when they 'spilt out from the train'.

He and the Gloucester captain Ben Lyon went out to inspect the pitch after rain and decided play wouldn't be possible until 4pm. Richardson says that when he returned to the Australian dressing room to tell the players they could relax he found them asleep.

Richardson won the toss and put Gloucestershire in on a difficult wicket. They were bowled out for only 72 and when the Australians batted on the second day they fared little better although Ponsford made 51 and Bradman 42. 'Bradman was in no mood for aggressive cricket but was content to turn the ball and place Goddard through the big gaps on the off side,' *The Times* reported. 'Bradman gave silly mid-off a catch after batting for an hour and three quarters, having played somewhat colourless cricket.'

They were all out for 157 and Gloucestershite, batting much better in their second innings (Hammond 89), set them 118 to win. The wicket had crumbled. Gloucestershire's Goddard and Parker exploited that after Jackson and McCabe put on 59 for the first wicket. Even Bradman could not halt a subsequent collapse. He made 14 before Parker bowled him – the second time Parker dismissed him in the match – and the crowd of 6,000 roared their approval. Bradman later told Wilfred Rhodes that Parker was 'the most difficult left-hander he ever played against'. (31)

In a desperate finish Walker and Hornibrook, the last wicket, ran a dangerous scrambled single off Goddard to make the scores level. The fielders closed in to block the winning single and the batsmen survived the remainder of Goddard's over. They then survived an over from Parker so that Hornibrook faced Goddard again. He was lbw amid what *The Times* called 'the wildest scenes of enthusiasm'.

No tied match had ever happened before in a match between English and Australian sides.

GLOUCESTERSHIRE V AUSTRALIANS

Bristol, 23, 25, 26 August. Tied.

GLOUCESTERSHIRE

R.A. Sinfield	c Walker	b Hurwood	1	c a'Beckett	b Hornibrook	16
A.E. Dipper	c Richardson	b Hurwood	1	c a'Beckett	b McCabe	26
W.R. Hammond	c a'Beckett	b Hornibrook	17		b Hornibrook	89
*B.H. Lyon		b Hurwood	5		b McCabe	8
+H. Smith	c Richardson	b Hornibrook	16		b Hornibrook	23
C.C.R. Dacre	c a'Beckett	b Grimmett	4	c McCabe	b Grimmett	17
F.J. Seabrook		c & b Grimmett	19	lbw	b Hornibrook	2
W.L. Neale	c Walker	b Hornibrook	2		b Hornibrook	0
C.J. Barnett		b Grimmett	2	c Walker	b Grimmett	6
C.W.L. Parker		not out	0		not out	3
T.W.J. Goddard	c Kippax	b Hornibrook	3		run out	0
Extras	(lb 2)		2	(b 6, lb 6)		12
Total			72			202

1-2, 2-3, 3-17, 4-30, 5-35, 6-53, 7-67, 8-69, 9-69

1-21, 2-101, 3-113, 4-166, 5-187, 6-192 7-199, 8-199, 9-210

	O	M	R	W	O	M	R	W
a'Beckett	8	4	9	0	9	4	16	0
Hurwood	11	5	13	3	11	4	29	0
Grimmett	19	3	28	3	28.2	4	83	2
Hornibrook	14.3	6	20	4	25	5	49	5
McCabe					10	3	13	2

AUSTRALIANS

W.H. Ponsford		b Sinfield	51		run out	0
A.A. Jackson		b Goddard	8	lbw	b Goddard	25
D.G. Bradman	c Sinfield	b Parker	42		b Parker	14
A.F. Kippaxlbw		b Sinfield	3	lbw	b Parker	0
S.J. McCabe	c Smith	b Parker	5		b Parker	34
*V.Y. Richardson	lbw	b Goddard	12	st Smith	b Parker	3
E.L. a'Beckett	c Sinfield	b Goddard	1	c Lyon	b Parker	2
A. Hurwood		b Goddard	0	lbw	b Parker	14
C.V. Grimmett		not out	7	c Seabrook	b Parker	12
P.M. Hornibrook		b Goddard	9	lbw	Goddard	4
+C.W. Walker	c Seabrook	b Parker	7		not out	0
Extras	(b 5, lb 7)		12	(b 2, lb 7)		9
Total			157			117

1-42, 2-78, 3-88, 4-96, 5-129, 6-131, 7-131, 8-131, 9-140

1-59, 2-63, 3-67, 4-73, 5-73, 6-81, 7-86, 8-108, 9-115

	O	M	R	W	O	M	R	W
Sinfield	14	5	18	2				
Barnett	4	3	3	0				
Goddard	26	7	52	5	34.1	10	54	2
Parker	30.5	9	72	3	35	14	54	7

Canterbury was hot – hotter than Sydney, Bradman felt, and although he didn't say this, hot for another reason. *The Sydney Morning Herald,* under a 'London,' 27 August dateline (the day the Kent match began) reported that the correspondent of the *Australian Press Association* [Tebbutt] at Canterbury had told Bradman of rumours he was 'to be carpeted' on his return to Australia. Bradman responded that nobody could be carpeted until then and only 'if Mr. Kelly so recommends. I have nothing to say about it.' Tebbutt explained that Kelly had 'informed the *Australian Press Association* that he could not well pass over Bradman's apparent defiance of the Board of Control'.

Tebbutt added: 'Bradman's team-mates say nothing, but it is believed that they naturally feel that Bradman's great success has enabled him to act in a manner in which others dare not. Bradman is a keen business man. He has been careful so far not to write about recent matches, so possibly a less serious view will be taken of the matter. However, it is difficult to reconcile Bradman's cinematic appearances and journalistic activities with the formidable contract the players signed.'

What specifically prompted Kelly to say what he did is unknown, and, incidentally the *Herald* put it at the bottom of a page beneath both the report of the Kent match and two paragraphs about the tour's finances, so even in the restrained context of 1930 it was being offered as a sober news item rather than something apocalyptic.

It is, however, one of those maddening items with clear subterranean aspects which are not explored (and presumably left the readers of the *Herald* on 29 August 1930 as curious and bemused as we are today).

The relationship between Kelly and Bradman can only be conjecture, although Bradman did say much later that Kelly was no diplomat and once burst into his – Bradman's – bedroom brandishing a newspaper which said he was to appear on stage. Bradman, in pyjamas, explained that he had not signed to do anything of the sort. [(32)]

To find a context, we must indulge in the conjecture. It was an age of deference to figures in authority, and Kelly – a formidable-looking figure with his moustache – represented that. It was an age of autocratic rule where employees did what they were told and kept their mouths shut, at least in public. Moreover, Kelly had charge of a young side who *were* innocents abroad and one of his prime considerations must have been *not* to lose control of them. England could have been a cavern of temptations. This explains the draconian initial contract from the

Board, the enforcement of silence to Press questions throughout the tour, Kelly's gruff way of dismissing journalists even when they were asking for team news, and the screening of the Australian dressing room – even at The Oval, when Kelly put up a sign saying unauthorised entry was forbidden. The Prince of Wales, visiting – and he owned the ground – said: 'You can't do that to me.'

It all represented a constant circling of the wagons.

Kelly had suddenly and quickly – no later than the second match, Leicester – found himself with a phenomenon on his hands, and, worse, a phenomenon which grew bigger day by day until it attained genuinely surreal proportions. *This* could get out of control at any moment, brushing aside the Board's contract, breaking up team morale and opening the gates to who knew what else? It may be that august, distant Mr. W.L. Kelly felt, in his private moments, bemused, angry and not a little fearful. Tebbutt, in his book at the end of the tour, wrote – it bears quoting again – that 'Kelly lacked the firmness to take the situation in hand before it got beyond him'. In an era when people *didn't* set down insights like that it remains a strong judgement to make.

Now extend the conjecture to Bradman himself. He came from a modest background and was only 21 when the tour began. He celebrated his 22nd birthday on this same 27 August as the match against Kent began and Tebbutt filed his subterranean paragraphs. Bradman, like Kelly, had a phenomenon on his hands: himself. It grew at the same speed for him as it did for Kelly. He had a chance to make a great deal of money and can anybody, contemplating a 21-year-old of the modest background in an Australia ravaged and humbled by the Depression, blame him for doing it after taking great care that it did not violate the Board's contract and in no way impaired his ability to function as a player?

In *Bradman: The Illustrated Biography* author Michael Page offers the opinion that 'it seems Kelly felt the need to "pull rank" on Bradman, or perhaps he felt more than a twinge of jealousy at his success'. The latter is extremely improbable because no manager expects to be lauded as a success in the way players are. He is of necessity a background figure, steering the ship in near silence, and in what way would he feel jealousy? Whatever Bradman (or any other player) got or didn't get, Kelly was never going to get anyway and he must have known that from the moment he agreed to manage the tour. Ordinarily a manager delights in the success of his players (and if he doesn't, what is he doing there?)

The former seems more likely. Kelly, living with the fact that the phenomenon was – in his eyes – stretching the limits of control, and maybe creating dissention in the ranks, vented his anger in what in context amounts to a significant outburst to Tebbutt, however subterranean.

The tensions would return and return, dogging the journey back to Australia and increasing when the team landed before reaching a climax when Kelly made his report to the Board. It may seem trite to say the tensions were inevitable, but postulating that one individual success – on this scale and in a team sport – could have happened without generating them is very, very difficult.

Keeping it subterranean, they played Kent quite normally.

Kent

Woodfull returned, won the toss and batted in front of 13,000 people. Warner thought the Australians looked tired and in their first innings were dismissed for 181 – Bradman lbw to Tich Freeman for 18.

The Times reported that Bradman 'played one beautiful stroke to fine leg for 3 off Freeman but his treatment of [Bill] Ashdown [right-arm medium-fast] and his tendency to play Freeman as that very astute bowler would have had him play, led the spectator to suppose that Bradman would have been far happier if Woodfull had taken him to open the innings, so giving him time to get the pace of the pitch before Freeman appeared. Both he and Jackson were leg before wicket to that ball of Freeman's that does not turn very much but comes quickly off the pitch.'

Kent replied with 227. Bradman joined Woodfull when Ponsford was out for 11. Woodfull played Freeman's mysteries with his pads while Bradman was 'on the look-out for any ball that could be hit hard and safely'. [33]

The Times reported: 'It was extremely interesting to watch Bradman playing Freeman. He used his feet well in playing him, and an overpitched ball was swept firmly round to the boundary at mid-wicket, but, although Bradman was obviously determined to show that he could play the spinning ball as well as the fast ball which comes straight through, Freeman would every now and again produce that ball which makes the batsman pray it has not touched either his bat or his stumps. The stand between him and Woodfull was full of good and courageous cricket, however.'

Bradman finished the day 68 not out and next day with Jackson did make the match safe.

'When the game was continued, five minutes after the advertised time, Bradman and Jackson walked through a crowd of admiring boys and girls, who actually followed them to the pitch, where a policeman or two shepherded them off in the gentlest manner possible,' Warner wrote. 'This certainly gave a rural touch to the match, but it was a most unusual sight at a first-class game, and on one of the most famous grounds in the world.' (34)

The *Australian Press Association* felt the locals might have had a 'premonition of dull cricket'. No more than 3,000 of them came and they saw Jackson and Bradman bat 'listlessly. Bradman showed a measure of enterprise. Freeman's perfect length commanded respect but more than an hour passed before Bradman pulled a ball, and was ironically applauded.'

Freeman impressed Warner, too, as something magnificent. 'There was a worn patch on the middle-and-leg stump and he made his leg-break turn several inches. I was sitting behind his arm with several pundits, and opinion was unanimous as to the greatness of his work.' Warner described the batsmen as cautious rather than listless and pointed out that they added only 50 in the eighty-five minutes to 1 o'clock.

Bradman was mildly barracked although his defensive mastery earned a grudging admiration and everybody knew what Freeman could do, particularly if a wicket fell. *The Times* however wondered why, if Bradman could defend like this and read the spin so well, he hadn't trusted himself to make the Australians safe from defeat in an hour.

The *Australian Press Association* used more trenchant words. It was a 'dreadful display on the part of both batsmen'. Bradman lingered for three quarters of an hour in the 90s before finally, with the Australians total at 175, jumping out to Hardinge and thumping a full-pitch to the long-on boundary to reach his eleventh century of the tour. This one took three hours twenty-five minutes, but the 32 this morning needed an hour and a half. In the same time Jackson made 14.

He accelerated, punishing Hardinge and Freeman, and that seemed to prove the earlier caution wasn't justified. He scored five boundaries – three off-drives, a pull and a hook – quickly and the Australians went in to lunch at 215 for 3 (Bradman 127, Jackson 27).

Though Bradman hit brilliantly, the sun-baked spectators lost interest after lunch because the Australians' refusal to force the game earlier made a draw inevitable. Bradman plundered the leg breaks of C.H. (John) Knott for three successive 4s: the off-glance for one of them, hooked a ball from his off-stump for another. He took 28 from Knott in two overs while Jackson, 'whose snail-like pace had not improved', (35) crawled to 37.

This was the other Bradman, the early-tour Bradman, and unrecognisable from the pre-lunch player. He'd made sure the Australians wouldn't lose and then cut loose, using his feet to go up the wicket, playing strokes all over the field and essentially doing whatever he wanted.

He'd reached 150 by playing a ball from medium-pacer Albert Wright off his legs effortlessly, except for the whip of his wrists. When he got to 200 Woodfull declared. It left enough time for Kent to make 82 for 2.

Bradman defended his slow scoring in *Don Bradman's Book.* He began by explaining that when the Test series ended he had an end-of-term feeling and wanted to entertain. That, however, did not extend endangering the Australians' situation in any given match. It took priority at Canterbury. He accepted that the batting might have been 'uninteresting' but hoped the spectators understood – and forgave.

The Australians travelled along the coast from Canterbury to Brighton where they played and drew with Sussex. Bradman was rested. They motored back along the coast to the Folkestone Festival and a match against a strong England XI.

England XI

A large crowd watched the England XI proceed circumspectly until Percy Chapman started to hit everything he could reach and at one point Bradman dropped him off a'Beckett. The England XI made 403 for 8 declared.

Bradman came in at 118 for 1 and, Warner wrote, 'played a characteristic innings in which were several fine late cuts and strokes to leg, while the certainty with which he can hit any full-pitch for 4 was again apparent. He practically never plays forward, relying almost entirely on back play for defence.' (36)

He and Jackson scored rapidly as the second day drew to a close (he was 30 not out) and next morning they put on 40 in half an hour. Here was Bradman the entertainer, batting easily, giving his armoury of

KENT V AUSTRALIANS

Canterbury, 27, 28, 29 August. Drawn.

AUSTRALIANS

*W.M. Woodfull	run out		16	lbw	b Freeman	45
W.H. Ponsford	c Ashdown	b Freeman	21		b Ashdown	11
D.G. Bradman	lbw	b Freeman	18		not out	205
A.A. Jackson	lbw	b Freeman	11		not out	50
V.Y. Richardson	c Ames	b Ashdown	45			
A.G. Fairfax		b Freeman	4			
E.L. a'Beckett		run out	4			
C.V. Grimmett	c Chapman	b Ashdown	0			
A. Hurwood	c Ames	b Hardinge	45		run out	0
T.W. Wall		not out	12			
+C.W. Walker	lbw	b Freeman	1			
Extras	(b 1, lb 1, nb 2)		4	(b 7, lb 2)		9
Total			181	(3 wkts dec)		320

1-39, 2-39, 3-65, 4-78, 5-98, 6-122, 7-122, 8-125, 9-178 — 1-18, 2-123, 3-125

	O	M	R	W	O	M	R	W
Wright	7	2	18	0	16	4	40	0
Ashdown	18	4	38	2	21	4	68	1
Freeman	39.2	8	78	5	33	12	68	1
Hardinge	21	10	43	1	31	6	86	0
Woolley					16	7	21	0
Knott					2	0	28	0

KENT

H.T.W. Hardinge	lbw	b Grimmett	39		not out	12
J.L. Bryan		b Grimmett	31	c Jackson	b Hurwood	11
F.E. Woolley	c a'Beckett	b Wall	3		not out	60
+L.E.G. Ames		b Wall	8			
L.J. Todd		not out	42		b Wall	0
W.H. Ashdown		b Wall	48			
A.P.F. Chapman	c Fairfax	b a'Beckett	1			
C.H. Knott		b Grimmett	3			
*G.B. Legge		b Grimmett	22			
A.C. Wright	c Walker	b Wall	19			
A.P. Freeman		b Wall	0			
Extras	(b 3, lb 7, nb 1)		11			0
Total			227	(2 wkts)		83

1-71, 2-76, 3-86, 4-86, 5-155, 6-155, 7-166, 8-198, 9-225 — 1-1, 2-31

	O	M	R	W	O	M	R	W
Wall	26.2	5	60	5	3	0	7	1
Fairfax	17	6	39	0	5	1	22	0
Grimmett	37	12	80	4				
a'Beckett	12	2	32	1	8	0	27	0
Hurwood	10	6	5	0	10	3	19	1
Richardson					1	0	8	0

strokes full expression. He took Australia to 200 with a rasping square cut to the boundary and his own 50 with an on-drive. Allom had the new ball and Bradman glanced him on the leg side but when he tried to do it again was lbw. He'd made 63 (six 4s) in an hour and a quarter. *The Times* described the innings as 'delightful'.

The England XI made 46 for 1 at the end. In the true spirit of a Festival match the Australians used a total of eight bowlers (Bradman 3 overs for 7 and no wicket), and the England XI ten.

Club Cricket Conference

The idea that a touring party of Australians, who had already played thirty-two matches in England since 30 April, would meet a team of club cricketers over two days at Lord's seems nigh incredible now. The Club Cricket Conference represented some 700 clubs in and around London and, as Bradman attested, came some way to producing an old-fashioned sporting shock in front of 5,000 people; London would not see the Australians again this tour. The larger wickets were used, incidentally.

The Australians batted, Ponsford went for a duck in the second over and Bradman turned the first ball he received to the long-leg boundary. He was then missed when he hit a catch to square leg. Thereafter he batted as if it was a Test match, finding so many gaps that the runs came in even time. He made 30 of the first 40 in half an hour and was 'dashing'. [37] The total reached 96 in an hour and a quarter when Bradman – 70, and with seven 4s – chased a ball moving away from him and was well caught low down at first slip.

The Australians made 278 and bowled the Conference side out twice to win it comfortably.

Bradman wrote nostalgically about 'good bye to Lord's' and recalled the farewell dinner by the MCC, in the magnificent oak-panelled hall of the Merchant Taylors' Company, where the author J.M. Barrie made a humorous speech calling him 'Mr. Badman'.

Barrie said:

> *'This Mr. Badman seemed to carry about his person the atom with which professor Einstein frightened us.* [38] *I had a horrible fear that Larwood or Tate would strike him on that spot and the earth dissolve, leaving only Chapman to catch what was left. [Loud laughter] I am very sorry for Badman. I have no doubt he meant to do better. [Loud laughter] When the*

ENGLAND XI V AUSTRALIANS

Folkestone, 3, 4, 5 September. Drawn.

ENGLAND XI

R.E.S. Wyatt	c Oldfield	b Hornibrook	51		
J.W. Hearne	c a'Beckett	b Wall	33		
W.R. Hammond	hit wicket	b Wall	54		
J.A.S. Langridge	c Jackson	b a'Beckett	23		
+L.E.G. Ames	c Oldfield	b Wall	121	c & b a'Beckett	5
*A.P.F. Chapman	c Ponsford	b a'Beckett	40		
R.C. Robertson-Glasgow	b a'Beckett		2	not out	9
M.W. Tate	c & b McCabe		50		
Hon. F.S.G. Calthorpe	not out		14		
M.J.C. Allom,	dnb			not out	27
A.P. Freeman	dnb				
Extras	(b 9, lb 4, w 2)		15	(b 1, lb 4)	5
Total	(8 wkts dec)		403	(1 wkt)	46

1-78, 2-108, 3-167, 4-171, 5-232,
6-249, 7-370, 8-403 — 1-7

	O	M	R	W	O	M	R	W
Wall	41.4	11	104	3				
a'Beckett	29	11	81	3	3	0	3	1
Grimmett	10	1	35	0				
Hornibrook	28	6	83	1				
McCabe	19	3	78	1	5	2	12	0
Bradman	3	0	7	0				
Kippax					4	0	23	0
Jackson					1	0	3	0

AUSTRALIANS

*W.M. Woodfull		run out	34
W.H. Ponsford	c Calthorpe	b Allom	76
D.G. Bradman	lbw	b Allom	63
A.F. Kippaxlbw		b Allom	0
A.A. Jackson		b Langridge	78
S.J. McCabe		b Allom	14
E.L. a'Beckett	c Hammond	b Freeman	53
+W.A. Oldfield	lbw	b Freeman	10
C.V. Grimmett	c Langridge	b Freeman	1
P.M. Hornibrook	c Hearne	b Freeman	43
T.W. Wall		not out	40
Extras	(b 9, lb 11)		20
Total			432

1-118, 2-119, 3-119, 4-222, 5-242,
6-307, 7-327, 8-341, 9-345

	O	M	R	W
Tate	14	5	31	0
Allom	32	5	94	4
Freeman	41.5	3	131	4
Robertson-Glasgow	11	2	12	0
Langridge	16	1	54	1
Hammond	5	1	10	0
Wyatt	5	0	32	0
Calthorpe	5	2	12	0
Chapman	1	0	5	0
Hearne	8	2	31	0

Australians return home, countless thousands will meet them, straining in the leash to hear from Woodfull which side won. They will all be taken to hotels and public places – except Badman. He has carried this plan of his, of not knowing how to get out, to such an extent that now he cannot get out of anything. He won't even be able to get out of the ship. When all the others are merry and bright, we leave him pacing the deck – a dark and gloomy figure [laughter].'

Leveson-Gower's XI

The Scarborough Cricket Festival, created in 1876, grew into an end-of-season institution where leading players indulged in serious cricket with a light heart. Moment by moment the matches were suspended between the two and obeyed the creed that players could show their skills but not too much of them. When a bowler took quick wickets he might expect to be taken off; when a batsman scored a hundred he'd be expected to get out. Everyone – players, umpires, officials, spectators – delighted in the whole thing and in its mood the Festival represented the perfect way for a touring side to complete their tour.

Leveson-Gower invited virtually a full current England side but also included Wilfred Rhodes, playing the final match of his career and who had already, of course, bowled at Bradman for Yorkshire at Sheffield. In a very poignant sense the match represented the end of an era, because Rhodes played under and bowled at W.G. Grace, and the beginning of another. By 10 September 1930, as the crowd of 10,000 gathered for the first day's play, none could doubt that they were living in the time of Bradman.

Richardson captained the Australians, won the toss and put the Leveson-Gower XI in. Showers restricted the day but 218 runs were scored and, because showers cut into the second day, Wyatt declared.

The *Scarborough Evening News and Daily Post* reported: 'There was a large crowd outside the gates today awaiting some decision and very few in the ground, the outlook appearing very dismal. This was unfortunate, as another huge gate was anticipated, most people being credited with the great desire of seeing Bradman bat in particular.'

(When the covers were taken off a crab measuring seven inches was found, presumed deposited by a gull, so even the birds were dropping their catches.)

CLUB CRICKET CONFERENCE V AUSTRALIANS

Lord's, 6, 8 September. Australians won by an innings and 41 runs.

AUSTRALIANS

W.H. Ponsford	c Summers	b Brindley	0
A. Fairfax		b Brindley	25
D.G. Bradman	c Whitehead	b Nazeer Ali	70
A.F. Kippax		b Smith	63
S.J. McCabe		b Brindley	0
E.L. a'Beckett		b Smith	14
*W.M. Woodfull	c Summers	b Brindley	69
W.A. Oldfield		b Smith	0
A. Hurwood		b Smith	0
P.M. Hornibrook	lbw	b Brindley	1
+C.W. Walker		not out	7
Extras	(b 18, lb 11)		29
Total			278

	O	M	R	W
Smith	23	3	70	4
Brindley	30.1	5	71	5
Nazeer Ali	25	5	52	1
Taylor	14	1	45	0
Jarvis	4	0	11	0

CLUB CRICKET CONFERENCE

T.G. Grinter		b Fairfax	5	c Hurwood	b Fairfax	8
L.W. Newman		b Fairfax	6		b Hurwood	8
T.N. Pearce	c a'Beckett	b Fairfax	7	st Walker	b Hornibrook	30
G.F. Summers	c a'Beckett	b McCabe	53		b Hornibrook	15
W.T. Brindley	lbw	b Hurwood	34		b McCabe	5
S. Nazeer Ali		b Hurwood	14		not out	24
H. Taylor		b Hurwood	0		b Hornibrook	6
F.E. Whitehead	c Hurwood	b Fairfax	3		b a'Beckett	1
V.E. Jarvis		b Hurwood	1	c Walker	b a'Beckett	0
H.T.O Smith		not out	4		b Hornibrook	0
H.E.L Piercy		b Hurwood	0		b a'Beckett	1
Extras	(b 3, lb 2, nb 1)		6	(b 3, lb 2, nb 1)		6
Total			133			104

	O	M	R	W	O	M	R	W
Fairfax	22	6	41	4	7	3	7	1
a'Beckett	15	3	35	0	4.5	4	1	3
Hornibrook	11	0	26	0	10	0	37	4
McCabe	9	3	11	1	8	2	20	1
Hurwood	8.3	4	14	5	10	0	33	1

Play eventually began at 2.45pm, Jackson and Fairfax opening to Larwood and Tate. After half an hour, with the score 17 and the ground full, Rhodes came on. Rhodes bowled Jackson with a ball which pitched on the leg stump. Jackson tried a big hit but it spun across him and took the off stump. There was something timeless about this ball: batsman had been seduced into big hits – and tempted by easy runs – against it since Rhodes first played for Yorkshire in 1898, and now at the very end they were still doing it.

'Jackson received a warm tribute as he retired after a pretty 24, and an outburst of loud applause showed unmistakedly what was the crowd's desire. Bradman was in no hurry whatever to reach the wicket, but once there his opening did not disappoint, 10 runs quickly accruing. His first scoring stroke, however, gave the crowd a jolt, as he returned a ball from Rhodes only just short of Wyatt at mid-on.' **(39)**

Rhodes remembered that 'with a little luck I should have had Bradman caught at mid-off before he had scored, if I had had a better fielder there. It would have been nice to have had Bradman out for a duck, but it is only fair to say that the wicket had been covered to protect it against the rain of the night.' However the rain had been so heavy some got through the covering and 'made the wicket patchy. It looked to me that the ball pitched on one of these spots and that this caused Bradman, who was playing a forcing shot through the covers, to mis-time it.' **(40)**

The Times felt he'd been 'deceived in the flight', Wyatt fielded a couple of yards too deep and 'so what, considering the positions in cricket held by Rhodes and Bradman, would have been an historical catch was never made.'

He took a single from Parker, struck him powerfully to leg for 3, turned Rhodes 'cleverly' for 2 deep on the leg side – Duckworth running for it in his pads – then played a tremendous straight drive from Rhodes to the boundary. That was the 10, quickly accrued.

He 'delighted the crowd with masterly batsmanship, placing the ball through the field. He had scored 21 against his partner's 2 in little more than a quarter of an hour, which, considering the slow travelling of the ball on the ground, was remarkable.' **(41)**

Bradman, however, took a different view. He described the wicket as a slow-turner in the English way and that made for dull cricket. **(42)** He punished anything short by pulling it but the slowness of the outfield stopped these shots reaching the boundary. Tate replaced Parker, who wasn't turning the ball, and Bradman straight-drove him so powerfully that it did go to the boundary – almost 6.

By tea he'd made 48 in forty minutes with four boundaries. He went to 50 by placing Rhodes for a single on the leg side. At 60 he jumped out to a ball from Rhodes which was crucially just shorter than the ones which had gone immediately before it and spun more. It beat Bradman and beat Duckworth, too. 'A difficult chance', Rhodes remembered. Another timeless ball . . .

Then Bradman mis-timed a hook which went to Sandham at square leg but the ball was spinning so viciously that Sandham didn't manage to get underneath it. 'An easy catch,' Rhodes remembered.

The light faded and he finished on 73 not out.

That evening a civic banquet was held in the Grand Hotel to commemorate the Jubilee of the Festival. The Australians attended and a great many speeches were made. Leveson-Gower talked whimsically about the Ashes. Lord Hawke proposed the toast and said: 'I am told that Australians or any of the people from our great dominions when they come here always talk of coming home. The great word was home and they could not come without coming to Scarborough. It is the finest place in the country and will remain so.'

Hawke added that he was not 'crying' about the Ashes because the better team won.

> *'When you first came over here you were very mild. You hoped to do well; but after a certain time our Press said there were only two to be feared – Mr. Bradman and Mr. Grimmett. We know Mr. Bradman has come over to this country and robbed our orchard, securing record after record. We don't mind that. He is a wonder. He is a brilliant player with an average at the end of a series of five Tests of 139. I don't believe he has played his finest innings yet. Mr. Hobbs, when asked which was the finest innings he had ever seen in Test cricket, said Macartney's 124 [it was 112] before lunch at Leeds, and I agree with him. I hope some day Mr. Bradman will have the chance to play as great an innings as that.'*

So the presence of Macartney was still there and clearly Hawke did not accept that Bradman's 254 at Lord's, or indeed his immense creation at Leeds, were superior. To make definitive judgements about anything like this is rather like giving marks to oil paintings or piano concerts, but in the years to come the sheer weight of Bradman's achievements would overwhelm what Macartney had done – and perhaps, that autumn day, had already done so.

Kelly made a gracious speech, speaking about Old Father Time creeping across the pitch to conclude the tour and how he hoped the team had showed true sportsmanship throughout. Within three years Jardine, Larwood and Voce would have redefined the atmosphere of cricket and made such a speech impossible.

Rhodes was called upon to speak but said he was no good at that sort of thing. 'I am very sorry to give up first-class cricket, but you cannot help Anno Domini. Thank you all again.'

Next morning Bradman went on to 96. He jumped out to try and hit a short ball from Parker to square leg but it kept low and bowled him. He had made 2,960 runs in first-class matches, and including a Scottish XI and the Club Cricket Conference, 3,170 in England – and 3,396 overall, including Tasmania, Perth and Colombo.

Up until 1930, the only comparison had been Trumper with 2,570 for the touring 1902 Australians. Trumper played 53 innings, Bradman only 36 for the 2,960, and these totals were reflected in their respective averages: Trumper 48.49, Bradman 98.66.

As the great cricket historian and philosopher C.L.R. James wrote (in another context altogether, but never mind): '*You need not build on this a monument but you cannot ignore it.*'

LEVESON-GOWER'S XI V AUSTRALIANS

Scarborough, 10, 11, 12 September. Drawn.

H.D.G. LEVESON-GOWER'S XI

J.B. Hobbs	c Oldfield	b Fairfax	24	st Richardson	b Hornibrook	59
H. Sutcliffe	c Fairfax	b Hornibrook	45		b Wall	27
K.S. Duleepsinhji	c Oldfield	b Hornibrook	29		b Hornibrook	41
A. Sandham	b Wall		59	c Wall	b Hornibrook	12
M. Leyland	c Oldfield	b Hornibrook	9	c Wall	b Bradman	50
*R.E.S. Wyatt	lbw	b Hornibrook	7	st Richardson	b Bradman	5
M.W. Tate		c & b Hurwood	1	c Grimmett	b Bradman	9
H. Larwood	c Bradman	b Hornibrook	11		b Kippax	9
W. Rhodes		not out	16		b Kippax	3
+G. Duckworth	b Wall		0		not out	13
C.W.L. Parker	dnb				b Kippax	10
Extras	(b 2, lb 14, w 1)		17	(lb 8, nb 1)		9
Total	(9 wkts dec)		218			247

1-39, 2-102, 3-105, 4-121, 5-143, 6-144, 7-165, 8-216, 9-218

1-39, 2-111, 3-131, 4-166, 5-183, 6-209, 7-220, 8-224, 9-225

	O	M	R	W	O	M	R	W
Wall	14	2	35	2	9	1	33	1
Fairfax	18	4	58	1	8	1	29	0
Hurwood	16	3	32	1	3	1	11	0
Hornibrook	34	11	69	5	18	1	100	3
McCabe	2	0	6	0				
Grimmett	1	0	1	0				
Bradman					7	0	52	3
Kippax					2.3	0	13	3

AUSTRALIANS

A.A. Jackson		b Rhodes	24
A.G. Fairfax	st Duckworth	b Rhodes	8
D.G. Bradman		b Parker	96
A.F. Kippax		b Larwood	59
S.J. McCabe	c Larwood	b Parker	24
*V.Y. Richardson		not out	8
A. Hurwood		b Rhodes	1
C.V. Grimmett	c Wyatt	b Rhodes	3
P.M. Hornibrook	lbw	b Parker	0
T.W. Wall	c Wyatt	b Rhodes	6
+W.A. Oldfield		absent hurt	
Extras	(b 6, lb 3)		9
Total			238

1-30, 2-53, 3-166, 4-214, 5-221, 6-222, 7-230, 8-231, 9-238

	O	M	R	W
Larwood	14	4	34	1
Tate	10	3	14	0
Parker	31	7	81	3
Rhodes	30.5	5	95	5
Wyatt	2	0	5	0

Chapter Ten

Life In The Hard Place

THE MATCH AT SCARBOROUGH FINISHED ON FRIDAY 12 SEPTEMBER and the Australians had free time at last until the first of the party set off from London a week later for an extensive Continental tour before they joined the *Oronsay* at Toulon. The remainder, including Bradman, would follow on 27 September.

What the Australians did in London after 12 September is not recorded by the newspapers because, in the era of non-intrusive journalism, the players seem to have been left completely alone. It may well be that Bradman and his co-author Ben Bennison were working hard to complete his book on the tour which was to appear in November. That represented a pressing deadline to deliver the manuscript but publication, even shortly after the end of the tour, did not violate the Board's contract – again. The manuscript went up to and included the Scarborough match, implying that perhaps all the text from before the Fifth Test to Scarborough had to be extracted from Bradman's daily diary entries, worked and added.

There were fragments about the Australians in the Press. On 15 September *The Evening Standard* reported that 'great interest is being shown by the public in the gramophone record made by six members of the Australian Test team [including Bradman] which can be heard daily in the Gramophone Department at Harrods, Knightsbridge, SW.' This was the record which the *Standard* had earlier offered as prizes. There were only three copies of it although 'by permission of the winners' a fourth had been made so 'that the public might hear it. It will be played until the end of the week, and then broken up.' The *Standard* added: 'The record was delivered at Harrods on Friday. Up to the closing hour on Saturday it had been played 200 times.'

That same day *The Sydney Morning Herald* reported that the *Daily Express* in London was reporting Bradman due to become engaged to an English girl and return to England the following year to play for a county as an amateur. Bradman said 'they are mere yarns'.

The *Express* also probed the question of whether Bradman faced disciplinary proceedings over the life-story instalments in *The Star* but said 'his closest friends do not expect suspension'.

On Wednesday 17 September Bradman, with Wall and Walker, went to watch the great Australian billiards player Walter Lindrum at the famous Thurston's Hall venue in Leicester Square.

Next day *The Sun,* Sydney carried two paragraphs about Bradman's plans after the return ship docked at Perth and he'd travelled to Adelaide. 'Don Bradman will be the first of the Australian cricketers to reach Sydney. He will come from Adelaide by aeroplane. This was announced today by Mr. W.H. Jeanes, secretary of the Board of Control, who stated that permission had been asked by Mick Simmons Ltd. and granted for that course to be followed. Bradman will land in Sydney about November 4.'

On the evening of 19 September the first of the Australians – including Woodfull, Richardson, Kippax, Grimmett and McCabe – left Liverpool Street Station in London for Harwich and the ferry to the Hook of Holland. It was miserable autumn weather, a gale threatening. Evidently they feared a rough night on the Channel. From the Hook they'd travel to Amsterdam, Berlin, Vienna, Budapest and Monte Carlo on the way to the *Oronsay.*

The Sydney Morning Herald reported: 'The public did not know the time of departure and consequently only a small party of friends, including Mr. Leveson-Gower, was there to say farewell. But the gathering grew as the time of departure neared, and everybody waved an enthusiastic good-bye. The Australian singer, Harold Williams, led Kippax, Grimmett and McCabe in a lusty chorus just before the train steamed out.'

The Evening Standard's Diary column noted that the Australians were able to reach Liverpool Street without trouble because, according to Richardson, their valet at the Midland Hotel – they called him Bert – marshalled all their luggage. 'In a no-man's-land of cabin trunks and suit-cases he was hard at work until just before the players left.' Woodfull said he didn't know if he'd be back on the next tour, 1934, but Grimmett said he would 'if they'll have me'.

Three days later deputy wicket-keeper Walker was fined £5 at Haywards Heath for dangerous driving and 10s for driving without a licence. The Magistrates' Court heard that Walker had been staying with friends near Haywards Heath on 31 August – during the Sussex match, in which he wasn't playing – 'and was being driven to the station by the daughter of the house. As a result of a remark, jokingly made, he took the wheel. When they got to Boltro-road, his companion told him that this was where they turned down. Walker put the brakes on suddenly, but the wheels did not lock properly and the car mounted the pavement.' It struck one Thomas Goldsmith, waiting for a bus, and knocked him against a fence. Walker paid him £30 compensation. [(1)]

The leaving became instructive. Far from the anonymity of the first group, the second group would be given extended publicity because of Bradman's presence in it. The day before departure *The Evening Standard* carried a photograph and caption of Bradman packing at the Midland Grand Hotel. No other player was pictured or mentioned.

Next day the *Standard* led one inside page with 'COO-EE (AND ALL THAT) TO DON BRADMAN' with three decks of smaller headlines underneath all about him and, beside the story, a picture across two columns. The caption read: '*Members of the Australian cricket team leaving St. Pancras today on their journey home. Don Bradman is seen in the centre, bareheaded, and on the left are Grimmett and Wall.*'

Quite unconsciously the *Standard* betrayed the real situation: he had become the centre. The writer of the farewell story, signing himself just H.T., essayed humour when he began like this:

> *'Good-bye, Bradman! Good-bye, Don!*
> *Coo-ee and all that.*
>
> *He left London today. A nice young fellow. Charming smile . . . Yet somehow it's a relief knowing he's on the high seas again, on his way back to Australia, bat and baggage.'*

H.T. went on to point out how rough the Bay of Biscay can be and savoured the fact that there would be no Bradman loose in England – until 1934. 'Bradman must have shaken 1,000 hands before he escaped to his compartment.' It was a precise picture of the rest of his playing career, a forest of strangers' hands, escape, sanctuary.

Bradman himself said: 'I will not say good-bye – it is only *au revoir*. I hope to see you all in 1934.'

The *Australian Press Association* reported that 'many friends farewelled them at St. Pancras Station' and a team of Australian women's hockey players, who happened to be there, 'gave a shrill chorus of coo-ees'. That created a 'real Australian flavour to the crowded send-off [. . .] As usual Bradman held an unceasing reception [. . .] There was great enthusiasm as the train left. Bradman was still hanging out of the window as the train disappeared.'

Tebbutt, in his book of the tour, wrote of this departure: 'Another member of the team, who has a dry wit [. . .] gave me a neat illustration of Bradman's position in the public eye compared with that of his comrades.' Tebbutt pointed out that when the first party left the previous week only 'a handful of intimate friends' and one cameraman had been there, but now there were 'twenty photographers and a great crowd'. The wit jerked a 'thumb in Bradman's direction' and said slyly: 'The team didn't leave until today.'

At Tilbury, Bradman said: 'This summer has been the happiest in my life, and I want to thank all the English people for the wonderful way I have been treated. I have made many friends in England, and I hope to renew these friendships when the next Australian team comes over. No, I am not leaving a sweetheart but I value tremendously all the friends I have made.'

Tebbutt filed: 'As few visitors were allowed to come to the dismal docks [at Tilbury] the players saw the last of England in the quietest fashion [. . .] Bradman seemed depressed at leaving the scene of his many triumphs, but the others were in high spirits.' (2)

The third party – Oldfield, Hurwood, Jackson, a'Beckett and Kelly – were due to leave on the Wednesday and, like the earlier party, they'd pick up the *Oronsay* at Toulon.

*

During the month-long voyage back to Australia something significant happened. The firm for whom Bradman had worked since 1929 – Mick Simmons Ltd. – sold sports goods in New South Wales and they now had a vast publicity coup on their hands. They intended to exploit it. Oscar Lawson, who 'handled advertising and public relations' (3) for the company – and who initially persuaded Bradman to join – cabled to ask him to ask for permission to leave the tour when the *Oronsay* docked at Fremantle and make his own way home. Bradman received the telegram at Colombo. The contract did not forbid this (provided no expenses incurred to the Board) and, while the other members of the team sailed from Fremantle to Adelaide and Melbourne and Sydney, he would go by train. That could be exploited for publicity all along the way.

The *Oronsay* docked at Colombo on Saturday 18 October and the Australians were given an official reception by the Ceylon Cricket Association whose officials went aboard to meet them. Before Bradman came ashore he was presented with a Ceylonese souvenir purchased in rupees with a local fund. Bradman wore a suit, collar and tie and looked a very neat young man as he held the souvenir for *The Times of Ceylon* photographer while a dozen people flanked him, including Wall, Fairfax and Macartney.

The newspaper reported that 'the team had taken part in all the competitions on board. Woodfull and his partner won the final of the mixed deck quoits; Bradman proved champion in the bat and ball tennis, in which Hurwood was the runner-up; Oldfield won the final of the peg quoits and was runner-up in the deck quoits.'

Woodfull wouldn't talk to reporters and Kelly said little. *The Times* added: 'Some members of the team, speaking about the Tests, attributed Bradman's amazing success to his uncanny discretion – his unerring ability to chose the right ball to hit. The team generally were proud of the fact that there was not a single instance in which one of their players was run out in the five Tests, while there were about six run-outs of England players.'

Woodfull, who had been joined by his wife and child, was the last to come ashore. The Cricket Association provided cars and the Australians broke up into parties to go sight-seeing. The *Oronsay* sailed at midnight.

General Motors, the American manufacturer who'd been making cars in Australia since 1926, saw the value in being associated with Bradman. They intended to present him with a new car and 'to combine with' Simmons 'in cashing in on his publicity value'. (4) General Motors would pay Bradman's fare from Perth to Adelaide and then fly him to Sydney.

Bradman cabled the Board and received permission. (At the Board meeting in Sydney on 18 September, Simmons had asked for permission for Bradman to fly from Adelaide to Sydney and received it.)

This meant that from the moment the *Oronsay* docked at Fremantle, whatever anybody said – and they would say a great deal – he was detached from the team. That it must have increased the tensions and resentments the other players felt would scarcely matter because, apart from the final formalities at the various ports of call beyond Fremantle, the tour was over. It might matter in the future, however.

The *Oronsay* docked at Fremantle at 8.30 on the morning of Tuesday 28 October. Subsequently *The Advertiser* in Adelaide put together what happened prior to this.

'It is said that the first intimation of Bradman's intention to leave the *Oronsay* at Fremantle was made to the manager of the team, Mr. W.L. Kelly, when he received a wireless message from Mr. Jeanes [Bill Jeanes, secretary of the Board of Control], informing him that Bradman had applied [. . .] for permission to disembark there, and that the chairman [Aubrey Oxlade] had approved.' Kelly was clearly angry about this because *The Advertiser* went on:

> *'It is probable that Mr. Kelly will make a protest to the Board for acting in such a manner without consulting him. Some of the other members of the team consider that an unfair distinction has been made in the case of Bradman. It was pointed out that whereas one member was anxious to remain in London for a fortnight in order to be coached in business matters by the firm he represents, he was refused permission. But Bradman, before the completion of the tour, was given special permission by the Board to undertake an individual trip.*
>
> *'How does Bradman stand with his team-mates?*
>
> *'This is a question the cricket public have repeatedly asked. The players generally realise that Bradman's outstanding ability renders his position unusual, but there were murmurs of resentment at the suggested favouritism shown to him.*
>
> *'When Mr. Kelly was approached [. . .] his replies were terse but significant.*
>
> *'The Australian team manager was asked whether he had any control over Bradman. "The Board of Control has taken Bradman out of my hands," he said.*
>
> *'"Did you have any trouble in England?" was the next question, and*

> *Mr. Kelly's reply was that he had had no trouble with any of the players in England.'*

As the *Oronsay* berthed an estimated 1,500–2,000 people crowded on to the quayside, among them Lawson. Bradman described this as 'one of the pleasantest shocks of my life'. [5] Lawson lost no time in getting on board and had a brief conversation with Bradman in his cabin. Bradman appointed him his manager during the trip from here to home and said: 'Right, manager, here you are. You can start right away.' Bradman then handed Lawson a huge sheaf of letters and telegrams.

From this moment one-to-one access to Bradman was through Lawson 'and only those whose business was of vital importance were permitted even a glimpse of him'. [6] Nor had the team abandoned the disciplines of silence. When reporters approached the players they said 'see our manager'.

The West Australian reported: 'Bradman, Woodfull and Jackson could be picked out as they leaned over the rail of the promenade deck. "Hey, Don, take that hat off," bawled a raucous voice, but Bradman merely grinned beneath his hood-brimmed headgear and resumed his Sphinx-like expression. When passengers began to disembark, all eyes were on the alert for a glimpse of Bradman, and there were many false alarms. As it happened, there was no ground for the suspicion that he might slip ashore unobtrusively because the team disembarked as a body.'

Cheers rang out as they came down the gangway.

Cars were provided by the West Australian Cricket Association but General Motors had one of their own for Bradman. Kelly refused him permission to use it and he joined the team motorcade. [7] On the journey to Fremantle Town Hall it 'made slow progress initially because it had to pass through a dense crowd.' Outside the Town Hall the crowd was so dense that the players took several minutes going in. Inevitably, the Mayor made a speech.

'Following the Fremantle civic reception, the visitors were motored to Perth, via King's Park, and groups of cheering people and school children were frequently encountered en route.' [8]

At Perth, they went to the Prince of Wales Theatre which had 2,500 people inside with an estimated further 2,500 outside. The Mayor gave the team a civic reception and to thunderous applause Woodfull made a speech. There were calls for Bradman to speak but he didn't. A wag called: 'They can't get him out, can they?' – meaning get him out of his modesty and speak. Kelly said he was 'astounded' that thousands of people had turned out to greet them. Before they left Woodfull introduced each member of the team to the audience.

The *West Australian* reported that the theatre, 'which was packed, resounded with tumultuous applause when members of the team walked down the centre aisle, the cheering being renewed in greater volume as outstanding players like Woodfull, Bradman and Grimmett were recognised. Outside, a surging crowd which had been unable to gain admission was kept under control by a possee of mounted and foot police. People at windows and verandahs of nearby buildings cheered lustily as the cricketers arrived.'

As the team emerged they were cheered again and 'so dense was the throng waiting in the street that they had to push their way along, and several minutes elapsed before the police were able to move the crowd sufficiently to let the official cars through.' **(9)**

The Advertiser reported: 'One woman was pushed over, but uninjured, by one of the slowly moving vehicles. Several members of the team escaped the attentions of the crowd by leaving through the rear of the theatre. Bradman waited until most of the people had left the building and then walked [. . .] into the hall, where he was besieged and kissed by a number of women.' **(10)**

They motored to the Palace Hotel where the executive of the Western Australian Cricket Association welcomed them to a luncheon.

Kelly made another speech, saying Woodfull was the most popular member of the side, praising Ponsford and Bradman for their centuries in the Tests and added diplomatically: 'I did not have the slightest trouble or difficulty with any member of the team.' Woodfull made another speech, saying that people might imagine the moment they regained the Ashes was the high point of the tour but no, it hadn't been that, it had been meeting the King and Queen at Sandringham.

After this luncheon when Bradman was 'leaving the dining room he was surrounded by about 100 girls and women who asked for his autograph. He sat down and spent half an hour complying with their wishes. On leaving the hotel he was greeted by a cheering crowd of about 500.' **(11)**

Bradman drove off in the General Motors car. Members of the party, including Bradman, visited Perth Hospital to meet wounded servicemen. Late that afternoon the tourists – except Bradman, of course – boarded the *Oronsay* and sailed towards Adelaide.

Bradman went to the Theatre Royal where a crowd of 1,000 mobbed him as he prepared to go on stage during a revue called *Splashes.* The *West Australian* reported: 'With the assistance of a squad of police under the charge of Sargeant Switsur, Bradman eventually gained sanctuary at the back of the stage, where he met members of the company.' He signed a lot of autographs and 'when he appeared on the stage with the full company, Bradman received a tumultuous welcome from a capacity house. He was then presented with a cheque for £100 by Mr. George Wallace [whose revue it was] who said he hoped it would be the first of many such presentations.'

Bradman did make a speech, 'speaking clearly and calmly'. He said he was pleased if his making runs gave pleasure to other people because it gave him pleasure. He stressed that it had been a team effort but 'if credit is due to any player more than another it should go to our captain Billy Woodfull'. That was greeted with loud applause. He said Woodfull's opening partnerships with Ponsford had made things much easier for those following them and paid tribute to the wizardry of Grimmett but returned to the theme of the team effort. He finished by saying that the finest sight of the whole tour had been the lights of Fremantle the previous evening – so, like Woodfull and Kelly, he understood the right things to say and when to say them.

Later that evening at the station, Lawson later revealed, the crowd were so enthusiastic that it had taken eight policemen to literally 'bundle' him and Bradman into their compartment on the Great Western express for Adelaide. Lawson and Bradman were not alone, however, on the journey. Mr. G.E. O'Callaghan of General Motors (Australia) was with them, no doubt keeping a watchful eye on the company's investment and exploiting it. He had every right. They'd paid.

The train left at 9.30pm and the journey would take the remainder of this Tuesday, then Wednesday, Thursday and Friday as it passed along the necklace of towns and small communities on its way to Adelaide. The journey became a triumphal procession.

Lawson recounted how (in the words of *The Advertiser,* Adelaide) 'all along the Transcontinental line crowds gathered to cheer the famous cricketer, and even at small wayside stations at all hours of the night and early morning Bradman was awakened by voices at his window appealing to him to "poke his head out" so that he could be seen.'

At Kalgoorlie, he was given a civic reception by the Mayor – but arranged by General Motors – and 3,000 people filled the Town Hall. Lawson tried to stem the flow of autograph hunters and tried to count how many he actually signed on the journey but gave up after 2,000. Nor did the absence of proper autograph books deter the hunters: he signed scraps of paper, handbags and, at one stop, even some 'fancy work' – embroidery?

On the Friday morning at Port Augusta, 186 miles (300km) from Adelaide, he was given a civic reception by the Mayor (who made the inevitable speech) and said he hadn't expected such treatment. He was 'swarmed' by young autograph hunters but hadn't the time to sign them before the train left.

At Peterborough 1,000 school children and about 700 adults thronged the platform to see him. A new record was established for platform tickets. The Mayor escorted him to a room at the rear of the station and congratulated him. Bradman said he hadn't seen so many children since he began the tour last March. He spoke about the cricket in England and when the train pulled out was given a rousing cheer.

At the little station of Terowie, 136 miles (220km) from Adelaide, a 78-year-old lady said she was anxious to speak to him and did for several minutes. Here he signed bats, books and cards.

The train pulled in to Adelaide Station shortly before six that evening and *The Advertiser* caught the moment:

> *'Immediately the express came to a standstill the familiar figure of the young batsman emerged from one of the carriages and there was a rush in his direction. A number of police constables and prominent officials of the South Australian Cricket Association quickly formed a cordon round him, and after preliminary hand-shaking and the extending of greetings to the international, a move was made to the assembly hall [in the station]. Here the crowd was much more thickly congregated, the stairways and ramp being packed with cheering admirers. Bradman and his escort turned towards the northern exit, and the crowd fought for vantage points from which to witness the departure of the party.*
>
> *'Before entering the motor car waiting to take him to his hotel, Bradman gave photographers an opportunity, and the crowd welcomed the chance to get a "close-up" view of the record-breaker. More cheers*

were given before the mounted troopers, foot constables and police sidecar outfits forced a passage through the crowd for the motor car. Escorted by the traffic police Bradman was taken to his hotel, among those accompanying him being [. . .] Jeanes and officials of the South Australian Cricket Association.

'During the evening large crowds gathered outside the Hotel Richmond in Rundle-street in the hope of catching a glimpse of Bradman, and several autograph hunters pestered porters with enquiries as to the young batsman's whereabouts. Troopers were stationed near the entrance and this had a restraining effect upon the crowd. Bradman, however, did not give his admirers any opportunity of repeating the idolising scenes staged in Western Australia.'

Next morning the *Oronsay* docked and Bradman, accompanied by Lawson, drove down to meet it at 7am. Then the party left by motorcade at 10am for a civic reception at the Town Hall (and the Lord Mayor). The public had been invited – the doors opened at 9.30am and a Mr. Edwin Dalby was due to 'render musical items on the Town Hall organ from 10.30 o'clock.' (12)

The Advertiser reported: 'Temporary fences had to be erected, and troopers summoned to keep the crowd in check. Bradman was always singled out for the loudest cheers.'

At 12.30pm the party had a luncheon at the Adelaide Oval. Kelly made a speech describing Grimmett as the outstanding success of the team, but equally paying tribute to Richardson, Wall and Walker – all, of course, from South Australia.

The Advertiser, which carried the story that Kelly might protest to the Board over the decision to let Bradman travel separately, also described a speech Bradman gave. He 'drew attention to the fact that General Motors had presented five motor cars to the Lord Mayors of the capital cities to be disposed of for the relief of unemployment, and one would also be presented to him. Although he did not express himself in so many words, those who heard the speech could not fail to understand that he had undertaken the trip in the interests of charity and that he was not actuated solely by personal motives.'

That evening, the party – minus Bradman and the four South Australians – re-boarded the *Oronsay* for Melbourne.

That evening Bradman was due at a radio studio to speak to the

Australia public for the first time since his return. When he got there he gave a 'racy' account of the tour and made an appeal on behalf of the Lord Mayor's Unemployment Relief Fund. Then he appeared at the Regent Theatre where he received a cheque for £50. He presented £5 to the Mayor's appeal.

On the Sunday morning, leading his own motorcade, he drove out to Parafield airfield some 11 miles (18km) north of Adelaide. There he boarded a Fokker plane called the *Southern Cloud* for Melbourne. It was due to reach Essendon airfield 8½ miles (14km) from Melbourne at 3.30pm but didn't land until 5.30pm. A crowd estimated at 10,000 had thinned by then although several hundred remained and they 'rushed the plane almost before it had stopped. When Bradman [emerged] he was immediately lost in the crowd, and only the forcible attention of a strong body of police enabled him to reach a lorry draped with the Australian flag that was to serve as a platform.' (13)

There Bradman was welcomed by Warwick Armstrong, captain of the victorious 1921 side to England. Bradman himself said this reception was the best he'd received and apologised for being late. The departure from Adelaide had been delayed and the plane encountered strong headwinds.

The *Oronsay* docked at the station pier at seven the following morning, greeted by a crowd of 1,000, and the players were driven in a motorcade to Melbourne for a civic reception. The Mayor said that listening to the radio broadcasts had 'proved a real tonic in the troublous times through which Australia was passing.' (14)

In the afternoon at the Tivoli Theatre Bradman received a cheque for £100 from Melbourne admirers. A woman presented him with a bouquet of roses for his mother from 'the mothers of Melbourne'. A wag called out to her: 'Why don't you give him a kiss?' She did, and kissed Lord Beauchamp – who'd handed over the £100 – too.

Next day Bradman flew in the *Southern Cloud* to Goulburn airfield and arrived at 3.15pm after battering against almost gale-force winds. As the plane landed it 'rocked freely' because of the wind. Only a few people went to the airfield, among them his father and brother who'd driven over from Bowral – evidently the Mayor and the local cricket authorities hadn't been invited.

Bradman was offered tea in Goulburn but accepted only on condition there'd be no official reception. He said: 'I want to push on home as soon as possible.' He'd just about had enough.

He was to be driven home by a leading Australian racing driver, 'Wizard' Smith, whom General Motors had hired. The road went past Moss Vale where in early March he'd caught the train which the other New South Wales players were already on.

At Bowral ten policemen were needed to control the crowds. A band played 'Our Don Bradman' as he, his father and mother, brother and sister, went to a dais to listen to the Lord Mayor make the inevitable speech. He spoke himself, briefly, covering the ground of the England tour again and saying that he'd had many welcomes bigger than this one but none better because of its sincerity.

And there he was, exactly back where it had all begun nine months before. An immense circle had been completed.

He was tired, so tired that he slept late next day while 'Wizard' Smith waited to take him to Sydney for what in a sense was the beginning of the rest of his life. It could never be the same again, never be only quiet, homely Bowral.

The day he flew from Essendon to Goulburn, Vic Richardson made a speech at a social event organised by an Adelaide radio station. It was to present Grimmett with a cheque for £160, the result of a fund organised by the station. Richardson said: 'We could have played any team without Don Bradman, but we could not play the blind school without Clarrie Grimmett . . .' – he was the only indispensable member of the side. Since the occasion was for and about Grimmett, what Richardson said is eminently understandable. Perhaps a more sensible course would have been to omit any reference to Bradman and simply play homage to Grimmett.

To defend his view, Richardson would have to have explained where Bradman's 974 Test runs would have come from if Bradman hadn't made them, which might have been a trifle difficult coming from a man who'd made 98 in five innings at an average of 19.60.

To speculate about Richardson's motives is one of those maddening, subterranean things we have come to know so well, but you can legitimately wonder if it was a product of the tensions within the team and the way Bradman had – or had not – handled that.

Bradman was fined £50 by the Board for the newspapers articles in *The Star.*

Kelly, upset by Tebbutt's book on the tour and the subterranean currents *there* about Bradman and the rest of the team, issued a statement refuting that Bradman had been 'aloof', claiming that preparing his book had occupied Bradman – removing him from the social whirl, as it were – and that, because of his success, he had a vast amount of correspondence to answer, again removing him from the social whirl. Kelly said he had not needed to show 'firmness' to any member of the team but had to one or two journalists, Tebbutt among them, for trying to get into functions meant for the team.

Tebbutt responded that Kelly had built his complaint on one paragraph of the book but the full context gave a much more balanced picture. Tebbutt, claiming friendship with Bradman, said he intended to send him a copy and their friendship would survive.

Natural justice, before we leave the tour, demands that Fender be heard. In his book ([15]) he wrote:

> *'He is an enormously improved player as compared with 1928–29, and has already made his place among the great ones of the game. I do not think one could quite call him an attractive bat to watch, but he is extremely effective, and his pull shot must surely be as much a milestone in batting as was that of George Hirst when the great Yorkshireman first used it. Bradman's pull shot is just as individual as Hirst's was when he introduced it and, although it must be called by the same name, it is an entirely different shot from the stroke normally known among batsmen to-day. His footwork in the making of a shot is different because he usually gets his right foot well across and outside the off-stump. The most distinctive difference between his pull and all others, however, is that he invariably hits the ball very hard and straight down on to the ground.*
>
> *'Bradman cut late, and at times drove with marked effect and tremendous accuracy, but great though his record may be, he has not impressed me as being comparable with such players as Charlie Macartney or Victor Trumper. Bradman may have all the strokes which these great players had, but if he has, he has not yet shown them to us. A Macartney innings was one around which controversy would often rage as to which of the shots he made was the best, and the same with Victor Trumper. Both men made so many brilliant shots, in so many different directions, that one had a wide range of choice, and if there were half a dozen spectators discussing a Macartney or a Trumper innings, they would each, according*

to their particular preference, be able to claim that a different stroke was the best one of all. Hours of Bradman, however, would never leave anyone in any doubt about his best stroke.'

Someone said that the great sin of the second half of the Twentieth Century was inefficiency. That's a very contentious statement, to put it mildly, but you know what he meant. The days of beauty for beauty's sake were going: you only have to look at the car designs, the architecture, the town plans, the offices, the clothes and so on to know that.

It was so in cricket, too. Trumper was clearly a genius of a very original and delicate kind; Macartney a sort of beautiful, terrible, irresistible force. Bradman was efficient. By the Oval Test, 1930, the world had changed and the future did belong to efficiency. Fender hadn't realised.

Many are the versions of the birth of Bodyline (which requires, I think, a capital letter by now) and we have already heard the most persuasive of them in Larwood's own words about The Oval.

The Bodyline series of 1932–33, the next in the Ashes series after 1930, was the first when winning overrode the wellbeing of the game. No such thing had ever been imagined before. It came into being as a weapon against Bradman, a way of reducing him to human proportions because, if you didn't find the way to that, he would surely repeat what he had just done – almost 1,000 runs – in every subsequent series.

England won at Trent Bridge because Bradman made only 8 and 131. Australia won at Lord's with his 254, and his 334 put them beyond defeat at Leeds. After the Manchester washout, Australia won at The Oval with his 232. To centralise the results on Bradman's performances may seem grossly unfair to what the other Australians were doing, especially Grimmett, but consider the team's totals without him: 729 at Lord's would have been 475; 566 at Leeds 232; 695 at The Oval 463. Bradman was the difference and, more even than that, other batsmen could play off him.

Nor, in the autumn of 1930, might anyone say that Bradman, 22, would not get *better.* He had already distorted the series and the question had to be faced: if we don't find the way, playing against Australia for twenty years will be futile. We will be supplicants before him, forever defeated.

The interplay between this and Larwood giving Bradman some hurry up at The Oval during the 232, Bodyline stemming from that and Douglas Jardine's implacable personality in carrying it through regardless, is intriguing in the way that so many historical *what ifs?* are. There may have been other ways to reduce Bradman but nobody found them. His average in 1932–33, a mere 56, became – after Bodyline – 94 in 1934, 90 in 1936–37, 108 in 1938, 97 in 1946–47 and 72 in 1948.

There's a subtle undercurrent here, one gathered from impressions so long afterwards rather than the accumulation of hard facts. In the 1928–29 season Hammond scored 905 runs (next Hendred 472; best Australian Ryder 492). In 1926 it had been Hobbs 486 (Macartney 473); in 1924–25 Sutcliffe 734 (J.M. Taylor 541). And so it went. The range was variations on a certain level until Hammond, and the subtle undercurrent – relying on contemporary sources and subsequent historians – is that Hammond pushed the possibilities of batsmanship on Australian wickets to a new place. Nobody (as far as I'm aware) suggested he had changed the nature of the game.

By July 1930 and the Headingley Test even the casual observer could not have failed to realise that Bradman had.

It needs saying: when England won The Oval Test match in 1953 they held the Ashes for the first time since Jardine. Bradman had seen off the four captains after Jardine (Wyatt, Allen, Hammond, Yardley) and two complete generations of England bowlers. None except Jardine found the way and it's a terrible paradox that the way Jardine found gouged so deep. You had to distort the game yourself to contain the Bradman distortion.

There's a further paradox. Across 1930 Bradman played entirely within the laws and spirit of the game. He made 974 without any controversy, even. You re-live the Test innings and don't find any 'incidents' at all except one brief example of possible dissent at The Oval when he felt he'd been wrongly given out. He batted more effectively than any batsman had ever done in the whole story of the game but it was just batting, if you can put it like that. The distortion he brought did not challenge, much less threaten, the customs and ethics of the game.

During the Bodyline series, the moment Woodfull told Plum Warner 'There are two sides out there and one isn't playing cricket' became unbearably poignant because, as we have seen throughout this book, the talk always was of the Empire, the bonds that bound, coming Home, the precious spirit of the game; and all perfectly modulated. Cricket was hard – always had been – but within a specific framework. When Woodfull made *the* speech, and when it was applauded from Tasmania to Perth and all over England, he and his audiences were being quite sincere. It was how they viewed the world and he was merely giving that expression in the formalised, expected, traditional way.

Jardine said different things. In the accepted wisdom of the game's history, Jardine's Bodyline broke no cricket law but it did something worse: it broke bodies and in breaking them broke the framework, making the game into something else altogether. In many significant ways 1930 seems far away now and 1932–33 very close.

To recapture the place where Woodfull lived is even more elusive because Jardine was *modern*. Any Test player today would recognise him and talk easily to him about the imperative of winning; no modern sports psychologist – proffering motivation and bonding and the rest – could teach him a thing. What do you do when you've thousands of Australians baying for your blood? Go and field in the deep, right in front of them so that, inevitably, you're pointing your backside at them.

The four-day Tests in England (Australia's had always been timeless), introduced in 1930, marked a fundamental change, too, and although it is important to stress that Bradman did not cause this he was able to exploit it. The three-day Tests did not allow enough time for a side to make a colossal total and bowl the other side out twice. At Leeds in 1926, or example Australia batted first and made 494. England replied with 294, followed on and made 254 for 3 to make the match a safe draw.

The four-day Tests changed that because Bradman, in the modern way, could bat England out of the match by scoring so heavily and so fast. Australia might not win but they wouldn't lose.

At Leeds in 1934 England made 200 and Australia 584 (Bradman 304): impregnable. England hung on to 229 for 6 in their second innings when heavy rain ruined the final day. At The Oval a month later, Australia closed the opening day on 475 for 2 and finished on 701 (Ponsford 266, Bradman 244). They won by an innings and 562 runs. This also was *modern* – you win ruthlessly and comprehensively. Any

Australian captain of the 1990s and 2000s would have said, immediately and without needing to think, *Yeah, that's what you do.*

Hadn't it happened before Bradman? Of course, but never so blatantly, so repeatedly, on such a scale and so deliberately. Before Bradman, circumstances sometimes created enormous totals and mostly circumstances didn't. Bradman used it as a tactic, and it became so much a norm that successive generations in world cricket who inherited it all knew *Yeah, that's what you do* without ever knowing where it came from, or when, or why or what had gone before it. When Ricky Ponting did not enforce the follow-on at Brisbane in November 2006 he was thinking just like Bradman. You destroy the opposition in *this* Test and it gets harder for them in the *next* Test, when you'll do it again if you can.

Trumper didn't think like that and Macartney didn't think like that.

Between Jardine and 1948 when Bradman retired, England played Australia 25 times and won 4 – the fourth in the timeless Test at The Oval in 1938 when Bradman couldn't bat. Hammond, captaining England, took one look at the wicket and said England needed at least 1,000 because Bradman might get that many. When Bradman fell injured, the match became a cruel parody of itself. Hammond declared at 903 for 7, which itself was a distortion created by the Bradman distortion.

Expanding on that, the other three wins were achieved when Bradman 'failed:' 36 and 13 at Lord's in 1934; 38 and 0 at Brisbane, 1936; 0 and 82 at Sydney, 1936.

I want to push the case further. Between Jardine and 1948, Bradman made twelve centuries and Australian won nine of the matches he scored them in. These are not statistics so much as the story of what actually happened.

The ruthlessness reached a terrible climax at Southend in 1948 when the Australians made 721 (Bradman 187) in a single day against a modest Essex bowling attack. All-rounder Keith Miller, by temperament uninterested in slaughter, was playing cards and when the wicket fell to bring him in famously put his hand face down on the table and said: 'I'll be back in a minute.' He walked all round his first ball, returned and picked the hand up again. Bradman *was* interested in slaughter, even if it took his team to the point where, towards the end of this day at Southend, 4s and 6s were being greeted with silence. The diet had been too rich for the crowd to digest any more.

Trevor Bailey played in that match and when he graduated to the England side had no hesitation in grinding the Australians down with the bat by spending whole lifetimes at the crease, or in making preposterous appeals against the light, (16) or deliberately bowling down the leg side where the Australians couldn't reach him. Bradman manifestly did not behave like that but he created the hard place where others felt they could, and should.

Len Hutton, one of England's greatest openers, said he found Australians harder to play against when he got to know and like them. He was captain when Bailey bowled down the leg side. This was Leeds in 1953, the Australians chasing 177 in two hours to win and retain the Ashes. They went for them and when the third wicket fell at 111 were within sight. Rex Alston wrote: 'As [Alan] Davidson was walking in, Bailey and Hutton were seen in deep conversation, with Bailey gesticulating to distant parts of the field. The upshot was that Bailey took over the end occupied previously by the two spinners and bowled wide of the leg stump to six men on the leg side. This move, made not a moment too soon, definitely snatched victory from Australia's grasp.' (17)

This was not, of course, Bodyline or anything like it and it was certainly not against the rules, it was just life in the hard place.

In 1964, Bobby Simpson captained Australia in England and, to retain the Ashes, reduced the Fourth Test to a farce by taking twelve and three quarter hours to score 311 out of 656 for 8 declared. He batted England out of the match in the sense that they could no longer win and did so despite universal condemnation that this sort of thing would kill the game. *Yeah, that's what you do.*

Always it was an uneasy balance between the demands of the hard place and the imperatives of the inherited ethics; and, from 1932–33, each generation had to find its own balance because, in life beyond, generally accepted conduct constantly changed. Cricket might want to remain pure and aloof but it could not any more than anything else could. Its players were always products of the age they lived in, and shaped accordingly.

The point: between the First Test in 1877 and the 1930s, generally accepted conduct changed very little, if at all. After 1945 it changed quickly and comprehensively. Bradman was raised on certainties which his descendants never knew. In 2001, when he died, the mighty British Empire spanning the globe had ceased to exist, Australia had become a multi-racial society and, for many of them, Britain was a distant foreign country. If you'd told them it was their Home they wouldn't have known what you were talking about.

This is not a lament for times gone by, just the way it is. The part Bradman played, however unwittingly, in raising Australian national consciousness is much more intriguing.

You can argue that cricket, like every other human activity, reflects with great accuracy the time in which it is played. You can gaze at the photographs of the early Test cricketers, faces always stern for the camera, moustaches drooping, and wonder how good they were, how they played. You can study The Golden Age, which may conveniently be put at 1899 to 1914, and wonder how much chivalry there really was, how much influence the amateurs – living at an exalted, untouchable social level – wielded. You cannot doubt that all these people took the game seriously because there is simply no evidence that they did not. The question is one of degree. You get a sense of shift during the 1920–21 series: Australia won by an innings and 377, an innings and 91, 119, eight wickets and nine wickets.

In those days there were certain things in life a gentleman would not do, and no doubt certain things cricketers would not do, either. At Leeds in 1930, when these ethics still existed in their traditional form, the England bowlers were confronted with Bradman utterly rampant as he moved to 309 in the day. Their reaction was to continue to try and bowl him out as well as contain him. It was not in their *mentality* to pull everyone back on to the boundary and give him singles. That would have been admitting defeat to themselves. Maurice Tate was asked to bowl to try and slow Bradman and he replied: 'I'll do better than that, I'll bowl the beggar out.'

Within two years Jardine and the other mentality had come. It has never really gone away.

Appendix 1
Every ball Bradman faced in the 1930 Tests

I've used Bill Ferguson's scorebooks (courtesy of John Kobylecky) to reconstruct each of the seven Test innings ball by ball.

Key:
The first column is the bowler, then the batsman on strike.

The second column is the batsman the strike has passed to. Sometimes this happens several times in an over and so there are several columns. In those overs, please read across left to right, then down and across left to right.

A ball from which the batsman did not score is designated 0.

The numerals are the runs he did score.

W = wicket

Byes and leg byes are given in brackets.

FIRST TEST: Trent Bridge

Thursday: *England won the toss and batted, finishing on 241 for 8.*

Friday: *Rain affected. England were all out for 270. The Australian innings began at 2.59pm.*

Larwood	Woodfull	0(4lb)01	Ponsford	00		
Tate	Woodfull	000000				
Larwood	Ponsford	0001	Woodfull	20		
Tate	Ponsford	000000				
Larwood	Woodfull	000000				
Tate	Ponsford	1	Woodfull	0001	Ponsford	1
Larwood	Ponsford	1	Woodfull	000W		

Woodfull caught Chapman bowled Larwood 4 (Australia 12 for 1, Ponsford 4)

	Bradman	1				
Tate	Bradman	01	Ponsford	0000		
Larwood	Bradman	1	Ponsford	00200		
Tate	Bradman	1	Ponsford	00004		
Robins	Bradman	21	Ponsford	01		
	Bradman	1	Ponsford	0		
Tate	Bradman	040000				
Robins	Ponsford	20001	Bradman	1		
Tate	Bradman	0001	Ponsford	1	Bradman 4	
Robins	Ponsford	1	Bradman	1		
	Ponsford	01	Bradman	1	Ponsford 4	
Tate	Bradman	002001				
Tyldesley	Bradman	400004				
Tate	Ponsford	000000				
Tyldesley	Bradman	000000				
Hammond	Ponsford	01	Bradman	0000		
Tate	Ponsford	002000				
Hammond	Bradman	1	Ponsford	1	Bradman 1	
	Ponsford	001				
Tate	Ponsford	000400				
Hammond	Bradman	000000				
Tate	Ponsford	000000				
Hammond	Bradman	1	Ponsford	00000		
Tate	Bradman	000000				
Hammond	Ponsford	01	Bradman	0000		
Tate	Ponsford	01	Bradman	001	Ponsford	0
Hammond	Bradman	000000				
Tate	Ponsford	1	Bradman	1	Ponsford	0000
Tyldesley	Bradman	000000				
Tate	Ponsford	0001	Bradman	01		
Tyldesley	Bradman	1	Ponsford	001	Bradman	0
Tate	Ponsford	000000				
Tyldesley	Bradman	01	Ponsford	1	Bradman	001
Tate	Bradman	00001	Ponsford	0		
Tyldesley	Bradman	00000(4b)				
Tate	Ponsford	000200				
Tyldesley	Bradman	01	Ponsford	001	Bradman	0
Tate	Ponsford	00000W				

Ponsford bowled Tate 39 (Australia 93 for 2, Bradman 42)

Tyldesley	Bradman	000001				
Tate	Bradman	001	Kippax	000		
Tyldesley	Bradman	1	Kippax	1	Bradman	000
Tate	Kippax	000000				
Tyldesley	Bradman	201	Kippax	1	Bradman	1
	Kippax	0				
Hammond	Bradman	01	Kippax	0000		
Tyldesley	Bradman	000000				
Hammond	Kippax	1	Bradman	00020		
Tyldesley	Kippax	000001				
Hammond	Kippax	000000				
Tyldesley	Bradman	21	Kippax	0000		
Hammond	Bradman	1	Kippax	001	Bradman	02
Tyldesley	Kippax	000204				
Hammond	Bradman	200000				
Tyldesley	Kippax	001	Bradman	001		
Hammond	Bradman	(1b)	Kippax	00000		
Tyldesley	Bradman	1	Kippax	1	Bradman	1
	Kippax	000				
Hammond	Bradman	201	Kippax	003		
Tyldesley	Kippax	0001	Bradman	1	Kippax	0
Hammond	Bradman	0001	Kippax	00		
Robins	Bradman	002(1lb)	Kippax	40		
Hammond	Bradman	0(1b)	Kippax	001	Bradman	0
Robins	Kippax	1	Bradman	02001		
Hammond	Bradman	1	Kippax	00(1b)	Bradman	0
Robins	Kippax	00W				

Kippax caught Hammond bowled Robins 23 (Australia 152 for 3, Bradman 74)

		McCabe 004				
Tate	Bradman	000000				
Robins	McCabe	4001	Bradman	1	McCabe	1
Tate	McCabe	000000				
Robins	Bradman	001	McCabe	404		
Tate	Bradman	00001	McCabe	0		
Robins	Bradman	1	McCabe	21	Bradman	01
	McCabe	1				
Tate	McCabe	0001	Bradman	21		
Robins	Bradman	1	McCabe	1	Bradman	201
	McCabe	4				
Tate	Bradman	01	McCabe	1	Bradman	000
Tyldesley	McCabe	001	Bradman	1	McCabe	20

Lunch Australia 198 for 3 (Bradman 88, McCabe 32)

Tate	Bradman	000200				
Hammond	McCabe	0001	Bradman	00		
Tate	McCabe	1	Bradman	1	McCabe	01
	Bradman	00				
Hammond	McCabe	040200				
Tate	Bradman	000000				
Hammond	McCabe	0001	Bradman	00		
Tate	McCabe	001	Bradman	01	McCabe	0
Hammond	Bradman	000000				
Tate	McCabe	01	Bradman	0000		
Hammond	McCabe	1	Bradman	0200 (1b)		
Tate	Bradman	000000				
Hammond	McCabe	001	Bradman	040		
Tate	McCabe	000000				
Hammond	Bradman	001	McCabe	040		
Tate	Bradman	001	McCabe	0W		

McCabe caught and bowled Tate 49 (Australia 229, Bradman 101)

[If you add Bradman's runs from 88 when Kippax was out to here they come to 100 not 101 – and nobody disputes he was 101. Somewhere, somehow a single has gone missing and remains missing despite thorough research and detective work. The problem is that if you give Bradman 1 more run to make him 101 you make Australia 230 – which they weren't. Worse, the single would naturally take him up to the other end, making nonsense of the whole sequence afterwards. If anyone can find this infernal single, please let me know!]

	Richardson	0				
Tyldesley	Bradman	01	Richardson	0000		
Tate	Bradman	0001	Richardson	00		
Tyldesley	Bradman	040020				
Tate	Richardson	000000				
Tyldesley	Bradman	204400				
Tate	Richardson	000000				
Tyldesley	Bradman	000000				
Tate	Richardson	200000				
Robins	Bradman	00001	Richardson	0		
Hammond	Bradman	004040				
Robins	Richardson	(1b)	Bradman	001	Richardson	00
Hammond	Bradman	1	Richardson	00000		
Robins	Bradman	1	Richardson			

Bradman bowled Robins 131 at 3.33pm (four hours eighteen minutes, ten 4s). Australia 267 for 7. Australia were all out for 335, losing the match by 93 runs.

SECOND TEST: Lord's

Friday: *Chapman won the toss and batted. England made 405 for 9 at the close.*

Saturday: *England all out 425. Australia begin their innings at 11.35am with Woodfull and Ponsford. They put on 96 at lunch and when Ponsford was out, caught by Hammond off White, they'd put on 162. Bradman came to the wicket at 3.29pm.*

White	Ponsford	0000W	Bradman	1		
Hammond	Bradman	000004				
White	Woodfull	000000				
Hammond	Bradman	000000				
White	Woodfull	1	Bradman	1	Woodfull	03
	Bradman	00				
Hammond	Woodfull	0001	Bradman	1	Woodfull	0
White	Bradman	001	Woodfull	040		
Hammond	Bradman	004001				
White	Bradman	400400				
Hammond	Woodfull	00021	Bradman	1		
White	Bradman	40001	Woodfull	0		

Australia 201 for 1 at 3.55pm (Woodfull 90, Bradman 27).

Allen	Bradman	40201	Woodfull	0		
Tate	Bradman	001	Woodfull	1	Bradman	1
	Woodfull	0				
Allen	Bradman	4201	Woodfull	20		
Tate	Bradman	1	Woodfull	00000		
Allen	Bradman	1	Woodfull	0001	Bradman	1
Tate	Bradman	22				

Bradman 50 at 4.15pm (forty-six minutes). Australia 228 for 1.

		001				
			Woodfull	0		
Hammond	Bradman	1	Woodfull	003	Bradman	1
	Woodfull	1				
Tate	Woodfull	000001				
Hammond	Woodfull	001	Bradman	(1b)	Woodfull	00
Tate	Bradman	1	Woodfull	00001		
Hammond	Woodfull	400000				

Tea: Australia 244 for 1 (Woodfull 105, Bradman 54).

Robins	Bradman	1	Woodfull	1	Bradman	1
	Woodfull	1	Bradman	1	Woodfull	1

Australia 250 for 1 at 4.50pm (Woodfull 108, Bradman 56).

Tate	Woodfull	001	Bradman	000
Robins	Woodfull	000040		

Tate	Bradman	041	Woodfull	1	Bradman	1
	Woodfull	1				
Robins	Woodfull	0001	Bradman	1	Woodfull	0
Tate	Bradman	000000				
Robins	Woodfull	1	Bradman	2001	Woodfull	1
Tate	Woodfull	000000				
Robins	Bradman	1	Woodfull	00400		
Tate	Bradman	0021	Woodfull	00		
Robins	Bradman	044004				
Tate	Woodfull	00003	Bradman	1		
White	Bradman	1	Woodfull	001	Bradman	01
Tate	Bradman	1	Woodfull	01	Bradman	01
	Woodfull	0				
Australia 300 for 1 at 5.25pm (Woodfull 127, Bradman 88).						
White	Bradman	400001				
Tate	Bradman	21	Woodfull	0000		
White	Bradman	01	Woodfull	01	Bradman	20
Hammond	Woodfull	0001	Bradman	01		
Bradman 100 at 5.35pm (one hour forty-six minutes). Australia 314 for 1.						
White	Bradman	400401				
Hammond	Bradman	002000				
Woolley	Woodfull	1	Bradman	1	Woodfull	1
	Bradman	1	Woodfull	0(4nb)0		
Hammond	Bradman	01	Woodfull	0000		
Woolley	Bradman	1	Woodfull	1	Bradman	1
	Woodfull	01	Bradman	(2b)		
Hammond	Woodfull	1	Bradman	1	Woodfull	0000
Woolley	Bradman	1	Woodfull	1	Bradman	0000
Hammond	Woodfull	000000				
Woolley	Bradman	401	Woodfull	1	Bradman	1
	Woodfull	1				
Australia 352 for 1 at 5.59pm (Woodfull 141, Bradman 124).						
Hammond	Woodfull	000000				
Woolley	Bradman	401	Woodfull	020		
Hammond	Bradman	3	Woodfull	001	Bradman	01
Woolley	Bradman	202200				
Allen	Woodfull	0001	Bradman	1	Woodfull	3
Robins	Woodfull	1	Bradman	1	Woodfull	1
	Bradman	21	Woodfull	1		
Allen	Woodfull	002000				
Robins	Bradman	1	Woodfull	001	Bradman	01
Allen	Bradman	1	Woodfull	001	Bradman	04
Bradman 151 (two hours thirty-four minutes) at 6.22pm.						
Robins	Woodfull	W				

Woodfull caught Duckworth bowled Robins 155 at 6.23pm. Australia 393 for 2 (Bradman 151).

	Kippax	41	Bradman	1
	Kippax	1	Bradman	0

Australia 400 for 2 at 6.27pm (Bradman 152).

Allen	Kippax	00001	Bradman	3

Close of play: Australia 404 for 2 (Bradman 155, Kippax 7).

Monday:

Tate	Bradman	000002				
Allen	Kippax	000000				
Tate	Bradman	000000				
Allen	Kippax	000000				
Tate	Bradman	000020				
Allen	Kippax	00003	Bradman	0		
Tate	Kippax	0021	Bradman	00		
Allen	Kippax	01	Bradman	2001		
Tate	Bradman	000000				
Allen	Kippax	00001	Bradman	0		
Tate	Kippax	000000				
Allen	Bradman	1	Kippax	00021		
Robins	Kippax	00001	Bradman	1		
Tate	Bradman	040000				
Robins	Kippax	1	Bradman	201	Kippax	01
Tate	Kippax	000000				
Robins	Bradman	1	Kippax	0001	Bradman	1
Tate	Bradman	004000				
Robins	Kippax	01	Bradman	001	Kippax	0
Tate	Bradman	000000				
Robins	Kippax	05	Bradman	X0001 (X=wide)		

Australia 450 for 2 at 11.57pm (Bradman 179, Kippax 28).

Tate	Bradman	001	Kippax	1	Bradman	00
Robins	Kippax	(lb)	Bradman	00021		
Tate	Bradman	000040				
Robins	Kippax	1	Bradman	1	Kippax	1
	Bradman	001				
Hammond	Bradman	020000				
Robins	Kippax	000021				
Hammond	Kippax	01	Bradman	03	Kippax	00
Robins	Bradman	020202				

Bradman 200 (three hours fifty-four minutes) at 12.16pm. Australia 479 for 3.

Hammond	Kippax	000000

White	Bradman	0001	Kippax	00		
Hammond	Bradman	000000				
White	Kippax	00001	Bradman	0		
Hammond	Kippax	040000				
White	Bradman	00001	Kippax	0		
Hammond	Bradman	1	Kippax	22000		
White	Bradman	002000				
Hammond	Kippax	00001	Bradman	0		
White	Kippax	000000				
Hammond	Bradman	00001	Kippax	1		
White	Kippax	000000				
Hammond	Bradman	000000				
White	Kippax	000020				
Hammond	Bradman	002002				

Australia 502 for 2 (Bradman 210, Kippax 49).

White	Kippax	0001	Bradman	1	Kippax	0
Hammond	Bradman	1	Kippax	1	Bradman	01
	Kippax	01				
White	Kippax	2001	Bradman	1	Kippax	0
Hammond	Bradman	1	Kippax	01	Bradman	01
	Kippax	0				
White	Bradman	01	Kippax	1	Bradman	004
Tate	Kippax	1	Bradman	1	Kippax	0000
White	Bradman	020000				
Tate	Kippax	1	Bradman	01	Kippax	000
Allen	Bradman	X000001 (X= 4 wides)				
Tate	Bradman	1	Kippax	4001	Bradman	0
Allen	Kippax	1	Bradman	00040		
Tate	Kippax	00001	Bradman	0		

Lunch: Australia 544 for 2 (Bradman 231, Kippax 65).

White	Kippax	004000				
Tate	Bradman	1	Kippax	01	Bradman	1
	Kippax	1	Bradman	0		

Australia 552 for 2 at 2.22pm (Bradman 233, Kippax 71).

White	Kippax	01	Bradman	41	Kippax	20
Tate	Bradman	1	Kippax	00000		
White	Bradman	1	Kippax	001	Bradman	1
	Kippax	0				
Tate	Bradman	1	Kippax	00000		
White	Bradman	0001	Kippax	00		
Tate	Bradman	00(1b)	Kippax	000		
White	Bradman	01	Kippax	0001		
Tate	Kippax	01	Bradman	1	Kippax	002

White	Bradman	401	Kippax	01	Bradman	0

Bradman 250 (five hours thirty-five minutes) at 2.44pm.

Tate	Kippax	01	Bradman	(1b)	Kippax	000
White	Bradman	400W				

Bradman caught Chapman bowled White 254. Australia 585 for 3.
Australia declared at tea at 729 for 6.
Close of play: England 98 for 2.

Tuesday:
England were all out for 375 at 5.25pm, Australia 72 to win.

Tate	Woodfull	000000				
Hammond	Ponsford	1	Woodfull	00000		
Tate	Ponsford	200400				
Hammond	Woodfull	000000				
Tate	Ponsford	200400				
Hammond	Woodfull	000100				

(because the batsmen did not cross, the single seems to have been a 2 called 1 short)

Robins	Ponsford	1	Woodfull	01	Ponsford	W

Ponsford bowled Robins 14. Australia 16 for 1. Bradman came in at 4.05pm.

	Bradman	1	Woodfull	0
Tate	Bradman	0	W	

Bradman caught Chapman bowled Tate 1. Australia 17 for 2.
Australia won by seven wickets.

THIRD TEST: Headingley

Friday: *Woodfull won the toss and batted.*

Larwood	Woodfull	01	Jackson	001
Woodfull		9		
Tate	Jackson	0000W		

Jackson caught Larwood bowled Tate 1. Australia 2 for 1. Bradman came in to bat at 11.38am.

			Bradman	0
Larwood	Woodfull	400000		
Tate	Bradman	020000		
Larwood	Woodfull	000002		
Tate	Bradman	040000		
Larwood	Woodfull	01	Bradman	0201
Tate	Bradman	000001		
Larwood	Bradman	40421	Woodfull	0
Geary	Bradman	000040		
Tate	Woodfull	000000		
Geary	Bradman	000000		
Tate	Woodfull	001	Bradman	000

Geary	Woodfull	000000				
Tate	Bradman	001	Woodfull	001		
Geary	Woodfull	000000				
Tate	Bradman	400000				
Geary	Woodfull	00001	Bradman	3		
Tate	Bradman	00201	Woodfull	0		
Tyldesley	Bradman	40401	Woodfull	0		

Australia 57 for 1 at 12.25m (Woodfull 11, Bradman 45).

Geary	Bradman	1	Woodfull	01	Bradman	004

Bradman 50 (forty-nine minutes) at 12.27pm.

Tyldesley	Woodfull	000200				
Geary	Bradman	440001				
Tyldesley	Bradman	200401				
Tate	Bradman	000040				
Geary	Woodfull	1	Bradman	001	Woodfull	00
Tyldesley	Bradman	1	Woodfull	0001	Bradman	1
Geary	Bradman	012	Woodfull	000		
Tyldesley	Bradman	004000				
Geary	Woodfull	0001	Bradman	1	Woodfull	0
Tyldesley	Bradman	000000				
Geary	Woodfull	1	Bradman	00020		

Australia 102 for 1 at 12.53pm (Woodfull 18, Bradman 83).

Tyldesley	Woodfull	0(lb)	Bradman	4000		
Geary	Woodfull	1	Bradman	0001	Woodfull	0
Tyldesley	Bradman	000000				
Hammond	Woodfull	000004				
Tyldesley	Bradman	01	Woodfull	0001		
Hammond	Woodfull	00001	Bradman	1		
Larwood	Bradman	000001				
Hammond	Bradman	000201				
Larwood	Bradman	400040				

Bradman 102 (one hour thirty-nine minutes) at 12.54pm.

Hammond	Woodfull	00001	Bradman	0
Larwood	Woodfull	000001		
Hammond	Woodfull	002000		
Larwood	Bradman	1	Woodfull	00000
Hammond	Bradman	000020		

Lunch: Australia 136 for 1 (Woodfull 29, Bradman 105).

Larwood	Woodfull	00001	Bradman	1		
Geary	Bradman	000040				
Larwood	Woodfull	1	Bradman	41	Woodfull	003

Australia 151 for 1 at 2.27pm (Woodfull 34, Bradman 115).

Geary	Woodfull	040000				
Larwood	Bradman	042420				
Geary	Woodfull	01	Bradman	01	Woodfull	00
Larwood	Bradman	1	Woodfull	00000		
Geary	Bradman	0001	Woodfull	00		
Tate	Bradman	1	Woodfull	01	Bradman	041
Geary	Bradman	01	Woodfull	0000		
Tate	Bradman	01	Woodfull	3	Bradman	000
Geary	Woodfull	004000				
Hammond	Bradman	1	Woodfull	00000		
Geary	Bradman	201	Woodfull	001		
Hammond	Woodfull	000001				
Geary	Woodfull	000000				
Hammond	Bradman	000000				
Geary	Woodfull	00001	Woodfull	0		
Hammond	Woodfull	00W				
Woodfull bowled Hammond 50. Australia 194 for 2 (Bradman 142).						
			Kippax	000		
Geary	Bradman	000000				
Hammond	Kippax	001	Bradman	03	Kippax	0
Geary	Bradman	000002				
Australia 200 for 1 at 3.14pm (Bradman 147, Kippax 1).						
Larwood	Kippax	000000				
Tate	Bradman	040000				
Bradman 151 (two hours fifty-four minutes) at 3.20pm.						
Larwood	Kippax	000000				
Tate	Bradman	20041	Kippax	0		
Larwood	Bradman	1	Kippax	00001		
Tate	Kippax	000000				
Larwood	Bradman	401	Kippax	400		
Hammond	Bradman	000401				
Tate	Bradman	1	Kippax	001	Bradman	22
Hammond	Kippax	1	Bradman	00004		
Tate	Kippax	01	Bradman	0200		
Hammond	Kippax	000000				
Tyldesley	Bradman	401	Kippax	201		
Hammond	Kippax	004000				
Australia 253 for 2 at 3.53pm (Bradman 186, Kippax 16).						
Tyldesley	Bradman	1	Kippax	00000		
Leyland	Bradman	220441				
Tyldesley	Bradman	001				
Bradman 200 (three hours thirty-four minutes) at 4pm.						
			Kippax	000		
Leyland	Bradman	01	Kippax	1	Bradman	01

	Kippax	0				
Tyldesley	Bradman	1	Kippax	1	Bradman	4000
Leyland	Kippax	1	Bradman	001	Kippax	1
	Bradman	1				
Tyldesley	Bradman	01	Kippax	0000		
Leyland	Bradman	0001	Kippax	00		
Tyldesley	Bradman	000000				
Leyland	Kippax	020001				
Tyldesley	Kippax	1	Bradman	001	Kippax	00
Leyland	Bradman	000001				
Tyldesley	Bradman	0001	Kippax	00		
Leyland	Bradman	0401	Kippax	01		
Australia 300 at 4.25pm (Bradman 219, Kippax 29).						
Tyldesley	Kippax	000000				
Leyland	Bradman	01	Kippax	0400		
Tea: Australia 305 for 2 (Bradman 220, Kippax 33).						
Larwood	Bradman	004003				
Tyldesley	Bradman	00(1b)	Kippax	001		
Larwood	Kippax	1	Bradman	1	Kippax	01
	Bradman	1	Kippax	1		
Tyldesley	Kippax	01	Bradman	0001		
Larwood	Bradman	000040				
Tyldesley	Kippax	01	Bradman	001	Kippax	2
Larwood	Bradman	400020				
Tyldesley	Kippax	1	Bradman	0001	Kippax	3
Tate	Kippax	0001	Bradman	00		
Tyldesley	Kippax	01	Bradman	1	Kippax	1
	Bradman	1	Kippax	0		
Tate	Bradman	004003				
Bradman 251 (four hours thirty-four minutes) at 5.22pm. Australia 352 for 2 (Kippax 48).						
Tyldesley	Bradman	001	Kippax	1	Bradman	02
Tate	Kippax	0001	Bradman	20		
Tyldesley	Kippax	1	Bradman	1	Kippax	2000
Tate	Bradman	1	Kippax	0021	Bradman	0
Tyldesley	Kippax	000000				
Tate	Bradman	02001	Kippax	0		
Tyldesley	Bradman	0001	Kippax	02		
Geary	Bradman	404000				
Tyldesley	Kippax	001	Bradman	1	Kippax	00
Geary	Bradman	02001	Kippax	0		
Leyland	Bradman	0001	Kippax	04		
Geary	Bradman	001	Kippax	1	Bradman	02
Leyland	Kippax	01	Bradman	0000		

Geary	Kippax	001	Bradman	1	Kippax	00
Leyland	Bradman	1	Kippax	00001		

Australia 400 for 2 at 5.56pm (Bradman 283, Kippax 68).

Larwood	Kippax	001	Bradman	03	Kippax	0
Tate	Bradman	041	Kippax	402		
Larwood	Bradman	0041	Kippax	01		
Tate	Kippax	0002W				

Kippax caught Chapman bowled Tate 77. Australia 423 for 3 (Bradman 293).

			McCabe	(1)		
Larwood	McCabe	1	Bradman	1	McCabe	0(4lb)00
Tate	Bradman	400000				
Hammond	McCabe	44(lb)	Bradman	1		
McCabe	0 (this over seems to be one ball short)					
Tate	Bradman	1				

Bradman 300 (five hours thirty-six minutes) at 6.22pm.

			McCabe	00001		
Hammond	McCabe	002(lb)	Bradman	1	McCabe	0
Tate	Bradman	040040				

Close of play: Australia 458 for 3 (Bradman 309, McCabe 12).

Saturday:

Larwood	McCabe	024000		
Tate	Bradman	0403	McCabe	00
Larwood	Bradman	1	McCabe	00000
Tate	Bradman	000000		
Larwood	McCabe	404000		
Tate	Bradman	1	McCabe	00040
Larwood	Bradman	1	McCabe	W

McCabe bowled Larwood 30. Australia 486 for 4 (Bradman 319).

	Richardson	1	Bradman	400
Tate	Richardson	000W		

Richardson caught Larwood bowled Tate 1. Australia 491 for 5 (Bradman 323).

			a'Beckett	00
Larwood	Bradman	1	a'Beckett	20000
Tate	Bradman	020004		
Larwood	a'Beckett	004000		
Tate	Bradman	04000W		

Bradman caught Duckworth bowled Tate 334. Australia 508 for 6. They went on to make 566, England 391 and, following on, 95 for 3 but weather ruined the match.

FOURTH TEST: Old Trafford

Friday: *Woodfull won the toss and batted. He and Ponsford opened and put on 106 for the first wicket before Woodfull was caught by Duckworth off the first ball of Tate's fifteenth over.*

Tate	Bradman	1	Ponsford	0000		
Peebles	Bradman	(4b)0001	Ponsford	1		
Tate	Ponsford	000001				
Peebles	Ponsford	01	Bradman	1	Ponsford	000
Tate	Bradman	003	Ponsford	01	Bradman	0
Peebles	Ponsford	1	Bradman	2001	Ponsford	1
Tate	Ponsford	000000				
Peebles	Bradman	1	Ponsford	1	Bradman	0(2b)00
Tate	Ponsford	0001	Bradman	00		
Peebles	Peebles	00001	Bradman	4		
Tate	Ponsford	0004(nb)0				
Peebles	Bradman	00W				

Bradman bowled Peebles 14. Australia 138 for 2. Australia made 345 and England 251 but the weather ruined this match, too.

FIFTH TEST: The Oval

Saturday: *Timeless Test which began on the Saturday. Wyatt won the toss and batted, England finishing the day on 316 for 5.*

Monday: *England 405 all out. Woodfull and Ponsford opened for Australia and put on 159. Peebles prepared to bowl his fifteenth over.*

Peebles	Ponsford	00W

Ponsford bowled Peebles 110. Australia 159 for 1 (Woodfull 40). Bradman came in at 4.30pm but rain caused two interruptions.

			Bradman	1	Woodfull	00
Tate	Bradman	200000				
Peebles	Woodfull	1	Bradman	00000		
Tate	Woodfull	000000				
Peebles	Bradman	20001	Woodfull	0		
Tate	Bradman	1	Woodfull	04000		
Peebles	Bradman	002000				
Tate	Woodfull	000000				
Peebles	Bradman	01	Woodfull	0000		
Tate	Bradman	21	Woodfull	1	Bradman	000
Peebles	Woodfull	0001	Bradman	3	Woodfull	2
Hammond	Bradman	0(b)	Woodfull	01	Bradman	00
Peebles	Woodfull	400W				

Woodfull caught Duckworth bowled Peebles 54. Australia 190 for 2 (Bradman 16).

			Kippax	1	Bradman	0

Hammond	Kippax	001	Bradman	000		
Peebles	Kippax	02000(1b)				
Hammond	Kippax	020000				
Peebles	Bradman	1	Kippax	00200		
Australia 200 at 6.15pm (Bradman 17, Kippax 8).						
Larwood	Bradman	2001	Kippax	1	Bradman	1
Peebles	Bradman	01	Kippax	1	Bradman	021
Larwood	Bradman	01	Kippax	1	Bradman	01

Close of play: Australia 215 for 2 (Bradman 27, Kippax 11).

Tuesday:	*Play resumes 11am.*					
Tate	Bradman	01	Kippax	01	Bradman	3
	Kippax	1				
Larwood	Kippax	01	Bradman	1	Kippax	0(nb)0
Tate	Bradman	200000				
Larwood	Kippax	003 (from nb)			Bradman	01 (one short)
Tate	Bradman	001	Kippax	000		
Larwood	Bradman	1	Kippax	0002(nb)		
Tate	Bradman	1	Kippax	1	Bradman	0400
Larwood	Kippax	01	Bradman	0200		
Peebles	Kippax	240000				
Australia 253 for 2 at 11.25am (Bradman 44, Kippax 27).						
Tate	Bradman	000001				
Peebles	Bradman	000000				
Tate	Kippax	000000				
Peebles	Bradman	401				
Bradman 50 (one hour thirty-nine minutes) at 11.39am.						

			Kippax	000		
Hammond	Bradman	000000				
Peebles	Kippax	1	Bradman	21	Kippax	W

Kippax caught Wyatt bowled Peebles 28. Australia 263 for 3 (Bradman 53).

	Jackson	02				
Hammond	Bradman	000000				
Peebles	Jackson	0(b)	Bradman	01	Jackson	1
	Bradman	1				
Hammond	Bradman	1	Jackson	0(2lb)001		
Peebles	Jackson	1	Bradman	01	Jackson	0(4b)0
Hammond	Bradman	1	Jackson	1	Bradman	0000
Peebles	Jackson	000(1lb)	Bradman	20		
Hammond	Jackson	000(4lb)00				
Peebles	Bradman	001	Jackson	004		
Hammond	Bradman	002000				
Peebles	Jackson	000000				
Hammond	Bradman	01	Jackson	01	Bradman	00
Leyland	Jackson	000000				
Hammond	Bradman	03	Jackson	0000		

Australia 301 for 2 at 12.20pm (Bradman 67, Jackson 11).

Leyland	Bradman	0001	Jackson	00		
Hammond	Bradman	01	Jackson	0000		
Leyland	Bradman	041	Jackson	002		
Hammond	Bradman	1	Jackson	00000		
Leyland	Bradman	004003				
Hammond	Bradman	0(b)0000				
Leyland	Jackson	001	Bradman	000		
Hammond	Jackson	000000				
Tate	Bradman	3	Jackson	1	Bradman	0000
Hammond	Jackson	000000				
Tate	Bradman	1	Jackson	00000		
Hammond	Bradman	000041				
Tate	Bradman	1	Jackson	00000		
Larwood	Bradman	201	Jackson	000		
Peebles	Bradman	1	Jackson	1	Bradman	01
	Jackson	00				
Larwood	Bradman	01	Jackson	0000		
Peebles	Bradman	1	Jackson	00004		
Larwood	Bradman	400000				

Bradman 103 (three hours five minutes) at 1.05pm (Jackson 20).

Peebles	Jackson	000000				
Larwood	Bradman	1	Jackson	01	Bradman	000
Peebles	Jackson	000020				

Australia 351 for 3 at 1.15pm (Bradman 104, Jackson 23).

Tate	Bradman	0203	Jackson	00		
Peebles	Bradman	01	Jackson	001	Bradman	0
Tate	Jackson	01	Bradman	0001		
Peebles	Bradman	1	Jackson	044(3b)0		

Lunch: Australia 371 for 3 (Bradman 112, Jackson 33).

Tate	Bradman	1	Jackson	00000		
Larwood	Bradman	01	Jackson	0000		
Tate	Bradman	01	Jackson	0000		
Larwood	Bradman	1	Jackson	003	Bradman	00
Tate	Jackson	001	Bradman	01	Jackson	0
Larwood	Bradman	0003	Jackson	00		
Tate	Bradman	020000				
Peebles	Jackson	000000				
Tate	Bradman	1	Jackson	00000		
Peebles	Bradman	00001	Jackson	0		
Tate	Bradman	00001	Jackson	0		
Peebles	Bradman	001	Jackson	004		
Tate	Bradman	001	Jackson	001		
Peebles	Jackson	00001	Bradman	2		
Hammond	Jackson	000(4b)				

Australia 402 for 3 (Bradman 129, Jackson 43).
Bad light

	Jackson	00		
Peebles	Bradman	0001	Jackson	00
Hammond	Bradman	000000		

Bad light. Close of play: Australia 403 for 3 (Bradman 130, Jackson 43).

Wednesday: *Play resumed 11am.*

Peebles	Jackson	000000				
Hammond	Bradman	001	Jackson	000		
Peebles	Bradman	00001	Jackson	1		
Hammond	Jackson	00001	Bradman	(1lb)		
Peebles	Bradman	001	Jackson	01	Bradman	0
Leyland	Jackson	000000				
Peebles	Bradman	01	Jackson	2001		
Leyland	Jackson	000000				
Peebles	Bradman	01	Jackson	0000		
Leyland	Bradman	04001	Jackson	0		
Peebles	Bradman	002040				
Leyland	Jackson	000000				
Tate	Bradman	200000				

Leyland	Jackson	000000				
Tate	Bradman	000000				
Leyland	Jackson	000000				
Tate	Bradman	200000				
Bradman 150 (five hours) at 11.32am (Jackson 49).						
Leyland	Jackson	000040				
Tate	Bradman	400000				
Leyland	Jackson	02201	Bradman	0		
Tate	Jackson	001	Bradman	000		
Hammond	Jackson	000200				
Tate	Bradman	3	Jackson	00000		
Hammond	Bradman	001	Jackson	000		
Australia 450 for 3 at 12.02pm (Bradman 158, Jackson 61).						
Tate	Bradman	20021	Jackson	0		
Hammond	Bradman	01	Jackson	01	Bradman	1
	Jackson	0				
Larwood	Bradman	040000				
Hammond	Jackson	000000				
Larwood	Bradman	002004				
Hammond	Jackson	000040				
Larwood	Bradman	00001	Jackson	0		
Hammond	Bradman	0221	Jackson	00		
Larwood	Bradman	1	Jackson	001	Bradman	1
	Jackson	0				
Hammond	Bradman	000000				
Larwood	Jackson	000000				
Wyatt	Bradman	3	Jackson	00000		
Larwood	Bradman	40201	Jackson	0		
Wyatt	Bradman	01	Jackson	0000		
Larwood	Bradman	21	Jackson	01	Bradman 01	
Australia 501 for 3 at 12.54pm (Bradman 198, Jackson 72).						
Wyatt	Bradman	004				
Bradman 202 (six hours twenty-three minutes) at 12.55pm.						
	Bradman	000				
Peebles	Jackson	00001	Bradman	0		
Wyatt	Jackson	00W				
Jackson caught Sutcliffe bowled Wyatt 73. Australia 506 for 4 (Bradman 202).						
			McCabe	1	Bradman	1
	McCabe	4				
Peebles	Bradman	4201	McCabe	40		
Wyatt	Bradman	004001				
Peebles	Bradman	1	McCabe	00001	Bradman	0
Wyatt	McCabe	00(lb)	Bradman	3	McCabe	42
Peebles	Bradman	00401	McCabe	0		

Tate	Bradman	1	McCabe	00200
Larwood	Bradman	1	McCabe	00000
Tate	Bradman	200000		

Lunch Australia 551 for 4 (Bradman 228, McCabe 18).

Larwood	McCabe	0001	Bradman	1	McCabe	4
Tate	Bradman	000020				
Larwood	McCabe	04001	Bradman	0		
Tate	McCabe	000041				
Larwood	McCabe	004000				
Tate	Bradman	0001	McCabe	00		
Larwood	Bradman	00W				

Bradman caught Duckworth bowled Larwood 232. Australia 570 for 5 (McCabe 33). Australia made 695, England 251 in the second innings to lose by an innings and 39 runs.

Appendix 2
The matches Bradman didn't play in

The fact that the Australian selectors only picked fifteen players for a tour lasting, in all, from March to October – and embracing the two matches in Tasmania, the one at Perth, the one at Colombo and thirty-four matches in Britain – meant that they would all be playing a lot of cricket. Bradman missed only four, and three of those were against weaker sides, Essex, Warwickshire and Sussex. They beat Essex comprehensively at unlovely, unloved Leyton and drew against Sussex, despite an inspired spell by Maurice Tate, without too many alarms. The Warwickshire match was ruined by rain.

By missing the Nottinghamshire match Bradman also missed the chance to play against Bill Voce, a fascinating imponderable in view of what was to come in Australia under Jardine. Vic Richardson did play and smote Voce mightily. Oldfield wrote in *Behind the Wicket* that the Australians realised, 'watching his hostile type of bowling, that if he succeeded to any great degree he would be certain to be included in the next Test team'.

Soon after the beginning of the tour an unstated pressure must have started gathering to play Bradman because he was filling grounds and, as we saw in Wales, the overnight prospect of seeing him continue his innings brought so many people in that Glamorgan emerged from the year solvent.

Of the six matches after the Fifth Test he missed only Sussex, and scored 508 runs when, young and fit and eager as he was, he had to be tired.

Here are the four matches he didn't play in.

ESSEX V AUSTRALIANS

Leyton, 7, 8, 9 May. Australians won by 207 runs.

AUSTRALIANS

*W.M. Woodfull		b Palmer	4	c Nichols	b Smith	54
W.H. Ponsford	st Sheffield	b Hipkin	39	c Cutmore	b Nichols	26
S.J. McCabe	c Nichols	b Palmer	5	c Bray	b Palmer	6
A.F. Kippax		b Nichols	57	lbw	b O'Connor	42
A.A. Jackson	c Nichols	b Hipkin	7	c Sheffield	b O'Connor	27
A.G. Fairfax		b Palmer	12		not out	53
E.L. a'Beckett		b Palmer	0	c Crawley	b O'Connor	30
+W.A. Oldfield		not out	16		not out	14
C.V. Grimmett	c Bray	b Nichols	0			
A. Hurwood		b Hipkin	1			
P.M. Hornibrook	c O'Connor	b Palmer	7			
Extras	(b 5, lb 3)		8	(b 6, lb 5, nb 1)		12
Total			156	(6 wkts dec)		264

1-9, 2-34, 3-74, 4-92, 5-119, 6-119, 7-138, 8-138, 9-143

1-56, 2-70, 3-128, 4-176, 5-176, 6-238

	O	M	R	W	O	M	R	W
Nichols	18	9	23	2	21	6	36	1
Palmer	20.4	5	40	5	21	7	37	1
Hipkin	25	7	44	3	21	4	70	0
O'Connor	12	3	25	0	19	1	57	3
Smith	7	2	16	0	23	3	52	1

ESSEX

L.G. Crawley		b Fairfax	8		run out	8
J.A. Cutmore	st Oldfield	b Grimmett	8	c Jackson	b Hornibrook	39
J. O'Connor		b Grimmett	1	st Oldfield	b Grimmett	26
C.A.G. Russell		b Hornibrook	19		b Hornibrook	6
M.S. Nichols		b Hornibrook	9		b Hornibrook	4
*C. Bray	c Woodfull	b Hornibrook	3	st Oldfield	b Hornibrook	32
D.F. Pope		b Fairfax	5	c Jackson	b Grimmett	4
A.B. Hipkin		b Hornibrook	0	c Jackson	b Grimmett	9
+J.R. Sheffield		b Hornibrook	0		b a'Beckett	1
H.T.O. Smith	c Fairfax	b Hornibrook	2		b a'Beckett	0
H.J. Palmer		not out	0		not out	3
Extras	(b 9, lb 3)		12	(b 9, lb 3, nb 2)		14
Total			67			146

1-17, 2-17, 3-19, 4-49, 5-54, 6-55, 7-61, 8-61, 9-67

1-8, 2-28, 3-39, 4-43, 5-81, 6-101, 7-130, 8-140, 9-141

	O	M	R	W	O	M	R	W
Fairfax	15.4	3	25	2	11	6	14	0
a'Beckett	2	1	2	0	16	9	13	2
Grimmett	8	2	17	2	27	9	57	3
Hornibrook	9	4	11	6	22	10	29	4
Hurwood					12	6	18	0
McCabe					1	0	1	0

NOTTINGHAMSHIRE V AUSTRALIANS

Nottingham, 5, 7, 8 July. Drawn.

AUSTRALIANS

W.H. Ponsford		b Larwood	6	c Larwood	b Voce	27
A.A. Jackson	c Whysall	b Voce	22	c S.J. Staples	b A. Staples	79
S.J. McCabe		c & b Larwood	58	c Gunn	b Larwood	79
A.F. Kippax	c Larwood	b Voce	93		not out	89
*V.Y. Richardson	c Rhodes	b A. Staples	55	c Walker	b A. Staples	69
A.G. Fairfax		b Larwood	3			
E.L. a'Beckett	c S.J. Staples	b A. Staples	38		not out	5
A. Hurwood		b Voce	0			
+C.W. Walker		b Voce	5			
P.M. Hornibrook		not out	5			
T.W. Wall		b A Staples	6			
Extras	(b 3, lb 1, w 1)		5	(b 7, lb 5)		12
Total			296	(4 wkts dec)		360

1-19, 2-41, 3-115, 4-198, 5-205, 6-260, 7-280, 8-281, 9-285

1-43, 2-165, 3-218, 4-339

	O	M	R	W	O	M	R	W
Larwood	19	1	59	3	9	1	35	1
Barratt	19	8	48	0	3	1	13	0
Voce	20	5	86	4	22	3	112	1
S.J. Staples	22	4	54	0	22	4	69	0
A. Staples	14.2	2	44	3	18	2	56	2
Rhodes					11	4	30	0
Gunn					4	0	33	0

NOTTINGHAMSHIRE

*G. Gunn	c Wall	b Hurwood	34
W.W. Whysall		b Hurwood	120
W. Walker		b Hurwood	53
W.D.R. Payton	lbw	b Wall	24
+B. Lilley		b Hornibrook	24
A. Staples		run out	29
S.D. Rhodes	c Hornibrook	b Hurwood	20
F. Barratt		b McCabe	0
H. Larwood	c a'Beckett	b Hornibrook	25
S.J. Staples	c Richardson	b Hurwood	62
W. Voce		not out	22
Extras	(b 14, lb 5, nb 1)		20
Total			433

1-64, 2-170, 3-223, 4-251, 5-294, 6-296, 7-296, 8-331, 9-387

	O	M	R	W
Wall	30	2	96	1
a'Beckett	30	10	57	0
Hurwood	37	6	111	5
Hornibrook	32	11	85	2
Kippax	7	0	26	0
McCabe	12	2	38	1

WARWICKSHIRE V AUSTRALIANS

Edgbaston, 6, 7, 8 August. Drawn.

WARWICKSHIRE

+E.J. Smith	c Woodfull	b Hurwood	0
A.J.W. Croom	c Hurwood	b Hornibrook	25
L.T.A. Bates	c Richardson	b Fairfax	22
*R.E.S. Wyatt	not out		22
Rev. J.H. Parsons	not out		26
Extras	(b 4, lb 3)		7
Total	(3 wickets)		102

Dnb: Hon. F.S.G. Calthorpe, G.D. Kemp-Welch, N.E. Partridge, N. Kilner, J.H. Mayer, G.A.E. Paine.

1-8, 2-45, 3-53

	O	M	R	W
Fairfax	13	7	13	1
a'Beckett	2	1	1	0
Hurwood	12	1	28	1
Hornibrook	20	7	29	1
Grimmett	7	2	14	0
McCabe	4.5	0	10	0

Australians: *W.M. Woodfull, W.H. Ponsford, A.A. Jackson, S.J. McCabe, V.Y. Richardson, A.G. Fairfax, E.L. a'Beckett, C.V. Grimmett, +W.A. Oldfield, P.M. Hornibrook, A. Hurwood.

SUSSEX V AUSTRALIANS

Brighton, 30 August, 1, 2 September. Drawn.

AUSTRALIANS

W.H. Ponsford		b Tate	0		b Tate	38
A.A. Jackson	c Duleepsinhji	b Tate	10	c Bowley	b Tate	12
S.J. McCabe		b Tate	15		b Tate	15
A.F. Kippax	c Langridge	b J.H. Parks	158		not out	102
*V.Y. Richardson		b Tate	2	st Cornford	b Bowley	24
A.G. Fairfaxlbw		b Tate	6	st Cornford	b Langridge	16
E.L. a'Beckett	c Wensley	b Tate	1	c Duleepsinhji	b Langridge	13
+W.A. Oldfield		b Bowley	7	c Cornford	b Wensley	1
C.V. Grimmett	c Duleepsinhji	b Bowley	38		b Wensley	0
A. Hurwood	lbw	b Wensley	61		run out	5
P.M. Hornibrook		not out	59		not out	2
Extras	(b 5, lb 5)		10	(b 2, lb 3)		5
Total			367	(9 wkts dec)		233

1-0, 2-22, 3-31, 4-33, 5-67, 6-69, 7-79, 8-199, 9-249

1-30, 2-66, 3-67, 4-122, 5-167, 6-205, 7-206, 8-212, 9-217

	O	M	R	W	O	M	R	W
Tate	39	8	82	6	13	0	39	3
Wensley	30.1	9	76	1	19	3	51	2
J.H. Parks	18	2	65	1	6	0	18	0
Langridge	14	1	50	0	21.2	3	52	2
Bowley	14	0	70	2	8	0	39	0
Cook	6	1	14	0	2	0	5	0
Duleepsinhji					6	0	24	0

SUSSEX

E.H. Bowley		b Hornibrook	34	c Hurwood	b Hornibrook	25
J.H. Parks		b Hornibrook	84		not out	39
K.S. Duleepsinhji	st Oldfield	b Hornibrook	15			
T.E.R. Cook		not out	67		not out	26
J.A.S. Langridge	c Richardson	b Fairfax	25			
A.H.H. Gilligan	c a'Beckett	b Fairfax	4			
H.W. Parks		b Hornibrook	1			
A.F. Wensley	c Jackson	b Grimmett	2			
M.W. Tate	c Ponsford	b Hornibrook	21			
+W.L. Cornford	c Kippax	b Grimmett	1			
*A.E.R. Gilligan	absent hurt					
Extras	(b 10, lb 5)		15	(b 2, lb 1)		3
Total			269	(1 wkt)		93

1-68, 2-98, 3-176, 4-223, 5-227, 6-237, 7-240, 8-267, 9-269

1-42

	O	M	R	W	O	M	R	W
Fairfax	19	6	41	2	4	2	9	0
Hurwood	10	6	16	0	7	2	10	0
Grimmett	32.5	5	115	2				
a'Beckett	13	2	21	0	6	0	17	0
Hornibrook	26	3	51	5	11	2	31	1
McCabe	3	1	10	0	4	3	1	0
Kippax					4	0	11	0
Jackson					4	0	5	0
Ponsford					1	0	6	0

Appendix 3

The terms of the tour*

All the players had to sign a thirty-six-clause contract drawn up by the Board of Control. The first two clauses covered the formalities of their departure from Australia.

CLAUSE 3 – During the tour players shall unless prevented by illness or accident, play in such matches as the manager, with the approval of the Selection Committee, may direct.

CLAUSE 4 – Players shall punctually attend at such times and places as the manager may, on the advice of the Selection Committee, appoint for the purpose of playing in matches or for practice or otherwise as the manager, with the approval of the Selection Committee may direct.

CLAUSE 5 – Players shall on the way to, or on arrival in England, and thereafter during the tour stay and reside in such place as the manager shall appoint or select and shall not without the consent of the manager, stay or reside elsewhere.

CLAUSE 6 – Players agree that they will not during the currency of this agreement commit any act or be guilty of any conduct which renders them unfit or uncapable of playing in any match or unfit to remain members of the team; and that they will at all times, obey the direction of the manager and/or the Executive Committee.

If any player commits a breach of this covenant the Executive

* These appeared in *The Evening Standard,* London, on Saturday 26 April 1930.

Committee may, in its absolute and uncontrolled discretion, by notice in writing to such player determine the agreement with the player; whereupon he shall at once, forfeit all claims to the fixed sum hereinafter mentioned, or to any other sum hereinafter mentioned, which shall not have been paid to such player at the date of determination of the said agreement. The Executive Committee shall in any such case provide such player with a first-class passage to Australia provided always and it is hereby mutually agreed, that such player, upon his return to Australia may appeal against any such decision to the Board, and the decision of the Board shall be final, and binding in all respects, as players do hereby agree.

CLAUSE 7 – Each and every member of the team covenants that he will not be accompanied on tour or any part thereof by his wife or any member of the family or any relative or connection.

CLAUSE 8 – Each and every member of the team covenants that during the period of the tour neither his wife nor any of his children under his legal control will be in England or outside Australia where the team, from time to time, may be touring.

CLAUSE 9 – Any breach of Clauses 7 or 8 by any player shall *ipso facto* render him unfit to remain a member of the team, and the Executive Committee shall forthwith exercise powers vested in them under Clause 6.

CLAUSE 10 – If the manager or treasurer commits any breach of Clauses 6 or 7 he shall forthwith be recalled to Australia by the Board and, in such case, shall not be entitled to fixed sum as hereinafter provided.

CLAUSE 11 – Neither the manager, Executive, treasurer, nor any player shall accept employment as a newspaper correspondent or do any work for, or in connection with, any newspaper or any broadcasting; and no member of the team other than the manager shall directly or indirectly in any capacity whatsoever communicate with Press nor give any information concerning matters connected with the tour to the Press or any member, servant or agent thereof.

CLAUSE 12 – No person shall be admitted to any room reserved for the use of the players or any car so reserved nor shall any person be permitted to travel with the team without the consent of the manager.

CLAUSE 13 – The treasurer shall pay out moneys advanced by the Board or resulting from the tour or expenses of the tour, including hotel, travelling, gratuities and reasonable laundry expenses, but not the cost of wine, other alcoholic liquors or tobacco.

CLAUSE 14 – The Executive Committee shall have full power to impose such fines and in such amounts as they shall think proper on any player failing to conform to the conditions hereof, or any of them, or failing to obey the directions of the Executive Committee or manager or misconducting himself in any manner whatsoever.

CLAUSE 15 (Unknown.)

CLAUSE 16 – Subject to the terms of this agreement the manager shall be entitled to £650 payable as follows: £50 before embarking for outfit purposes, £450 during the progress of the tour, but not more than £90 in each calendar month and £150 on his return to Australia. The treasurer and each player shall be entitled to receive £600, payable as follows: £50 prior to embarkation for outfit purposes, £400 during the tour but not more than £90 in each calendar month and £150 on his return to Australia. The last mentioned payment to a player shall be dependent upon a satisfactory report being made by the manager, and upon the chairman receiving such satisfactory report shall authorise payment thereof.

If the report is unsatisfactory to the Board it may determine that the sum be forfeited to the Board wholly or in part and the Board shall be the sole authority in deciding the matter, and the decision shall be final.

CLAUSE 17 – To cover expenses of the players for tramcar and taxicab fares to and from hotels and grounds at which their matches are played, also for incidental expenses of players on land and sea, an allowance shall be made to each player of 30s weekly, payable fortnightly from the date of embarkation at Melbourne to the date of disembarkation in Australia at the close of the tour, which shall not form part of the £600 aforementioned.

CLAUSE 18 – It is naturally agreed by, and between the parties herein, their and each of their heirs, Executors administrators and assigns, that, if any members of the team during the continuance of the tour, shall die or suffer any injury or illness, thus rendering himself incapable of performing his duties, then such player and, in case of death, his personal representative shall be entitled to receive only such proportion of sums in Clause 16 as shall have been paid and due upon date of such death, injury or illness provided always that if such death, injury or illness shall have been brought about in course of the performance of his duties, then above-mentioned conditions shall not be applicable, but the player or his personal representative shall be entitled to receive full benefits under the agreements in all respects.

CLAUSE 19 – The manager and treasurer shall have control of all matters relating to the finance of the tour.

CLAUSE 20 – The captain, vice-captain and one other member of the team appointed by the Board shall form the Selection Committee.

CLAUSE 21–24 (Unavailable.)

CLAUSE 25–26 (Relate to travelling by the steamer.)

CLAUSE 27 – Every player specifically undertakes and agrees that he will not return to England within two years of the completion of the official tour for the purpose of cricket.

CLAUSE 28 – No person shall invite or permit any other person to travel with the team, or enjoy the privileges and concessions granted to the team unless permission is previously given by the chairman or manager, and no visitors shall be entertained at the expense of the Board except with the approval of the chairman or manager.

CLAUSE 29 – No monetary allowance shall be charged against the tour expenses by members of the team, or subscriptions to ship's sports or liquid refreshments on land or sea.

CLAUSE 30 – On his return to Australia each member shall disembark at his home port; if any member does not so disembark he shall himself pay his own expense from the port of disembarkation to his home town.

CLAUSE 31 – No player is entitled to be reimbursed for any meals not taken at official hotels where the team is staying.

CLAUSE 32 – No player shall employ any ground bowler at the Board's expense except in very special cases of the consent of the Executive.

CLAUSE 33 – All excess freight and luggage shall be payable by the member concerned and any member carrying dutiable goods shall declare same to customs, and pay the duty thereon.

CLAUSE 34 – No member shall absent himself from any function which has been duly designated as official by the Executive without the sanction of the Executive.

CLAUSE 35 – Neither the treasurer nor any player shall be permitted to accompany or invite any person to attend any function as a member of the Australian team except with the permission of the manager.

CLAUSE 36 – The board shall provide each player with a blazer, cap, sweater and tie only.

Appendix 4

The tour averages

FIRST-CLASS MATCHES

	M	I	NO	R	HS	Av
D.G. Bradman	27	36	6	2960	334	98.66
A.F. Kippax	23	32	7	1451	153	58.04
W.M. Woodfull	23	26	1	1434	216	57.36
W.H. Ponsford	24	33	4	1425	220*	49.13
A.A. Jackson	26	35	3	1097	118	34.28
S.J. McCabe	26	33	2	1012	96	32.64
V.Y. Richardson	26	32	1	832	116	26.83
A.G. Fairfax	23	27	6	536	63	25.52
E.L. a'Beckett	17	21	5	397	67*	24.81
W.A. Oldfield	16	16	4	225	43*	18.75
P.M. Hornibrook	26	26	8	232	59	12.88
C.V. Grimmett	26	23	3	237	50	11.85
A. Hurwood	20	19	1	188	61	10.44
T.W. Wall	22	19	6	107	40*	8.23
C.W. Walker	16	14	5	43	10*	4.77

	O	M	R	W	Av
C.V. Grimmett	1015.1	262	2427	144	16.85
P.M. Hornibrook	819.2	240	1802	96	18.77
D.G. Bradman	76	12	301	12	25.08
A. Hurwood	354	116	752	28	26.85
S.J. McCabe	281	69	723	26	27.80
T.W. Wall	610.2	111	1638	56	29.25
A.G. Fairfax	535.4	150	1218	41	29.70
E.L. a'Beckett	343	112	628	20	31.40
Also bowled:					
A.F. Kippax	253	2	91	4	—
A.A. Jackson	5	0	8	0	—
W.H. Ponsford	1	0	6	0	—
V.Y. Richardson	1	0	8	0	—

TESTS

	M	I	NO	R	HS	Av
D.G. Bradman	5	7	0	974	334	139.14
W.M. Woodfull	5	7	1	345	155	57.50
W.H. Ponsford	4	6	0	330	110	55.00
A.F. Kippax	5	7	1	329	83	54.83
A.G. Fairfax	4	5	2	150	53*	50.00
A.A. Jackson	2	2	0	74	73	37.00
S.J. McCabe	5	7	1	54	210	35.00

	M	I	NO	R	HS	Av
E.L. a'Beckett	1	1	0	29	29	29.00
V.Y. Richardson	4	5	1	37	98	24.50
W.A. Oldfield	5	6	1	43*	96	19.20
C.V. Grimmett	5	5	0	50	80	16.00
P.M. Hornibrook	5	5	1	7	16	4.00
T.W. Wall	5	5	2	8*	12	4.00

	0	M	R	W	Av
S.J. McCabe	87	21	221	8	27.63
A.G. Fairfax	134.2	34	335	12	27.92
C.V. Grimmett	349.4	78	925	29	31.90
P.M. Hornibrook	196.1	50	471	13	36.23
T.W. Wall	229.4	44	593	13	45.62
E.L. a'Beckett	39	12	66	1	66.00
D.G. Bradman	1	0	1	0	

TESTS (ENGLAND)

	M	I	NO	R	HS	Av
H. Sutcliffe	4	7	2	436	161	87.20
K.S. Duleepsinhji	4	7	0	416	173	59.43
A.P.F. Chapman	4	6	0	259	121	43.17
R.E.S. Wyatt	1	2	0	71	64	35.50
R.W.V. Robins	2	4	2	70	50*	35.00
W.R. Hammond	5	9	0	306	113	34.00
E.H. Hendren	2	4	0	134	72	33.50
J.B. Hobbs	5	9	0	301	78	33.44
J.C. White	1	2	1	33	23*	33.00
G.O.B. Allen	1	2	0	60	57	30.00
M. Leyland	3	5	1	103	44	25.75
F.E. Woolley	2	4	0	74	41	18.50
M.W. Tate	5	8	0	148	54	18.50
H. Larwood	3	5	1	63	19	15.75
G. Duckworth	5	8	2	87	33	14.50
W.W. Whysall	1	2	0	23	13	11.50
I.A.R. Peebles	2	3	2	9	6	9.00
R.K. Tyldesley	2	3	0	12	6	4.00
G. Geary	1	2	1	0	0	0.00
M.S. Nichols	1	1	1	7	7*	
T.W.J. Goddard	1	(did not bat)				

	O	M	R	W	Av
M.S. Nichols	21	5	33	2	16.50
T.W.J. Goddard	32.1	14	49	2	24.50
R.K. Tyldesley	89	23	234	7	33.43
R.W.V. Robins	85.2	7	338	10	33.80
M.W. Tate	280.1	82	574	15	38.27
I.A.R. Peebles	126	17	354	9	39.33
J.C. White	53	7	166	3	55.33
R.E.S. Wyatt	14	1	58	1	58.00
W.R. Hammond	148.2	35	302	5	60.40
H. Larwood	101	18	292	4	73.00
G. Geary	35	10	95	1	95.00
G.O.B. Allen	34	7	115	0	
M. Leyland	35	9	95	0	
F.E. Woolley	9	1	38	0	

Bibliography

Alston, Rex – *Over To Me,* Frederick Muller, London, 1953.

Barker, Ralph and Rosenwater, Irving – *Test Cricket: England v Australia,* Batsford, London, 1969.

Bowes, Bill – *Express Deliveries,* Stanley Paul, London, undated.

Bradman, Don – *Don Bradman's Book,* Hutchinson & Co., London, 1930.

– *My Cricketing Life,* Stanley Paul, London, undated.

– *Farewell to Cricket,* Hodder & Stoughton, Third Impression, London, 1952.

Docker, Edward Wybergh – *Bradman and the Bodyline Series,* Angus & Robertson, Brighton, 1978.

Fender, P.G.H. – *The Turn of the Wheel,* Faber & Faber, London, undated.

– *The Tests of 1930,* Faber & Faber, London, 1930.

Hammond, Walter – *Cricket My Destiny,* Stanley Paul, London, undated.

Larwood, Harold – *Bodyline?* Elkin Mathews & Marrot, London 1933.

Oldfield, W.A. – *Behind the Wicket,* Hutchinson, London, 1938.

Page, Michael – *Bradman: The Illustrated Biography,* Macmillan, London, 1983.

Peebles, Ian – *Spinner's Yarn,* Collins, London, 1977.

Richardson, V.Y. – *The Vic Richardson Story,* Angus and Robertson, London, 1968.

Rogerson, Sidney – *Wilfred Rhodes,* Hollis & Carter, London, 1960.
Rosenwater, Irving – *Sir Donald Bradman: A Biography,* B.T. Batsford Ltd., London 1978.

Streeton, Richard – *P.G.H. Fender: A Biography,* Faber, London, 1981.

Tebbutt, Geoffrey – *With the 1930 Australians,* Hodder & Stoughton, London, 1930.
Tennyson, Lionel Lord – *Sticky Wickets,* Christopher Johnson, London, 1950.

Wakley, B.J. – *Classic Centuries in the Test Matches between England and Australia,* Nicholas Kaye, London, 1964.
Warner, P.F. – *The Fight for the Ashes in 1930,* Harrap, London, 1930.
Webber, Roy – *The Australians in England,* Hodder & Stoughton, London, 1953.
Wyatt, R.E.S. – *Three Straight Sticks,* Stanley Paul, London, 1951.

Footnotes

Quotes from page viii

1. B.T. Batsford Ltd., London 1978.
2. Angus and Robertson, London, 1967.
3. Faber & Faber, London, 1930.
4. Collins, London, 1977.

Introduction

1. *Don Bradman's Book,* Bradman.
2. *The Turn Of The Wheel,* Fender.
3. Bradman op. cit.
4. Fender op. cit.

Chapter One

1. *Don Bradman's Book,* Bradman.
2. *Sydney Morning Herald.*
3. Ibid.
4. *The Mercury.*
5. *The Vic Richardson Story,* Richardson.
6. *The Adelaide Observer.*
7. *The West Australian.*
8. reported in the *Sydney Morning Herald.*
9. *The West Australian.*
10. Charles Macartney, a pugnacious Australian batsman who last toured England in 1926 and with whom Bradman would be constantly compared. Warren Bardsley, prolific left-hander Australian opener who also last toured in 1926.
11. *With the 1930 Australians,* Tebbutt.
12. Ibid.
13. *Don Bradman's Book*, Bradman.
14. *Australian Press Association.*
15. *The Vic Richardson Story*, Richardson.
16. *Don Bradman's Book*, Bradman.

Chapter Two

1. *Don Bradman's Book,* Bradman.
2. *Australian Press Association.*
3. George Robert Canning Harris, 4th Baron Harris, was a cricketer and latterly a leading cricket administrator.
4. *Don Bradman's Book*, Bradman.
5. *Beyond A Boundary,* James.
6. *The Vic Richardson Story*, Richardson.
7. *The Age,* Melbourne.
8. www.urban75.org/london/st_pancras.html
9. *With The 1930 Australians,* Tebbutt.
10. P.F. (Plum) Warner, former England captain and pillar of the game.
11. *Don Bradman's Book*, Bradman.
12. Gallipoli, a First World War campaign against Turkey involving the Australian and New Zealand Arms Corps (ANZAC).
13. *The Evening News,* London.
14. Ibid.
15. *Evening Standard,* London.
16. *The Vic Richardson Story*, Richardson.
17. *Don Bradman's Book*, Bradman.
18. *Behind The Wicket,* Oldfield.

Chapter Three

1. *The Evening Standard,* London.
2. *The Sun,* Sydney.
3. *The Times.*
4. *The Sun,* Sydney.
5. *Bradman: The Illustrated Biography,* Page.
6. *The Times.*
7. *Daily Mail,* 13 January 1933.
8. *The Fight For The Ashes In 1930,* Warner.
9. www.britainexpress.com/counties/**worcester**shire/az/**worcester**/**guildhall**.htm
10. *Bradman And The BodyLine Series,* Docker.
11. *Bradman: The Illustrated Biography.*
12. *The Sun,* Sydney.

13. *The Leicester Mercury.*
14. *The Evening News,* London.
15. *Don Bradman's Book*, Bradman.
16. *Farewell To Cricket,* Bradman.
17. *Express Deliveries,* Bowes.
18. *Don Bradman's Book*, Bradman.
19. *The Times.*
20. *Sheffield Daily Telegraph.*
21. Ibid.

Chapter Four

1. *With The 1930 Australians,* Tebbutt.
2. *Liverpool Post & Mercury.*
3. Bradman, in *Don Bradman's Book,* says it hit the middle stump.
4. *My Cricket Book,* Bradman.
5. *Evening Standard,* London.
6. *The Manchester Guardian.*
7. *The Times.*
8. *Spinner's Yarn,* Peebles.
9. Ibid.
10. *The Times.*
11. Ibid.
12. *Derby Daily Telegraph.*
13. *Don Bradman's Book*, Bradman.
14. *Evening Standard.*
15. *Australian Press Association.*
16. *Evening Standard.*
17. *Fight For The Ashes In 1930,* Warner.
18. *The Times.*
19. *Australian Press Association.*
20. Tebbutt wrote that Bradman 'had never, he said, seen Macartney bat'. The description of the dinner appeared in Tebbutt's book and the preface to that was dated October 1930, implying it was done after the end of the tour. We must assume that Tebbutt had simply forgotten what he'd written at The Oval – it is very difficult to believe that Bradman said at the dinner he'd not seen Macartney.

    In *Don Bradman's Book,* also published after the tour, Bradman wrote that his father had taken him to Sydney at the age of thirteen to see the Fifth Test between Australia and England, and 'although I was quite a boy then, I have vivid memories of seeing [. . .] Macartney, in all his glory making 170'.

The explanation seems simple: Tebbutt mis-attributed whatever Bradman had said.

21. *Don Bradman's Book*, Bradman.
22. Quoted in *P.G.H. Fender,* Streeton.
23. *Australian Press Association.*
24. *The Times.*
25. *Don Bradman's Book*, Bradman.
26. *Spinner's Yarn.*
27. *Don Bradman's Book*, Bradman.
28. Ibid.
29. *The Sun,* Sydney.
30. *Sticky Wickets,* Tennyson.

Chapter Five

1. In the Press coverage of the tour there are various, usually slight, references to Archie Jackson's health. He was to die in February 1933 of tuberculosis, which is still regarded as one of cricket's greatest sadnesses.
2. *Nottingham Evening News.*
3. Ibid.
4. Ibid.
5. Ibid.
6. *Maurice Tate,* Arlott.
7. *The Times.*
8. *Cricket My Destiny,* Hammond.
9. Because of the importance of what followed, then and now, I have tried in the reconstruction to trace every run Bradman scored and how he scored them. To do this with complete accuracy is impossible because most contemporary newspaper reports don't, for all the understandable reasons, mention most of the 80 singles he scored. This is frustrating but unavoidable.

However, courtesy of John Kobylecky, I've been able to use scorer Ferguson's original spreadsheets for Bradman's Test innings at Leeds and The Oval. You'll see when we get to them. Ferguson noted each run under headings – for example *Leg* meaning on the leg side. Where on the leg side we cannot know because the only two other headings are *Mid-on* and *Sq leg.* The presumption must be that he divided the leg side into three segments: *Leg* meant anywhere from long leg up to square; *Sq leg* meant anywhere from there up to mid-on, and *Mid-on* meant anywhere from there up to the sightscreen.

Confining ourselves to *Leg,* you can of course play several shots to send the ball into that segment – pull, sweep, hook and glance not to mention snicks. However, although Ferguson is not geographically definitive his shorthand does help to give an innings its true shape, not least by demonstrating how hard Bradman worked certain segments and how rarely he worked others.

Mr. Kobylecky alas did not have the spreadsheet for Nottingham and I've been unable to find it anywhere else.

10. *Sydney Morning Telegraph.*
11. *The Times.*
12. *Fight For The Ashes In 1930,* Warner.
13. *Don Bradman's Book,* Bradman.
14. *Evening Standard,* London.
15. *Don Bradman's Book,* Bradman.
16. *The Vic Richardson Story,* Richardson.
17. *The Sun,* Sydney.

Chapter Six

1. *The Manchester Guardian.*
2. Quoted in *Wilfred Rhodes,* Rogerson.
3. *The Times.*
4. *The Sun,* Sydney.
5. *Yorkshire Evening Post.*
6. *The Sun.*
7. *Evening Standard,* London.
8. *Australian Press Association.*
9. *Don Bradman's Book,* Bradman.
10. *The Fight For The Ashes In 1930,* Warner.
11. *The Tests Of 1930,* Fender.

Chapter Seven

1. *The Times.*
2. *Yorkshire Post.*
3. *The Sun,* Sydney.
4. *Yorkshire Post.*
5. *Don Bradman's Book,* Bradman.
6. *Yorkshire Evening News.*
7. *Yorkshire Telegraph & Star,* Sheffield.
8. Ibid.
9. *Yorkshire Evening Post.*
10. Bradman's 334 at Leeds was, and remains, one of the greatest innings ever played (in the authentic sense of that term) and because of that I have tried to recreate it in very great detail. The innings expressed itself in the two basic contexts, runs and time, the former keeping pace uncannily with the latter.

Using scorer Ferguson's 'all-in-a-line' spreadsheets – which (as I mentioned in the footnote to the Nottingham Test) divide the pitch into six segments, three on either side of the wicket – it is possible to see where all the runs came from. Contemporary newspaper accounts, much longer than today, essentially recorded each day's play in chronological order. This was particularly true of the evening papers, then more numerous, with later deadlines and giving Test cricket much more prominence. Using these sources it is possible to track down a surprising number of individual run-getting strokes, particularly the boundaries and significant milestones, 50, 100, 150 and so on. The spreadsheets place every scoring shot into a segment so we know approximately where they went.

What time the runs were scored is itself important because that gives a progressive overall framework, and shows how fast – or slowly – the innings was progressing. John Kobylecky has employed detective work as well as all the known times – when play began, lunch, tea, individual milestones, times in the scorebooks, mentions in the Press – to create a starting time for every over. By definition these cannot be absolutely exact because, to achieve them, you'd have had to be at Leeds with a stopwatch. Equally, even if they are wrong it can't be by much. I have used these throughout. A random example from the evening session of day one:

Larwood bowled the first ball of an over in a new spell to

Kippax at 5.57pm. Kippax took a single from the third ball, Bradman 3 from the last ball to make his score 283.

Tate began the next over at 6pm and thirty seconds.

I therefore give the time Bradman moved to 283 as 6pm, because it came at the end of Larwood's over.

11. *Yorkshire Telegraph & Star.*

12. The controversy about this ball is further explored in Rosenwater's *Sir Donald Bradman: A Biography.*

13. *Cricket My Destiny,* Hammond.

14. *Yorkshire Evening Post.*

15. *Don Bradman's Book,* Bradman.

16. *Yorkshire Telegraph & Star.*

17. Ibid.

18. *The Tests Of 1930,* Fender.

19. *Evening Standard,* London.

20. Sixpence: as I pointed out at the beginning of this book, a £ was divided into 20 shillings, and each shilling into 12 pence. The sixpence was a common coin.

21. *The Fight For The Ashes In 1930,* Warner.

22. *The Times.*

23. *The Star,* London.

24. *The Sun,* Sydney.

25. *Bradford Telegraph & Argus.*

26. *The Sun.*

27. *Evening Standard.*

28. *Yorkshire Telegraph & Star.*

29. *The Times.*

30. *Don Bradman's Book,* Bradman.

31. Warner op. cit.

32. Mailey in *The Sun,* Sydney.

33. *The Sun,* Sydney.

34. *Yorkshire Evening Post.*

35. *Yorkshire Evening News.*

36. *Evening Standard.*

37. *Don Bradman's Book,* Bradman.

38. *Evening Standard.*

39. *Yorkshire Telegraph & Star.*

40. *Bradford Telegraph & Argus.*

41. Ibid.
42. *Evening Standard.*
43. *Nottingham Journal.*

Chapter Eight

1. *Don Bradman's Book,* Bradman.
2. *My Cricket Life,* Bradman.
3. *Glasgow Herald.*
4. *Australian Press Association.*
5. *Don Bradman's Book,* Bradman.
6. *Spinner's Yarn,* Peebles.
7. *Manchester Evening News.*
8. Ibid.
9. *Don Bradman's Book,* Bradman.
10. *Evening Standard,* London.
11. *Spinner's Yarn.*
12. *With The 1930 Australians,* Tebbutt.
13. *The Sun,* Sydney.
14. In Rosenwater's *Bradman.*
15. *The Times.*

Chapter Nine

1. *Three Straight Sticks,* Wyatt.
2. *Don Bradman's Book,* Bradman.
3. *Three Straight Sticks.*
4. Ibid.
5. *The Sun,* Sydney.
6. *Three Straight Sticks.*
7. Ibid.
8. *Australian Press Association.*
9. *The Tests Of 1930,* Fender.
10. *Australian Press Association.*
11. *The Sun,* Sydney.
12. *Yorkshire Evening Post.*
13. *Australian Press Association.*
14. *The Sun,* Sydney.
15. *Evening Standard,* London.
16. Peebles makes no mention of this in *Spinner's Yarn.*

17. *Three Straight Sticks.*
18. *Australian Press Association.*
19. *Don Bradman's Book*, Bradman.
20. *Yorkshire Evening Post.*
21. *The Sun,* Sydney.
22. *Spinner's Yarn.*
23. *Bodyline?* Larwood.
24. *Don Bradman's Book*, Bradman.
25. *Evening Standard.*
26. *The Fight For The Ashes In 1930,* Warner.
27. *The Tests Of 1930,* Fender.
28. Ibid.
29. *The Fight For The Ashes In 1930.*
30. *The Vic Richardson Story,* Richardson.
31. Quoted in *Rhodes,* Rogerson.
32. *Illustrated Bradman,* Page.
33. *The Times.*
34. *The Fight For The Ashes In 1930.*
35. *Australian Press Association.*
36. *The Fight For The Ashes In 1930.*
37. *Evening Standard.*
38. Barrie, who wrote *Peter Pan,* seems to be getting Einstein (and the theory of Relativity) confused with splitting the atom, which was nothing to do with him.
39. *Scarborough Evening News & Daily Post.*
40. Quoted in Rogerson.
41. *Scarborough Evening News & Daily Post.*
42. *Don Bradman's Book*, Bradman.

Chapter Ten

1. *Evening Standard*, London.
2. *Australian Press Association.*
3. *Illustrated Bradman,* Page.
4. Ibid.
5. *The Advertiser,* Adelaide.
6. Ibid.
7. *Sydney Morning Herald.*
8. *West Australian.*

9. Ibid.
10. *The Advertiser.*
11. Ibid.
12. Ibid.
13. *Sydney Morning Herald.*
14. *The Advertiser.*
15. *The Tests Of 1930,* Fender.
16. Laker told a hilarious story of how Bailey instructed him to appeal against the light – each batsman was allowed one appeal per session and Bailey had already used his. It was perfect daylight and Laker, sheepish, ambled up to one of the umpires and said: 'You're not going to believe this, but . . . '
17. *Over To Me,* Alston.